THE BLACK TAX

THE BLACK TAX

150 YEARS OF THEFT,

EXPLOITATION, AND

DISPOSSESSION IN AMERICA

ANDREW W. KAHRL

The University of Chicago Press

Chicago and London

The University of Chicago Press, Chicago 60637
The University of Chicago Press, Ltd., London
© 2024 by Andrew W. Kahrl
Published 2024
Printed in the United States of America

33 32 31 30 29 28 27 26 25 24   1 2 3 4 5

ISBN-13: 978-0-226-73059-2 (cloth)
ISBN-13: 978-0-226-73062-2 (e-book)
DOI: https://doi.org/10.7208/chicago/9780226730622.001.0001

Library of Congress Cataloging-in-Publication Data

Names: Kahrl, Andrew W., 1978– author
Title: The black tax : 150 years of theft, exploitation, and dispossession in
America / Andrew W. Kahrl.
Description: Chicago : The University of Chicago Press, 2024. | Includes
bibliographical references and index.
Identifiers: LCCN 2023037914 | ISBN 9780226730592 (cloth) |
ISBN 9780226730622 (e-book)
Subjects: LCSH: Property tax—United States. | African Americans—Taxation. |
African Americans—Civil rights.
Classification: LCC HJ4120.K347 2024 | DDC 336.22—dc23/eng/20231023
LC record available at https://lccn.loc.gov/2023037914

♾ This paper meets the requirements of ANSI/NISO Z39.48-1992
(Permanence of Paper).

To Elodie and Muriel

CONTENTS

INTRODUCTION

When Jean Wright purchased a house on Long Island in the late 1970s, she believed she was investing in her family's future. The modest two-bedroom house in the town of Roosevelt, New York, could barely fit the single Black mother and her four young children. She knew that, before long, they would need more space. At least now, though, she wasn't fattening a landlord's pockets. She had a stake in the American Dream.

But it was a costly one. In addition to paying down the mortgage on the $50,000 house, Wright paid over $200 each month in property taxes. "From the day I bought this house I knew that my taxes were too high," Wright remarked. In fact, her annual tax bill was roughly the same as that of the typical owner of a $200,000 house in a wealthy white neighborhood in the same county. Soon, homeownership was consuming well over half of Wright's income, and she had to take a second job. Any hope of saving toward a larger house was soon dashed. Instead, "I feel like I spend my life robbing Peter to pay Paul," she explained. "And there's never anything left over for me."[1]

Elizabeth Milton shared Wright's frustration. In 1984, the thirty-five-year-old Black working mother also purchased a modest house that had a high tax bill. Hers, on a $35,000 house in the Long Island town of Wyandanch, amounted to 6 percent of the property's overall value. This was six times more than what many white homeowners in neighboring towns paid. She struggled to make it work. Some nights Milton sent her children to bed hungry. Some years, she wasn't able to "buy my girls new sneakers." And then, "sometimes, you know, you just can't do it. You just can't do the things you want to do or have to do."[2]

While paying the highest taxes, residents of Roosevelt and Wyandanch and the other predominantly Black towns on Long Island got the least in return. Both Wright and Milton sent their children to two of the most underfunded and lowest-performing school districts in the state. Milton's neighborhood was pockmarked with abandoned houses and empty lots littered with garbage, rusted-out cars, and broken appliances. And if they wanted to leave, neither had much hope of realizing any return on their investments. Home values flatlined the moment a neighborhood became Black, and the high tax bills that followed Black people wherever they went drove those values down further still.[3]

And if they missed a tax payment, even greater hardships awaited. Annie Kennedy had spent most of her life working and living in white people's homes as a housekeeper, and she dreamed of one day having a place she could call her own. In 1973, she put a $2,000 down payment—her entire life savings—and secured a $10,000 mortgage on a small house in Hempstead, in the heart of Long Island's Black Belt. She continued to work into her seventies and paid off the mortgage. But when she looked to sell the house in 1986, Kennedy learned that it was no longer hers. Years earlier, she had failed to pay a $92.07 school tax bill. Kennedy never received any notices of the missing payment, but that didn't save her: the law required only that the county send out notices, not that they be received. Nassau County sold the debt to tax-lien investor Charles Solomon, who took ownership of her home for just $92. All those mortgage payments, she remarked, "might as well [have been dumped] in a garbage pail."[4]

* * *

Why has racial inequality remained such an enduring problem in America, and what forces fuel its persistence? In recent years, pathbreaking works by scholars and journalists have called attention to the legacy of housing policies and real estate industry practices that powered the growth of the white middle class and white household wealth-building in mid-twentieth-century America while simultaneously constraining Black mobility, deepening racial segregation, and subjecting Black Americans to numerous and devastating forms of economic predation and plunder.[5] Others have pointed to America's retreat from the promise of educational equality and to its broader disinvestment in public schools, public services, and public institutions in the half-century since the civil rights movement toppled Jim Crow.[6]

Wright, Milton, and Kennedy's experiences in suburban Long Island in the 1980s—-and those of the people whose stories are told in this book—point to an engine of inequality that has been missing from these discussions, one that is as old as Black freedom itself and that firmly but quietly binds together so many of the problems and challenges Black Americans have faced in the past and continue to struggle against today: local tax systems.

"Taxes," the Supreme Court justice Oliver Wendell Holmes remarked, "are what we pay for civilized society." Throughout American history and still today, the delivery and distribution of vital public goods and services that promote a civilized society—from clean water, sewerage, and fire protection to public safety, recreation, and education—have been entrusted to local governments. And the bulk of the funding that local governments have relied on to perform these functions and deliver these services comes from a locally administered and enforced tax on local property. These features of America's federated system of taxation and public spending have made the property tax ripe for manipulation and abuse and prone to inequitable results.[7]

Black people have paid the heaviest cost. From the late nineteenth century to today, local tax assessors have consistently overtaxed the lands and homes that Black people own and the neighborhoods where they live. For all the taxes they have paid, Black Americans have struggled to receive anything close to their fair share of the public goods and services that local governments provided. And when they failed to pay on time, African Americans were—and continue to be—

subjected to the harshest consequences and most predatory features of tax delinquency laws that, in most states, permit local governments to sell liens on tax-delinquent properties to private investors, who can then saddle delinquent taxpayers with crippling debts and, should they fail to pay, take their property.

The Black Tax tells this history—the history of taxation in America as seen through the lives and experiences of Black Americans—and tallies its costs. It is the story of Black people's struggles against local tax systems that forced them to pay more for less and subjected them to heavy financial penalties and the threat of dispossession when they failed to pay on time. It is the story of how these tax structures were built and maintained and of whose interests they served. It is the story of those who exploited the machinery of local tax enforcement, and Black people's vulnerabilities and disadvantages as property owners, to amass wealth and property at their expense; of the riches they accumulated; and of the trail of destruction they left behind. It is the story of how Black Americans resisted exploitation, guarded against predation, fought for an equitable distribution of public goods and services, and fought to be recognized as taxpayers. And it is the story of how matters of local taxation and public spending shaped the struggle for racial equality as a whole, made the America we live in today, and shape the battles being waged over its future.

The history this book tells might come as a shock to many readers, for it is the exact opposite of what many of us have been led to believe about the distribution of tax burdens and public spending in America. From the moment Black people began making claims on the state, whites in power have responded by peddling the canard that Blacks paid little in taxes and, by implication, were undeserving of the rights, benefits, and protections of citizenship. Following the Civil War, white southern elites deployed racist tropes of Blacks as "freeloaders" and Republican-controlled state governments as profligate spenders of white taxpayers' dollars to overthrow Reconstruction. The myth that Blacks paid no taxes served to justify paltry spending on "colored" schools and wanton neglect of Black civic needs under Jim Crow. During the civil rights movement, segregationists invoked the myth to oppose equal access to public goods, services, and benefits, most especially public schools. In the decades that followed, the modern Right stoked the perception that Black people paid no taxes and consumed the bulk of white taxpayers' dollars to build popular support for tax cuts that mainly benefitted the wealthy and spending cuts that disproportionately harmed Black Americans and deepened inequality. The political saliency of these myths has contributed in no small measure to the hollowing out of the public sector, evisceration of the social safety net, and privatization of public goods and services in recent decades. These myths remain powerful today. And, as this history shows, they could not be further from the truth.[8]

* * *

The property tax is the most local of all taxes in America, and its local nature is key to understanding how it works and how it became a force of bureaucratic racism and structural inequality.[9]

Let's begin with the office in charge of administering local property taxes: one of the thousands of local tax assessors. Some of them are elected to office, others are appointed. Most assessors' offices are based at the county level, but many others are at the city or township level; sometimes, assessors' jurisdictions overlap. Assessors' methods for determining values—and the basis of valuation itself—vary by state and locality and have changed over time. The frequency with which local governments are required to update assessments also varies dramatically. Some states require that assessments be updated annually, others only every four or five years, and still others have no requirements whatsoever. In practice, local assessors have operated as they pleased, with minimal state supervision and virtual immunity from federal oversight or accountability. Whereas Congress and the federal judiciary took concrete steps to restrict local governments' ability to discriminate in regards to voting rights, public education, and housing in the mid-twentieth century, they left control over local tax administration firmly in the hands of local officials.[10]

Property taxes are different from other taxes in several key respects. With sales or income taxes, for example, the government first sets a tax rate and collects revenue based on the amount of taxable goods sold or income earned, which determines the size of its budget. With the property tax, that order is reversed. Local governments first determine their budget; they then set the tax rate to generate that amount based on the size of the tax base. Unlike the case of a sales tax, which is collected when someone makes a purchase, or an income tax, which is collected when someone earns money, it is entirely possible for someone to own property but be unable to pay the tax on it. The value of any home or piece of land can only be realized upon sale. Until then, a property owner must utilize other resources to pay their taxes. And when they cannot, or refuse to do so, the consequences can be dire.

In every state, failing to pay property taxes on time results in a lien being placed on the property. A lien is like a cloud on a title, reducing a property's uses and salability. To remove the lien, the delinquent taxpayer has to satisfy the debt and pay some penalty. But many states have not been content to wait for delinquent taxpayers to do so—yet neither do they actually want to foreclose on and assume ownership of their properties. So, instead, local governments hold auctions. There, the liens are sold to private investors, who pay the overdue taxes to the government. The winning bidder (known as a tax buyer) then takes over the job of pressing the homeowner to repay that debt. In the meantime, the tax buyer can charge interest on the debt (interest that, in some states, can run as high as 48 percent) and assorted charges and fees (which, in some states, have been virtually unlimited). If the debt remains unsettled long enough, the tax buyer can take the property.[11]

Tax-lien sales serve as the primary method for collecting unpaid property taxes and enforcing taxpayer compliance in the majority of US states. Under these systems, the punishments for late payments are quite explicitly not meant to fit the crime, as it were, but to incentivize investing and serve the interests of the tax-lien market. The nature of these markets varies according to state rules, the real estate markets these investors are speculating on, and the interests and intents of the tax buyers themselves. At some tax sales, tax buyers' sole interest is the interest they can collect, with the loss of property strictly a threat to extract payments from debtors. But other times, the liens themselves are the opening wedge for property acquisition, especially if the tax liens being auctioned are on potentially valuable property. In these instances, tax buyers bet on the prospect that delinquent property owners will be unable to pay these mounting debts, and they will utilize every legal tool available to them to ensure that outcome.

* * *

The Black Tax tells the history of racialized tax structures and the predatory practices that flourished within them in five chronological parts spanning the period from Reconstruction to the first two decades of the twenty-first century. Within each of these parts are chapters that broadly focus on the three core features of local fiscal systems: tax administration, public spending, and tax enforcement.

Part I tells the story of how these systems built and sustained the Jim Crow order. In the half-century following emancipation, African Americans managed to accumulate nearly 16 million acres of land. But as they did, local white tax administrators worked to make it more expensive to hold and easier to lose. Black disfranchisement gave local tax administrators free reign to treat Black people less as constituents to serve and more as subjects to exploit and punish. By the early 1900s, local tax assessors in counties across the South overvalued the often small, less valuable plots of land Black people had managed to acquire in order to squeeze more taxes out of them. They sharply increased assessments on properties whose owners had threatened the status quo, or whom local authorities wanted to force out. Few of the tax dollars Blacks paid ever found their way back into their neighborhoods or schools. In cities and towns, where Black neighborhoods began, paved streets, sidewalks, and water and sewer lines ended. White local officials plundered Black school dollars at will and forced Black taxpayers to heavily subsidize whites' public education.

Black property owners, meanwhile, remained forever vulnerable to having their property unjustly taken and sold for nonpayment of taxes. Those most vulnerable were those whose land was seen as valuable. When a Black person owned property that became "enhanced in value by either a real-estate development or expansion of business areas," NAACP special counsel Thurgood Marshall wrote in 1940, local officials could simply fail to send their tax bill or fail to record a payment. And then, "when the taxes are past due and are in arrears for the statutory period, the property is quietly sold at a tax sale without notice to the owners."[12] "That's how a lot of them lost their land," one Black Mississippian said of the tens of thousands of African Americans dispossessed of millions of acres of land during these decades. "White folks stole a lot of it for taxes."[13] In 1920, the great-great-grandfather of George Floyd, whose murder by a police officer in Minneapolis in 2020 sparked global protests, lost twenty-four acres of land he owned in Harnett County, North Carolina, at a tax sale under dubious circumstances over a $18.83 tax debt. At the time, a single acre of land in the county sold for $62. The loss plunged the family back into poverty.[14]

Freedom from kleptocracy drove millions of African Americans to migrate to northern cities in the first half of the twentieth century, the setting for part II. But as they did so, the system of financing local governments in America was changing in ways that would structurally disadvantage Black neighborhoods and fuel the forces that were segregating housing markets and schools across the country. Beginning in the 1910s, states began adopting new, more reliable and efficient sources of tax revenue—like income taxes—and ceased relying on property taxes. Local county and city governments, which had long been in charge of assessing property and collecting the tax within their borders, could now keep all of it.[15] But the amount of revenue any locality could derive from the property tax, the rate at which it taxed each property, was determined by the total assessed value of all property within its boundaries, otherwise known as its tax base. The larger the tax base, the lower the rate at which it needed to tax property to generate the same amount of revenue.

As these changes to the fiscal structure were unfolding, a burgeoning real estate industry consisting of banks, realtors, and developers, working in collaboration with public officials, were systematically segregating cities by race and herding Black people into racialized ghettos, where they were denied financing to buy homes and forced to pay exorbitant rents for inferior housing or lured into risky, predatory home-buying schemes. The color line in housing reaped rich rewards for the banks who financed it, the realtors who designed it, and the sea of speculators who exploited it, and it became the basis for white household wealth accumulation in the twentieth century. It made property in the hands of a Black person worth less because it was in their hands, while making white-owned homes and neighborhoods worth more because they were white.[16]

The racialization of urban housing markets, and cities' dependence on tax revenues derived from those markets, also gave cities a strong fiscal incentive to cater to the interests of white homeowners, all the more so as new suburbs, with their own separate school systems and tax bases, proliferated and competed with them for white residents and white tax dollars.[17] Cities did so by under-assessing the value of properties in white residential areas, an informal but pervasive feature of local tax administration in mid-twentieth-century America, and devoting a disproportionate portion of local budgets to public goods and services there.[18] Black homeowners and Black neighborhoods did not receive such favorable treatment. Instead, the homes they owned or paid rent to live in were prone to being overassessed and taxed at higher rates, and their neighborhoods and schools were chronically underserved.

High taxes and costly, risky home-financing arrangements also made Black homeowners in these cities more susceptible to tax delinquency. And when they failed to pay on time, tax buyers pounced. In cities like Chicago and Detroit, tax buying grew into a lucrative enterprise in the 1950s and 1960s, practiced by shadowy groups of lawyers and investors whose ruthlessness and clannishness was only matched by their lack of conscience. Financed by local banks, tax buyers like Chicago's Allan Blair and David Gray bought thousands of tax liens in Cook County as well as other public auctions across the state each year. Then, after they sent threatening letters to each homeowner, they waited for the checks to start pouring in. The longer it took for a delinquent taxpayer to settle, the more profits they could make. The biggest profits—the big score—came when a homeowner simply couldn't pay, or when they could but (for any number of reasons) failed to do so in time. That's when tax buyers could claim ownership of the property. Then, they could sell it back to the former owner and make an obscene profit. Or, if the former owner couldn't buy it back under any terms—and most could not—they could rent it back to them. And, if the former owners refused to play along, the buyers could always just evict them and sell it. That's what usually happened. It was all legal.

"They wanted to buy liens on properties where people were living there," one public-interest lawyer who fought on behalf of tax-sale victims said of tax buyers' tactics. "They wanted live bodies inside."[19] Tax buyers targeted tax-delinquent homes whose owners wanted to hold onto them—even better, who valued those homes more than the market did—and from whom they could more easily compel payments, or sell or rent back to. They did not invest in the abandoned properties that posed the greatest fiscal problems for local governments, not to mention residents of disinvested neighborhoods. Rather, they preyed on those who had missed a tax payment by accident or due to financial distress. Often, their victims were elderly, or ill, or confused. "They would've screwed over anybody regardless of the race to make a buck," the son and nephew of two of Chicago's most prolific tax buyers during these decades later said.[20] But because Black neighborhoods offered tax buyers not only greater volume but also greater profits, tax buyers mostly screwed over Black people.[21]

Part III tells the history of the Black freedom movement in the 1960s and 1970s South through the lens of local taxation. During these decades, Black people in towns and rural counties across the South challenged bureaucratic racism in local tax administration and organized to protect their property from predation. Protesters marched on city halls, demanding "covered sewers, street lights, playgrounds, postal service, libraries, [and] free access to public services and facilities."[22] They filed federal lawsuits challenging cities and towns' denial of these and other municipal services or their vastly unequal provision to Black neighborhoods. They attempted to pry open the federal courthouse doors to cases of discriminatory taxation by local governments against Black citizens, a key (and previously unrecognized) weapon in white segregationists' arsenal. And, backed by the protections of the 1965 Voting Rights Act, Black candidates ran for tax assessor and, once in office, attempted to reverse-engineer decades of racism in local tax administration.

But during the same years when the civil rights movement was scoring its greatest victories, Black people across the South were rapidly losing the one kind of wealth—land—they had managed to accumulate under Jim Crow. Not coincidentally, the areas where Blacks experienced some of the heaviest losses were those where real estate prices were rising most rapidly. In places like Hilton Head Island, South Carolina, sharp spikes in property taxes, administered by local officials eager to do their part to promote regional growth, forced countless numbers of Black families to sell their properties under duress and led many others to fall into tax delinquency and lose their homes at tax sales. More than a few owners landed on the tax delinquency rolls by acts of fraud and deceit. In the midst of a crisis of Black land loss unfolding across the 1960s and 1970s South, organizations like South Carolina's Black Land Services and the region-wide Emergency Land Fund formed and devised strategies for combatting predatory land grabbing.

In northern cities during these same decades, Black-led movements for tax reform worked to dismantle racist fiscal structures, secure a more equitable distribution of public expenditures, and rid lower-income and Black neighborhoods of predatory tax buyers, the subject of part IV. As growing numbers of Americans, white and Black, expressed discontent with the inequities and unfairness of local property taxes, Black organizers and activists like George Wiley worked to build interracial movements for tax justice that would relieve the poor of unfair burdens and force the wealthy and advantaged to pay their fair share. But they did so within a fiscal structure that racialized those advantages and disadvantages and was designed to divide. During the 1970s, crusading attorneys like Chicago's Marshall Patner fought on behalf of victims of tax-lien predation and challenged the constitutionality of the laws that allowed these practices to flourish. Public outrage over the unconscionable practices of tax buyers increased pressure on state lawmakers throughout the decade to abolish the practice.

But these government-administered marketplaces in tax debts would prove to be uniquely well suited to thrive in the age of neoliberalism, as described in part V. Beginning in the 1980s, the federal government and states slashed support for local governments and made them even more reliant on their own sources of revenue. In response, cities and counties aggressively pursued growth strategies through fiscal policy and administration. They embraced trickle-down fiscal policies of targeted tax cuts and raided their own treasuries to woo capital and spur development. They became more dependent on and beholden to municipal-bond markets. They slashed public services for those most in need and turned to tickets, fines, and fees to pay for services and replenish local coffers. And they partnered with tax-lien investors in devising new methods for generating revenue and accumulating capital from tax-delinquent properties. During these decades, the business of tax-lien investing grew in size, scope, and sophistication to become what it is today: a multibillion-dollar industry heavily financed by Wall Street investment banks, increasingly dominated by hedge funds and private equity, and featuring a widening array of financial products and investment strategies. But one thing remained the same: the source of investors' profits—financially distressed homeowners, disproportionately nonwhite, and living in revenue-starved, economically disadvantaged cities.

* * *

This history sheds new light on the forces generating economic inequality in America and the racial character of those inequalities. In America today, one in four Black families have zero or negative net worth, as compared to less than one in ten white families.[23] The absence of wealth among vast numbers of Black Americans—and the massive concentration of wealth in America, more generally—grew, as the writer Trymaine Lee aptly put it, "by plunder."[24]

The Black tax nourished its growth. Racial discrimination and inequity in local tax systems were forms of exploitation and plunder that begat other exploitative and predatory practices, each compounding and mutually reinforcing the other, with devastating long-term effects.[25] Higher property taxes sapped the earnings of Black households and relentlessly undermined their struggles to save and build wealth. They devalued the property Black people possessed, while enhancing the value and security of white property. They increased the odds of Black homeowners falling into tax delinquency and suffering additional financial losses to tax buyers. And they made Black-owned land and homes more vulnerable to dispossession, no more so than when these properties became valuable. Local tax structures and practices not only imposed a form of compound interest in reverse on generations of Black Americans, they turned the tax assessor's office and tax auction block into instruments of capital accumulation through dispossession.[26]

While it is impossible to quantify the total amount of wealth and property that overtaxation and tax-lien predation stole from Black Americans over the past one hundred and fifty years, the most conservative estimates of these losses are staggering. In 2020, the economists Carlos Avenancio-León and Troup Howard found that, nationwide, the assessed values of properties in Black and Hispanic neighborhoods are 10 to 13 percent higher than those of properties in predominantly white areas within the same jurisdictions, forcing the median African American homeowner in the US today to pay an extra $300 to $390 annually in property taxes, with those families at the widest end of the assessment gap paying up to $790 more in taxes annually. These disparities are place-based, meaning that they fall on both owner-occupied and rental properties alike. By the most conservative estimate, their findings suggest that every Black person in America today pays an extra $100 in property taxes annually. As this book shows, these disparities are nothing new; indeed, all evidence suggests that the 10 to 13 percent race tax that Black people pay on their property taxes today falls on the low end of historic rates of overtaxation. Given Avenancio-León and Howard's findings, and this history, a very conservative estimate of the total amount Black Americans have been overtaxed between 1870 and 2020 adds up to (in 2023 dollars) over $275 billion.[27]

The material losses Black people suffered from tax sales and tax-lien predation are even greater. For many of the owners of the over 11 million acres of land Black people lost in the twentieth century, it was a tax bill that they could not pay that sealed their fate and opened the door for land speculators who flocked to local tax sales to profit at their expense. A 2022 study found that the compounded value of Black land lost in the twentieth century amounts to roughly $326 billion today. We'll never know how much of the land taken from Black people was the direct or indirect result of tax delinquency or of the financial pressures of paying taxes on over-assessed land. Nor is it possible to get an accurate estimate of the amount of wealth extracted from Black property owners in cities and towns across the US through exorbitant interest payments and fees to tax buyers. But a conservative estimate of the total losses (in 2023 dollars) from dispossession and exploitation of tax-delinquent Black property owners over the past century and a half easily exceeds $300 billion. Because these losses fueled others' gains, the roughly $600 billion taken from Black Americans through these mechanisms resulted in a difference in wealth today of trillions of dollars.[28]

* * *

These figures and estimates underscore the gravity of this history. But they cannot adequately convey its meaning. Only the stories of people and places can. People like Evelina Jenkins, a Black woman living in Jim Crow South Carolina who had sixty-six acres of coastal land she owned—property that today is worth tens of millions of dollars—legally stolen from her via a fraudulent tax sale in 1932. And people like Louis and Doretta Balthazar, African American migrants to postwar Chicago, who bought a three-flat apartment on the city's West

Side with the money Louis earned as a barber, where they raised their nine children and made steady progress toward financial security. That was, until a single missed tax payment allowed the city's largest tax buyer the opportunity to claim their home for himself. Places like the small town of Edwards, Mississippi, where in 1966 Black residents waged a prolonged boycott of local white-owned businesses to force the town to extend sewer lines, paved streets, and other public services and amenities into Black neighborhoods, for which the town retaliated by grossly overtaxing all of the boycott participants' homes. And places like Gary, Indiana, the most struggling of all Rust Belt cities, whose decline in the 1960s and 1970s was accelerated by the massive local tax breaks its largest industry enjoyed and fought to protect, and by the deprivations its predominantly Black population suffered as a result. It is their stories and these experiences that frame the history that follows.

PART I

JIM CROW'S

FISCAL ORDER

1

UNACCOUNTABLE

On January 12, 1865, fresh from his victorious march through the heart of the Confederacy, Union general William T. Sherman asked a delegation of Black leaders in Savannah, Georgia, what their people needed to truly become free. "Land," they said in unison, to own and farm for themselves. Four days later, Sherman issued Special Field Order 15, carving up all the abandoned coastal plantations from Charleston, South Carolina, more than two hundred miles south to the mouth of the St. Johns River in Florida into forty-acre plots for the formerly enslaved. Sherman also directed that the new owners of the land be loaned a "partially broken down" mule or horse from the Army's stockades.[1]

But less than ten months later, President Andrew Johnson restored ownership of sea-island plantations to former slaveholders. When Union general O. O. Howard delivered the news on Edisto Island, South Carolina, the freedmen and women responded in disbelief, some shouting, "No, never." Later, they petitioned the Freedmen's Bureau and President Johnson for the homesteads "we were promised." "Without some provision [of land]," they implored Johnson, "our future is sad to look upon." Johnson ignored their pleas. It was among the first of many broken promises that Black people encountered on the crooked road from slavery to freedom.[2]

Yet Blacks' dreams of landed independence continued to burn bright. In the coming decades, and against all odds, African Americans built a substantial land base in the rural South. By 1900, one in

PLOWING IN SOUTH CAROLINA.—FROM A SKETCH BY JAS. E. TAYLOR.

Figure 1.1 A freedman's farm in South Carolina, 1866.

four Black farmers in the US owned their own land.[3] Owning a plot of land, no matter how small, did more than provide its owners with the means of growing their own crops and feeding their own families. It symbolized freedom. Land ownership vested its holders with rights as property owners that seemed, to the formerly enslaved, more tangible and more secure than the civil rights that white "redeemers" were so intent on denying and the federal courts were so reluctant to enforce.[4]

But along with those property rights came responsibilities. As the white ruling class overthrew Reconstruction, fended off populist insurgencies, and wrested back control over state and local governments across the South in the late nineteenth century, they utilized the powers of tax administration—and Black people's property tax obligations—to re-establish and reinforce systems of economic exploitation and Black subjugation.

* * *

"The power to tax," US Supreme Court chief justice John Marshall famously intoned, "is the power to destroy." As they plotted to regain control over their former property, restore plantation labor regimes, and snuff out Black notions of freedom, defeated former Confederates took those words to heart. Before Congress took control over Reconstruction in 1866, southern states enacted a flurry of taxes targeted at the formerly enslaved. They enacted poll taxes, like the one Mississippi imposed on all Black males between the ages of eighteen and sixty. Those who failed to pay were arrested and forced into plantation labor. They imposed onerous license fees for working in certain occupations or businesses. Virginia, for example, required aspiring oyster harvesters to post a $500 bond. Many cities imposed heavy fees on Black artisans, barbers, shopkeepers, and other self-reliant occupations. Unable to afford such licenses, Blacks were effectively barred from earning money using their own skills. They, too, were forced back, as one white put it, "to work on the farms at such prices as their former masters might allow them."

Once they forced Black men and women back onto plantations, southern states aimed to keep them there through taxes. North Carolina imposed an $8 annual poll tax, the equivalent to more than a month's wage for plantation laborers, which sheriffs required freedmen to pay before they could collect their wages. As a result, and by design, Black workers began the year in debt and remained there. Some of them, denied the ability to earn enough money to live on, turned to begging and theft.[5]

Former Confederates' relentless efforts to exploit and oppress freedmen and women and nullify the results of the war outraged the North. It compelled Republicans in Congress to pass, over Johnson's veto, the Reconstruction Act of 1867, which dissolved southern state governments, placed the entire region under military occupation, and imposed requirements for readmission—including ratification of the Fourteenth Amendment and provision of universal male suffrage. With military protection, Black citizens worked to build a new fiscal foundation for the South. At southern state constitutional conventions, Black delegates called for bold measures to expand their states' revenue-raising capacities and support new and expanded public services and institutions. At Mississippi's 1869 Constitutional Convention, Black delegates introduced a resolution calling for "a system of free schools" alongside one calling for "reform of the 'iniquitous and unequal' system of taxation and assessments which discriminated against labor." In Louisiana, Black delegates "demanded at least one free public school in each parish, to be provided for by public taxation." Black political organizations pressed for progressive taxes in support of public education, welfare, and social services. Delegates to a Black political convention in Louisville, Kentucky, in 1869 adopted a resolution calling for "equality of taxation." The National Negro Convention in Washington, DC, that year similarly called for "a national tax for Negro schools," alongside demands for "universal suffrage, and the opening of public land especially in the South for Negroes."[6]

Reconstruction state governments sharply broke with the tax policies and practices of the past. Whereas antebellum officials had taxed land at low rates if at all, under Reconstruction southern states increased those rates, began assessing property at its full value, and worked to standardize assessment practices. They created state agencies to oversee local administration and empowered them to adjust assessments to ensure accuracy and equality across jurisdictions. They also adopted measures to shield small landowners from being taxed out of their homes. Several states passed laws designed to help small farmers and tenants by exempting a certain amount of a property from taxation.[7]

These measures dramatically increased the amount of revenue state governments collected and radically shifted the burden of taxation. In Mississippi, the effective tax rate on the largest landowners quadrupled between 1860 and 1870. By taxing land at its full value and at higher rates, Reconstruction governments forced such landowners to sell excess land. More than any other, this policy fueled the sharp increase in Black landholdings during these years. In Mississippi, such land sales opened up vast amounts of acreage in the Delta region to small farmers, briefly earning the region a reputation as a "poor man's paradise." In South Carolina, much of the land in Black people's possession in 1890 had been acquired during Reconstruction as a result of tax policies explicitly aimed at breaking up the largest plantations.[8]

While Reconstruction governments did take steps to shield small landowners from heavy tax burdens, many whites were paying taxes for the first time at a moment when the rural backcountry was reeling in the aftermath of war.[9] Sensing a political opportunity, white planters and elites sought to stoke broad-based opposition to Reconstruction by appealing to poorer whites as fellow taxpayers. Beginning in the early 1870s, taxpayer leagues and organizations formed across the South, largely organized and led by former Confederate officers and members of the planter aristocracy but quickly gaining mass followings. By 1874, there was a taxpayer organization in nearly every county in South Carolina.[10]

White taxpayer organizations complemented the work of terrorist groups like the Ku Klux Klan. As these vigilante groups terrorized and murdered Black citizens and white Republicans, and as white newspapers deployed racist images of Black misrule to stir the passions and fears of the white electorate, taxpayer leagues framed white opposition to Republican rule as a principled stand against fiscal irresponsibility. To be sure, white taxpayers also engaged in acts of political violence and terror. In 1874, members of a taxpayer group laid siege to the county courthouse in Vicksburg, Mississippi, and demanded that all its Black officeholders resign, then opened fire on Black militia members, killing between seventy-five and three hundred men.[11]

These efforts to organize cross-class alliances of white southerners under their shared identity as taxpayers seeded the ground for reactionary tax politics for generations to come. Taxpayer groups worked to divide the electorate between "taxpayers and tax-layers" and to make the former synonymous with white people and the latter with Blacks and their allies. They worked to delegitimize Reconstruction governments with the notion that those who "paid little or no taxes" had no right to "levy taxes" on others; in other words, they had no right to participate in government. Taxpayer groups made a point of spotlighting the Black beneficiaries of tax-funded institutions, to convince the white poor that the taxes they were struggling to pay were aiding and assisting former slaves exclusively. As one white upcountry farmer in South Carolina wrote in disgust, "Every little negro in the county is now going to school and the public pays for it[.] ... [Our] lands principally are taxed to pay for them."[12]

This message, crafted by economic elites, resonated among the region's poor whites. Taxpayer groups devised the most effective political messages against Republican rule, building a political movement that couched elite policy objectives in populist terms.[13] Though most taxpayer groups disbanded following the overthrow of Reconstruction in 1877, the stoking of white taxpayer grievance remained a staple of white supremacist politics throughout the Jim Crow era and beyond.

The poorer whites who joined taxpayer leagues celebrated the defeat of Reconstruction and the restoration of the "rule of the taxpayer," as Redemption governments fashioned themselves. But in practice, white "redeemers" were concerned with slashing taxes only on the wealthy and industries, starving the newly formed public institutions that had been aiding and educating Blacks and poor whites alike, and limiting the state's revenue-raising capacity.[14] They quickly reinstated low assessments on the most valuable farmlands and exempted many industrial assets from taxation. In Mississippi, assessed values on 160-acre farms fell by nearly half after white Democrats returned to power in the 1880s.[15] In Alabama, whites drew up a new constitution in 1875 that placed strict limits on the powers of the state and localities to tax property and on the amount of state revenue that could go toward public education. To make up for those losses, the constitution also authorized the state to lease convicts to private corporations.[16]

During the Redemption era, southern state governments shifted the burden of public finance back onto the poor and disfranchised. They redesigned state tax codes to serve the interests of the white planter class. Some states replaced tax exemptions for small landowners with exemptions for machinery and other items found only on large plantations. "The result," historian Eric Foner notes, "was that blacks now paid taxes on virtually every piece of property they owned—tools, mules, even furniture—while larger farms had several thousand dollars exempted."[17] These regimes also dismantled oversight and equalization boards, slashed assessors' salaries, and repealed laws mandating full-value assessments. Some states resumed allowing property owners to submit their own estimates of their property's worth, a practice that allowed the wealthiest landowners to pay only so much as they wished.[18] The result was what historian J. Morgan Kousser described as "a regressive, malapportioned, and often dishonestly administered state and local tax system."[19] Even as they condemned federal power, white redeemers harbored no ideological commitment to ensuring local control over political and fiscal affairs. In states where pockets of Black political power still remained at the county and municipal levels, Redemption-era governments worked to constrain the exercise of local power. As the legal scholar Daniel Farbman put it, "the question for Redeemers was never whether, as an abstract matter, local control was preferable to centralized control. Rather, . . . the question was how the balance between local and state power could be manipulated and adjusted to protect the Redeemers' political power and further the struggle for white supremacy."[20]

* * *

As white "redeemers" dismantled Reconstruction and as the US Supreme Court gutted the civil rights and protections of the Fourteenth and Fifteenth Amendments, Blacks became even more dogged in their pursuit of landownership and the rights that owning property conferred. During these years, "the development of a strong land base became," as historian Manning Marable put it, "an ideological imperative of black thought."[21] Land and the availability of mortgages to Black borrowers seeking to buy some were most in abundance in Virginia. Here, in the cradle of the former Confederacy, Black landownership rates soared at the turn of the twentieth century. Between 1891 and 1910, the historian Loren Schweninger found, Black landholdings in the state more than doubled, from 698,074 acres to 1,551,153 acres.

By then, more than one-half of the total farm acreage Black Virginians tilled was on land they owned.[22]

African Americans bought land wherever they could get it, and from whomever was willing to sell it. Often, that meant settling for the "less fertile, worn-out tracts" that white farmers had "worn out and abandoned as unproductive."[23] "The Negroes, as a rule, must buy rocky or swampy land far removed from town, from the railroads, or from the navigable streams," Carter G. Woodson wrote.[24] Throughout the South, the land that Black people owned tended to be "out-of-the-way, or neglected[,] . . . in the nooks and corners between creeks and between white communities," in "areas characterized by economic deterioration" or "disadvantageously situated as regards a market."[25] In Georgia, Black ownership was most prevalent on the coast, where the soil was less productive and there were violent storms, and in the hillier regions, "where the soil is relatively poor."[26] In Virginia, one white writer observed, "The characteristic negro farm . . . is of thin soil and removed from the streams."[27] In the state's northern neck, whites claimed a monopoly on land "on the river front and on the rich river bottoms," where oyster beds were abundant. These "strip[s] of land . . . can not, as a rule, be bought by Negroes."[28] The 1900 US Census estimated that the average value of a Black-owned acre in Virginia was $6.49, whereas the average value of a white-owned acre of land in the state was $13.15, roughly twice that amount. At the same time, whites owned more of this more valuable land: 115.2 acres on average, as compared to 49.7 acres among Blacks.[29] Nearly 70 percent of Black-owned farms in the state were fewer than forty-nine acres in size. By contrast, 64 percent of white-owned farms in the state were over forty-nine acres in size.[30]

Owning land might have afforded Black people a measure of freedom and independence, but it did not shield them from exploitation at the hands of local tax administrators. In Virginia, the restoration of elite white rule in the 1890s was followed by a steady decrease in the assessments of white-owned property along with a "constant increase" in the assessed value of Black-owned property.[31] In 1901,

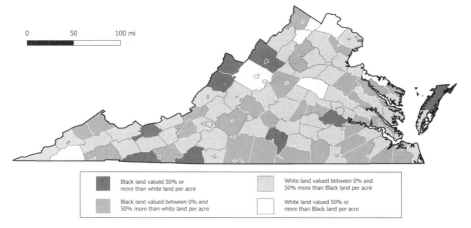

Figure 1.2 Per-acre tax assessments on Black-owned land relative to white-owned land in Virginia counties in 1901. The 1900 US agricultural census estimated Black-owned farmland in Virginia to be worth, on a per-acre basis, one-half as much as white-owned land.

the statewide average assessed value of a Black-owned acre there was $4.08, while the average assessed value of a white-owned acre was $4.68—yet the US Census estimated that the average actual value of that Black-owned acre was roughly half that of the average white-owned one.[32] A 1916 study found that white-owned land was assessed, on average, at 33.1 percent of its full value, while Black-owned land was assessed at 45.3 percent.[33] Virginia tax assessors also tended to grossly undervalue or omit entirely the buildings, improvements, and personal holdings of white landowners, while being scrupulous in their accounting of Black property holdings.[34]

Across the South, the results of white "redemption" and Black disfranchisement were written on the tax bills that white and Black landowners received. In Georgia, W. E. B. Du Bois found, the property held by the wealthy enjoyed "wholesale undervaluation," while the "very small estates of the poor" were overvalued, with Black-owned land the most overassessed.[35] In South Carolina, the African Americans who succeeded in building a substantial land base along the Sea Islands in the late nineteenth century found themselves overtaxed throughout the twentieth.[36] In Mississippi, the practice of overassessing Black-owned homes and land became, one study found, "system-atic." In some counties, Black-owned property was assessed upwards of 330 percent higher than white-owned property.[37]

It wasn't just Black-owned land and homes that were subject to overtaxation. One researcher found that Black-owned cattle were valued, on average, at 40 percent above white-owned cattle in one South Carolina county. In another, Black-owned sheep were assessed, on average, at over three times the value of white-owned sheep, and hogs at nearly a dollar more per head.[38]

Assessors' inactions proved just as consequential in generating these results. In some states, assessors were mere recorders of the values that property owners submitted, which they could correct if they chose. These minimalist administrative systems predict-ably resulted in assessments that nakedly reflected the power and standing of their holders. Small landowners and Black landowners, especially, were more likely to submit accurate valuations *and* were more likely to have their valuations adjusted upward.[39] Larger and politically powerful landowners, in contrast, grossly undervalued their holdings, which administrators never dared—or wanted—to correct.[40] What a property was initially valued at for tax purposes, it tended to remain at. Poorly funded, understaffed, and under no compulsion to tax fairly and accurately, assessors rarely if ever con-ducted reassessments, and instead habitually copied the assessment rolls from year to year, only updating properties when they changed hands. This system meant, in practice that the longer a person held a piece of land, the lower its effective tax rate. This policy structurally advantaged white, wealthier landowners, who had much longer land tenures than did small Black landowners who had acquired their land more recently.[41]

When assessors did adjust assessments, it was often to give tax breaks to favored constituents. During the Great Depression, Nor-folk's Board of Tax Equalization reduced the total assessed value of white-owned real estate by $1,634,730, while raising the assessed value of Black-owned real estate by $241,000.[42] Statewide, between 1921 and 1932, the average assessed value of a Black-owned acre in

Virginia increased relative to white-owned acres.[43] In two Georgia Black Belt counties, the per-acre assessment on Black-owned land steadily increased and surpassed white assessed values during the 1920s, a decade that saw land and agricultural prices plummet. In Greene County, the per-acre assessed value of Black land went from 59 cents below the rate on white land in 1919 to $1.13 above it in 1934. Similarly, in Macon County, Black-owned acres went from $1.51 below white acres in 1919 to 9 cents above them in 1934.[44]

Local tax administration made a mockery of Blacks' citizenship and equality. But unlike the violence and terror that stalked Black families and communities throughout the Jim Crow era, racist tax assessments were subtle and meant to be imperceptible. "Such exploitation," one ethnographer remarked, "has little of the race antagonism which accompanies Jim Crow regulations, segregation, or violence."[45] Black property owners whose assessments remained static while whites' were lowered across the board had no reason to suspect that they were being overtaxed, even though the reduction in the overall size of the tax base meant that they were.

Even still, Black people knew they were being unfairly taxed. Those Blacks who were fortunate enough to own taxable property were more aware of this reality than others were, even as these practices sapped the earnings of all Blacks living under the Jim Crow fiscal order. "It is generally understood that the Negro who owns real estate and other visible property, is assessed in a higher valuation than anybody else," Black journalist William Pickens remarked in 1916.[46] Black landowners groaned under the weight of tax bills for which, as we'll see in the next chapter, they got little to nothing in return. "The Negro hardly has his furniture arranged before the real estate taxes have been increased on his newly acquired property," one Black homeowner commented.[47] The Black press investigated cases where Black-owned homes that were "generally identical to white homes in other sections" were given higher assessments—but to little effect.[48]

Some white assessors made no secret of their intentions, using their powers as a weapon against Black mobility. In 1928, the assessor in Prince George's County, Maryland, increased the assessed value of real estate acquired by a Black land-development syndicate to nearly three times its market value and twenty times the assessed value of comparable white lots. The developers alleged the assessments were "imposed for the purpose of discouraging buyers and . . . driving [Black] owners out of the county."[49] During the real estate boom in 1920s Florida, tax assessors facilitated speculation by selectively reassessing Black-owned land in areas targeted for development. A 1931 report found instances of "Negroes who own farms and homes [being] assessed at a higher value of taxation than white citizens in the same community," and of "Negroes [who were] restricted from purchase" or forced to sell under duress after sharp spikes in their tax assessments.[50]

Black disfranchisement created the conditions for bureaucratic racism to thrive. Writing in 1903, W. E. B. Du Bois lamented, "To-day the black man of the South has almost nothing to say as to how much he shall be taxed, or how those taxes shall be expended; as to who shall execute the laws, and how they shall do it; as to who shall make the laws, and how they shall be made."[51] And because Black people living under Jim Crow did not have any such say, one Black writer remarked, "the white officials miss no opportunity to impose all the taxes they can on [us]."[52] Reflecting on the rampant overtaxation of Black-owned land on the Sea Islands, T. J. Woofter remarked, "White communities, in the same situation . . . may be and probably are the victims of similar kinds of injustice; but once aroused to the situation these communities have redress at the polls which is denied to Negro communities."[53] Arthur Raper similarly attributed higher assessments on Black-owned land to "the Negro's restricted opportunity to be felt politically." Unlike white property owners, "[A Black landowner] cannot go to the Black Belt courthouse office and demand a tax-valuation adjustment from a county official he did not help to elect—he is equally impotent should he wish to help unseat some office-holder for lack of proper consideration of him."[54]

After 1937, Black people could not go to the federal courthouse, either. At the same time as white assessors across the South were systematically overtaxing Black property owners, the federal judiciary and Congress were making it impossible for victims of discriminatory taxation at the hands of state and local governments to pursue justice at the federal level. In 1932, the US Supreme Court ruled that, in local tax disputes, the federal courts must defer to state remedies.[55] Then, in 1937, Congress passed the Tax Injunction Act, which stated that federal district courts "shall not enjoin, suspend or restrain the assessment, levy or collection of any tax under State law where a plain, speedy, and efficient remedy may be had in the courts of such State."[56] The Act aimed to prevent multistate corporations from contesting their assessments in federal court and withholding payment, a common tactic they used to bargain down their tax bills, and one that compounded local governments' fiscal crisis during the Great Depression.[57]

But while it curbed one form of corporate tax avoidance, the Tax Injunction Act expanded the discriminatory powers of local tax assessors. By cutting off local taxpayers' access to the federal courts, the Tax Injunction Act effectively exempted the tax assessor's office from the civil rights legal revolution that was about to unfold. Tax assessors' immunity from legal challenges outside state and local courts would not go unnoticed among the defenders of the Jim Crow order.

2

ACROSS THE TRACKS

In Indianola, Mississippi, whites referred to the area where Black people lived as "across the tracks." In other southern cities and towns, Blacks lived in low-lying and flood-prone areas known as "the bottoms." Whatever the Black area was called, by the early 1900s, these places were easy to identify by the public goods and services residents lacked and the health and environmental conditions they were forced to endure. During these years, southern cities, towns, and school districts began investing in modern civic improvements, building electrical grids, laying water and sewer lines, paving and repairing streets and sidewalks, and increasing spending on public education. But even as Blacks paid more than their fair share of the taxes that supported these public expenditures, they received few of taxation's benefits. Across the tracks or down in the bottoms, the sidewalks stopped, paved streets turned to dirt, garbage went uncollected, and water became contaminated. "No signs are needed to identify the white and black residential areas," a northern white visitor said of the typical southern town. The Black area began where "the paved roads turn to dirt. The storm pipes become open ditches." Children there were forced to walk for miles to attend schools that only began after the cotton had been picked or were so overcrowded they had to operate on double sessions, and that rarely went past seventh grade.[1]

These were the bitter fruits of Blacks' disfranchisement. The stripping of Black people's civil rights led inevitably to denying them their civic rights: the services, benefits, and improvements that cities and counties began to provide around the turn of the twentieth century.[2] Moreover, it allowed for the improvements and benefits whites enjoyed to come at African Americans' expense and on their dime.[3] To manage urban growth, cities and towns placed garbage dumps and concentrated noxious industries on the Black side of town. When heavy storms and overuse caused wastewater systems to break down, the waste flushed from white people's toilets flowed down into Black neighborhoods, contaminating drinking water and spreading disease. And as more whites poured into cities and enrolled their children in public schools, school districts plundered ever-greater amounts of "colored" school budgets. To live under Jim Crow meant, as Booker T. Washington once explained, "that the sewerage in his part of the city will be inferior; that the streets and sidewalks will be neglected, that the street lighting will be poor; that his section of the city will not be kept in order." It meant that Black people would be forced to "receive inferior accommodations in return for the taxes [they pay]."[4] Even more outrageous, it meant, as the Black writer William Pickens fumed, that Black people's local tax dollars went toward "paying to improve other people's property."[5]

Across the early-twentieth-century South, Black people helped to pay for the better schools white children attended and the better services white neighborhoods enjoyed. For whites, preserving those benefits required denying their source. Even as local tax administrators schemed to overtax Black people's land and homes, throughout the Jim Crow era whites insisted that Blacks paid no taxes at all, that any public dollars spent on Black people came solely from white people's pockets, and that Blacks should be grateful for whatever crumbs dropped from white taxpayers' tables. These crumbs included the public dollars that flowed into southern cities and towns from federal agencies and programs launched under the New Deal. The myth that Black people paid no taxes formed the ideological foundation of the Jim Crow fiscal state and served to justify all of its exclusionary and exploitative practices and inequitable outcomes. Writing on Indianola in the 1930s, ethnographer Hortense Powdermaker described how whites not only "justif[ied] the disparity in educational facilities, upkeep of roads and streets" on the notion "that the Whites pay the taxes and therefore should enjoy the benefit of public works." They also invoked this myth to argue that only "Whites should be employed on public works, paid out of tax money. Therefore, too, they should control the vote determining how taxes are to be levied and disbursed."[6] As public spending disparities widened, Black local politics increasingly centered on calling out white lies and making claims on the local state, not as citizens deserving of equal rights but as taxpayers deserving of their fair share.

* * *

Prior to the Civil War, southern states and localities provided little in the way of public goods and services. For many, the central organizing unit was the plantation, with governments and their agencies—such as law enforcement—mirroring its interests and serving strictly in support of its operations. Public education was virtually nonexistent and was, of course, denied to enslaved populations. Where public schools did exist, they were entirely funded by local sources.

Following the war, white former Confederates resolved that not a dime of white tax dollars would aid the formerly enslaved. Before Republicans in Congress dissolved their state governments and placed the region under military occupation in 1867, southern states rushed to enact laws aimed at taxing freedpeople to pay for their own care and support. South Carolina tied funding for its Board of Relief of Indigent Persons of Color to the proceeds from a $1 poll tax on all freedmen between ages of eighteen and fifty and a 50-cent tax on all unmarried freedwomen. Mississippi paid for its Freedmen's Pauper Fund with the revenue from the state's poll tax on Black men between the ages of eighteen and sixty. These taxes served the dual purpose of forcing Black people to work for wages.[7]

White southerners denied any responsibility for supporting freedpeople's needs and dismissed out of hand Black people's entitlement to equal benefits from the state. As they worked to shift the costs of emancipation onto the emancipated, white southerners crafted a logic that would undergird white supremacist fiscal policy and politics for decades to come. They simply denied that Black people paid any taxes, and they proceeded from this lie to argue that Black people were therefore not entitled to any publicly funded goods or services, nor to any say over tax policy or administration. Across the postwar South, as one white Tennessean wrote, "all [whites] complain that it is not right to tax the white population to support the Negros; they paying [*sic*] no tax."[8]

Freedpeople struggled to answer these lies with the truth and to claim their equal right to public entitlements. In Vicksburg, Mississippi, a group of Colored Citizens protested being forced to pay school taxes so long as "our schools are not to share in the common benefit." As one freedman argued, "As the Steat has not taken any Steeps towards Careing for our poor people we dont thinke the Steat has any right to our Suport."[9]

During Reconstruction, Republican-controlled state governments worked to create uniform systems for funding public schools.[10] Some states such as Mississippi earmarked a portion of the property taxes collected by local governments for public education and then distributed those funds to public schools according to the number of school-age children in each district. These funding models aimed to ensure that the benefits of public education would be broadly shared and equally distributed and to serve as a check on local attempts to deny education to Black children. With Blacks and Republicans wielding power at the state level, the politics of public education became a contest over local versus state control. "Local control," as W. E. B. Du Bois wrote, "meant the control of property and racial particularisms. It stood for reaction and prejudice."[11]

After white "redeemers" seized control of state governments, salaries for Black school teachers plummeted, and annual budgets for "colored" schools were decimated.[12] The bulk of the proceeds plundered from Black schools went to white schools in counties with large Black populations, which meant that they mostly went toward educating the children of the white aristocracy in the richest agricultural areas. By preserving school funding models that distributed public education dollars on a per capita basis but allowing local authorities to use those monies as they pleased, counties with large Black populations continued to receive all the intended funds but could now spend the bulk of those funds on white schools only. White children living in predominantly white counties, conversely, saw no increase in funding. As a result, school-funding disparities among whites widened dramatically. In Mississippi, white schools in the all-white Itawamba County spent $5.65 per capita, while in Washington County, where Blacks comprised over 75 percent of the population, per capita spending on white schoolchildren was over $80.[13]

As southern states disfranchised Black voters and began rewriting state constitutions in the 1890s, the politics of public education funding became, among whites, a struggle over who was entitled to the spoils of raiding "colored" school funds. State lawmakers representing heavily white districts outside the Black Belt denounced funding models that distributed school funds to counties on a per capita basis. In its place, they called for the division of tax dollars by race and distribution of school funds in accordance with each race's tax payments. Making Black schools solely reliant on Black tax dollars first emerged as a popular rallying cry among poor whites and taxpayer leagues during Reconstruction, and subsequently several state legislatures considered such plans. However, those plans that were enacted were overturned by state courts, and other legislatures backed down under the threat of federal lawsuits.[14] In the 1880s, southern white Populists demanded greater school funding for all and higher taxes on corporations and industries to pay for it. But as populist insurgencies collapsed in the 1890s, poor whites returned again to demanding a racial school tax division as a means of achieving greater funding equality among whites.[15] Legislatures responded with symbolic gestures that portended substantive change.

Beginning in the 1890s, several southern states ordered local tax collectors to divide tax records by race. The aim was to prove how great the gap was between Black people's direct tax payments and public spending on them, and thus provide the basis for further cuts in funding for Black schools. As Virginia's state auditor, Frank G. Ruffin, argued, separate tax books would "let the white men know how much

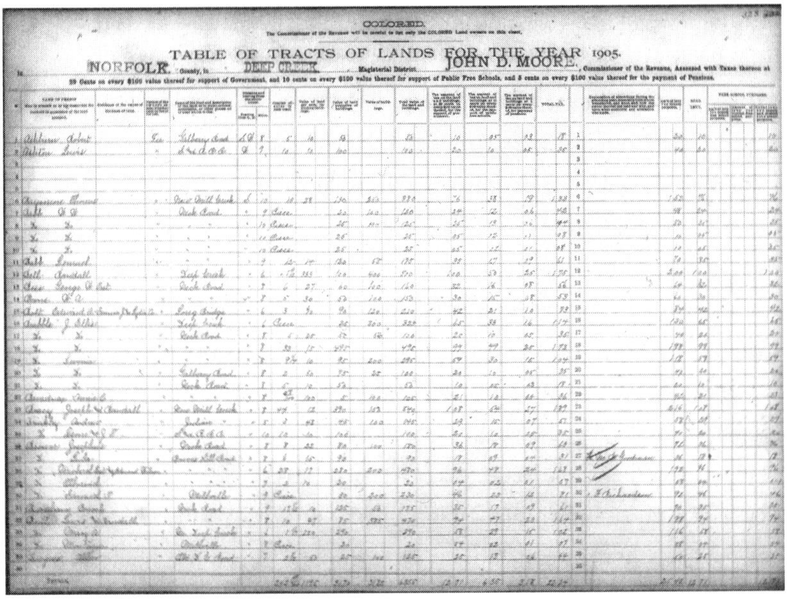
COLORED.

TABLE OF TRACTS OF LANDS FOR THE YEAR 1905.

NORFOLK County, in DEEP CREEK Magisterial District. JOHN D. MOORE, Commissioner of the Revenue

Figure 2.1 Norfolk County, Virginia, "colored" land tax book, 1905.

of their money is squandered on negroes."[16] "The object" of Virginia's 1891 law dividing land tax records by race, one newspaper remarked, was to not only "show the proportion of taxes paid by the negroes," but to also "furnish the data upon which a separation of the school [tax] would be based."[17]

By the early 1900s, white supremacist politicians like Mississippi's James K. Vardaman and Georgia's Hoke Smith made the racial division of tax revenues part of their campaign platforms.[18] These proposals would, they claimed, relieve white taxpayers of any obligations to support "colored" schools. The most vocal white supremacists would accept nothing less. "Let the white people's taxes go to white people's children, and the negro's taxes to his children," Rebecca Latimer Felton demanded of Georgia lawmakers.[19] But equally importantly, they would also prevent whites in heavily Black counties from exploiting per-capita funding formulas to hoard public dollars.[20] The strongest support for such measures came from heavily white districts that stood to benefit most. In 1901, when lawmakers in Alabama

met to adopt a new constitution that disfranchised the Black population, whites representing poorer counties proposed a provision to
divide school tax revenues by each race's tax payments.[21] Lawmakers
from Black Belt counties shot down the proposal and instead placed
extremely low statutory limits on property tax rates and erected a host
of procedural barriers preventing state and local governments from
raising taxes in the future.[22]

Other states responded to poorer whites' demands for a racial division of school taxes by decentralizing public funding for education.
Virginia's new state constitution (adopted in 1902) slashed state funding for public schools while authorizing counties, cities, and school
districts to raise additional funds themselves through property taxes.
The only requirement was that districts provide primary schools for
at least four months each year. "This plan," Virginia lawmaker Walter
A. Watson argued, "would permit local authorities to give the negroes
only such schools as they deem proper."[23]

Across the South, states shifted funding for public education from
the state to the local level. Between 1900 and 1915, the proportion
of public school expenditures provided by local taxes in Virginia,
North Carolina, South Carolina, and Georgia rose from 42.4 percent to 72.4 percent.[24] School-funding decentralization did little to
help white schools in poorer, heavily white counties, while allowing
white schools across the Black Belt to continue to pillage Black tax
dollars with impunity. One 1941 study found that not a single county
in the South with a population over 50 percent Black annually spent
more than $14.99 per Black pupil.[25] In the majority-Black Bruns-
wick County, Virginia, white officials annually allotted $45 per white
schoolchild and only $3 per Black child. At the time, Black property
owners there contributed in direct tax payments over one-fourth of
the county's school funds.[26] Failing to address the inadequacies of
white public schools in poorer regions of the South, these reforms also
did little to quell white demands for separating tax revenues along
racial lines, a plank that remained a staple of white-supremacist politics for years to come.

Black and white scholars and educational reformers attempted, often in vain, to inject facts into these debates and reveal the erroneous assumptions behind white demands for fiscal apartheid. In 1906, W. E. B. Du Bois published research showing that, in Georgia, only 20 cents of every dollar spent on public education went toward "colored" schools, though roughly half of all the state's schoolchildren were Black.[27] In 1909, Charles Coon, a leading white educational administrator in North Carolina, compared the actual tax contributions of whites and Blacks in Georgia, North Carolina, and Virginia to the funding white and "colored" schools there received. Significantly, Coon allocated railroad and corporate tax revenues by population. He found that, were there to be a strict division of school taxes by race, Black schools in Virginia would be *owed* $18,077 annually, those in North Carolina would be owed $26,539, and those in Georgia a whopping $141,682.[28] Contrary to white supremacists' claims, African Americans were, indeed, "pay[ing] more than their share for public education."[29] Dividing school funds by race would, if anything, be beneficial to Black schoolchildren. Subsequent studies confirmed Coon's findings. Between 1880 and 1910, one economic historian estimated, "black taxpayers were subsidizing white school systems in every southern state." In Mississippi, annual net transfers of Black tax dollars to white schools rose to over $1 million by 1910.[30] Coon presented his findings at a major conference for southern educators. He compared white southerners' insistence that the overindulgence of "colored" schools was holding the region back to the "farmer who always complained that the heavy doctor's bills prevented his success. On questioning the doctor," Coon deadpanned, "it was discovered that the farmer had not paid his bill for twenty years."[31]

Coon's findings made front-page headlines in several northern newspapers. Liberal reformers cited them as proof of the South's deplorable neglect of Black education. Coon's white peers in the South at first tried to dismiss his findings. "It is so absurd to contend that the white people pay nothing to the education of the negro," the *Raleigh News and Observer* said.[32] Richmond, Virginia, school superintendent J. D. Eggleston accused Coon of "utter ignorance" on "fiscal matters" and scoffed at his distribution of railroad taxes on a per capita basis.

Everyone knows "that no negroes own railroad stock," he chuckled.[33] (Coon responded, "If you bring the matter down to that, then most school teachers and other whites would fare rather slim when the school funds derived from railroad taxes are passed around!")[34] Others sidestepped the claims and instead expressed anger at Coon giving fodder to those who took delight in "the opportunity to disparage the white people of this section."[35] Others took offense at the mere suggestion that Black taxpayers were helping to pay for white children's education. "Is [Coon] a white man or a negro?" one asked, calling his report "an insult as deep and infamous as it would be possible to conceive of. It is enough to make the blood of a Southern white man boil!"[36] Coon's findings undermined claims that education for Blacks was a "gift" from white taxpayers, one that they could withdraw on any whim. It made the Black taxpayer newly visible. And it raised difficult questions about the relationship between the sources of taxes and the recipients of public spending that white proponents of fiscal apartheid were not prepared to address. Even as school-tax divisions never materialized, in practice, whites got the lion's share of the railroad tax, along with all the other tax revenues.

Black people paid taxes to fund white school systems, and then taxed themselves a second time to provide their children the education those systems denied. Black communities were in a constant state of fundraising—to pay teachers' salaries, to provide schoolhouses, and to purchase books and supplies. This form of double taxation was common throughout the South, and actively encouraged by white officials, who stood to benefit politically—and materially—from Blacks' self-sacrifice. One study estimated that 1,816 Black schools (nearly 44 percent) in the South were on land or in buildings Black property owners had donated to the local school boards. Expropriating Black school funds and spending as little as possible on "colored" schools paid rich dividends for white-controlled school districts, not only lowering the cost of educating white children for white taxpayers but allowing them to acquire property from Black people for free.[37]

Forced to pay taxes in support of white schools, and forced to hand over their own property just to provide their own children with the

Figure 2.2 African Americans segregated school, 1939.

education they were denied, Blacks came to see their oppression in fiscal terms and couched their demands for equal treatment in the language of taxpayer citizenship. They pointed out the obvious: that Blacks contributed far more taxes than what appeared on the "colored" pages of property tax ledgers. Incredulous over white officials' claims that the pitiful salaries for Black school teachers in Alabama were justified by Black taxpayers' supposedly meager contributions, Booker T. Washington noted that the state annually generated over $900,000 from leasing Black convicts to private contractors: "While $900,000 is turned over to the state treasury from Negro convict labor, to say nothing of Negro taxes, there came out of the state treasury to pay Negro teachers, only $357,586."[38]

Washington and others pointed out that every Black person paid taxes for the roof over their heads and the lands they farmed, whether they received a tax bill or not. "The man who pays house rent pays large taxes, for the price paid for the rent included payment of the taxes on the property." William Pickens characterized the region's large landowners with hundreds of tenants as "but a tax-agent appointed by the laws of society to gather the taxes of those tenants and turn the same over to the tax-collector. He raises rent or lowers wages in proportion to the taxes he must deliver to the state." White southerners' claims of having to shoulder the cost of educating Black children just "because their names are in the majority on the tax books," the author and future NAACP executive secretary James Weldon Johnson wrote in 1915, "is as absurd as it would be for the relatively few landowners of New York City to complain that they have to stand the financial burden of educating the thousands and thousands of children whose parents pay rent for tenements and flats."[39]

* * *

A growing portion of the taxes that Blacks paid directly or indirectly went toward urban infrastructure and civic improvements. Throughout the 1800s, urban centers in the South remained small and sparsely developed; most functioned as trading centers for agricultural commodities. They issued few bonds, collected few taxes, and spent little on public services. In 1880, the largest southern city, New Orleans, spent less than one-fifth per capita as Boston did.[40] What little cities did spend went strictly toward the areas where elites lived and whose interests urban governments served.

That state of affairs began to change in the 1900s. Between 1880 and 1910, the number of people living in cities, towns, and villages across the South increased by over five million. In 1880, fewer than three thousand people lived in Birmingham, Alabama. By 1910, the city had grown into an industrial behemoth of more than 133,000 residents. In 1881, roughly four hundred people lived in Roanoke, Virginia. One decade later, the city claimed a population of more than twenty-five thousand. Between 1890 and 1910, the population of Norfolk, Virginia, nearly doubled from thirty-five thousand to over sixty-seven thousand. In response, southern cities adopted sweeping political reforms, replacing elected officials with city managers, adopting modern city-planning methods, and investing in street paving, water and sewerage systems, and public education. The South's urban white professional and middle classes led the push for progressive reform and enjoyed its benefits.[41] The areas within and around urban centers where Blacks lived, on the other hand, became defined by the absence of such services and amenities. There, as W. E. B. Du Bois described, "the streets are unpaved; sidewalks are in dilapidated condition; the drainage is bad; the garbage is not cared for, . . . much of it . . . due to the deliberate refusal of the city to spend any public money on city improvements in the Negro district."[42]

In many cities, municipal services did not follow the color line in housing markets so much as help to draw it. At the same time as southern cities and towns embarked on major infrastructure projects and expanded services, they worked to segregate residential areas by race and confine Black people geographically. As historian Edward L. Ayers observed, "the faster a Southern city grew, the faster it became segregated."[43] Beginning with Baltimore in 1910, several southern cities and towns adopted racial zoning ordinances. After setting the boundaries, cities allocated services accordingly. In Baltimore, the city sewerage commission systematically bypassed Black neighborhoods as it expanded. Louisville, Kentucky, scaled back street cleaning and repair in areas designated for "Negro" occupancy, and removed these areas from consideration for future infrastructure expansion.[44] Into the 1930s, over one-third of Black homes in the city remained unconnected to sewer lines.[45] In Houston, the city's "Negro sections" were notable for their "absence of drainage, lights, and paving."[46] Smaller cities in Virginia, like Lynchburg and Charlottesville, had by the 1920s extended paved streets into most of their residential areas, except its "Negro districts," all of which remained "wholly lacking" in pavement.[47] In Athens, Georgia, sanitation in Black settlements "receives practically no attention or supervision from the city."[48] In Martinsville, Virginia, one reporter wryly remarked, "sidewalks seem to stop where Negro property begins."[49] In Richmond, Virginia, over half the blocks in the Black districts lacked pavement, and over one-third were without sidewalks.[50]

These racially uneven patterns of growth and infrastructure development posed significant threats to the health and safety of urban

Black populations. In many cities, the unpaved and ungraded streets in overcrowded Black areas became virtually impassible, preventing wood and coal from being delivered in the winter months and impeding fire trucks year-round.[51] In early-twentieth-century Atlanta, the public wastewater system that served middle-class white neighborhoods would, during heavy storms, overflow and drain into low-lying Black neighborhoods.[52]

Blacks understood the intent behind residential-segregation ordinances and strained to couch their opposition to them in material terms. When the NAACP challenged Louisville's racial-zoning ordinance, which resulted in the practice being deemed unconstitutional in 1917, the organization's lawyers attempted to undermine the city's claim that Black people's mere presence as residents in white neighborhoods lowered property values. During cross-examination, one of the city's leading real estate dealers conceded that, after an area became designated for Black occupancy, the city withdrew services it previously provided. Similarly, landlords ceased to improve or repair properties as soon as they began renting to Black tenants.[53] In Birmingham, Black civic leaders stressed that their opposition to a proposed racial-zoning ordinance was not due to any desire to live among white people. "Nothing is further from the truth," one of the city's Black newspapers exclaimed. "They oppose the measure because Negroes are unprotected when they are not near white people. They don't have police supervision, lights are not given, streets are not kept up and a general lack of interest is exercised in any absolute Negro community."[54] In Richmond, one study found that the "general lack of paving in the Negro residential areas ... constitutes a chief cause of complaint and is the reason most generally assigned for the aggressiveness in pushing into white areas."[55]

Across the urban South, Blacks resisted residential segregation statutes on the grounds that they would exacerbate these disparities. When city commissioners in Roanoke, Virginia, drafted a resolution calling for white and Black residents to adhere to the city's color line in 1921, a group of leading Black citizens came to the public meeting with its own set of resolutions. Speaking for the group, the Rev. L. L.

Downing first sought to clear up any "misunderstanding" as to why Black people might be seeking housing opportunities in white neighborhoods. It was "absolutely not," he explained, due "to a desire of any group of citizens to have as neighbors any other particular group." Rather, it was due to the "crowded and congested condition[s]" in Black neighborhoods and to the city's neglect of Black residents' most basic needs. "In our residential section we have not a single decent street." When a street crossed over from the white to Black section of town, he noted, it went from being "well kept" to "the way nature left it." Whereas white neighborhoods had been outfitted with water and sewerage lines, in Black sections "there is no sewerage, no water facilities, [no] gas or electricity. . . . In many cases our people obtain water from three or four blocks away and from dangerous unsanitary springs and wells." Little wonder, he added, "that our morbidity and mortality rate is high." The group's resolution went on to detail the sordid state of the "colored" schools, which were "unsanitary and antiquated," with leaking roofs, "tissue paper" dividing walls, and dangerous playgrounds. "Therefore," it concluded, "it is the consensus of our people, who are law-abiding citizens, tax payers, that these conditions . . . if properly looked into and remedied accordingly, will do more to bring about a better understanding" between the races than any segregation statute could hope to accomplish. "All we are after," Downing closed, "is civic advantages we deserve and are justly due." Blindsided, Roanoke's white city commissioner sputtered, "Council has done everything in its power to give the colored sections everything possible" and gaveled the meeting to a close without holding a vote on either resolution.[56]

When it came to passing the bond referenda that financed civic improvements, white officials could not so easily dismiss Blacks' demands. To conform with the narrowest interpretation of the Fifteenth Amendment's voting rights protections, southern states adopted a host of ostensibly racially neutral barriers to voting—such as poll taxes, literacy tests, and understanding clauses—which they then applied on a discriminatory basis. To make Blacks' exclusion from electoral politics complete, they made the South a one-party region, with the only contested election being the Democratic primary, and then banned Black people from becoming members of the Democratic Party. But Blacks who successfully navigated the gauntlet of voter suppression measures could still vote in general elections, which meant that they could vote on bond issues. In 1919, Atlanta called on voters to pass a bond referendum to fund the city's schools. Previous bond issues—which Black residents paid taxes to pay down—had funded new schools for white children and higher salaries for white teachers. Meanwhile, the Black schools suffered from severe overcrowding and chronic underinvestment. Schooling for Black children ended at the seventh grade. For nearly a decade, most ran on "double sessions," where students attended for half a day. With the new bond measure on the table, Black civic leaders demanded that the city include in it funds for new grammar schools for Black children and the elimination of "double sessions," increased salaries for Black teachers, and the construction of a Black high school. When city and school officials offered only vague assurances, Black community activists and organizers went door-to-door, helping to register Black voters and getting them to the polls, to defeat the measure. "What guarantees shall we have of the faithful carrying out of these promises?" NAACP leaders asked, and added, "What about our miserable streets, our inadequate police and fire protection? What about our schools? Shall promises be made only to turn out to be mere 'scraps of paper'?"

At the same time as they demanded their civic rights as taxpayers, Black Atlantans' efforts to secure more school funding also challenged the insidious notion that Black people—or any group—only deserved in public goods and services as much as they paid in taxes. This, the NAACP had to remind white officials, was not how taxes worked. Whether or not a new "colored" school or library, or paved streets or sewer lines in Black neighborhoods, would result in Blacks "receiving more money than we contribute as taxpayers" did not matter, they argued. Just as taxes should be assessed fairly, "public funds" should be allocated "in the interest of all of the people."[57]

In three consecutive elections, Black voters cast the decisive margin defeating bond measures. Following one defeat, members of the school board called on the state legislature to override the vote and permit the city to raise the school tax rate, anyway, because "the majority of white voters approved it." Instead, the city agreed to negotiate, and in 1921 included funding for its first "colored" high school in its bond issue. The measure passed. The city then tried to rescind its promise, and only agreed to build Booker T. Washington High School under threat of lawsuit. It would be the last "colored" high school—or any "colored" school—the city would build for over a quarter century, during which time its Black population increased by nearly forty thousand.[58]

While these voting efforts could claim some success, too often they led only to dead ends. In 1935, Atlanta's NAACP chapter threatened to mobilize Black voters in opposition to a bond issue unless the city agreed to provide more funding for Black schools. But they were unable to generate enough voters who could overcome enhanced voter-suppression measures to sway the election. By then, double sessions had spread to virtually every Black school in the city, as they had in most southern cities.[59]

* * *

Federal spending on cities' and towns' local infrastructures grew dramatically in the 1930s. Seeking to address glaring public needs and put the nation's ranks of the unemployed back to work, the Franklin D. Roosevelt administration created a series of public works programs as part of its New Deal. Among others, the Works Progress Administration (WPA) and Public Works Administration (PWA) allocated federal dollars toward local infrastructure projects in cities and towns across the country. Local governments across the South grasped for these federal dollars with both hands. In Mississippi, hundreds of cities and towns applied for and received funds to build and pave streets and sidewalks, create storm and wastewater sewer systems, build and improve school buildings and public libraries, improve water systems, and build new parks and playgrounds, among other projects. The town of Edwards received WPA funds to build a new public swimming pool and improve its sewer system. The town of Shaw secured WPA funds to pave town streets, lay sidewalks, repair the town's reservoir, and build a new bathhouse and jail. Port Gibson used a combination of federal and local dollars to build a swimming pool, man-made lake, and country club. In 1935 alone, the PWA allocated $47,929,944 in funds for 202 projects in the Magnolia State.[60]

Few of the federal dollars southern towns secured in the 1930s made it "across the tracks," though. New Deal agencies afforded state and local administrators wide discretion over their use of federal funds. Local officials submitted project proposals, state administrators sent these proposals to Washington for approval, and the federal agencies approved them with few strings attached. As a result, nearly all the projects approved for cities and towns in Mississippi and other southern states, not to mention most of the public works jobs these projects created, primarily if not exclusively benefitted white residents. Cities and towns used federal dollars to pave streets and lay water mains and sewers exclusively on the white side of town, and they limited access to new, federally funded swimming pools and public libraries to whites only.[61]

During these same years, the African American populations of southern cities and towns continued to swell. New Deal agricultural policies and programs resulted in the mass displacement of rural farm laborers. The displaced sharecroppers, tenant farmers, and agricultural laborers who didn't leave the South entirely tended to move into southern cities and towns in search of work, schooling for their children, and community.[62] As they did so, local governments and real estate dealers worked to keep the influx contained within Black residential areas or push them into unincorporated areas on the outskirts of town. Once Black people settled in an unincorporated area, that area tended to remain unincorporated, even when a neighboring city or town annexed surrounding areas and expanded town boundaries.[63]

Within these neglected areas, Black residents battled against daily threats to their health and safety and innumerable indignities. New wastewater systems that enabled indoor plumbing rarely extended into Black residential areas. Instead, Blacks continued to rely on out-houses, cesspools, and straight piping of raw sewage into backyards, which caused illness and disease to spread. In Tunica, Mississippi, a fetid stream known as Sugar Ditch formed behind a string of con-crete and clapboard houses for Black families.[64] When cities and towns did extend water and sewerage into Black areas, they invari-ably did so on the cheap. Some, like the town of Shaw, Mississippi, cut costs by using narrower pipes (which provided less water pres-sure) and placing fewer fire hydrants in Black neighborhoods. On the Black side of Shaw, water mains were 1.25 inches wide as compared to the 6-inch mains for white residents. Such drastically reduced water pressure, combined with the sparse number of fire hydrants, meant that blazes that broke out in Black homes were more destructive. In one year alone, seven Black homes in Shaw burned to the ground, resulting in one death.[65] In Port Gibson, Mississippi, as one investi-gator described, "sewerage pipes run along the sidewalk about five to ten yards in front of the homes. People say that these [pipes] back up a lot causing overflows and a heavy stench of sewer water."[66] In Bolton, Mississippi, Bennie Thompson (who would later become the town's mayor and a US Congressman) recalled, "On the white side of town, all the streets were concrete. On the Black side of town, they were either gravel or asphalt base. On the white side of town, there were sidewalks. On the Black side of town, no sidewalks. On the white side of town, there was six-inch water mains. On the Black side of town, there were two-inch water mains."[67]

Meanwhile, Black children spent their summers dripping in sweat while the sounds of white children splashing and playing in pub-lic swimming pools they were barred from using rang in their ears. As a Black child in Edwards, Jean White heard the sounds of white children playing in the town swimming pool from her home. "You couldn't swim, but you wanted to get in the water because they was having such a good time," she recalled. "None of us knew how to swim," K. C. Morrison said of the Black children he grew up with in Edwards.[68]

* * *

More than the indignity of being forced to drink from a "colored" water fountain or sit in the "colored" section of a train, Black people experienced segregation as the threat of being sickened from untreated water or sewage, of dying in a house fire for lack of fire hydrants or water pressure, of their children attending school in a dilapidated structure and for only half a day, and of being forced to pay taxes in support of services, protections, and improvements they were denied. Southern cities and towns' public spending policies and priorities would also become the terrain on which Black people waged local struggles against Jim Crow in the decades to come.

3

TAKEN

In 1884, Caesar Scott purchased 40 acres of land on St. Helena Island, South Carolina. Over the next fifty years, the former slave, his children, and his grandchildren grew rice and vegetables, raised livestock, fished, and tried to live as self-sufficiently as they could. By the early 1930s, the family's homestead, which had grown to sixty-six acres and included two barrier islands, had passed down to Scott's granddaughter, Evelina Jenkins. The family held tight to their independence. To meet expenses, Jenkins sold some of the okra, tomatoes, and sweet potatoes she grew at the market in the town of Beaufort on the mainland, and as a young woman she had worked in white families' homes, but otherwise she lived off the land. Among those expenses were property taxes. Jenkins struggled each year to round up the cash needed to pay the bill to Beaufort County. Jenkins, like many of the Gullah families living on the Sea Islands, rarely ventured into town, much less into the county's courthouse. So she, like many others, entrusted a white person—in this case, attorney William Levin, for whom she had previously worked as a domestic servant—to take her tax payment to town and pay it on her behalf. Levin shared an office building with the county sheriff, J. E. McTeer, the man in charge of collecting tax payments. Each year, McTeer was also in charge of auctioning off the liens on properties that had become tax delinquent.

Jenkins's 1931 tax payment never arrived. But she did not know this. Nor did she know that McTeer would assess a lien on her land and put it up for auction the following year, which he did. The price:

$26. The buyer: William Levin.[1] After a year passed, Levin claimed the deed to all of Jenkins's sixty-six acres—another thing Jenkins did not know. For Levin, it was a speculative investment that he could wait to cash in. For decades afterward, Levin kept up the ruse of taking Jenkins's tax payment into town—having her pay, that is, on property that was no longer hers. It was one of sixty properties in Beaufort County that Levin had claimed at the tax sale.[2]

Jenkins's grandfather Caesar was one of the many former slaves who had succeeded in acquiring land after the Civil War. But from the moment Black people began buying property, they struggled to retain it. "Probably for every acre owned by a black man to-day," W. E. B. Du Bois wrote in 1909, "an acre has been lost by some other."[3] To finance their purchases, Blacks often had to settle for high-interest and high-risk loans. To keep them, they had to pay higher property taxes to local governments than whites did. And then they had to hope that no white person ever resented their successes or wanted their properties for themselves. Across the Jim Crow South, armed bands of white terrorists (known as "whitecappers") descended on Black landowners without warning, forcing them to abandon their homes at gunpoint. Whites in competition with Black-owned businesses for Black people's dollars led lynch mobs against their competitors. As the crusading journalist Ida B. Wells wrote in 1892 following the lynching of a Black grocery store owner in Memphis, Tennessee, who had the audacity to defend his property from white attacks, these acts of racial terror were "an excuse to get rid of Negroes who were acquiring wealth and property."[4]

Black property owners remained on guard against these threats. The threat of losing your land at a tax sale, however, could strike without warning. Black landowners in the late-nineteenth- and early-twentieth-century South fell into tax delinquency for the same reasons that white property owners did: due to financial hardship, negligence, or accident. Many Blacks also landed on the delinquent tax rolls because someone conspired to put them there. Regardless of how, once a Black person fell into tax delinquency, they struggled to climb out from under crippling debts, satisfy confusing legal requirements and procedures for redemption, or escape from traps that were often set from inside local tax offices. Many Black people lost their land or home to taxes without ever fully understanding why. In contrast to whitecappings, lynch mobs, and other forms of violent Black land taking, the tax sale became, as NAACP special counsel Thurgood Marshall described, a means of "depriving Negroes of their property through subterfuge."[5] Those most endangered were those whose land was most valuable.

* * *

The melding of state power and private interests has long been a feature of tax collection and enforcement. In ancient Greece, governments auctioned off the right to collect taxes, with the winning bidder entitled to a share of the proceeds. The Roman empire introduced the practice of "tax farming," a system of awarding contracts for the right to collect taxes on behalf of the state, which was later adopted by England in the thirteenth century. No matter where it was practiced, the collection of taxes by private actors generated controversy. Public outrage over tax farming became a rallying cry during the English Revolution, leading to its abolishment.[6] But for governments, the prospect of farming out tax collection and enforcement held a seductive appeal. Doing so ensured a steady revenue stream, lowered administrative costs, and, when a property was seized for want of payment, deflected anger away from public officials. In the United States, state constitutions put tax collection in the hands of public officials, but they often turned to private actors to combat tax avoidance and collect late payments. Most states had statutes allowing for the sale of liens on tax-delinquent property, and all had procedures for foreclosures and resales.

Wherever counties held tax sales, a class of investors formed. In midwestern states like Illinois and Iowa in the mid-1800s, local lawyers, bankers, and realtors—as well as a handful of outside investors—crowded into tax auctions. They were joined by handfuls of one-time bidders, many of whom were drawn in by the prospect of acquiring land for pennies on the dollar.[7]

As the Union Army laid siege along the South Carolina Sea Islands at the outset of the Civil War, the federal government imposed a land tax that they knew white Confederates had no intention of paying. And when they didn't, the government seized the property as tax delinquent and sold it. Much of it was acquired by Union soldiers and white northerners, but some of it fell into the hands of the formerly enslaved. Tax sales of abandoned plantations afforded former slaves the first opportunities to acquire plots of land in America for themselves and formed the basis for early attempts at land redistribution.[8] After President Johnson ended such efforts at the federal level, radical Republicans in newly reconstructed southern state governments attempted to continue them. In South Carolina, state senator Beverly Nash, who had been born enslaved, called for heavy taxes on the largest plantations to force their sale. "I want them taxed until they put these lands back where they belong, into the hands of those who worked them," Nash said. To fellow freedmen and women, he added, "You toiled for them, you labored for them, and were sold to pay for them, and you ought to have them."[9] "We must drive them to the wall by taxation," radical Republican J. P. M. Epping said of the state's landed aristocrats at South Carolina's 1867 Constitutional Convention. Absent a federal policy, radicals argued, doing so was the only way to expand opportunities for landownership among former slaves and nourish a democracy of small landowners. Along with voluntary sales and adverse possession of abandoned lands, tax sales provided one of the means by which Black people began to build a land base in the post-emancipation South.[10]

But that base was a fragile one. Even as property taxes remained comparatively low in southern states, they imposed heavy burdens and posed innumerable challenges and hazards to many Black landowners. Virtually all Black landowners remained dependent on white merchants and lenders for food, clothing, and other necessities, which the merchants supplied at exorbitant prices and on highly usurious terms. Carter G. Woodson estimated that one-fourth of all Black farm owners also worked as tenants on white-owned farms, with their own landholdings used merely "to raise a few vegetables and fruits required by the family."[11] Unable to save, many turned to those same usurious lenders to pay their taxes.[12] Borrowing money to pay taxes, invariably at exorbitant interest rates, became a common practice, and informal tax lending services formed wherever large numbers of cash-poor landowners lived. So, too, did networks of mutual support and aid. Across the Sea Islands, many Black families designated certain crops to be grown and sold to pay annual tax bills. On Hilton Head Island, South Carolina, Black families planted pecan trees for that purpose. Each fall, parents sent their children out to fill up burlap sacks with pecans, which they sold.[13] Others harvested oysters and other shellfish, or they sent their children out to work on shrimp boats, in oyster canneries, or phosphate mines just long enough to earn the money needed for taxes.[14]

Black property owners took pride in paying their taxes and staked their claim to equal rights and protections on their status as taxpayers. But the act of paying their taxes was one that many dreaded. Under Jim Crow, even paying a bill became, for Black people, an exercise in humiliation and a reminder of their proscribed status. As a child growing up in segregated Alabama, Ann S. Pointer remembers:

> My grandmother . . . would get up in October, and I would walk to town with her, to pay her taxes . . . and she'd be the first one there in the courthouse at the tax office, and the man the tax collector and assessor all was in there. He knew my grandmother[,] he'd talk to her 'hey how you doin' hi there' and he'd be . . . getting his books and things down, and . . . he'd sit down and start writing in the book you know whatever he's writing up her taxes. A white man walk in, later on, '[. . .]I'll be back with you in a minute' and she would sit there just about all day long.[15]

African Americans ventured into these spaces with trepidation. "It's a funny thing," Money Alan Kirby of Magnolia, Arkansas, observed: "They'd always have where you'd have tax offices and business offices[,] . . . they always had police stationed close to those places."[16] They never failed to notice the recording of the race of taxpayers in

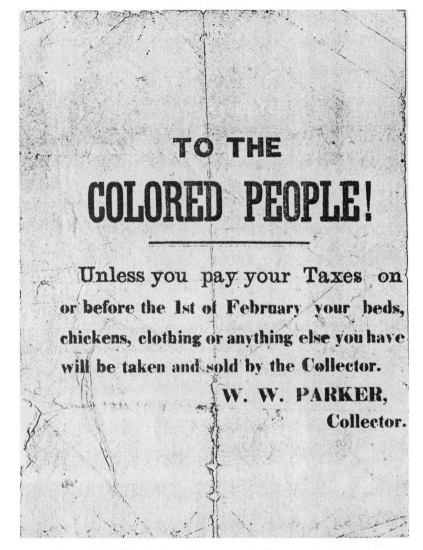

TO THE

COLORED PEOPLE!

Unless you pay your Taxes on or before the 1st of February your beds, chickens, clothing or anything else you have will be taken and sold by the Collector.

W. W. PARKER,
Collector.

Figure 3.1 Tax collection notice in Halifax County, NC, 1874, *Documenting the American South*.

tax records, as many states required under law. "I went into the Tax Office one day and they had all these [pages that] had W all the way down," Milton Douglas Quigless of Tarboro, North Carolina, bitterly recalled. "Back over the corner they had some with C all the way down. [Even] the tax books were segregated. Everything."[17]

Black landowners struggled to sock away savings to pay annual tax bills. Across much of the rural South, Black people had few places to safely deposit earnings and plan for future expenses.[18] Referring to the sharecroppers and tenant farmers of the Georgia Black Belt, where savings banks were virtually nonexistent, Du Bois commented, "Usually, the only dependence of these poor peasants is the personal honesty of some white landlord. Much of [rural Blacks'] accumulated wealth is a monument to the honesty of such men. But alas! there is no corresponding record of the loss of money and courage through systemic cheating and chicanery."[19]

All these circumstances made Black property owners much more vulnerable to tax delinquency. Between 1893 and 1900, the rate of tax delinquency on Black-owned property in Virginia was nearly three times the rate of white tax delinquency.[20] These disparities were not solely due to Blacks' financial circumstances and white assessors' discriminatory methods. Other Jim Crow practices also contributed. Just as assessors favored white property owners through reduced valuations, so too did they tend to protect them from tax sales. A simple promise by a white property owner to pay their bill could be enough to convince a tax collector or county treasurer in a rural southern county to remove a property from delinquent tax lists or otherwise prevent it from being sold off. In one portion of Greene County, Georgia, Arthur Raper found that officials withheld from its tax sales practically all white-owned farmland.[21]

Black property owners could never expect such protections. Instead, a tax-delinquent property owner often found themselves thrust into a confusing, hostile, and punitive legal and administrative environment marked by innumerable roadblocks and misdirections. All states mandated counties and cities to publicly list all tax-delinquent land prior to a sale. Some states required listing such lands in a local newspaper, others that they be posted in a public place like the front door to the county courthouse.[22] Invariably, these legal notices were printed in publications they didn't read and posted in places they rarely entered. Black Floridian Cornelius Speed recalled that "many black people . . . didn't take [news]papers. I could name 25 to 30 people who lost property for nonpayment of taxes, and they didn't know it. I don't know if [the government] advertised it, but [people] had no way of knowing [even if] they advertised."[23] Even when Blacks received notices in the mail or gained access to public information, many of them struggled to understand what they owed, when it was due, how they could pay it, and how they could verify that their payment was received and recorded. As Armstrong Edward Manuel of New Iberia, Louisiana, explained: "A lot of [Black] farmers . . . had been poorly educated so often times they didn't know how to read or write and they didn't understand all the finagling that was going on or sometimes the legalities involved. Sometimes they discovered that when they thought they were paying property taxes, in fact the records didn't reflect that they had paid property taxes."[24]

In oral histories of life under Jim Crow, many African Americans distinctly recalled family members losing land due to unpaid taxes. A common thread was their struggle to understand how, exactly, it had happened. "Somehow or another, he didn't have much education and he didn't pay his taxes. [That's how] they took it back from him," Robert Georgia of Summerton, South Carolina, said of his great-grandfather's land losses.[25] "He didn't pay his taxes," Lillie Pierce Fenner of North Carolina said of her father, and "they took [his land]."[26] Pointing to farmland outside New Bern, North Carolina, that her family had once owned, Ernestine Foy Clemmons explained, "My father left it to me when he died." But then, for reasons she could not understand, the county "took my property and sold it. Auctioned it off. I didn't even know nothing about it."[27] "When they knew anything," Cornelius Speed said of Blacks in Florida who lost their land to taxes, "they were being moved out."[28]

White land grabbers saw the tax sale as a bloodless means of property taking, but some were prepared to do it the hard way, as well. In 1906, Thomas M. Turner, a Black farmer in Prince George's County, Maryland, was shot dead by white tax buyer Edwin Gibbs, who had obtained a tax deed to Turner's land. Turner claimed he had never received the tax bill in question, a notice of

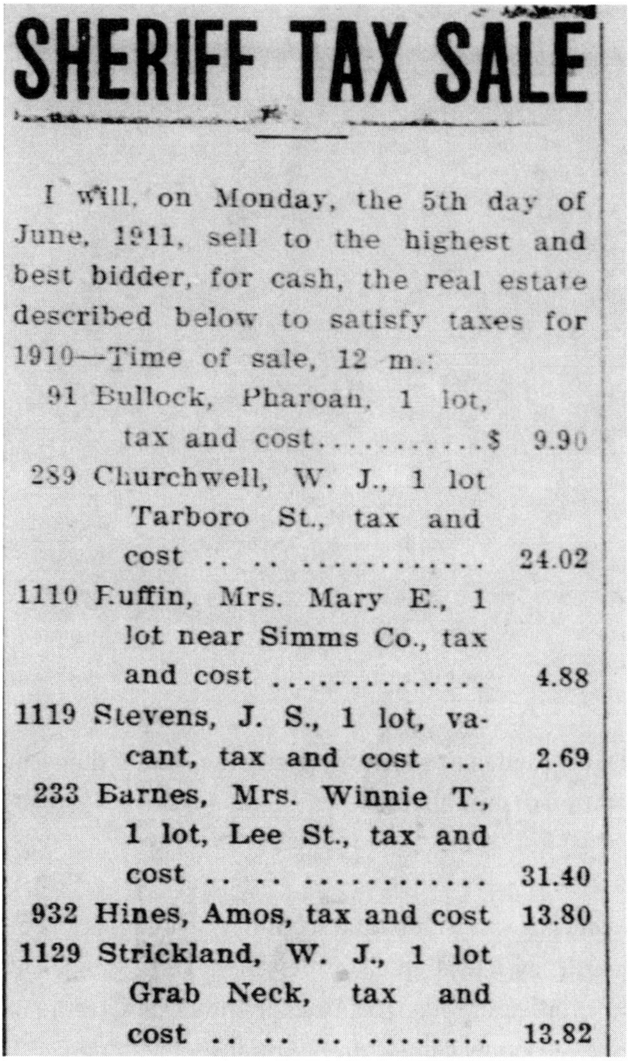

SHERIFF TAX SALE

I will, on Monday, the 5th day of June, 1911, sell to the highest and best bidder, for cash, the real estate described below to satisfy taxes for 1910—Time of sale, 12 m.:

  91 Bullock, Pharoah, 1 lot,
      tax and cost...........$ 9.90
  289 Churchwell, W. J., 1 lot
      Tarboro St., tax and
      cost 24.02
1110 Ruffin, Mrs. Mary E., 1
      lot near Simms Co., tax
      and cost 4.88
1119 Stevens, J. S., 1 lot, va-
      cant, tax and cost ... 2.69
  233 Barnes, Mrs. Winnie T.,
      1 lot, Lee St., tax and
      cost 31.40
  932 Hines, Amos, tax and cost 13.80
1129 Strickland, W. J., 1 lot
      Grab Neck, tax and
      cost 13.82

Figure 3.2 "Sheriff Tax Sale," [Wilson, NC] *Daily Times*, May 26, 1911.

tax delinquency, or the required notice from Gibbs that he held the tax deed. Nevertheless, Gibbs strode onto Turner's land and began uprooting Turner's crops. When Turner ordered Gibbs to leave, Gibbs shot Turner twice, killing him instantly. Turner left behind a wife and ten children, two of whom witnessed his murder. The *Baltimore Afro-American* described it as "one of the most unprovoked

Figure 3.3 "Tax Sale in Pinellas County, Florida," *Tampa Bay Times*, May 30, 1950.

murders recorded in this state for sometime." Later that year, Gibbs was acquitted of murder.[29]

* * *

But it wasn't just white mobs and scammers whom Black landowners had to fear. They, like all small farmers in the rural South, had to contend with crop-eating pests, usurious creditors, and, by the 1920s, an agricultural economy in free fall. The rural South—and Black farmers, especially—plunged into the Great Depression years before it gripped the rest of the nation. By the early 1920s, rates of tax delinquency and mortgage and tax foreclosures on southern farmland skyrocketed. Following the high-water mark of Black landownership in 1910, Blacks' land holdings began to fall sharply during the decade. Rising tax-delinquency rates both reflected and accelerated those losses.

Small farmers' land losses became large white landowners' gains. In Virginia, declines in the number of Black-owned acres were accompanied by an increase in the size of the average white farmer's landholdings.[30] In Arkansas, counties with the largest numbers of landowning Blacks experienced the highest tax-delinquency and forfeiture rates. The overall proportion of land owned by Blacks there fell from 21.3 percent in 1920 to 11 percent by 1933. That year alone, nearly 1.5 million acres of rich farmland in the state's Delta region had been forfeited for unpaid taxes. The number of farm operators there fell by 13 percent. During those same years, the holdings of the Delta's largest planters swelled. Between 1931 and 1934 alone, large Delta planters acquired 11 percent of their total landholdings, much of it through purchasing tax-foreclosed property from the state. Whereas in 1910 the average plantation in the Delta was 616 acres, by 1943 it had grown to 828 acres.[31] Similar patterns of tax-sale losses leading to white planter gains prevailed across the South. In the Georgia Black Belt, Arthur Raper observed, "The greatest number of sales [of tax-delinquent lands] were made to a few of the largest resident landowners."[32]

Rather than reverse these trends, agricultural recovery programs implemented under the New Deal accelerated them. By acquiring Black-owned farmland through mortgage and tax foreclosure sales, white plantation owners could enlarge their share of federal relief funds while also undermining Black attempts at propertied independence. At a time when few had cash on hand, some of the rural South's largest landowners had the resources to invest heavily in tax liens and tax foreclosed property.[33]

In some instances, whites were not content to wait until Black property owners fell into tax delinquency before they took their land. In the Arkansas Delta, large white plantation owners in Crittenden County had eyed the Black town of Edmondson warily since its founding in 1901. In 1888, white supremacist mobs had regained control over the county from Black and white Republicans, murdering hundreds and driving out its Black leaders. But in 1901, two of them, Anthony Fleming and J. R. Rooks, returned to farmland they still owned, launched the Edmondson Home and Improvement Company, and founded the town. The partners laid streets and subdivided land into lots that they sold on contract, holding title until

Figure 3.4 Residents of the Black town of Edmondson, Arkansas, n.d. In 1933, white planta-tion owners conspired to seize ownership of the entire town through a fraudulent tax sale.

the owners had paid in full.[34] Fleming and Rooks vowed that "none of the land in or near the town was ever to be sold to whites."[35] They used the proceeds of sales to acquire more land. By 1911, Edmondson had grown to thirty square miles and included a bank, ten stores, two restaurants, one hotel, three churches, a post office, a school, and a sawmill. Residents later founded the region's first NAACP branch.[36] "Edmondson's success," one historian wrote, "made it a destination for black migrants at a time when Jim Crow laws and disfranchise-ment had stymied opportunities for blacks elsewhere."[37] It became, as one observer described, "a monument to the wisdom of colored people, and is destined to become one of the leading centers in this country to show what the Negro race is capable of doing when it is left to its own judgment and will."[38]

Which was why, Delta planters agreed, Edmondson needed to go. A town consisting of Black homeowners and small proprietors and farmers was bad for labor management. "It might make the Negro tenants and laborers" of the surrounding white-controlled planta-tions "dissatisfied with their lot."[39] So, white officials began disman-tling the town's social infrastructure, piece by piece. First, the county closed the "colored" school, which served 515 children, and diverted the funds to the white school district.[40] Next, white planters enlisted a Black man to make a straw purchase of a lot in the downtown commercial district, ostensibly to open a large mercantile business and cotton gin. He acquired the lot and, as H. L. Mitchell of the Southern Tenants Farmers Union described, "The store building was erected, and in came a white man to operate it. The outsider had tricked his fellow black people into selling property to the white man."[41] White planter Harold Weaver had concocted the scheme. Instead of a mercantile business, Weaver opened a commissary, whiskey store, and honky-tonk catering to the sharecroppers and tenant farmers who worked the white-owned farmlands that surrounded the town.[42]

Finally, with the revitalization of plantation agriculture and rising land values resulting from the New Deal's Agricultural Adjustment Act, Weaver and his confederates conspired to take the land itself.[43] They used Crittenden County's tax-enforcement machinery to do so. County officials surreptitiously created a new special-improvement district (ostensibly to provide better drainage) that covered the entire town. This move gave the county the authority to assign a new special-assessment tax on all lots. In court filings, residents claimed that they never received any notice of the establishment of the district or of the tax bills that followed. Indeed, there was no evidence that the tax was ever levied, nor that any improvements to the town's drainage were ever provided.[44] Nevertheless, the county used residents' failure to pay a tax they claimed they never knew about for services never provided as the basis for declaring all the lots tax delinquent. If a tax sale was subsequently held, no one in town or elsewhere knew about it. There was no evidence that the county followed the statutory procedures for public notification, and in these years not a single parcel of land in the county was bought for taxes. In Arkansas, tax-delinquent property not sold at a tax sale reverts to the state. That's what happened to all of Edmondson in 1933. After the state took ownership, the Commissioner of State Lands deeded all six hundred lots to Weaver.[45]

It all happened so suddenly. One day they were property-owning residents of an independent Black town. The next day they were disfranchised tenants in homes that legally belonged to one of the county's largest plantation owners. Weaver began evicting residents and replacing them with sharecroppers who worked on his farm. He tore down houses, shuttered businesses, dug up fruit trees and vegetable gardens, plowed up streets and replaced them with rows of cotton, or simply kept the rich farmlands (whose value had grown thanks to the New Deal) fallow and pocketed checks from the federal government. For those who resisted, "terror was resorted to. . . . [O]ne family had gasoline spread about their home and it fired in the dead of night." What was once a "well laid-out and planned municipality, of great attractiveness, with many modern conveniences" had been laid to waste.[46]

In 1936, organizers for the Southern Tenant Farmers Union (STFU) came to Edmondson and found a pitiful sight: former homeowners and independent farmers reduced to abject poverty, dependence, and dissolution. The STFU hired an attorney, K. T. Sutton, to figure out what had happened. It did not take Sutton long to find that county officials had flagrantly violated numerous statutory requirements. The county sheriff had made no attempt to collect the tax. The taxes were never entered into county ledgers. Once they went unpaid, the tax collector failed to file tax-delinquency notices with the county clerk. The clerk subsequently failed to file public notices of the pending tax sale in a local newspaper or to post in a public place the list of tax-delinquent properties. The clerk of court failed to record the list of delinquent properties. The state issued deeds granting Weaver clear title to all tax-delinquent properties in the town prior to the end of the statutory two-year redemption period.[47]

Any one of these errors—if they were errors—should have invalidated every tax deed Weaver had acquired and restored ownership to the Edmondson Home and Improvement Company. In 1940, the company filed suit against Weaver in Crittenden County Chancery Court over what it described as "pretended conveyances from the State." Sutton charged that Weaver's actions "constituted fraud, unfairness and inequitable conduct" and claimed that they "were actuated by sinister motives, conceived in inequity, born of sin and nurtured in corruption."[48]

All these assertions were true, but in this court, none of it mattered. Indeed, Weaver had little to fear. The conspirators who seized Edmondson controlled local government and the courts. Nevertheless, Weaver still retaliated against the residents who supported the lawsuit and had filed complaints, evicting them from their homes and, now also operating as the town's marshal, arresting several on charges of trespassing.[49]

As residents struggled to continue fighting the case, Sutton pleaded with the NAACP to provide help. He begged executive secretary Walter White to send $100 to cover legal expenses.[50] During a stop in Memphis, NAACP special counsel Thurgood Marshall agreed to meet with Sutton and a group of residents.[51] But he and fellow attorneys in the NAACP main office felt powerless to do anything other than publicly decry the injustice. Since Congress and the federal judiciary had effectively slammed the federal courthouse doors shut on matters of local taxation, if the people of Edmondson wanted to prove that their property had been stolen by the state under illegitimate tax-delinquency proceedings, they would need to argue their case in state court.

After numerous delays, the chancery court judge dismissed the suit in 1948. By then, Weaver had already begun mechanizing cotton harvesting and evicting most of the sharecroppers, too. The children and grandchildren of the people who had, a generation earlier, migrated to the Arkansas Delta and built a town that embodied their dreams of independence, now joined the exodus north.[52]

* * *

Along with the threat of targeted land takings, Black landowners had to guard against predatory investors who made a business of exploiting people's mistakes and hardships to accumulate profits and property at tax sales. For those in the business of plundering the property of the weak and disadvantaged, Black people became a natural target, their race (and all of the vulnerabilities attached to it) functioning as a predictor of profit. Retired white businessman A. J. Day had begun investing in tax liens at the annual tax sale in Yazoo County, Mississippi, both to earn interest from others' debts and to accumulate farmland. Day speculated on tax liens that would be redeemed (at interest) and those on properties that he wanted to add to his holdings. By the early 1940s, Day had become one of Yazoo County's largest landowners, just as Black landownership in the county was in sharp decline. One of the pieces of land Day sought to acquire via the tax sale belonged to Andella Jackson, a fifty-six-year-old Black woman who lived a hundred miles north in Clarksdale. Jackson's brother rented the land to Black tenant farmers. After the Jacksons missed a single tax payment in 1932, Yazoo County promptly sold a lien on the land to Day. Neither Jackson nor her brother had received any notice of a tax bill or that a lien had been placed on the land and subsequently sold. In order to get ownership of her land, Day either needed to file suit in local court or get Jackson to sign a quitclaim deed.[53]

Day bet that he could trick Jackson into signing her land away by convincing her that the confusing language on the tax-lien certificate meant that he already owned the land. (He did not.) Day enlisted a local Black man to accompany him on a trip to Clarksdale. There, Day dropped his companion off at Jackson's home, where they got to talking about her old family farm down in Yazoo County. After Jackson expressed a desire to "visit her old home," Jackson's friend mentioned that Day was in Clarksdale and "would be glad to take her [there] without charge." The next morning, on their way toward Yazoo County, Day proceeded to tell Jackson "that her land had sold to the State for taxes and that" he now held title to it. The cost of redeeming it, he said, was $300, an amount he knew she could not pay. But because he felt bad for her and her loss, Day offered to give Jackson $40. The land, he stressed, was already his. He flashed a stack of legal documents to prove it. If she wanted to get anything for it, Day counseled, she needed to sign a document executing the deed. "Thinking she had lost her land," Jackson did so.[54]

The following day, Day brought Jackson to a justice of the peace to sign some forms so that she could get her $40 check. The court officer asked Jackson "if she understood" what she was signing. She said she did, and then signed the form with an "X." Day handed her $40 and bid her farewell. Afterward, Jackson learned from her brother that, contrary to Day's claims, "all of the taxes had been paid on the land," and moreover, that she had still owned the land when Day first approached her. As court documents later described, Jackson then "promptly went to see Mr. Day and offered to repay him the $40 which he refused to accept, seeking a reconveyance to her of the land, which he refused to do."[55]

Throughout the late 1930s, Thurgood Marshall traveled throughout the South, investigating civil rights cases and meeting with heads of local branches. Wherever he went, he heard local people tell of these kinds of tax-sale abuses. They told him of Black property owners who were "not sent tax bills on their property." And when they "inquire[d] about the tax bills[,]" they were "either not given any information or are put off with the statement that 'everything is all right.'" And then, Marshall later wrote, "When the taxes are past due and are in arrears for the statutory period, the property is quietly sold at a tax sale without notice to the owners. The Negroes are not notified until after the statutory period of redemption has passed. They are then forced to leave the property." This tended to happen, Marshall learned, to those "Negroes [who] own property which becomes enhanced in value."[56]

Not all Black victims of these schemes went quietly. After discovering that she had been defrauded, Jackson filed suit against Day for gross misrepresentation and deceit and petitioned the court to nullify the tax deed. She sued Day not as a Black person victimized by a white man but as a property owner who had been deceived and defrauded. This approach, as other historians have argued, constituted one of the few viable pathways for Black persons seeking justice in Jim Crow courts. In contrast to civil rights claims, which white jurists took delight in rejecting, "when it came to black people's legal claims on property," historian N. D. B. Connolly notes, "courts and other adjudicating bodies generally proved more responsive, for there it was often the integrity of capitalism, not white power, that was at issue."[57] So it was for Jackson. Ruling in her favor, chancery court judge J. Roberds wrote, "It is very evident that [Jackson] understood from the acts and statements of Mr. Day . . . that she had entirely lost title to her land, or that it would require the payment of over three hundred dollars to redeem it, one situation as hopeless of remedy by her as the other. Neither was correct. This woman," the court continued, "was ignorant, did not know her rights or the facts, and had no one to advise her. Situated as these parties were, this transaction cannot stand."[58]

Under Jim Crow law, white land grabbers stood on firmer legal footing when they coupled their theft of Black people's property with deadly assertions of white supremacy. In Amite County, Mississippi, Isaac Simmons inherited a 220-acre farm from his father in 1929. There, the African American minister farmed a variety of crops, periodically sold some of its timber, and raised his seven children. Soon after he had acquired it, though, a rumor began to spread around the county that there were huge oil deposits under the Simmons farm. In 1942, the county sold 141 acres of Simmons's farm for delinquent taxes. The winning bidder, Noble Ryder, fetched it for $190. The tax sale of Simmons's farm lacked any semblance of legitimacy. At the time, Simmons was enrolled in a government-administered tax installment plan. He was current on his payments and had kept the receipts to prove it.

When Ryder moved to take possession of Simmons's land and sell its mineral rights, Simmons reached out to Frank Mize, a white attorney in Jackson. Mize filed suit to have the tax sale declared invalid. With the suit pending, Ryder struggled to find anyone interested in buying mineral rights. So, Ryder took matters into his own hands. Along with six other white men, he traveled to Simmons's farm in the summer of 1944. First, they abducted Simmons's son, Eldridge, and beat him viciously. Then, they tracked down his father. For being a "smart n——r" and having the audacity to hire a white attorney and contest Ryder's tax deed, the men brutally tortured Isaac Simmons, kicking in all of his teeth and cutting out his tongue, before blasting three shots into his back. The inquest listed that Simmons had "met death at hands of unknown parties."[59]

After escaping to New Orleans, Simmons's son Eldridge submitted an affidavit describing his father's murder and naming his assailants, which was later forwarded to the NAACP's office in New York. Marshall called on the US Justice Department to investigate the killing.[60] The Justice Department agreed and, in a victory of sorts, in October 1944 a local grand jury indicted Noble Ryder and his co-conspirators. But after a one-day trial, a jury spent only thirty-five minutes deliberating before acquitting Ryder of all charges. The prosecutor declined to file charges against the other indicted co-conspirators. Simmons's children, having fled the state, dropped their suit against Ryder, who assumed ownership of the property.[61]

PART II

BLACK IN THE METROPOLIS

4

CAPTIVES

Following the brutal murder of Isaac Simmons for daring to contest a fraudulent tax deed in 1944, Percy Greene, the editor of Jackson, Mississippi's Black newspaper the *Jackson Advocate*, remarked that the "complete break-down of law enforcement and justice in the courts where a Negro is concerned . . . has caused thousands of Negroes to leave the state, and is causing other thousands to make ready to leave."[1] Greene wildly underestimated the extent of the exodus. During the first half of the twentieth century, millions of African Americans migrated to northern cities seeking freedom from a system of rural land tenure and farm labor that kept them permanently indebted and impoverished, from kleptocratic local governments and schools that quietly overtaxed and flagrantly underserved them, and from a host of economic predators who stole whatever property they possessed the moment it became valuable.

Black people came North seeking opportunities to work for wages and save their earnings, and to enjoy the benefits of public services and public education that Jim Crow denied. Much of their earnings, though, went toward paying exorbitant rents for inferior housing, outrageous prices for food and other necessities, and innumerable other expenses. The added costs that ghettoization imposed on Black populations came to be known collectively as the "race tax." The creation of racially segregated housing markets in the urban North, the racist devaluation of Black-owned and -occupied property within these markets, and the changing fiscal structure and mechanics of local property taxation, also forced Black people to pay a race tax *on their taxes*. Wherever Black residential areas formed in northern cities, higher effective property tax rates soon followed. The causes were both structural and political, the result of preexisting formulas and general procedures being applied to racially segregated housing markets in which race determined value combined with the fiscal pressures and political calculations that suburban growth and urban decline produced. This emerging fiscal structure and political economy took shape quietly, and its draining effects on the pocketbooks of Black urban populations were often imperceptible. But despite its subtlety, the effects of overtaxation would prove no less consequential than the other, more flagrant forms of exploitation that urban Blacks were forced to endure, and far more revealing of the broader forces fueling the racial segregation of cities and suburbs as a whole.

* * *

The roots of structural racism in mid-twentieth-century urban tax systems grew out of the changing fiscal structure of state and local governments in the early twentieth century. Throughout the nineteenth century, property taxes served as one of the main sources of state *and* local revenue. Often, property was assessed and property taxes collected at the local level before being handed up to state taxing bodies, which subsequently redistributed that revenue back to local governments and school districts in accordance with state funding formulas. This system incentivized local assessors to undervalue property within their jurisdictions so as to lighten their constituents' relative tax contributions to the state. Of course, other counties did the same, and a race to the bottom ensued, with each county competing to value their property lower than others and gain a relative tax advantage. States struggled to rein in these practices, but a system reliant on local administrators answering to local constituents to produce revenue for the state offered few viable solutions.[2] So, instead, states went in search of other means of generating tax revenues. In 1911, the state of Wisconsin developed the nation's first effective and efficient income tax. Other states soon followed their lead and adopted state income taxes modeled on Wisconsin's. As they did so, they ceased relying on property taxes for revenue. The county and city governments that had been in charge of assessing properties and collecting property taxes could now keep those funds.[3]

By the 1920s, the property tax was well on its way to becoming in most states what it is today: a strictly local tax raised by local governments in support of local needs.[4] But among the features of property tax administration that were carried over from the old structure into the new was the practice of assessing properties at a fraction of their full value. As local governments began adopting land-use zoning, some states adopted classification schemes that required local assessors to value different types of property at different percentages of their actual value. Other states required all properties to be assessed at the same fractional percentage but did not specify at what percentage. Still others kept laws on the books requiring that properties be assessed at their full value but, since they no longer had any stake in the outcome, had given up on trying to enforce those laws. In one sense, it did not matter if a tax assessor assessed properties at their full value or at a fractional percentage. Since the property tax was being collected and spent locally, a locality that assessed all properties at a small fraction of their full value but then taxed those same properties at a higher rate could have generated the same amount of revenue had it assessed properties at full value and taxed them at a lower rate.

But in practice, fractional assessments disguised inaccuracies and kept taxpayers from knowing whether they were being fairly taxed. This lack of transparency was especially the case in the vast majority of states and localities where the practice of fractional assessments remained informal and unsanctioned under law, and where tax statements only listed a property's assessed value, not the percentage at which it was assessed, much less how that percentage compared to the percentages applied to other properties. Indeed, one of the reasons why tax assessors liked fractional assessments was because they led many taxpayers to believe (incorrectly) that they were getting a deal. Even if a taxpayer suspected otherwise, the process of discovery was an exercise in frustration. As one study of assessment practices in New York noted, "the assessment formulas and methods . . . are so complex that it is impossible for most taxpayers to figure out what their rate of assessment is."[5] The very complexity of fractional assessments and lack of transparency helped, as one legal scholar remarked, "to conceal errors and inequity, and protect[ed] [assessors] from a feared swarm of assessment appeals."[6]

The appeals process itself constituted another barrier. Even if taxpayers believed they were being unfairly taxed, local governments made a point of keeping them unaware of their rights to appeal and of making the appeal process as inaccessible to average citizens as possible. In Cook County, Illinois, the tax appeal process was, as one report described, "veiled . . . in a shroud of secrecy." The only people who knew how to successfully navigate the appeals process were tax lawyers, and the only people who availed themselves of the right to appeal were, by and large, corporate and industrial property owners and wealthy individuals. As such, these were the property taxpayers to whom local assessors were most attentive.[7]

In addition to assessing properties at various (and often unknown) fractional percentages, many assessors did not even base assessments on market values. In Chicago and many other cities, assessments on residential properties were based on their "replacement cost," a formula that used the size and age of the structure and the materials used in its construction, but not its location, to determine its value. In other cities, assessors' offices adopted formulas that prioritized residential properties' structural features and did not give "much weight" to locational factors. Even among those that used market-value assessments, the actual assessments (full or a fractional percentage thereof) often bore little relation to a property's market value at any given time. That's because tax assessors rarely updated the values they assigned to properties. Most states required tax assessors to conduct reassessments of all properties within their jurisdictions on a regular schedule. Some required it be done annually, others every four years, others on assessment cycles longer still, and some not at all. Once states stopped collecting property taxes, they stopped caring how local governments administered it.

By mid-century, a majority of states lacked any standards that local assessors were bound to follow and any training or certification requirements to hold the office. Among those states that did hold such standards or requirements, the rules governing assessments were, as one policy analyst wrote, "very general, imprecise, and ambiguous." Regardless of what a state's laws said, assessors routinely ignored them without consequence. State supervisory bodies were nonexistent in a majority of states; in the rest, they were practically so. Assessors answered only to local power and served local interests.[8]

Outside their respective cities and counties, tax assessors were virtually unknown. But within their jurisdictions, assessors' decisions carried enormous consequences for the businesses and industries whose properties they valued, and for area real estate markets as a whole. And because they did, and because they possessed such extraordinary discretionary powers, assessors occupied one of the most powerful positions within urban political systems. In Chicago and other cities governed by political machines, the tax assessor's office sat at the center of an intricate system of funding and mobilization, the end results of which were drastically reduced assessments on the property holdings of major donors and of neighborhoods comprised of the most loyal and connected voting blocs. The Cook County assessor functioned as the fundraising arm for the city's Democratic machine. In Gary, Indiana, a parade of tax assessors throughout the first half of the twentieth century grossly undervalued the property holdings of the city's main industry, US Steel, annually costing the city millions of dollars in tax revenue.[9]

All these features of property tax administration would have significant—and uniformly negative—implications for African Americans entering into urban housing markets in the early twentieth century. During these years, a burgeoning real estate industry developed and applied what Charles Abrams later described as a "racist theory of property value" to shape and mold US housing markets. Industry actors worked to establish race as a key variable in property valuation. White-owned homes in racially homogeneous neighborhoods that effectively excluded people of color were worth more because those neighborhoods were white. Conversely, property in the hands of a Black person was worth less because it was in their hands. The concept was embedded in the business of buying, selling, and financing real estate and enshrined in federal housing policies and programs. It provided the economic rationale for lenders to deny Black people mortgages to buy homes in white neighborhoods, for realtors to refuse to show homes to Black homeseekers there, and for policymakers to craft housing policies that worked to contain Black people within racialized ghettos (where they were also denied mortgages to buy homes), all so as to ensure the continued appreciation of white housing markets and the financial security of white homeowners.[10]

These policies and practices gave all white Americans a material interest in maintaining the residential color line. They closed off routes to homeownership for generations of Black Americans. More than that, they ensured that, even when Black people acquired homes, their properties would never appreciate in value the way white-owned homes in white neighborhoods did. Instead, this racist theory of value meant that the neighborhoods where Black people lived were devalued simply because Black people lived there. And because they were devalued in this way, and because of the formulas and practices used to assess residential properties for taxes, the places where Black people lived in cities were, consequently, taxed more. Replacement-cost formulas such as the one used in Chicago resulted in properties in rapidly appreciating, all-white neighborhoods receiving the same tax bill as those located in areas where values were plummeting and housing stock deteriorating due to overcrowding and neglect—simply because they were built in the same year and shared the same structural features. The gap between reassessments, and the fact that reassessments rarely resulted in meaningful updates and adjustments, ensured that the effective tax rates on properties in areas appreciating in value would shrink over time, while those in areas where values were dropping would increase.

Replacement-cost formulas and gaps between reassessments were two among many factors that contributed to making the property tax regressive in practice. Regardless of race, higher-valued properties were taxed relatively less than lower-valued properties. But because of how race determined those underlying values, regressive property taxes became racist property taxes. These results would have been the same had assessors simply been disinterested bureaucratic cogs in local tax machinery. And they were far from disinterested. Because property in all-white neighborhoods was worth more and could generate more tax revenue, assessors had strong incentives to protect and enhance the value of white property by taxing it favorably. Those incentives were made even stronger and more urgent as urban white populations spilled out into newly formed suburbs following World War II.

Throughout the late nineteenth and early twentieth centuries, when residential development spread into outlying areas, cities usually responded by annexing these areas, and they did so at the behest of residents seeking access to the services and amenities that cities provided. During these years, cities also routinely absorbed smaller municipalities, also without much of a fight. With major industries and commercial properties still firmly entrenched in central cities, suburbs lacked the taxable resources needed to develop their own infrastructure, and they saw little point in establishing their own water and sewer infrastructure, police and fire services, and other public amenities that could just as easily be provided by neighboring cities, and at lower cost. Only the oldest, wealthiest suburbs, like Brookline, Massachusetts, or Evanston, Illinois, possessed both tax bases large enough to go it alone and the political will to resist cities' annexation attempts.[11]

The relationship between central cities and surrounding suburbs changed dramatically beginning in the 1940s thanks to the housing programs launched under the New Deal. Both the Federal Housing Administration and Veterans' Administration's mortgage insurance programs unleashed an unprecedented wave of mortgage financing for new homeowners. The very design of these programs also encouraged developers to target undeveloped areas outside of central cities for new home construction. Rather than seeking annexation by a larger city, the developers who rushed to take advantage of these federal programs saw distinct advantages in suburban incorporation. A small suburban government, developers assumed, would be easier to control and influence, less likely to adopt and enforce regulations that cut into profits, and more likely to cater to their demands. Businesses and industries also saw much to be gained from suburban incorporation. The greater the number of local governments within a given region, the greater the ability of businesses to play one government against another when bargaining for tax reductions, exemptions, and abatements. They saw in suburban incorporation the opportunity to shape the tax and regulatory environments to their liking. These groups led the push for new suburban developments to form separate governments.[12]

The white families who moved into these new suburbs also came to see incorporation as offering distinct advantages. By clustering together, middle-class white homeowners could create tax bases large enough to generate the revenues needed to build and maintain high-quality public schools and provide residents enviable public goods and services at a lower cost. They could do so, that is, if they kept Black people and other threats to area home values out. The benefits of suburban tax-base formation was predicated on Black exclusion. Black exclusion enhanced home values, which funded the schools and local services whose quality affected home values. It was integral to maintaining the virtuous cycle of ever-increasing home values, ever-improving goods and services, and ever-falling tax burdens that suburban incorporation promised. This overriding objective guided the path of suburban development and infused every aspect of suburban fiscal politics and planning.

New suburban municipalities spread like wildfire across the postwar metropolis. Between 1945 and 1950, the St. Louis metro area added forty-four independent local governments.[13] In total, over a thousand new local governments formed in the US in the 1950s alone.[14] Wherever they encountered existing Black suburban settlements, newly formed suburbs surgically drew their boundaries around them. At the dawn of the age of mass suburbanization, the sparsely developed areas surrounding cities housed nearly one-fifth of the entire African American metro population located outside the South.[15] Most Black suburban settlements were unincorporated, and as new white suburbs formed into municipalities, they would remain so.[16] Across greater Los Angeles, not a single municipality formed in the 1950s had a Black population greater than 1 percent.[17] New or old, suburbs increasingly targeted existing Black or lower-income residential areas within their borders for removal. In the suburban township of Mount Laurel, New Jersey, officials adopted a "policy of waiting for dilapidated premises to be vacated and then forbidding further occupancy."[18] On one occasion, local officials prevented a nonprofit agency from improving housing conditions in a working-class neighborhood. As historian Andrew Wiese documents, suburban governments also used federal urban-renewal and slum-clearance programs to forcibly displace Black suburban communities.[19] In Pasadena, California, a city manager disclosed how the suburb planned to deal with one its few minority neighborhoods: "build a freeway [and] wipe out that section of town."[20]

Once removed, land-use controls ensured that people seen as threatening home values and tax bases could not come back. Exclusive suburbs over-zoned for nonresidential use, designating large swaths of land for industrial use only, while also placing restrictions on the types of permissible uses—typically, light manufacturing, office parks, or distribution centers. In most suburbs, only a small fraction of areas zoned for industry were ever developed. The point was to keep that land from being developed as affordable housing. This maneuver created a scarcity of residential properties that drove up home prices and grew the local tax base, while limiting the population and ensuring that residents would enjoy better public services at a lower cost. In areas zoned for residential use, suburbs placed minimum lot-size and minimum floor-space requirements, and they banned multifamily housing, apartment units, mobile homes, and tract housing.[21] If they did allow multifamily units, exclusive suburbs added requirements for costly amenities aimed at driving up rents, or imposed strict limits on the number of bedrooms and school-age children who could occupy a unit, or required numerous public meetings and votes by multiple governing bodies to determine the suitability of a project.[22] Exclusive suburbs invoked concerns about the environmental effects of overdevelopment to preserve woods, wetlands, and open spaces and limit the availability of land for mixed-income housing. Successful land-conservation campaigns provided a double win for exclusive suburbs, preventing the introduction of threats to real estate values while providing environmental amenities that further enhanced those values.[23]

By the early 1970s, the metro areas spreading out from many American cities had become a crazy quilt of small, independent, and often racially exclusive local governments. The typical metropolitan area in the US contained over one hundred local government units, with the numbers far greater in the largest and most segregated cities. Detroit was surrounded by 338 suburban governments and 116 school districts. The greater Chicago region became home to over 1,250 local units. Even mid-tier cities like Pittsburgh and Baltimore sprouted over three hundred and 350 local governments, respectively.[24] Each of these new local governments was formed in order to wield greater control over its housing markets, schools, and tax bases, and each followed the same exclusionary playbook for achieving its objectives. Together, they formed a fiscal white noose around central cities, the effects of which would fall most negatively on those who enjoyed the least mobility.

* * *

Facing the continued drain of people and taxes to the suburbs, cities similarly worked to calibrate their tax bases to achieve an optimum level of services and tax burdens in the postwar decades, and they similarly prioritized fiscal interests in urban land-use policies and planning. But increasingly, they did so from a position of weakness. As early as the 1950s, many cities found themselves surrounded on all sides by suburban municipalities with whom they now competed for residents, employers, and tax dollars.

Unable to grow their tax bases through expansion, cities turned

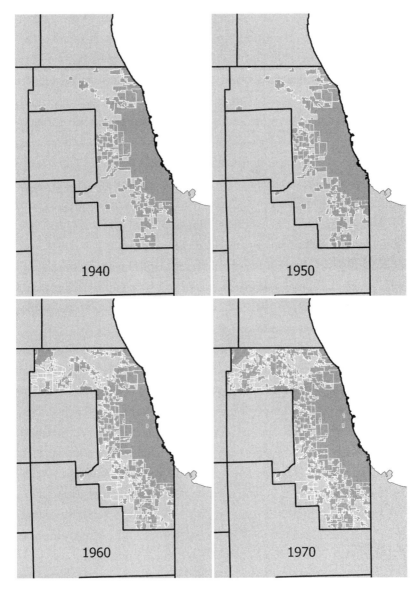

Figure 4.1 Municipal boundaries in Cook County, Illinois, from 1940 to 1970. The number of municipalities, school districts, and special districts grew exponentially in the post–World War II era.

instead to the real estate within their borders. Urban-growth coalitions consisting of corporate, financial, commercial, and real estate interests, building and construction trade unions, and middle-class professionals coalesced around the need to invest heavily in urban redevelopment. Federally funded urban-renewal projects promised to revitalize urban economies and improve cities' fiscal fortunes by removing blighted properties (which were tax liabilities) and opening up urban real estate for investment and redevelopment. Cities dove in headfirst. They floated scores of municipal bonds to fund major projects, facilities, and programs. They chased after federal funds for urban-renewal projects to clear thousands of acres of real estate, guided by the assumption that, once central cities had been cleared of "incompatible" people and land uses, capital would flow back in and cities' tax bases would emerge even larger than before. They sank unprecedented sums into public projects and programs that would, promoters promised, pay for themselves.[25]

Instead, these projects did the opposite. Rather than bring people and industries back into cities, urban-renewal projects more often turned taxable residential areas and commercial districts into tax-exempt freeways or empty lots waiting, often in vain, for investors. Nationwide, more than 20 percent of all land cleared out by urban-renewal projects remained vacant and unsold ten years after a project had been completed.[26] As these projects failed to bear fruit, cities' fiscal outlooks darkened, and their strategies grew more desperate.

Fearing any increase would drive more white residents away, urban assessors worked to keep taxes low for middle-class and more exclusive white neighborhoods. They made a point of not updating assessments. After 1946, Boston would not conduct another full reassessment for thirty years.[27] In other cities, assessors reduced assessments on some of the city's more exclusive residential areas.[28] They did so by design: low property assessments functioned, in effect, as bribes to wealthy white residents to stay. Whether through deliberate undervaluation or merely by failing to update assessments, assessors assigned lower values to "higher income residential property because," one federal study concluded, "they knew that the consequences [of valuing it accurately] would be to drive households into the suburbs."[29] In Boston, officials admitted to fears that valuation increases in white middle-class neighborhoods would "hasten the exodus."[30] In New York, city officials systematically undervalued single-family homes, which were disproportionately white, in order "to deter middle-income families from leaving the city for the suburbs," one state report found.[31] Studies found that the underassessment of the highest-end residential markets was a universal practice across postwar urban America.

As they provided white residential areas tax advantages, postwar urban-assessment practices pushed property tax burdens onto Black neighborhoods. By sheer inaction, Boston forced residents of its poorest neighborhoods and most depressed housing markets to assume a heavier property tax burden. By the 1960s, the average assessments in Boston's Black ghetto, Roxbury, were one and one-half times greater than a property's actual value. (By comparison, assessments in more affluent neighborhoods were, on average, 40 percent of market value.)[32] In New York City, assessments in predominantly Black and poor Red Hook were 82.4 percent of full market value, while those in the whiter, and wealthier, neighborhood of Brooklyn Heights were 11.8 percent. That meant that a person living in a $20,000 home in Red Hook paid the same amount in taxes as a person living in a $139,000 home in Brooklyn Heights. Across New York City, one study found, "all types of residential properties in low-income areas [we]re over-assessed compared to the same types of residential properties in higher-income areas."[33]

The story was the same in cities across the US. In Philadelphia, twelve of the sixteen city wards with the highest assessment ratios were Black.[34] In Buffalo, assessments on the predominantly Black inner east side were, on average, 111 percent of market value, while in middle-class white neighborhoods, they averaged 23.3 percent.[35] In Syracuse, New York, property assessments in disinvested urban Black neighborhoods were two to three times higher relative to property values than those in white residential areas.[36] In Norfolk, Virginia, the highest assessment ratios were in areas of the city with the lowest property values and largest concentrations of Black residents.[37] In Fort Worth, Texas, Black residential areas were assessed, on average, at 94 percent of market value, as compared to the 84 percent average for white homes.[38]

Tax assessors were well aware of how their actions and inactions shaped area real estate markets and individual and household tax burdens. Studies and investigations conducted at the time found that racist biases and assumptions saturated the decisions emanating from these offices. A 1973 study of Delaware County, Pennsylvania, supported by the National Science Foundation concluded that the assessor's office based its valuations on the supposed amount of taxes different groups consumed, rationalizing its overtaxation of Black neighborhoods on the basis of its residents' supposed consumption of more public goods and services.[39] A study in Virginia concluded that assessment bias was due to "local assessors . . . seek[ing] to impose the characteristics of a user charge on the property tax system" and that it "represent[ed] an attempt to pattern tax liabilities so they better match the pattern of public services people consume."[40] A Baltimore official went so far as to admit to a reporter that, in the reporter's words, "discriminatory assessments [we]re done by design" in order to "sock it to low-income areas as a means of collecting taxes from them to offset what they can't fork over because of meager incomes."[41]

Given the racial dynamics of urban housing markets and cities' fiscal interests, overassessing Black neighborhoods made fiscal sense. "If their goal is to maximize revenue," property tax policy expert Diane Paul remarked, "then discrimination against blacks . . . is rational."[42] Black people were, in the words of social scientists, "price inelastic"; that is, they were captive taxpayers.

Excluded from suburban housing markets, confined to urban ghettos, Black people were forced to pay more for housing, more for consumer goods, more for insurance, and more for food and other basic necessities. These were the race taxes Blacks were forced to pay. African Americans' unequal access to credit and opportunities—their captivity—created the conditions for their exploitation within these marketplaces.[43] As urban fiscal systems followed the market, they embraced its logic. To cities, white homeowners and white-owned properties were treated as appreciating assets, to be protected and nurtured through favorable assessments and enhanced services. Black homeowners and Black neighborhoods, on the other hand, were extractive assets to be pillaged for tax revenue and neglected and underserved by local governments.

But because so many urban Black residents during these years paid property taxes in the form of rent to landlords, during the years when these practices were becoming encoded into urban fiscal administration and logics, the overassessment of lower-income and predominantly Black residential areas remained entirely invisible to many of those whom it adversely affected. Even if few could see it, Blacks felt unequal assessment practices in their pocketbooks and in the housing conditions they were forced to endure. Like the segregated and exploitative housing markets upon which the property tax drew, this emerging fiscal structure increased housing costs for urban Black residents while driving down property values and housing conditions in the neighborhoods where they lived.

What Black arrivals to northern cities did see, though, was that for whatever taxes they paid, they received little in return. Addressing these inequities would become a preoccupying concern and a basis for political organizing throughout the Great Migration era, which we will turn to in the next chapter.

5

DISSERVICE

In the 1910s, John Williams and his young family joined the Black exodus from rural Georgia. They were among the millions of African Americans who migrated to northern cities during the first half of the twentieth century. The Williamses eventually settled into a cramped apartment on South Prairie Avenue in the heart of Chicago's Black Belt. They came there in search of jobs and dignity, and in flight from racial terrorism, grinding poverty, and unremitting economic exploitation. John found work in the stockyards while their teenage son Eugene got a job as a porter for a grocer.[1] They also came seeking the civic rights that the Jim Crow order denied, including a decent education for their children and equal access to the goods and services of modern cities. The pictures and articles in the issues of the *Chicago Defender* that were smuggled into rural southern communities told prospective migrants of all that the bustling metropolis had to offer: the wide, paved streets and sidewalks teeming with life; the modern schoolhouses; the spacious public parks, playgrounds, and ballfields scattered across the city's grid; the beaches and piers along Lake Michigan.[2]

But when they arrived, Black migrants like the Williamses found severely limited housing options that forced them to pay outrageous rents for inferior accommodations, city services that mirrored and worsened racial inequities, and schools that were effectively segregated and inferior. Their children might have been able to go to school for a full year, and past the seventh grade. But across the urban North, many Black children had to attend schools that were so overcrowded they could only attend for half a day. They could walk down the streets freely, but on the streets and sidewalks in their neighborhoods, garbage that the city refused to regularly collect accumulated. And the city's public spaces, they soon learned, were not, in fact, open to all.

On a brutally hot afternoon in July 1919, Eugene Williams and a group of friends ventured to Chicago's lakefront to swim along one of its public beaches, the one that had been unofficially designated for Black use. But when Williams inadvertently floated across an invisible color line in the water, a group of Irish youth began pelting him with rocks from the shore. One struck Williams in the head, causing him to drown. As an angry crowd gathered on shore, a Black man exchanged fire with a police officer. Within hours, violence had spread across the South Side. Williams's death sparked one of the deadliest and most destructive racial conflicts in US history, lasting nearly two weeks and resulting in thirty-eight deaths (twenty-three Black, fifteen white), hundreds of injuries, and thousands of properties burned to the ground and families (nearly all Black) left homeless.[3] Williams's death, and the bloody conflict that followed, would serve as a painful reminder to Black Chicagoans that the public spaces, services, and amenities northern cities provided, and that they paid to support, they could not enjoy equally.

Wherever Black people settled and Black neighborhoods formed in the Great Migration–era North, higher tax bills followed, but the goods and services those taxes paid for lagged far behind. Political scientist Jessica Trounstine found that, nationwide, "between 1900 and 1940, neighborhoods that were identifiably poor or inhabited by minorities were allocated lower-quality services, including road paving, public-health efforts, and sewer extension."[4] This finding would have come as no surprise to the people living in Black urban neighborhoods. "We'd laugh about how when the big snowstorms came, they'd have the snowplows out downtown as soon as it stopped, but they'd let it pile up for weeks in Harlem," the protagonist in Claude Brown's novel *Manchild in the Promised Land* remarked.[5] In a speech to the Chicago Urban League in 1936, Harold Ickes, the secretary of the interior, acknowledged this reality. "[Al]though [the Negro] . . . is paying more than his fair share of local taxes," Ickes remarked, "the municipal services supplied him compare unfavorably with those furnished to more prosperous sections of the community. The Negro's streets are the last to be cleaned or put in repair. His garbage receptacles may be overflowing with decomposing waste while the collectors are busy in other sections of the city. His requirements for water and sewage are the last to attract the annoyed attention of the city officials."[6] When it came to paying taxes and getting services, Blacks living in mid-twentieth-century cities received the short end of both sticks.

During these years, civic groups and organizations formed to press cities to extend water and sewer lines into Black neighborhoods, collect garbage, pave and repair streets, build parks and playgrounds, and provide fire and police protection. They insisted that their children receive an equal education—a full day of learning, taught by qualified teachers in fully equipped schools. They demanded these rights as citizens and as taxpayers. They had to fight for every cent.

* * *

The drawing of the color line in housing led to the severe overcrowding of the areas in northern cities where Black people were permitted to live. Beginning in the 1910s, property owners in places like Chicago's Black Belt scrambled to subdivide single-family residences into minuscule apartments that could net massive profits. As they did, and as Black urban populations swelled, living conditions in these areas quickly deteriorated. Landlord neglect was compounded by cities' neglect. An autopsy report on the 1919 race riot found that, once an area of the city became absorbed into the Black Belt, public authorities paid "less attention . . . to the condition of streets and alleys" and became increasingly lax in the "collection and disposal of rubbish and garbage" there.[7] The city's parks department likewise turned a blind eye to the exclusion of Black people from many of the city's parks, including those near Black neighborhoods. The report found that only a handful of the thirty-seven city-operated parks, playgrounds, and beaches in or near Black residential areas were, in fact, available to Blacks. In all of the public recreation centers, "the hostility of whites, especially gangs of hoodlums, attacks on Negro children, and the indifferent attitude of the director render[ed] attendance by Negroes extremely hazardous."[8] The same patterns of exclusion and neglect could be found in virtually every city where Black migrants settled in large numbers.

Beginning in the 1930s, New Deal agencies like the Works Progress Administration put the vast ranks of the urban unemployed to work building new parks and playgrounds, school buildings, and other urban infrastructure. Administration officials like Secretary Ickes sold these programs to Black Americans on the promise of closing the gaps in access to public goods and services. But in practice, these programs did little to overcome local policies of segregation and neglect. Funded federally, New Deal programs were administered locally, and they came to reflect and extend local biases. With few strings attached, local administrators applied federal dollars toward improving middle- and upper-class white residential areas while leaving Black ghettos to starve. In New York City, only one of the 255 playgrounds built with funding from the WPA was located in Harlem.[9] In an exhaustive study of Black life in Chicago in the early 1940s, the sociologists St. Clair Drake and Horace Cayton found that, for city services, little had changed since the deadly summer of 1919. The city's Black Belt, they found, still suffered from "inadequate recreational facilities." They wrote: "In matters of street-cleaning, garbage disposal, and general city services, Negro areas are neglected."[10]

These inadequacies imposed significant risks to public health and safety. As slumlords crammed Black families into dilapidated homes and crumbling tenements, the garbage that accumulated along streets and alleys and hallways fed rats and other vermin and spread disease. Fires became a deadly menace. The paper-thin dividers that landlords used to split single rooms into separate apartments served as kindling for blazes, made all the worse by the broken fire hydrants and low water pressure that became a common feature of

Figure 5.1 Street in Harlem, New York, 1965.

Black neighborhoods, and by the reluctance of firefighters to battle blazes that threatened Black lives.[11]

As urban Black ghettos became overcrowded, the schools that Black children attended did, as well. That's because school boundaries followed the color line in housing. In cities like Chicago, there were no white and "colored" schools, per se. (In fact, most northern school systems made a point of not recording students' race.) But the practical effects were virtually indistinguishable from the openly segregationist system found down South. As Black neighborhoods swelled in size, school administrators crammed in ever more Black students into Black "neighborhood" schools. It did not take long before the numbers of children there far exceeded the schools' capacities. Beginning in the 1910s, Chicago began adopting double shifts in some South Side elementary schools.[12] By 1935, twenty-two schools were on double shifts, all of them serving predominantly or exclusively Black student populations.[13] By the 1940s, following a decade that saw no new school construction and a second wave of migration, overcrowding in Black schools had grown so dire that some schools adopted triple shifts.[14] By the 1950s, Doolittle Elementary School on the South Side had achieved the "dubious distinction of being the largest elementary school in the world."[15] In some elementary schools, nearly three thousand students passed through its doors in two shifts each day. Mere blocks away, across the color line, sat white neighborhood schools, some of which were operating at less than half capacity, with empty classrooms.[16]

As more white families relocated to suburbs in the postwar years, school administrators did not dare adjust attendance zones to balance classroom sizes, and they readily accommodated white parents' demands to transfer their children from predominantly Black schools.[17] By the 1950s, roughly 40 percent of all African American students in Chicago's public school system attended school for only half the day. In contrast, only 2 percent of the predominantly white schools in the city operated on double shifts.[18] Chicago was far from alone. Urban school systems across the North confined Black school children to overcrowded, run-down schools, and when those classrooms burst at the seams, they converted those schools' cafeterias, gymnasia, and even hallways and janitor's closets into classrooms. And, when all else failed, they stole a half-day of schooling from all the children and all their parents.

For the children attending schools on double shifts, the costs were even greater. During the critical first six years of schooling, a child forced to attend a school on double shifts received roughly 2,700 fewer classroom hours than children who attended on a full-day schedule. That was equivalent to two and one-half years of elementary education.[19] But in reality, the loss was still greater. Overworked and underpaid, only the most heroic and self-sacrificing teacher in a double-shift school could provide anything approximating the kind of attention that school children elsewhere received. Along with the teachers, the textbooks and other learning materials also worked a double shift, preventing children from taking them home. And, of course, there was the other half of the day, when children weren't in school but their parents were still at work.[20]

* * *

From the earliest days of the Great Migration, Black neighborhood politics and organizing centered on securing an equal distribution of public goods and services and addressing the problems that these inequities caused. Often, the nature and focus of these efforts reflected the class biases and orientations of the urban Black professionals and social reformers leading them. On Chicago's South Side, leading Black citizens formed neighborhood improvement associations aimed at promoting better race relations, in part by combatting negative stereotypes of Black neighborhoods. They lobbied aldermen to repair streets, collect garbage, and address health and sanitation problems, and they policed the conduct of new arrivals.[21] The Chicago chapter of the Urban League scolded newcomers who failed to keep the streets, alleyways, and sidewalks surrounding their homes in good order. The *Chicago Defender* ran a regular column listing addresses of violators of proper conduct, good order, and neighborhood cleanliness. It also sponsored an annual "clean-up week" and contests for best-kept lawns and blocks.[22]

In Dayton, Ohio, Black civic groups filed numerous petitions seeking the extension of water and sewerage services into neighborhoods where residents were forced to drink water from contaminated wells and whose roads were so impassable postal carriers refused to deliver mail there. Between 1944 and 1945, residents of Benn's Plat, a Black neighborhood along the Miami River, spoke on this subject at twenty-six straight meetings of the board of commissioners. The city refused every request and, following World War II, took steps toward condemning the properties and buying out residents with lowball offers.[23]

In Pittsburgh, Pennsylvania, Black residents of the Schenley Heights neighborhood spent years calling on officials to address the area's low water pressure, which prevented firefighters from battling blazes in the neighborhood's older, overcrowded housing stock. After another uncontrolled fire resulted in a death in 1962, hundreds of residents flooded a city council meeting, demanding action. "We don't care what you have to do to correct this situation, or how you go about it," a neighborhood spokesman told council members, "just so long as when [fire]men . . . turn on their hoses, water will pour forth."[24]

Out of these neighborhood fights for equal public services, broader strategies for securing equal education within northern school systems came into focus. In 1939, the Chicago Council of the National Negro Congress organized protests against the school board over its "criminal neglect and segregation of Negro children in over-crowded, part-time" schools, and framed its double-shift policy as amounting to a form of "robbery" of Black school children and Black taxpayers. In 1957, one Chicago PTA group found that every single student attending school on double shifts could receive a full day of education if they could transfer into one of the dozens of white schools operating under capacity. The Chicago NAACP similarly found that there were 22,284 surplus seats in white schools, roughly equal to the demand. As white flight to the suburbs accelerated, the number of empty classrooms in predominantly white schools grew. By 1958, Chicago school board president R. Sargent Shriver noted, all of the children attending double-shift schools in severely overcrowded North Lawndale could have been transferred into under-enrolled schools nearby. But Chicago's school superintendent Benjamin Willis refused to budge and insisted that preserving neighborhood schools trumped all other concerns.[25]

In 1960, the Chicago NAACP launched "Operation Transfer," flooding school administrators with transfer requests from Black parents. Willis denied every parent's request to transfer their child to a predominantly white school. Protests erupted and demands grew for Willis to resign. Calling for his removal, the *Chicago Defender* accused Willis of "perpetuating racial segregation in the public schools" and "gerrymandering school districts for the primary purpose of 'containing' Negro children."[26] In January 1962, Black parents and students began staging sit-ins at the overcrowded Burnside Elementary School after school officials ordered thirty-four seventh-grade students who had sought transfers to be moved

Figure 5.2 Participants in a citywide boycott of Chicago Public Schools on October 22, 1963, to protest against the gerrymandering of school placement zones to maintain racial segregation.

to an equally overcrowded and predominantly Black school sixteen blocks away, rather than to an under-enrolled and predominantly white school eight blocks away. The second week of the sit-in, police began arresting parents.[27] The sit-in ended when the parents filed a federal lawsuit against Willis and the school board. *Webb v. Board of Education* sought a permanent injunction against the school board's attempts to "[maintain] and operat[e] a racially segregated public school system," which included gerrymandering school boundaries, granting transfer requests to white parents while denying them to Black parents, and refusing to fill empty seats in white schools to alleviate overcrowding in Black ones. (The suit was settled out of court, with the school board agreeing to study segregation in the schools.)[28]

Willis pulled out all the stops to forestall desegregation. As pressure to end double shifts mounted, in the spring of 1962 Willis ordered the placement of mobile classroom units in areas suffering from school overcrowding. Some crammed next to busy thoroughfares, these mobile units lacked anything but the most basic accommodations. It was plainly obvious that these units served no purpose other than to alleviate overcrowding and provide Black children a full day of schooling, while maintaining segregation. As teachers and members of PTAs came to inspect the units that spring, crowds of demonstrators greeted them, holding signs and chanting "No Willis Wagons."[29] Protests and direct actions continued over the school year, many led by the Coordinating Committee of Community Organizations (CCCO), formed in 1961. In one South Side neighborhood, parents and children staged sit-ins, sitting in front of moving equipment and climbing utility poles in order prevent the installation of a unit. Arsonists set fire to two units in other neighborhoods.[30] On October 22, 1963, over 224,000 students boycotted school in what the CCCO dubbed Freedom Day. Across the city, groups conducted freedom

Figure 5.3 To alleviate school overcrowding in Black neighborhoods while maintaining segregation, in 1963 Chicago Public Schools superintendent Benjamin Willis placed mobile classroom units in the most overcrowded areas. In August 1963, CORE led protests at the proposed sites, demanding that Black students be sent to under-enrolled white schools rather than be placed in temporary units.

schools, picketed outside school board members' homes, and staged a mass march to the offices of the Board of Education. Months later, the CCCO organized a second Freedom Day and school boycott. By the spring of 1965, the steady drumbeat of protests and demonstrations forced Willis's resignation.[31]

* * *

If school administrators in cities with sizable Black populations like Chicago's seemed to cater to white parents and real estate interests as if their budgets depended on it, it's because they did. Every white pupil they lost to a new suburban school district was another white household whose taxes had also exited the city. By the late 1950s, suburban school districts (initially deemed inferior to the more established urban school systems) had gone from being a deterrence to an asset for suburban developers seeking to attract middle-class whites from the city.[32] These schools offered more than just a sanctuary from the threat of integration: because of the fiscal architecture of the postwar metropolis, they also provided white suburban taxpayers a greater return on their public school investment. By effectively limiting the presence of people seen as threatening their tax bases and raising costs, exclusive suburbs could tax homeowners at relatively lower rates while generating more revenue.

As the number of school districts in metropolitan areas proliferated, per-pupil expenditures became inversely proportional to local tax rates. Residents of the wealthiest and whitest school districts, which enjoyed large tax bases and relatively smaller numbers of school-age children, paid relatively the least in school taxes, while those living in poorest and most diverse districts, where the tax bases were smaller and the needs greatest, paid the most.[33] In suburban St. Louis, the wealthy residents of the Clayton school district possessed $45,619 in assessed property value per pupil. The smaller, predominantly Black, and poor neighboring school district of Kinloch, meanwhile, could only generate $3,373 in assessed value per pupil. As a result, Clayton's school district could tax property at one-half the rate of Kinloch, while generating much more revenue per pupil.[34] In

Los Angeles, the Beverly Hills school district contained $50,885 in assessed property value per pupil, while the Black suburb of Baldwin Park contained only $3,706 per pupil. This discrepancy allowed the former to tax property at less than half the rate of the latter while spending twice as much per pupil.[35] In South Carolina, school districts with a median property value of $50,000 or more per pupil taxed property at $2.94 per $1,000, and in return generated $510 per pupil. By contrast, districts with median property values of $20,000 or less per pupil taxed property at $6.63 per $1,000, and from that generated only $393 per pupil.[36]

The fiscal ground rules of school funding gave the advantaged a strong incentive to protect their advantages, and for those caught in the middle to climb up by holding others down. In San Antonio, Texas, the suburban Alamo Heights School District encompassed high-end residential neighborhoods whose original property deeds contained racial covenants and which remained, into the 1960s, overwhelmingly white. The school district attracted the area's top teachers with salaries 25 percent higher than the metro average, and it showered its students with amenities such as an Olympic-sized swimming pool and clubhouse. All the while Alamo Heights's residents paid one of the lowest tax rates of any school district in the region. The schools in Alamo Heights stood in stark contrast to those on the opposite side of the city, in the predominantly poor and Latino Edgewood School District. There, students were forced to attend crumbling schools where rats scurried across classroom floors and buckets gathered rainwater from holes in roofs. Students there read from decades-old textbooks. Twenty percent of Edgewood's teachers lacked a college degree.[37]

School districts with robust tax bases resisted merging with average ones, and average ones refused to merge with poorer ones. In the late 1940s, Alamo Heights refused to join a consolidated school district encompassing metro San Antonio. That consolidated district (known as the Independent School District, or ISD), meanwhile, refused to admit Edgewood, despite three attempts. The reason, as one commentator put it: "Edgewood simply had too poor a tax base to adequately support education and the San Antonio ISD had no desire to acquire responsibility for such a burden." The result was school districts with the greatest needs having the fewest resources. By the late 1960s, Edgewood was responsible for educating over twenty thousand children in a district where the median family income was $4,686. By contrast, Alamo Heights educated a mere five thousand children in a district where the median family income was $8,001. Edgewood's tax base equaled $5,429 per student, while Alamo Heights enjoyed $45,095 in taxable property per student. Edgewood taxed its residents at the highest rate of any school district in greater San Antonio; Alamo Heights at the lowest.[38]

Widening tax base disparities were the predictable, intended outcome of suburban growth and fragmentation. By the 1960s, the National Commission on Urban Problems found 10-to-1 differentials in per-capita tax bases of governments within many of the nation's metro areas.[39] In Chicago's suburbs, wealthy school districts enjoyed per-pupil tax bases in excess of $500,000, while in some of the poorest districts the bases were as small as $6,000.[40] Especially in states, like Illinois, that provided little state funding toward local schools, living in poor districts meant paying more for less.

The structure of local taxation was not only responsible for the high quality of education enjoyed by students at well-resourced schools and the deprivations suffered by students at under-resourced ones. By incentivizing exclusionary housing and fiscal policies, it relentlessly worked to widen those disparities.[41] No matter where one stood on the fiscal ladder, the way up was by keeping others down. In the fragmented metropolis, "upward mobility," historian Emily Straus notes, "was predicated on the power of exclusion."[42]

This was the marketplace that metropolitan fragmentation created. It was not the frictionless sorting of people into local units of government, each of which properly calibrated its tax rates and range of services to suit its residents' preferences, as the popular and oft-cited theorist Charles Tiebout contended.[43] It was a marketplace that generated value by restricting access to goods, services, and benefits, one in which some people enjoyed mobility, opportunity, and the wealth-generating possibilities of homeownership because others did not. Whites enjoyed a bevy of options when searching for the ideal housing market, school district, and municipality *because* Blacks lacked options. Middle-class white neighborhoods paid less in local taxes for better services *because* poorer, Blacker neighborhoods paid more. Whites' mobility, and the material benefits that it conferred, depended on Blacks' immobility. Residential advantage was the objective; suburban incorporation was the means; racial segregation was the result. Writing on postwar Los Angeles, Gary Miller remarked, "The motivation for incorporation . . . had little to do with the gratification of distinct collective tastes for public goods. . . . [Rather, it] can easily be explained in economic terms as the gratification of the shared desire to have adequate or better urban services at little or no tax price by maximizing resources per capita."[44]

* * *

These dynamics did more than shape suburban fiscal strategies and taxpayer politics. By steadily draining cities of tax revenues while raising costs, they also worsened the conditions that fueled Black urban unrest. In the summer of 1965, simmering tensions in the Watts section of Los Angeles erupted following a police assault on a Black motorist and his mother. Six days of street conflict resulting in several dozen deaths, thousands injured and arrested, and millions of dollars of property destruction followed. In the aftermath, residents pointed to racist law enforcement as the proximate cause, but to the city's wanton neglect of the area as one of the underlying causes. Like other Black and brown areas of Los Angeles, Watts suffered from a dearth of city services and protections. Residents charged that police only came to harass, never to protect them; that firefighters arrived late if they came at all; that the city looked the other way at flagrant violations of land-use ordinances, such as the use of empty lots as unregulated dumps, or the operation of heavy industries in residential areas; that it failed to respond to repeated demands to redesign dangerous intersections that residents described as "death traps"; that street cleaners only came around once a year, if residents were lucky. "Just as drops of water are said to wear away stone," one Watts residents told a reporter, "these things build up and often cause a more violent explosion than would one large overt act."[45] On the eve of an uprising that engulfed the city of Detroit in flames in the summer of 1967, the president of an area block club voiced frustration over her repeated attempts to promote self-help in the face of public neglect. City officials told Black residents to lift themselves and their communities up, yet refused to regularly collect garbage from back alleys or enforce sanitation codes, Minnie Jones vented in frustration. "What is the use of cleaning up my yard if the garbage just blows on it from the alley?"[46]

Many urban Black residents felt they knew why cities were slow to address these problems. Pointing to a storm sewer in her neighborhood in West Philadelphia that had been clogged for over three years, with trash piled high and stagnant water pooling on all sides, resident Okella Mitchell muttered in disgust, "If we lived in a white neighborhood, they'd have fixed it long ago. They get around to us after taking care of the white folks. Then they accuse us of running down property."[47] In the Boston neighborhood of Roxbury, where studies in the mid-1960s had found extremely high assessments resulting in "exorbitant" effective tax rates that vastly exceeded those found in wealthier, whiter areas of the city, Black residents struggled to get even the barest services and attention. As one resident told the US Commission on Civil Rights, "we have been fighting for street lights for quite some time. But they have completely ignored us. Our street is dark and though we have been writing letters . . . nothing has happened." The reason, they believed, was "because this area is predominantly Negro. If it was any other area they would have gotten action."[48] Black and white residents of racially transitional neighborhoods often remarked that services seemed to decrease in direct proportion to an increase in Black residents. In the Merced Heights neighborhood of San Francisco, one white resident told an investigator, "back when we were a neighborhood in transition . . . we began to notice little things, . . . [like] the streets didn't seem to be cleaned as often as they were previously."[49] In the Corona section of Queens,

Figure 5.4 An African American reverend points out cracked cement at Douglass High School in Baltimore, Maryland, while protesting the city's failure to maintain the school, January 8, 1966.

in New York City, one Black resident fumed, "as soon as a few Negro families move into a community, the sanitation moves right out."[50]

In the summer of 1967, Black anger and rage over a litany of injustices spilled into the streets of dozens of major and mid-sized cities. These uprisings led President Lyndon B. Johnson to form a commission to study their underlying causes. In its report in February 1968, the Kerner Commission (named after its chair, Illinois governor Otto Kerner) listed the twelve most intense grievances expressed by Black Americans living in the cities that had experienced uprisings. Of these grievances, five of them (police, education, recreation, political structure, municipal services) were tied to functions and responsibilities of local governments, and their inequities were tied to local spending.[51] Locally commissioned reports made similar findings. In Dayton, Ohio, a report by the Committee on Civil Rights in 1967 highlighted the "poorer municipal services" provided to Black neighborhoods, the lack of "adequate recreational facilities," and the fact that "streets and alleys [in the city's Black ghetto] seemingly never get cleaned" as key factors fueling unrest.[52] The Kerner Commission indicted structural racism for these conditions. "White institutions created [the ghetto], white institutions maintain it, and white society condones it." It concluded: "Our Nation is moving toward two societies, one black, one white—separate and unequal," and it warned that, without action, these divisions and inequities would only deepen. It counseled that "hard choices must be made" and "new taxes enacted."[53]

But what forgotten and neglected Black neighborhoods got instead was a flurry of one-time expenditures aimed at addressing the immediate causes of unrest. In Chicago, where a conflict between police and Black youth over their use of a fire hydrant to cool off in a West Side neighborhood lacking public swimming pools sparked three days of civil unrest in the summer of 1966, the Richard J. Daley administration and the federal Office of Economic Opportunity placed dozens of portable swimming pools and spray nozzles on fire hydrants in Black neighborhoods.[54] When Black residents of North Lawndale loaded up nine oil drums with garbage and placed them in front of Chicago's City Hall in the summer of 1967, the city responded by cleaning all the neighborhood's streets and alleys within twenty-four hours.[55] In Dayton, Ohio, officials ordered enhanced garbage collection and alley cleaning on the Black west side following an uprising in 1966. After uprisings in Atlanta in the summer of 1967, the Kerner Report noted, "the city began replacing street lights, repaving streets, and collecting garbage in the disturbance area."[56] After protesters in Brownsville, Brooklyn, set fire to garbage piles and arson attacks spread to vacant buildings in June 1970, sanitation crews removed over 135 tons of garbage from the neighborhood in a matter of hours.

When it came to capturing the attention of neglectful authorities and securing immediate action to address dire conditions, "riots" worked. "Nobody pays any attention to us unless we resort to violence," a Black resident of Brownsville remarked as a fleet of garbage trucks barreled down the neighborhood's streets.[57] After the violence and disorder subsided, though, the fiscal structure that compelled cities to neglect poorer neighborhoods and immobile residents remained. For organizers, activists, and citizens alike, the fate of this fiscal structure would determine the fate of the struggles ahead.

6

LABORATORIES OF PREDATION

Louis Balthazar returned to his hometown of Natchitoches, Louisiana, following military service in World War II and, like many southern Black men of his generation, caught the first train headed north. In 1946, the twenty-seven-year-old arrived on Chicago's West Side, the chief destination for southern Blacks riding the second wave of the Great Migration, and enrolled in barber school. A year later, he sent for his sweetheart from Natchitoches, Doretta Rachal. The young couple married and settled into the East Garfield Park neighborhood alongside other families from Louisiana and Mississippi. While Louis was in school, the couple bounced from one relative's apartment to the next. After he obtained his license, Louis went into barbering with his friend Richard Brownlee. The pair rented a storefront on the corner of Kedzie and Fourteenth in North Lawndale and opened B&B Barbers. That same year, Brownlee and Balthazar each bought neighboring three-flat apartments, Richard's at 3161 West Monroe Street, Louis and Doretta's at 3163 West Monroe.[1]

Like every other Black family aspiring toward homeownership in postwar America, the Balthazars could not obtain a mortgage from a bank to buy the property, and instead had to buy it using a land contract. But unlike many Black families, the Balthazars secured the property on comparatively reasonable terms. The couple rented out the top two apartments and raised a family on the first. The two buildings became a landing spot for migrants from their hometowns. The block became one big family, sharing a common past, culture, and determination to make it in their new home.[2]

Balthazar invested the money he earned barbering, and every spare moment, into the building. He replaced the coal stoker with an oil furnace, then later upgraded to gas heat. He replaced the roof. Louis and Doretta were constantly tending to the property, painting the hallways and stairwells, fixing the porches. The couple did well enough to send their nine children to a Catholic school and paid off the contract loan in twelve years, a remarkable achievement in a housing marketplace that preyed on Black ambition. After having invested over $16,000 in the property, in 1961 the Balthazars owned it free and clear.[3]

That's when their troubles began. After Richard died unexpectedly, Louis relinquished the storefront and started cutting hair in the basement of 3163 West Monroe. But it wasn't long before the city's building department began fining him for operating a business out of his home. For years, Louis struggled with various ailments and periodically checked into the VA hospital for what his doctors described as a "nervous condition." And the Balthazars still had plenty of bills left to pay, like their children's tuition to Our Lady of Sorrows and, of course, their property taxes. By 1964, "I wasn't making no money and things had gotten kind of rough with me," he described. That fall, he checked in to the VA hospital. While being treated, a bill for one installment of his annual property taxes arrived in the mail. The deadline came and went. "I was sick and nervous, not able to work, and when the tax bills came I just didn't have the money to pay them. So I didn't do anything."[4] And for months afterward, the Balthazars didn't hear anything about it. The unpaid bill receded from their minds. Louis knew he would eventually have to pay it, and assumed that "when the day come," he could "always go and borrow some money."

What they didn't know was that the taxes had already been paid.

The following spring, the taxes to the Balthazars' property were sold at the annual Cook County Tax Auction to one of the nation's largest tax-lien investors, Interstate Bond Company. Afterward, the

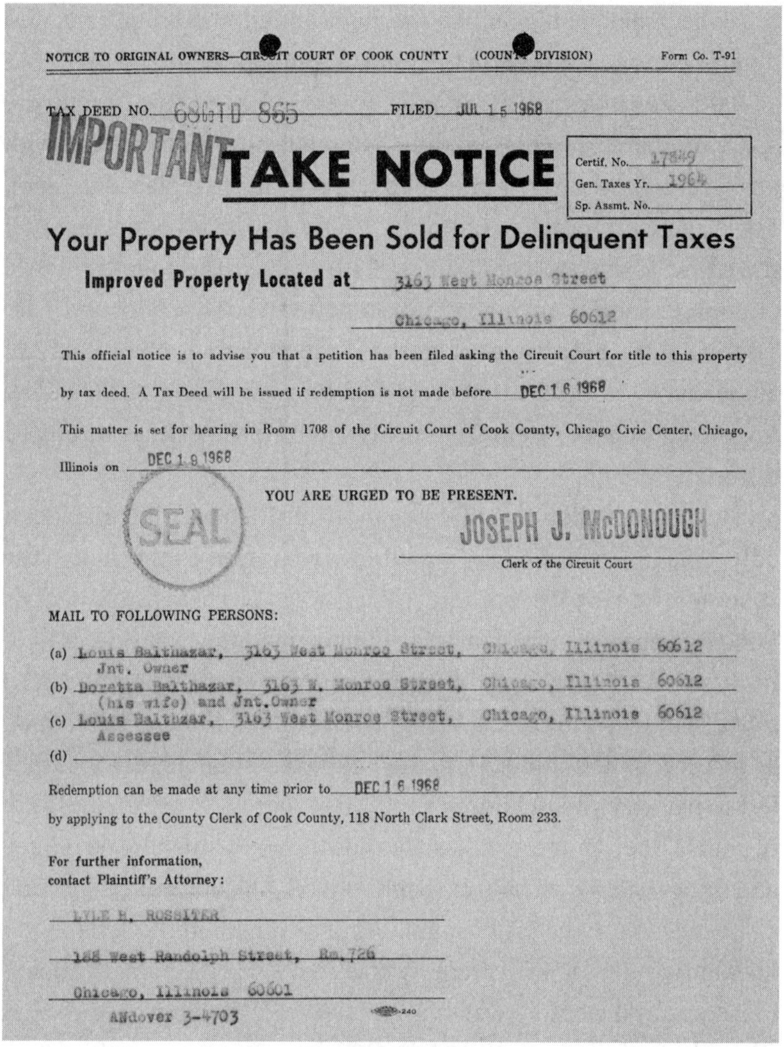

NOTICE TO ORIGINAL OWNERS—CIRCUIT COURT OF COOK COUNTY   (COUNTY DIVISION)   Form Co. T-91

TAX DEED NO. 68-TD 865 _____ FILED JUL 15 1968 _____

Certif. No. 17849
Gen. Taxes Yr. 1964
Sp. Assmt. No.

IMPORTANT TAKE NOTICE

Your Property Has Been Sold for Delinquent Taxes

Improved Property Located at ___ 3163 West Monroe Street ____

Chicago, Illinois 60612

This official notice is to advise you that a petition has been filed asking the Circuit Court for title to this property by tax deed. A Tax Deed will be issued if redemption is not made before ___ DEC 16 1968 _____

This matter is set for hearing in Room 1708 of the Circuit Court of Cook County, Chicago Civic Center, Chicago, Illinois on ___ DEC 18 1968 ____

YOU ARE URGED TO BE PRESENT.

(SEAL)

JOSEPH J. McDONOUGH
Clerk of the Circuit Court

MAIL TO FOLLOWING PERSONS:

(a) Louis Balthazar, 3163 West Monroe Street, Chicago, Illinois 60612
    Jnt. Owner
(b) Doretta Balthazar, 3163 W. Monroe Street, Chicago, Illinois 60612
    (his wife) and Jnt. Owner
(c) Louis Balthazar, 3163 West Monroe Street, Chicago, Illinois 60612
    Assessee
(d) _____

Redemption can be made at any time prior to ___ DEC 16 1968 ____
by applying to the County Clerk of Cook County, 118 North Clark Street, Room 233.

For further information,
contact Plaintiff's Attorney:

LYLE B. ROSSITER

188 West Randolph Street, Rm.726

Chicago, Illinois 60601
    ANdover 3-4703

Figure 6.1 Notice sent to Louis and Doretta Balthazar from the Cook County, Illinois, Circuit Court after the sale of their home to tax buyer Allan Blair for delinquent taxes, July 15, 1968.

Balthazars received a confusing letter from the Clerk's Office, filled with legalese that neither of them could make sense of. It seemed to indicate that the property belonged to some company he didn't recognize. Louis assumed it must be a mistake. He held a copy of the deed in his hands. It was in his name. He had paid off the contract seller. The property was his. They set the letter aside.

Another year passed, and still nothing. Then, in the fall of 1968, they received another notice, this one from a different unfamiliar name, Mari Ltd., informing them that they had less than six months to "redeem" their property. "Redeem?" Louis might have wondered. He owned it. He was living in it. None of this made any sense. Louis might have suspected that they were being scammed. He didn't respond. Then, in March 1969, he received another letter, this one from an attorney with an office downtown. The man insisted that Balthazar come to his office.

Louis and Doretta arrived at 1 North LaSalle and the receptionist led them into the office of attorney Allan Blair. Dark green curtains shaded the windows, glass-covered bookshelves lined the walls, a fine Turkish rug covered the floor. The couple took seats in front of the attorney's large mahogany desk. Blair swung around in his chair, leaned forward, and skipped the usual pleasantries. As Louis recalled, Blair said with a smirk, "You know, you don't own [your] property [any]more." "What?" Louis responded. Blair repeated, "You don't own the property at 3163 West Monroe [any]more." To make his point clear, he recalled, Blair added, "I can evict you anytime I want." "Well, is that why you called me down here?" a stunned Louis asked. "Yes," Blair shot back, and henceforth, "you are going to pay me rent." "Pay *you* rent?" Louis sputtered. "Yes," Blair answered flatly. And as for those two other tenants, "When you collect any money [from them], you [have] to send that to me."

Louis and Doretta could not believe what they were hearing. Doretta, dumbfounded, leaned into Louis and whispered, "What is this?" Louis asked Blair, "Well, what can we do?" Blair, he recalled, answered, "Well, you sign these papers here and you pay me rent that you get from these people on the second and third floor. You send that to me," along with $50 monthly rent for the Balthazars' own apartment.

Louis again asked Blair, "Is there anything else I can do?" "There is nothing you can do," Louis later testified Blair said, "because the property [doesn't] belong to you anymore." And, Blair added, if Louis refused to sign the papers, he would have his family evicted and all their belongings tossed to the curb by the weekend.[5] Seeing no other choice, the Balthazars signed, surrendering all "right to title in the above property other than as tenant at the sufferance of the owner" and waiving "any and all right to any clause of action which I may have against said owner."[6] Louis and Doretta stumbled out of Blair's office, scared and confused, their property and life savings seemingly gone, all over a single missed tax payment. They were not alone. It was one of more than two hundred properties in Illinois to which Blair's firm had acquired a tax deed that year.

During the same decades when African Americans like the Balthazars were migrating north, states like Illinois were sharpening tax-delinquency laws and tax-sale procedures to make outstanding tax debts more attractive to investors and failure to pay on time more painful for taxpayers. They did so in order to bring in more revenue and promote greater compliance following the explosion in tax-delinquency rates that had started in the Great Depression. But in so doing, they created a predatory marketplace. Exploiting laws they lobbied for and helped to write, tax buyers amassed fortunes purchasing liens to tax-delinquent properties and charging owners onerous interest and fees. And if the owners failed to pay, they took their homes outright. Because Black neighborhoods were overtaxed and Black homeowners more likely to experience some form of financial distress causing them to miss a tax payment, and because the color line created scarcity and ensured the profitability of properties in Black ghettos, tax buyers like Blair did much of their business there.

* * *

Laws authorizing counties to auction liens on tax-delinquent properties were as old as many states' constitutions. To the local governments that began conducting them regularly in the mid-nineteenth century, tax sales offered a means of securing unpaid tax revenue and transferring ownership of abandoned property into the hands of persons who would use and pay taxes on it. But to the persons who purchased liens on tax-delinquent properties, tax sales were, as one historian described, "mainly a moneylending mechanism to circumvent usury laws." In rural counties in midwestern states like Illinois and Iowa, tax buyers functioned as lenders of last resort to farmers who were unable to pay their property taxes on time. In exchange, tax buyers could charge interest and fees on those debts that, in some states, netted four times the profits allowed by conventional lending under state-mandated interest-rate caps.[7]

By its very nature, tax-lien investing profited from others' misfortunes and hardships. And in the fast-growing industrial cities of the Midwest, there was plenty of hardship and misfortune to go around. As early as the 1870s, a class of investors specializing in tax liens formed in cities like Chicago. People like Jacob Glos, one of the city's earliest known tax buyers, specifically targeted owner-occupied properties whose owners had failed to pay their taxes due to a mistake or financial distress but who desperately wanted to hold onto their homes. Many of them were recently arrived immigrants who might have been tricked into buying a home they couldn't afford, or who had suffered a temporary loss of income or experienced any of the number of calamities that befell working families in turn-of-the-twentieth-century industrial cities. And when their tax bills went unpaid, people like Glos pounced. By possessing a tax lien, which placed a cloud over someone else's property title, tax buyers could use the threat of dispossession—and the reality that the property owner could never sell their property until the cloud was removed—to compel payments. That's why, from the start, urban tax buyers avoided empty or abandoned properties (those that cities were otherwise most eager to convey to a new owner via tax sales) and instead zeroed in on those that had improvements (such as homes and buildings) and were held by individuals of modest means, preferably lacking in formal education or knowledge of the law, and who had an otherwise good history of tax compliance. These were property owners who, Glos estimated, had missed a tax payment due to temporary hardship or by mistake, and for whom the land was likely to hold value in excess of its market price. They would be most desperate to hold onto their property and most likely to comply with tax buyers' demands.[8]

Tax buyers' investing strategies varied by the laws governing tax sales in each state. At the time when Glos was growing his business, Illinois directed counties to sell a lien on a fraction of a delinquent taxpayer's property. Under this system, bidding at tax sales would start at the amount of land necessary to satisfy the tax debt, and bidders would bid down to ever-smaller portions of the land. In theory, the law was meant to ensure that the property owner did not lose property in excess of the amount owed, and that, if not redeemed, the tax buyer could obtain clear title to a piece of real estate. But this law was written with rural farmland in mind and was ill-suited to the city lots that Cook County auctioned off each year. Seeking only to place a cloud on a tax-delinquent property, tax buyers competed to accept ever-more-minuscule portions of it. Throughout the late 1800s and early 1900s, Glos outbid competitors by purchasing liens on the tiniest possible fraction of land and then hounding delinquent taxpayers for payments to remove the cloud.[9] Glos's strategies became so notorious that, in 1910, Illinois changed the way it administered tax sales. Instead of auctioning a fraction of a property for taxes, it had bidders compete for a lien by bidding down on the interest rate.[10]

Bid-down auctions were treated as a progressive reform that protected homeowners from exploitation. In theory, they lessened the penalty for the delinquent taxpayer. The bidding on each tax lien began at the maximum rate, the next bidder agreed to a lower one, and so on. But under this system, competition among tax buyers diminished the profitability for all of them. It thus encouraged tax buyers to collaborate and collude. Tax buyers entered into noncompete agreements and divided up the liens prior to the sale. Tax buyers also shared the costs of investigating tax-delinquent properties and determining which ones to bid on. By the date of the tax sale, tax buyers had already determined what properties they would be acquiring liens on and at what rate (invariably, the maximum under law).[11]

The more the public learned about the business of tax buying and the work of tax buyers like Glos, the more disgusted they became. Early-twentieth-century muckraking journalists explained the mechanics of the trade to readers and condemned its profiteers as "tax sharks" who preyed on the poor and vulnerable. For some in the business, the weight on their conscience proved too great. In 1911, the president of a New Jersey–based investment firm that specialized in tax liens grew so horrified by the "character of the business and realizing that its success depends upon taking advantage of the misfortunes of others" that he resigned and convinced its stockholders to dissolve the company. "It's too much like 'picking pennies off a dead man's eyes,'" he remarked.[12]

But to public officials, these tax sharks brought in revenue, absorbed public anger, and, they believed, compelled taxpayer compliance. To them, the cruel, heartless tax buyer was an asset. In Chicago, officials were quick to remind tardy taxpayers that "the tax buyer was neither gentle in his ways nor kindly in his disposition."[13] In Detroit, the county treasurer used press coverage of the city's largest and most notorious tax buyer, Charles H. Wiltsie, to compel tax payments in advance of the annual tax sale. "Upon the approach of Wiltsie," the *Detroit Free Press* described, the treasurer "would run up the danger signal and money would pour into the city coffers."[14] Tax buyers, in turn, cultivated close ties with local officials and leveraged their investments to secure exclusive access to information on properties. The auditor for the District of Columbia, where Wiltsie had reportedly invested over $1 million in tax liens over a ten-year span in the early 1900s, granted him access to tax arrears cards housed in the assessor's office, "so that he might bid intelligently."[15]

But when people paid their taxes, it was not because they feared the tax shark, and rising rates of tax delinquency were not due to lax enforcement. They were signs of distress. This fact became evident as the nation plunged into the Great Depression. Along with mortgage foreclosures, tax-delinquency rates skyrocketed to unprecedented levels in the early 1930s as housing markets collapsed. In some cities, delinquency rates crept above 65 percent, at a time when, in many states, the property tax supplied over 50 percent of all state and local revenue. In the depths of the Depression, many major cities, like Detroit and Chicago, failed to bring in over 30 percent of expected property tax revenues. Nearly every large and mid-sized city teetered on the edge of bankruptcy. Developers of failed subdivisions and other unfinished and abandoned real estate ventures were responsible for the largest amount of unpaid property taxes, with the second largest amount due from owners of income-producing properties like apartments and of commercial and industrial properties. Among residential properties, the highest rates of tax delinquency were often found in higher-valued neighborhoods.[16] Local governments' failure to reassess property to reflect market changes exacerbated the problem, making what began as a response to financial distress into a protest against unfair taxation.[17]

Prior to the Great Depression, tax buyers welcomed volatility in housing markets: delinquency was how they made their money, after all. But the market did need to be functional. The property had to have value that the delinquent taxpayer wanted to protect and preserve; there had to be market demand for the property that removing a cloud on the title would unlock. That framework broke down during the Great Depression when housing markets collapsed. And because of this collapse, tax liens became essentially worthless. So tax buyers walked away.

At the very moment when local governments needed them the most, tax buyers were nowhere to be found. In 1928, Cook County sold 18,753 tax-lien certificates netting $3,776,631. In 1933, it sold only thirteen certificates for a total of $557.[18] Participation in tax sales plummeted so rapidly that many cities simply cancelled them. On the Great Plains, besieged farmers staged hostile takeovers of tax auctions, buying delinquent properties for the bare minimum and returning title to the owners.[19]

In desperation, states enacted a flurry of legislation designed to cajole property owners into settling their debts. They extended payment deadlines and redemption periods. They waived or reduced fees and interest penalties. They created installment plans. Some even adjusted the amount of taxes due.[20] Such measures outraged tax buyers. In Milwaukee, tax buyers staged a boycott of the 1933 tax sale in response to the passage of a law that lowered the interest penalty on tax debts from 10 to 8 percent. But this protest was all for show. Few bidders would have come, and few liens would have been sold, regardless. Still, it signaled the approach that tax buyers and the nascent tax-lien industry planned to take, going forward, toward fiscally distressed local governments.[21]

To tax buyers' threats to boycott tax sales, critics responded: good riddance. The *Milwaukee Journal* asked, "Is there anything inherently sound about selling past due bills to somebody else? Is there anything constructive about handing delinquencies over to private individuals who hope to collect heavy interest charges or seize the properties of home owners or business men? It is better," they argued, "that government should hold these claims." Critics of tax sales hoped that the fiscal crisis—and tax sales' demonstrated incapacity to mitigate it—would compel states to devise their own tax-collection machinery, one that operated in the public's interest. A better model for enforcing taxpayer compliance and addressing government's fiscal needs, they argued, would begin by training its sights on "the cunning men who deliberately postpone or evade tax payments" and "bear down hard and compel payment [from them] by every proper use of persuasion or law." And it would work with, rather than against, those "honest home or other property owners who worry much and try hard to pay taxes, though they may be unable to do it on time." With these taxpayers, tax authorities should exercise "leniency, with every possible resort to co-operation."[22]

Tax enforcement in the public interest was the exact opposite of how tax buyers worked. For them, the tax liens on properties owned by "cunning men" were risky bets to avoid, while tax liens on the properties of "honest men" were the most enticing.[23]

Influencing the entire process were the cities' creditors and bondholders. And as the fiscal crisis in the 1930s deepened, bond markets made clear the kind of measures they wanted to see governments adopt: aggressive enforcement, higher penalties, more fees tacked onto unpaid debts, and, finally, more incentives to lure in tax buyers. In Westchester County, New York, banks refused to refinance municipal loans unless cities agreed to hold tax sales. Financial advisers implored cities to go tough on property owners, no matter their circumstances, and to indulge the demands of tax buyers. Taxpayers needed to know that nonpayment was not an option, and that if they shirked their tax obligations, no matter the reason, the consequences would be severe. "Municipal credit is founded, in the last analysis, upon the ability of the taxpayers to make prompt payments," municipal tax consultant Paul Studenski argued. "If taxes are not paid properly, municipal credit grows weak. Under such conditions, loans cannot be obtained and tax arrears cannot be converted into cash." The "steadiness of primary income," municipal financial advisor Frederick Bird counseled, "has come to be a very influential factor in a municipality's ability to sell bonds advantageously. Few items are scanned more carefully by prospective creditors than the record of tax collections." Now was not the time to go soft on delinquent taxpayers, no matter their debts or circumstances, nor make any moves that might reduce the profitability of tax-lien investing, these advisers argued. For them, the solutions were clear: "greater severity of penalties, higher interest rates, and stricter administration of collection laws." As if to underscore their point, credit-rating agencies improved the credit scores of cities that adopted tough measures. In 1938, Boston secured a favorable interest rate on a $4 million general-obligation bond after it announced plans to, among other measures, slash public employee salaries, close two hospitals, and begin holding regular tax sales.[24]

Calls to step up enforcement all operated from a common premise: that people chose not to pay their taxes; that tax delinquency was, in essence, voluntary; and that without strong disincentives it would become contagious. "Delinquency and a tolerant attitude toward tax delinquency breeds further tax delinquency," the Chicago Bar Association intoned. In order to check this virus, governments must "revive tax buying."[25] Even in the depths of the Great Depression, as tax-delinquency rates in many cities climbed above 50 percent, this view was commonly held among fiscal policy analysts: that most property owners were perfectly capable of paying their property taxes but chose not to do so because they knew that cities were helpless to do anything about it.

Even as tax buyers scaled back investing during the 1930s, they continued to press fiscally distressed governments. In New York, lobbyists for tax-lien investors succeeded in pushing through a major reform to the state's tax-delinquency law that awarded them clear and incontestable title to the property at the close of the redemption period. This reform, they argued, would incentivize tax buying and compel tax payments, since owners would now be assured of losing their property (and all its equity) if they didn't redeem.[26]

Tax-delinquent homeowners did not need such threats to compel them to pay. They needed incomes sufficient to meet their expenses. And, as soon as the economy stabilized and rates of unemployment dropped, so too did tax-delinquency rates. By 1940, property tax collection rates in Chicago had rebounded to pre-Depression levels. Revenue from Cook County's annual tax sale also sharply rebounded, as tax buyers dove back into the recovering market.[27]

But while the revenues from tax sales returned, the number of bidders at them remained low. In their place, large tax-buying investment firms took command. Operating in multiple states and with massive capital reserves, firms like the Interstate Bond Company began dominating tax sales. Founded in 1927 in Georgia, Interstate Bond was a creature of the Great Depression. As tax delinquency spread across the Georgia Black Belt and Piedmont in the 1920s, and the numbers of pages listing tax-delinquent property owners in newspapers multiplied, bringing shame and humiliation to countless numbers of hard-pressed farmers and homeowners, the company's founders saw an opportunity. Interstate turned the informal practice of tax lending into the business of tax financing: they would pay the taxes of those who could not and save them from "undue embarrassment in the publication of their homes being sold for past-due taxes."[28] Instead of being in debt to government, the taxpayer would be in debt to the Interstate Bond Company, at greater long-term cost. Distressed property owners flocked to their service. Four years after it was founded, Interstate Bond claimed over $2,225,000 in assets, which it subsequently invested in the very thing their clients wanted so desperately to avoid: tax sales.[29]

Interstate Bond soon expanded into several states, and in 1943 it

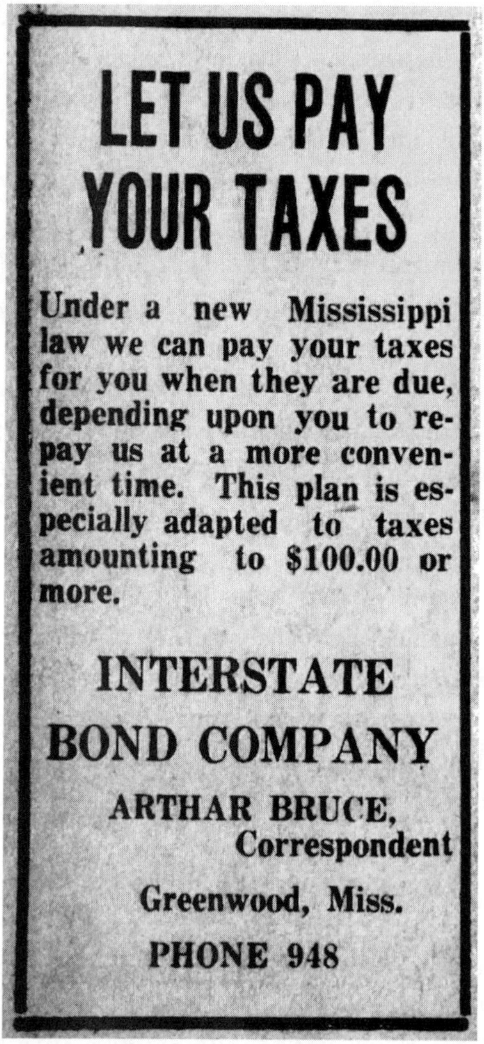

Figure 6.2 Interstate Bond Company advertisement, *Greenwood* [MS] *Commonwealth*, January 13, 1932.

secured a corporate charter in Illinois. Its Chicago team rented office space at 120 North LaSalle Street, on the same block where Jacob Glos had plied his trade a half-century earlier.[30] One block away sat the offices of the Tax Lien Corp., a consortium of tax buyers formed in the wake of the 1930s market collapse. The two firms would, in the years that followed, dominate the Cook County Tax Sale. With massive capital reserves, the two firms jointly financed investigations of tax-delinquent properties, divided up the profitable liens ahead of the sale, and proceeded to crowd all smaller investors out. By 1947, the two companies annually purchased upwards of 95 percent of all tax liens sold. "Page after page of the sale record shows two sales to Interstate Bond Co., one sale to Tax Lien Corp., two sales to Interstate, and one to Tax Lien, and so on," one observer described.[31] In other cities, heavily capitalized tax-buying firms began dominating tax auctions. When Milwaukee resumed tax sales in 1939, the heaviest bidder was the Florida-based Atlantic Municipal Corp.[32]

In Illinois, Interstate Bond also began lobbying state lawmakers to enact reforms to its tax-delinquency law. They pushed to increase the interest penalties tax buyers could collect and to make it easier for tax buyers to secure title to properties at the close of the redemption period, changes similar to the reforms enacted in New York. Even as Interstate Bond harbored no desire to accumulate property, there needed to be a credible threat of loss to compel payments, they argued. Otherwise, tax buyers' threats would ring hollow, delinquency rates would rise, and Illinois counties would soon slide back into fiscal crisis. Similarly, if governments made redemption too cheap, tax buyers would stop investing or would invest in other states' tax sales. Tax buyers found a champion in the *Chicago Tribune*, which ran numerous editorials throughout the 1940s parroting tax-lien lobbyists' arguments.[33] The Chicago Association of Commerce also called on lawmakers to make it easier to obtain clear title and provide other "safeguards to the 'tax-buyer.'"[34]

In 1951, these lobbying efforts paid off, as Illinois lawmakers passed major reforms to its tax-delinquency laws. The bill, which Interstate Bond's own attorney, Robert S. Cushman, helped to draft, established an escalating interest-rate scale that kicked in following the tax sale. If a property owner settled their debts within six months of the tax sale, they would have to pay the tax buyer 12 percent interest on the debt. After six months, the rate doubled to 24 percent; and after 12 months, it increased to 36 percent. During the last six months of the two-year redemption period, the interest rate rose to an incredible 48 percent. These exorbitant rates were coupled with mandatory fees—

for the issuing of the certificate, for the costs of serving, publishing, and mailing notices—that the property owner also had to pay in order to redeem. The most consequential change of all, though, was what happened after the end of the redemption period, when the tax buyer could now petition the circuit court to issue a tax deed, which made it incontestable. If the property owner failed to settle their mounting debts within two years, and the tax buyer followed every requirement, the property would be as good as gone. And the owner would be left with nothing. The formerly worthless tax deed, which, critics charged, had never withstood the slightest judicial scrutiny, had now been made "immune from collateral attack."[35]

The 1951 Revenue Act came in the midst of the second wave of the Great Migration. In the segregated housing markets of northern cities, property in Black neighborhoods derived its value from its extractive potential.[36] Tax sales provided a lucrative vein of extraction. Slum investors bought abandoned, often-dilapidated properties at tax sales and, in most cases, realized a full return on their investment in a matter of months. One Chicago slumlord acquired an abandoned two-story frame house on the west side at a tax sale for $475. She promptly divided the home into four apartments and began renting each to Black families for $75 per month. Another acquired tax deeds to ten West Side properties for a total of $5,739, which he subsequently converted into dozens of one-room kitchenettes, each netting monthly rents ranging from $40 to $60.[37]

But in Black neighborhoods nationwide there were also sizable numbers of African American homeowners. In Evanston, Illinois, nearly one-third of Black residents were homeowners in 1930.[38] The number of Black homeowners in cities grew at a faster rate than white homeownership during the 1940s.[39] Many of these Black homeowners were working people who had been forced to pay exorbitant prices on risky terms and had made enormous sacrifices to acquire and pay off their homes. Many others had acquired properties with the intention of supplementing their income from renting out apartments and spare rooms; in the process, many became emmeshed in the exploitative economy in Black housing.[40] Others had purchased empty lots and built their homes themselves, brick by brick. Regardless of how they acquired their homes, nearly all Black homeowners in mid-twentieth-century cities lived in segregated neighborhoods, where demand for housing was great, and experienced the financial hardships, uncertainties, and vulnerabilities that came with being Black in Jim Crow America. As a result, they became the most attractive of targets for tax buyers.

After Illinois passed the 1951 Revenue Act, lawyers and lobbyists for the Interstate Bond Company began filing test cases and pushing for additional reforms that lowered tax buyers' costs and strengthened their hand over delinquent taxpayers. These reforms included lowering notification requirements to delinquent taxpayers and automatically granting tax-certificate holders the right to pay subsequent taxes on the property during the redemption period at a statutory interest rate, which a delinquent taxpayer would also have to pay in order to redeem the property. These additional tweaks ostensibly removed roadblocks that delinquent taxpayers used to delay or prevent forfeiture. But for tax buyers, these same reforms lowered overhead costs and made it easier for buyers to acquire clear title when they wished. For institutional tax buyers like Interstate Bond, making it easier for tax buyers to gain ownership of tax-delinquent properties was a means to compel payments. But these reforms also vastly increased the potential spoils for tax buyers. Each amendment and test case, as one reporter summarized, "tightened the noose on the property owner, making it more difficult for him to comply with the law and retain title to his home."[41] It ensured that tax buyers wielded total control over negotiations with delinquent taxpayers, and could steer the redemption process toward whatever outcome they desired. As one legal scholar described, these changes "left the redemption laws, both case and statutory, in such a state of confusion that only those members of the bar whose regular practices include tax sales and tax deeds are able to deal with them with any degree of comfort."[42]

In Illinois, one of the lawyers who began working to enhance tax buyers' profits was Allan Blair. After graduating from the University of Illinois School of Law in 1954 and passing the state's bar exam in

1955, Blair joined Cushman's team of attorneys working on behalf of Interstate Bond.[43] He argued his first case before the Illinois Supreme Court in 1958, a successful appeal of a lower court decision voiding a tax deed on a technicality.[44] The goal, for Interstate Bond, was to increase the profits on tax liens to properties that were ultimately redeemed. The company was not interested in accumulating real estate. But Blair was. Blair saw—scattered across the lists of unredeemed tax certificates on Interstate Bond's books—properties worth tens of thousands of dollars or more. Many of them were in neighborhoods where segregation had created high demand or were held by owners who had missed a payment and who, following the tax sale, had been unable to crawl out from under mounting debts but desperately wanted to remain in their homes.

Blair saw his opportunity. He struck a deal with Interstate Bond to purchase in bulk all of its unredeemed tax certificates six months prior to the close of the redemption period. Then, Blair would comb through the list, inspect each property, find those that had value, wait until the close of the redemption period, and take ownership. The arrangement was mutually beneficial. Interstate could clear its books and realize a return on all its investments. Blair could score windfall profits from acquiring deeds for pennies on the dollar; those he did not want to acquire he could simply chalk up as losses and forget.[45]

After Blair received his stack of tax certificates from Interstate Bond each year, he or one of his associates conducted drive-by inspections of all the properties. From their car window, they assigned a rating for each—A, B, C, D, or E—based on its projected value. Value could come in several different forms. The property could acquire value simply by virtue of being owner occupied, allowing Blair to attempt to sell it back to the owner. It could be valuable because it was located in an area with high demand for housing and therefore could easily be resold. It could be generating revenue through rents, which Blair could then compel the former owner to collect on his behalf in exchange for remaining in his home. It could be valuable because it was in an area that the city was eyeing for an urban-renewal project or looking to condemn, or that a private developer needed to complete a project. In all of these cases, the tax buyer could realize a substantial return on a minimal investment.

Because the color line constrained the quantity of housing for urban Black populations, and because Black areas were targeted for slum-clearance and urban-renewal projects, through the 1950s and 1960s there was no such thing as a worthless property in the Black ghetto. Tax buyers could rest assured that tax-lien certificates on properties in Black neighborhoods could net a handsome return on investment, whether from the property owner seeking to redeem it or by acquiring the deed and flipping it to another (often, fellow) slumlord, adding it to their own rental-property portfolio, selling it on contract, or taking a government payout.

There were other reasons why tax buyers saw Black neighborhoods—and especially, Black homeowners—as attractive targets. Because the interest rate in states like Illinois doubled every six months after a tax sale, delinquent owners would want to redeem their property as quickly as possible. (This was not the case in all states. In others, the interest rate remained fixed throughout the redemption period, which made it easier for delinquent taxpayers to wait longer to redeem and less profitable for tax buyers the longer they did.) A tax-delinquent property owner who could obtain a loan from a bank or from a family member, could save themselves from paying significantly more to redeem, in turn diminishing the profitability of those tax-lien certificates. Whites enjoyed significantly greater access to financial assistance than African Americans did, along with earning higher wages and possessing greater household savings than Blacks. Tax-delinquent whites were thus more likely to redeem their properties much sooner, and at lower interest rates, than Blacks, which of course made their properties less attractive to tax buyers. Tax-sale records in Cook County reveal that, among redeemed properties, tax certificates to properties in predominantly Black townships generated higher returns than did those in predominantly white townships. Tax certificates in the largely white North and Rogers Park townships brought, on average, a 23 percent return on investment; in contrast, those in the South township, which covered much of the heavily Black South Side, generated a 37.7 percent return.[46]

Not only did Black homeowners generate more interest and fees for tax buyers. They were seen as more likely to not redeem for lack of funds, or because they didn't fully grasp the consequences of non-payment. Take the case of William Parks. By the time the factory worker had finally paid off his land-installment contract in 1962, he had invested over $19,000 in the modest two-story townhouse he'd purchased in 1946 on Chicago's South Side. Parks had labored for decades at the Sherwin-Williams paint-manufacturing plant and looked forward to retirement and collecting his pension the following year. After all those years of work, Parks was still earning a little over $5,000 a year in wages, and his pension would provide a paltry $48.41 a month. But it was enough, he hoped, to live out his retirement with some comfort. But soon after retiring in 1963, Parks fell ill. During his recovery, he missed paying a property tax bill. It was the only time Parks had ever failed to pay his taxes on time. It would cost him dearly. The following year, Interstate Bond purchased a tax certificate on his home. Parks, like many other Black men who had come North, had only attended school through the eighth grade and struggled to make sense of the confusing notices he received from the clerk's office. He failed to redeem before Interstate Bond sold his tax certificate to Blair. Blair conducted a drive-by inspection of Parks's townhouse. The property was in good condition. The townhouse had been brand new when Parks bought it and had been well maintained. Moreover, it was in the heart of the Black Belt.[47]

Blair gave Parks's home his highest rating (A++) and then laid his trap. Prior to the close of the redemption period, Parks received from the county treasurer a final estimate of what he owed. Interest plus fees had ballooned Parks's bill to nearly twice the original amount. Parks struggled to round up enough cash before the deadline and missed paying a subsequent property tax bill. Seeing his opportunity, and using a provision of the law he had authored, Blair paid Parks's most recent bill, which was then added on to the final bill. But Parks didn't learn this until he arrived at the clerk's office, check in hand, on the final day of the redemption period, and was told he hadn't brought enough money. Parks scrambled to round up the additional cash, but it was too late. Parks missed the deadline by one day. Blair had already filed for a tax deed to his home, which he offered to sell back to Parks for $12,000.[48]

Whether they took their homes or used the threat to extract onerous payments, tax buyers traumatized their victims. They not only stripped individuals and families of their assets and property but left individuals and families devastated and broken.[49] Mattie Coleman Burleson had inherited the home her father, Adam Coleman, had bought when he came north to Chicago from Mississippi in 1944. Arriving with only a fourth-grade education, he labored for years to save and stay one step ahead of the bill collectors. He had succeeded in doing so until 1962, when he failed to pay an installment of his property taxes. Interstate Bond bought a tax certificate on the home in 1964, which it subsequently sold to one of Blair's partners, Fred M. Horne, for $128 in 1966. Burleson, who was living in the home, received the final notice before the end of the redemption period, but mistakenly assumed that her

Figure 6.3 Chicago attorney and tax buyer Allan Blair in his office. *The Chicagoan*, September 1974.

father had handled it. In the spring of 1967, Coleman was informed that he no longer owned his house, but, Blair offered, he could buy it back for $12,000. The shock sent Coleman reeling, and he soon died. Burleson was devastated and, her friends said, blamed herself for failing to take care of it. Blair evicted Coleman's children. "Maddie was never the same after she lost her daddy and that home," her aunt said, and Burleson died shortly thereafter, at age forty-six.[50]

In Peoria, Blair obtained the deed to a home that an African American couple owned and rented out, after the tenants had failed to forward the tax bill to them. Speaking to a reporter, the couple remarked, "You struggled and sacrifice and buy property—miss meals, don't buy shoes or clothes, and then it is taken away from you like this. You wonder why people get bitter? This is the reason why."[51]

* * *

By the mid-1960s, Blair's tax-buying operation was in full swing. The money just poured in—from elderly widows who had overlooked a tax bill that their late spouse had once handled, from the siblings or children of mentally or physically ill people who were incapable of handling their own affairs, from working men and women who had fallen on hard times, from homeowners who insisted they had never received a bill or notices. All of them were forced to scramble to pay off mounting debts before the deadline or to negotiate with Blair in order to "buy" their house back. Blair drove a hard bargain. For a property he had paid a couple hundred dollars to acquire the tax certificate to, Blair offered to sell it back to the owners at upwards of 80 percent of its market value. If the former owner was unable to buy it back, and elderly, and if Blair was in a generous mood, he might offer to rent it back to them, only selling it upon their death. If they refused to play along, Blair could always evict them and sell. Since many of the properties tax buyers acquired were in neighborhoods that conventional mortgage lenders shunned, the business of tax buying also became, for many, a contract-selling business. Working through real estate brokers, Blair annually sold dozens of homes to the largest and most notorious contract sellers, and he later began directly selling homes and collecting payments from contract buy-ers.[52] His various LLCs held the deeds to numerous properties in the city's most depressed neighborhoods. These included the dilapi-dated tenement building that Martin Luther King Jr. chose to live in during the summer of 1966 to call attention to racial segregation and inequality in the urban North, which Blair's First Lien Co. owned.[53]

As he built his tax-buying enterprise, Blair rose through the ranks of Chicago's legal community and became a respected expert in real estate tax law. He became the lawyer whom other tax buyers and real estate investors called for advice, and the expert that law schools and bar associations invited to speak on real estate tax law. He became a leading member of the Chicago Bar Association (CBA); in 1968, he was named chairman of the CBA's ethics committee. Blair and his wife, Jocelyn, became a staple on the city's social circuit, appearing in the society pages and on the guest lists of charity balls and other high-profile social affairs. Blair purchased a luxury apartment on the fiftieth floor of a high rise on Lake Shore Drive, which he stocked with antiques, high-fidelity stereo equipment, a grand piano, and expen-sive art. He bought a summer house on a lake in northern Wiscon-sin.[54] The riches he and other tax buyers could extract from desperate homeowners and their missed tax payments seemed limitless.

PART III

A LOCAL STRUGGLE

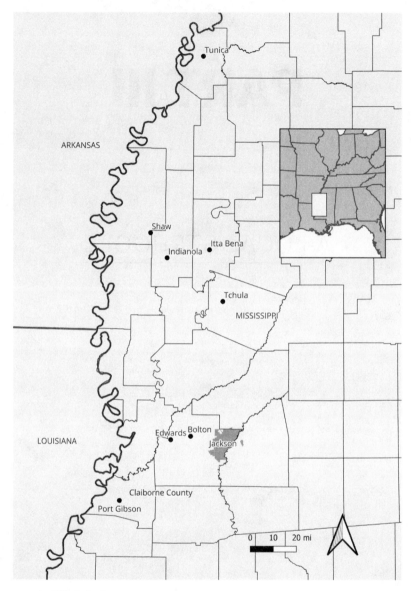

Figure 7.1 Mississippi.

7

CITIZENS AND TAXPAYERS

Blacks in 1960s Edwards, Mississippi, were well aware of how their tax dollars were spent. They were reminded every time they stepped onto a sidewalk or paved street on the white side of town, cleaned a flush toilet in a white family's home, or heard the sounds of white children splashing and playing in the town's swimming pool. Their taxes had helped to build and maintain all these public amenities, none of which they were allowed to enjoy. In this and hundreds of cities and small towns across the South, Blacks paid taxes for the roofs over their heads, for the food on their tables, and on every other possession their meager incomes could afford. But, as one Black Edwards resident put it, "you did not receive the benefits." Along the streets, "when the white houses ran out, the sidewalks ran out." As did pavement, streetlights, and sewer lines.[1]

Fifty years later, Jean White could still recall the stench of the outhouse and the slop jar in her family's house. She remembered feeling jealous of the few Black families who, by happenstance, enjoyed these modern amenities and tax-funded services. "Those that had the restrooms inside, you would call them the higher ups." One Black family happened to live in between two white neighborhoods, and because of that, had a sidewalk in front of their home. Their daughter, another Black resident recalled, "was the only Black girl who could [roller] skate in town." She remembered how the "colored" school let out "at twelve o'clock . . . so that the kids who lived on plantations could go and pick cotton," while white schoolchildren enjoyed a full day of education.[2]

So many of the daily indignities and injustices that White and other Black southerners of her generation experienced under Jim Crow had their origins in the budgetary decisions of white-controlled local governments. So many of the issues that drew people into the movement, so many of the items on local movements' agendas, concerned matters of local public spending. Indeed, what became "the movement" did not take shape in the seminal moments and major events that captured the nation's attention and fill the pages of history books today. Rather, it grew out of what the historian Charles Payne described as a "tradition of struggle," one that was forged at the local level and inseparable from Black people's intimate, place-bound experiences of oppression and exploitation.[3] It was through their encounters with local authorities that African Americans formed their understandings of power and devised modes of resistance. It was through local fights over matters of public concern—and, invariably, over matters of public spending—that communities became organized. And it was through the places where they lived, worked, and called home that Black people formed their visions of freedom, and from which those visions became something worth fighting and dying for.

It was also through the deployment of local powers and circumvention of federal authorities that white segregationists fought to preserve a crumbling Jim Crow order.[4] Of the local powers in whites' arsenal, few made it through the civil rights revolution of the 1960s more unscathed than local taxing powers. Amidst the movement's successful battles for expansion of federal power and authority in the workplace, places of public accommodations, and voting booths, the discretionary powers of local tax authorities and their use as a weapon of intimidation and retaliation remained unchecked. And thus it was here, in the tax assessment offices of small towns like Edwards, Mississippi, where Jim Crow took his last stand.

* * *

Black people entered into the fight against Jim Crow bearing tax receipts. By the late 1930s, African Americans in cities and towns across the South invoked their status as taxpayers to prod local governments and school systems to distribute public dollars more fairly. They filed lawsuits challenging the use of public dollars to fund the construction of white-only public facilities. They threatened to stage protests and direct actions against segregated beaches and parks unless cities agreed to provide them with public facilities of their own. Making claims on the local state as taxpayers was a tactical maneuver, a means, as historian N. D. B. Connolly described, for local Blacks to reset the terms of "Jim Crow's evolving racial contract."[5]

But as it became apparent that whites only honored that contract in the breach, civil rights organizers and strategists began to see taxpayer-based claims as a means of attacking Jim Crow's legal foundations. In 1938, NAACP attorneys in Oklahoma contested a $275,000 bond issue passed by white voters in Muskogee to fund the construction of a new white school and football stadium. Black resident Willie Eva Simmons, mother of three children in the "colored" school system, challenged in federal court the constitutionality of the bond issue on equal-protection grounds, since it used Black people's tax dollars to pay down the bond but legally barred them from enjoying any of its benefits.[6] In a narrow sense, Simmons's lawsuit simply challenged the city's funding scheme, which placed "colored" schools in the county system but still forced Black Muskogee residents to pay taxes in support of a city school district that barred Black students. But white segregationists well understood the lawsuit's purpose. "If they win," the state's assistant attorney general J. Henry Johnson warned, "it would break down the entire school system of the whole South."[7] That's because what was really at stake was not so much separation of the races as it was the gross inequalities in public funding and school quality between white and "colored" schools, and the denial of decent schools and educational opportunity to Black children.

Yet the District Court sided with the school district, ruling that Blacks' "failure to receive benefits from taxes" did not violate the Fourteenth Amendment. The NAACP appealed to the US Supreme Court, which opted not to take up the case and upheld the district court ruling on the grounds that the questions of federal invention in state and local school-funding decisions were "so unsubstantial as not to need further argument."[8]

In the years that followed, the NAACP's legal attack on school segregation drifted away from fiscal matters and funding inequalities and toward the intangible factors that would form the heart of the Supreme Court's 1954 decision in *Brown v. Board of Education*. But Black parents and taxpayers never lost sight of Jim Crow's material dimensions. Throughout the 1940s and early 1950s, local and statewide groups and organizations stepped up demands for school districts to close spending disparities, pay white and Black teachers equal salaries, and address the overcrowding of urban Black schools that had made double sessions (and even triple sessions) a common experience for Black children. Parents and protesters couched their demands as being for benefits they earned from paying taxes, and they used their limited powers to affect spending decisions to force change. In 1940, over two thousand Black voters in Atlanta went to the polls to defeat a school-bond issue that earmarked less than one-eighteenth of total spending on "colored" schools at a time when those schools were suffering from extreme overcrowding and neglect, with some still lacking running water and flush toilets.[9] In 1946, a group of Black educators and civic leaders in Mississippi publicly called on the governor and legislature to reform a funding scheme that, they charged, "taxes both whites and Negroes equally to build schools, but uses all the money as a rule ... [on] white schools only." The group contrasted the enhanced spending on white schools and expansion of white public universities during the 1940s with the innumerable inadequacies of "colored" schools. They stressed that "the Negro wants no special tax levied for him," calling simply for an "equal pro rata share of all monies levied by the state, counties and municipalities."[10]

By the early 1960s, local Blacks in hundreds of cities and towns across the South were engaging in protests and organizing campaigns aimed at forcing wholesale changes to the spending practices and priorities of local governments. In Thomasville, Alabama, Black residents threatened to conduct marches, sit-ins, and boycotts of white-owned businesses unless the town agreed to provide Black neighborhoods with sidewalks, streetlights, sewer service, and paved streets."[11] In Americus, Georgia, eighteen-year-old activist Lena Turner spent fifty-two days in jail for marching without a permit. Upon release, she told reporters what led her and others into the streets: Blacks in Americus wanted "more and better jobs, paved streets, sewers, voting rights, [and] better education."[12] In Plaquemine, Louisiana, local Blacks took to the streets in the summer of 1963 to protest against the town's intentional underdevelopment and neglect of Black neighborhoods. There, white officials had surgically drawn municipal boundaries around the two Black residential sections (despite both being in the geographical center of town) and used their unincorporated status to deny them access to the city's sewerage system and other infrastructure and services.[13] As a result, one civil rights worker described, "When it rains, the sewers back-up and flood over into the streets, giving off a terrible stench. Small children are often found playing in the overflow."[14] That summer, hundreds of local Blacks descended on Plaquemine's City Hall demanding to be able to "enjoy the benefits and fulfill the duties of citizenship by being a part of the city."[15] Among the hundreds of demonstrators beaten, arrested, and jailed in Plaquemine that summer included Congress of Racial Equality (CORE) co-founder James Farmer, one of the lead organizers of the March on Washington for Jobs and Freedom held in Washington, DC, in late August. Scheduled to speak at the historic event, Farmer instead spent it in a crowded cell in a Louisiana jail protesting municipal neglect.[16]

Organizers in CORE and the Student Nonviolent Coordinating Committee (SNCC), in particular, saw just how much the denial of these basic needs—"covered sewers, street lights, playgrounds, postal service, libraries, free access to public services and facilities"—drove people into the movement, and made it the basis for community organizing efforts.[17] *You think voting makes no difference?* One SNCC pamphlet asked. "Take a look at your curbs, your sewers and sidewalks, at the lighting and pavement of your streets, at the progress of your renewal projects; or do dirt roads coat your house with dust or mud while your children walk down the middle of unlighted streets for lack of sidewalks?"[18] In the summer of 1963, SNCC staffers fanned across the Black neighborhoods of Atlanta's south side, gathering information from residents on grievances and needs. City officials, residents charged, failed to provide Black Atlantans with parks and recreational facilities; streetlights, crosswalks, and traffic signs; sewerage and garbage service; sidewalks and pavement. Black Atlantans, SNCC's 1963 report stressed, "are tired of taxation without representation."[19]

* * *

Nowhere were local public spending disparities greater, and kleptocratic governance more nakedly apparent, than in the small towns of Mississippi's Delta and southwestern counties. In the town of Edwards, the white mayor, Clark Robbins, ignored Black residents' requests for extending sewer lines, paved streets, and other improvements into Black neighborhoods. He refused to meet with Black constituents and dismissed petitions from Black residents of the unincorporated Fairgrounds neighborhood for annexation. As civil rights protests and organizing swept across the state, Robbins hung a sign in his office window that read, "We'd rather fight than change."[20] Rather than extend services to Blacks, white officials were more intent on cutting them off. The bill collector, Ruth Harrel, notoriously failed to keep regular hours, preventing many Black residents from paying their water bills on time. Yet she was, Black residents complained, "quick to cut off service to Negroes for delayed payment but does not use the same policy on whites."[21] Because of this practice, many Blacks could be found carrying buckets of water from neighbors' homes. In response, the town council voted to double the rates for "water customers found to be providing water to other residents who had had their services cut off." Later, it voted to reduce the cutoff date for water services after a missed payment from ninety to sixty days.[22]

In the spring of 1964, as lawmakers in Washington worked toward passage of a historic civil rights bill desegregating public facilities and accommodations, Edwards's town council was exploring public options for preserving segregation. Days after the 1964 Civil Rights

Act became law, the town began requiring all swimmers to present a health certificate verifying that they were "free of contageous [sic] and communicable diseases," signed by a physician who had graduated from a Class A medical school and who was a member of the Mississippi Medical Association (MMA). At the time, none of the medical schools in the state that admitted Black students were Class A, and the MMA barred Black members. This measure kept Blacks out of the pool for the remainder of the summer and bought white town leaders some time to plot their next move. The following spring, the council voted to sell the pool to the newly formed Edwards Recreation Club, a private corporation headed by Alderman H. R. Bryant Jr., for $2,000. The minutes made sure to note that the town had sold off its pool solely "because of financial burden."[23] The new owners placed a tall wooden wall around the facilities and affixed signs around the premises that read, "Edwards Recreation Club, Inc. Private Members Only." It was one of many signs meant to convey to the Black population, as one Black resident put it, that the Civil Rights Act "didn't apply to Edwards."[24]

That same year, though, one of the state's leading civil rights organizations, the Delta Ministry, arrived in Edwards, renting the former campus of the Southern Christian Institute, one mile outside of town. The 1,200-acre campus, known as Mount Beulah, served as the headquarters for the Delta Ministry and became a leading site for civil rights organizing in the years that followed, hosting major conferences, workshops, training sessions, orientations, and retreats for organizers and activists.[25]

Mount Beulah also provided jobs for Blacks in Edwards and a place for area youth to socialize and become involved in the movement. Mary White took a job as the switchboard operator. In her early twenties, White had been thrust into adulthood as a teenager after both her parents died, leaving her to raise her younger siblings, Irene and Annie Thompson.[26] As Mary worked the switchboard, Irene became involved in local organizing activities and movement building. "It was a unique place and a unique moment," K. C. Morrison, who grew up with Irene, said of those days. "Some of the richest conversations, the richest thinking I did about my place in the world as an African American and the importance of being engaged in the movement occurred there," he recalled. "It was a rich commingling of ideas and people from everywhere, literally, all around the world." Conversations and debates invariably turned toward Edwards and its litany of outrages and indignities. Where to begin, they wondered. Where to take a stand? Under the punishing heat of a Mississippi summer, their thoughts turned to the town's pool. "It was such an obvious example of worst-case disparity," Morrison later said. "Recreation was something that was so simple." It was also "so obviously public."[27] No matter how many private club signs were hung, everyone knew that the pool had been "built with taxpayers' dollars."[28]

At the start of the summer of 1966, Irene, her sister Annie, K. C., his sister Elizabeth, and Monica Williams walked to the pool entrance and asked to be admitted. They were each handed an application for membership and told to complete and submit it, then await the board's decision. Weeks later, they were notified that their applications had been rejected. Irene called a mass meeting for Blacks in Edwards to plan their next action. What began as a discussion of the pool's exclusionary policy soon grew to include a broad range of grievances, from the plumes of toxic smoke that enveloped Black homes near the chemical plant in the Fairgrounds neighborhood, to the disrespectful conduct of the tax collector, Ruth Harrell, to the town's refusal to even mow the grass in the Black cemetery, as it did in the white one. Thompson announced that she and others planned to picket outside the pool, starting the following weekend, and that she had agreed to be the named plaintiff in a federal lawsuit contesting the pool's sale.[29] At the following town council meeting, the town's marshal "asked that the Mayor and Board consider the purchase of HELMETS, GAS, MASKS and any other equipment necessary for the keeping of the peace should the occasion arise."[30]

Days later, Irene Thompson led a group of fifteen picketers outside the pool, carrying placards that read: "We cannot swim in a public pool"; "U.S. Government is behind us. Edwards is against us"; and "We Want to Swim."[31] Every day for the remainder of the summer,

Figure 7.2 Mary White, one of the leaders of the Edwards, Mississippi, boycotts, standing outside the town's swimming pool, *JET Magazine*, September 29, 1966.

they returned, and their numbers grew. As teenagers marched, growing numbers of adults lent support. "They didn't get out there marching," Jean White recalled, "but when it came to cooking those meals, when we were out there, we had meals three times a day. They made sure we ate."[32] Percy Bland, a Black World War II veteran who lived across the street from the swimming pool, opened his house to picketers and provided water and refreshments throughout the day. The Kingsley Methodist Church hosted mass meetings where clergymen and movement activists spoke, residents aired their grievances, and the community formulated its demands.[33] Afterward, some retired to the handful of Black-owned cafes and joints, where music, conversation, and drinks flowed deep into the night. As Irene Thompson led the youth, adults such as domestic worker Willie Crump and Nerissa Gray, who ran one of the cafes in town, formulated plans for a work strike and boycott of white-owned businesses.[34]

Of the eighteen demands Blacks in Edwards settled on, seven directly dealt with matters of public spending and taxation. Domestic workers drew up their own list of demands of their employers, including a $1.25 hourly wage and the right to use the restrooms in the white homes where they worked, and vowed to walk off the job on the day the boycott launched. The Black residents of unincorporated Fairgrounds, likewise, submitted a petition to the county board of supervisors demanding that it pave its streets and install streetlights.[35] On Monday, August 8, fifty maids and cooks walked off their jobs in white homes. Later, protesters picketed businesses in the commercial district. Organizers set up a shuttle service to grocery stores in Vicksburg and Jackson. Residents planted community gardens. "We are closing the town up if they don't give up first-class citizenship," Nerissa Gray announced.[36]

Store owners were terrified. They relied overwhelmingly on Black dollars, even as they refused to hire Black people, another of the movement's demands. Some begged their Black customers to return. Others threatened and assaulted picketers. Days after the boycott began, town officials retaliated by imposing a 7:00 p.m. curfew on all establishments, a move meant to cripple the Black-owned cafes and restaurants that did much of their business in the late evening.[37] Lawyers with the Delta Ministry helped file an injunction against the curfew in federal court. The Mount Beulah campus became subject to frequent attacks from white terrorists. On three occasions, organizers awoke to find a burning cross on the campus lawn.[38]

White attacks fueled Black solidarity. "This town needs us more than we need it," Nerissa Gray told fellow protesters. "They think we are stupid children . . . but we are grown adults, thinking citizens and we are on our way to becoming first-class citizens. We're not going to let Mr. Charlie get us back to where we were."[39] "Our money is the one thing they can't rule," Irene Thompson added.[40] The Edwards Freedom Movement launched a newspaper that shared information on the boycott, sustained morale, and ran the names of persons who violated the boycott. Others took more extreme measures. Jean White recalls, "If you weren't part of [the boycott], then some men, they would make a visit to your house at night." She stressed: "They didn't do anything to them, but they would shoot over their houses, they would scare them."[41] They confronted Blacks found shopping in whites' stores. Gray caught a man leaving a grocery, bag of items in hand. She asked him why he wasn't honoring the boycott. As an observer described, "He said he didn't know [about it]. So she said well now you do. What are you going to do about it[?] He said I'll show you and then he tossed his whole load of groceries onto the street. He said he wanted to show that he was with the Freedom 100 per cent."[42]

Weeks passed. White officials continued to ignore Blacks' demands. The boycott remained "air-tight."[43] As fall approached, organizers' thoughts turned to the start of the school year. Irene Thompson had accepted an offer to attend the University of Michigan.[44] Before she left, Irene organized a mass march for the last Saturday in August, from the Black side of town to the mayor's office, where Irene would post a copy of the eighteen demands, signed by the "Negro Citizens and Tax Payers of Edwards, Mississippi," on the front door.[45] Jean White was among the dozens of teenagers who took part. "I will never forget, we started . . . off marching, we were singing our songs, everything. . . . When we turned the corner to go to the mayor's office, they had all of the county folks [sheriff's deputies] waiting on us. [When] Irene went to stick [the list of demands] on the door, they grabbed her . . . then they started grabbing [other] people." The sheriff's deputies quickly ran out of spaces to hold protesters. Then, as White recalls, white merchant and alderman S. K. "Knocky" Askew shouted to one of the deputies, "Don't worry about it. I got my cattle truck."[46] Moments later, protester Connie Williams remembers, dozens of Black teenagers were being violently pushed into a cow pen, covered in manure, and driven off to the county jail. That night, Black homeowners and landowning farmers, Williams recalls, "put up their property to bail us out."[47]

The summer ended, the pool closed for the season, Irene Thompson began her freshman year in college, and Black youth returned to school. Whites in Edwards were confident that the boycott would soon fizzle out. They were wrong. Throughout the fall, the boycott remained, as one investigator reported, "almost 100% effective." The furniture store "was doing absolutely no business." The gas station was losing $100 a week. The theater had been forced to close. The laundromat's weekly revenues dropped from $200 to $15. The sales tax revenues evaporated.[48] Into the fall and winter, Black residents lined up to speak at town council meetings, and made formal requests for streetlights, fire hydrants, and other services. A group submitted a request to relocate the Tesco chemical plant.[49] Organizers implemented plans to open a Black grocery store and food cooperative. They all vowed to maintain the boycott until Blacks' demands were met or "until the next election when the local Negroes will defeat the present white officials and any other white candidates who might seek office by vote of three to one."[50]

The boycott inspired other movements. In the town of Itta Bena, members of the local Mississippi Freedom Democratic Party submitted a petition demanding paved and graded streets and other basic services on the Black side of town. When the town refused to acknowledge the petition, they began staging call-ins to the mayor's office and confronting him in public.[51]

Mayor Robbins insisted that the northern white radicals encamped at Mt. Beulah were the source of Edwards's troubles. "Our local Negroes have been brainwashed by Mt. Beulah and if we just wait long enough they will learn better."[52] But white-owned businesses privately implored Robbins to agree to some of the movement's demands. Robbins promised Blacks he would "take a closer look at the streets, sidewalks, and the water and sewer facilities in every section of the corporate limits," and vowed to "give prompt consideration to any petition for paving streets or constructing sidewalks." But he insisted, "We are very limited in tax moneys available for community facilities and maintenance."[53] Robbins didn't need to worry about the loss of sales tax revenue, though. Throughout the boycott, the State Tax Commission sent the town checks for the amount of excess sales taxes collected by the stores in neighboring towns where boycotters shopped.[54]

But Edwards officials were determined to make Black protesters pay for the damage the boycott inflicted on local businesses. That fall, Robbins and fellow aldermen came up with their plan. David Magee, one of the movement's leaders, caught wind of what they had in store. "I was in the downtown area" he later testified, "[when] Sam Tupper, a member of the board of aldermen at the time, approached us." Tupper reminded Magee of all the damage the boycott had already inflicted, how "some of the stores might have to be closed." Then, Tupper said to Magee, "You all are going to pay for it. Your taxes are going to be doubled." And then he stormed off.[55]

Over in the mayor's office, Ruth Harrell pored over the assessment rolls, adjusting the property values for every resident who honored the boycott. Movement leaders and prominent supporters received the greatest adjustments; in many cases, the assessed value of their homes was doubled. The assessments for those Blacks who continued to shop in white stores or served as informants on the movement remained unchanged, as they did for nearly all the white homeowners. In total, Harrell increased the total assessed value of Black-owned property in town by 51 percent; the total value of white-owned property, by comparison, increased only 5.4 percent.[56]

On November 19, 1966, a public notice appeared in the town newspaper that the assessment rolls had been updated and residents had ten days to come to the town hall and inspect them in person and, if they wished, file a written objection. It was a standard, perfunctory announcement required under state law that, as usual, attracted little notice. The ten days passed without any Black residents coming in. On November 29, the mayor and board met to hear any objections to the tax rolls. "No protests were received by letter. No persons appeared to protest, and assessments were declared approved."[57] Under state law, taxpayers still had another twenty days to appeal their tax bills. After that date, Mississippi taxpayers had no legal standing to contest their assessment. Edwards began mailing out tax bills in late December, after the twenty-day window had closed.[58]

Figures 7.3 and 7.4 The homes of Edwards, Mississippi, residents Sam Jordan (African American, left) and Zeith Tupperfield (white, right). In 1967, town officials assessed both properties' value at $1,000. The previous year, Jordan's property had been valued at $500. Following Black residents' boycott of white-owned businesses in Edwards in 1966, town officials sharply increased property assessments on the homes of Black residents who participated in the boycott in retaliation. These images and each property's assessments were submitted as evidence in a federal civil rights lawsuit against the town over its assessment practices.

Days later, Black homeowners received their new tax bills in the mail. Some went to the town office and demanded an explanation. Harrell remained tight lipped. "I asked her why my taxes were so high," one resident testified. "She said she didn't know. She said everybody's taxes were up. That's all she gave me."[59] Other white officials were more candid. "You all got messed up with that boycott, so you have to pay more taxes," Sam Tupper told Black resident Percy Horton.[60] Another official confided that the new tax assessments were meant "to teach [Blacks] a lesson."[61] Horton and others turned to Mount Beulah for advice. As Charley Horwitz recalled, "Mr. Percy Horton came to my office and reported that his taxes had been raised. I inquired . . . if he had made improvements on his property to justify the increase, and he said that he had not."[62]

While Horwitz had not been in Mississippi long, he knew something smelled rotten. White segregationists had previously weaponized tax law and administration to suppress the movement. For her leading role in desegregating Central High School in Little Rock, Arkansas, African American journalist and activist Daisy Bates had the tax assessment on her home raised.[63] In Georgia, state officials used a minor oversight by Martin Luther King Jr. on a tax form to charge him with felony perjury in 1960. After an Alabama jury found the Reverends Ralph Abernathy, Solomon Seay, Joseph Lowery, and Fred Shuttlesworth guilty of libel in what would become the landmark case of *New York Times v. Sullivan*, state authorities promptly began seizing whatever property of the ministers they could.[64] As Black churches became sites for mass meetings and civil rights organizing, several southern states debated removing tax exemptions from churches that hosted integrated meetings or congregations.[65] After state troopers forced Black inmates to brutally assault sharecropper Fannie Lou Hamer in her cell for registering to vote, the pastor at Hamer's church, which had been hosting voter education workshops, was notified that its property tax exemption had been rescinded and its water service would be cut off.[66] Black property owners who defied white authority or challenged white supremacy could expect to receive, as Victoria Jackson Gray of Hattiesburg described, "reassessed property taxes, or newly discovered violations of building codes."[67] Throughout the years Nathan Jones was active in Claiborne County's movement, the assessed value of his farm acreage rose while that of all white-owned land remained the same.[68] Indeed, the constant threat of retaliatory tax increases made Black landowners' pivotal role in the Black freedom movement—being the first to register to vote, hosting mass meetings, providing shelter for organizers and activists, using their land as collateral to bail out protesters—all the more remarkable.

After speaking with Horton, Horwitz went into town and secured a copy of the entirety of the tax rolls for the 1967 and the previous year, noting which properties received an increase. Then, he and Nerissa Gray went through and identified the race of each homeowner. When they were finished, Horwitz got on the phone with civil rights attorneys to discuss their options.[69]

Tensions ran high at the next town meeting. Mayor Robbins began by announcing that the town planned to meet several of the protesters' demands: it had issued a $375,000 revenue bond to pay for the extension of sewer lines into Black neighborhoods, it planned to install streetlights in unserved areas, and it agreed to raise the hourly wage of garbage workers to $1.25.[70] But all Black residents wanted to talk about were their tax bills. The aldermen insisted that the increases were normal, that all public notices had been made, that a "meeting for objections had been held according to Laws of the State of Mississippi and that there have been no objections."[71]

The boycott was back on, as were plans to sue the town. Percy Bland, who had helped picketers and seen his tax assessment more than double as a result, agreed to be the named plaintiff in a federal lawsuit against Edwards officials. It would be a tall order. The 1937 Tax Injunction Act had effectively barred the federal courts from intervening in local tax disputes. But Edwards's Black taxpayers had no other choice. Mississippi state courts did not allow for class-action lawsuits in tax cases, did not permit an injunction against the collection of illegal taxes or suspension of tax collection based on a charge of illegality, and penalized a taxpayer who lost an appeal the full contested amount plus 10 percent and court costs.[72] So, Horwitz and attorneys George Peach Taylor and Frank R. Parker, with the support of the umbrella organization Lawyers' Committee for Civil Rights under Law, decided to challenge the assessments as a violation of section 1983 of the 1871 Civil Rights Act, which guaranteed citizens relief from violations of their constitutional rights by state actors, in federal court. They had to make the case that Mississippi had failed to meet the requirements of section 1341 of the Tax Injunction Act, which prevented taxpayers from filing suit in federal court if a "plain, speedy, and efficient remedy" was available in state court.[73]

The actions of Edwards town officials came at a moment when federal courts were wrestling over the question of whether disparate impact violated the equal protection clause. While the disparate impact of town assessments was not in doubt, lawyers for the town would argue there was no intent to discriminate. Since the town had done the bare minimum as required under state law, and since public officials had been careful not to refer publicly to the race of affected taxpayers in any official proceedings, the plaintiffs had to prove that the assessments were discriminatory on the basis of visual and statistical evidence.

The Lawyers' Committee hired James W. Loewen, a young sociology professor and researcher at Tougaloo College, to determine if race had been a factor in Edwards's property assessments. Loewen identified twenty white-owned and twenty Black-owned properties that had received identical assessments. Then, he sent a team of Tougaloo students to take photographs of each property (being careful to avoid capturing the image of any residents) and write up a detailed, standardized description of each. Loewen then brought in an outside appraiser, who did not know the town or the race of the owners, and asked him to compare two properties from the same assessment category and determine which home was worth more and by how much. The results were conclusive. In each case, the appraiser assigned a higher value to the white-owned home, in many instances by a wide margin. Loewen thus found "conclusive evidence of bias."[74]

Edwards officials struggled to explain the tax increases. Alderman V. J. Angelo testified that the fiscal crisis caused by the boycotts had required the town to raise assessments on properties that had historically been undervalued. These undervalued homes just happened to be Black owned. Other officials, though, said it was because of improvements made to the properties. This assertion was factually untrue, and flatly contradicted by Mayor Robbins, who admitted that the changes had been made "without any formal on-site inspections to observe any construction or improvement to provide a basis for changing assessments, without any professional outside appraisals or surveys."[75] They then claimed that the increases were in anticipation of future improvements resulting from the laying of sewer lines and other services. But at the time of the reassessments, the town had not signed a contract for that work, much less identified the areas that would receive sewer services. The financing mechanism for these improvements—a revenue bond—would be paid down by the fees charged to users, not from general tax revenues. What's more, a few of the affected African American homeowners were already connected to the sewer system.[76]

Despite the wealth of evidence, Edwards's Black homeowners still faced long odds in federal court. To win, they had to make the case that the violations of section 1983 required federal action. That same year, the American Law Institute called on Congress to formally exempt civil rights cases from the Tax Injunction Act. There was at least one case the lawyers could point to for precedent. In *Monroe v. Pape* (1961), the US Supreme Court ruled that federal remedies could supplement state remedies, and that the latter need not be exhausted before turning to the former.[77] The lawyers therefore argued that the Black taxpayers of Edwards still deserved to have their federal case heard, because there was no "plain, speedy, or efficient remedy" available to them in Mississippi state courts.

Neither argument held any sway in US district judge Harold Cox's courtroom, where *Bland v. McHann* was first heard. A notorious racist and arch-segregationist appointed to the federal bench by President John F. Kennedy in 1961 in an attempt to curry favor with Cox's college roommate, Mississippi senator James O. Eastland, Cox held (and still holds) the dubious distinction of having the most decisions on civil rights cases reversed on appeal. Cox not only dismissed the charge that Mississippi had failed to provide an adequate remedy, labeling the state's appeals process "perfectly expeditious and valid," but also ruled in favor of the defendants on the merits. He dismissed as inconclusive the statistical evidence and the testimony of threats by town officials. And he concluded that the plaintiffs had failed to present "any evidence which impugned the honesty, or integrity, or fairness of any member of the Board of Aldermen . . . [or] the Mayor."[78]

The plaintiffs appealed the decision to the Fifth Circuit Court of Appeals. That court vacated Cox's judgment on the merits of the case, which it ruled was "inappropriate . . . [and] went beyond that issue," but determined that Mississippi's remedy did meet the bare-minimum standards of adequacy; the taxpayers were thus not entitled to injunctive relief. "Taxpayers' complaints that the Mississippi remedy is inadequate," the court ruled, "appear in reality to be an argument that a better remedy would be available in the federal courts." In such a scenario, federal restraint and deference to the states must prevail. In order for a victim of tax discrimination to get a hearing in federal court, the Fifth Circuit ruled, the taxpayer must first "assert his federal rights in the state courts" by making the case to Mississippi that its own appeals process was inadequate.[79]

The US Supreme Court declined to hear the case, upholding the Fifth Circuit ruling. The Court grounded this decision in a decision rendered earlier in the term. In *Lynch v. Household Financial Corporation* (1972), it rejected the distinction between personal rights and property rights, suggesting that charges of discrimination in matters of taxation would now fall under civil rights statutes. But in a footnote, the Court also reaffirmed the federal policy against intervention in state and local tax affairs. In effect, the Court granted the property tax an exemption and designated the right of property owners to a fair system of taxation as a civil right that was not protected by federal civil rights laws.[80]

* * *

Mississippi could tax Black property owners as it pleased. But could it also deny Black people any of the services that those tax dollars paid for? Another federal case, originating in another Mississippi town, attempted to resolve that question. Andrew and Mary Lou Hawkins lived in the town of Shaw, on the Black side, where the roads turned to dirt and raw sewage pooled in yards after heavy rains. During the 1960s, the couple had emerged as leaders of the local freedom movement. In 1963, Andrew had led a voter registration drive that cost him his job on a plantation. In 1965, he and Mary Lou led the formation of the Mississippi Freedom Labor Union, a daring if ultimately unsuccessful attempt to organize farm laborers, domestic servants, and sharecroppers to secure pay raises, eight-hour workdays, health insurance, and other employment protections and benefits.[81] That same year, he and thirty other residents filed a complaint with Shaw officials over its refusal to extend public services to Black homes. The town dismissed their request. "What did you expect?" Mary Lou bitterly remarked. "It's always been the first-class citizens that get everything. The second-class citizens get nothing." As far as whites were concerned, "Negroes don't need nothing—just a cow pen to sleep in. It don't make any difference."[82]

But just then, the NAACP Legal Defense Fund (LDF) was embarking on a drive to attack Jim Crow in municipal services. LDF attorneys ultimately aimed to take on the maldistribution of public funding and services in major cities. But first they wanted to establish the unconstitutionality of discriminatory municipal service distribution. Shaw seemed the perfect municipality to test this argument. The town was, lawyers argued, a "model of the way municipalities throughout the country blatantly short-change their black ghettoes in services."[83] On December 2, 1967, the LDF filed a federal case asking for preliminary and permanent injunctions to compel improvements on the Black side of town and to prevent the town from making any further improvements to white areas until it had addressed these disparities.[84]

When the LDF began work on the case, Hawkins recalled, whites in Shaw "thought it was a big hoax. . . . But when they started getting subpoenas, they got hostile."[85] The mayor, P. M. Bennett, quickly grew agitated during court hearings. At one, he blurted out, "I think [the town council] has been doing a fine job in the n—— neighborhood."[86] White plantation owners, employers, and property owners threatened to fire and evict workers and tenants unless they removed their names from the complaint. Fear of further immiseration and starvation compelled nearly every Black resident to back out. By the time LDF lawyers were ready to file suit, only Hawkins remained. Whites would make sure he and his family would pay for their defiance. In 1969, their home burned down in what they believed was an arson attack. The narrow water mains and low water pressure prevented firefighters from battling the blaze. Law enforcement refused to investigate. LDF attorneys added these facts to its case against the town.[87]

In 1969, LDF attorneys Melvin Leventhal and Jonathan Shapiro filed a class-action lawsuit against Shaw, accusing it of violating Black residents' Fourteenth Amendment rights to equal protection in the provision of municipal services. District court judge William C. Keady dismissed the case as one that needed to be resolved at the ballot box, not in court. Hawkins appealed to the Fifth Circuit. In 1971, Judge Elbert Parr Tuttle overturned the district court ruling and found Shaw in violation of the Fourteenth Amendment. "Referring to a portion of a town or a segment of society as being 'on the other side of the tracks' has for too long been a familiar expression to most Americans," Tuttle wrote. "While there may be many reasons why such areas exist in nearly all of our cities, one reason that cannot be accepted is the discriminatory provision of municipal services based on race." Tuttle ordered the town to form a biracial commission to develop a plan detailing how it would correct these disparities.[88]

Civil rights lawyers and activists hailed the ruling in *Hawkins v. Town of Shaw* as historic. Some compared it to *Brown v. Board of Education.* The *Shaw* case, Marian Wright Edelman remarked, "establishes a terribly important principle for equalizing facilities between the black and white communities." "Now there is a new legal thrust to dismantle the prejudicial delivery of basic city services," Whitney Young exclaimed. *Time* magazine predicated that "*Shaw* could force big as well as small cities across the U.S. to reallocate everything from police patrols to garbage pickups and parkspace."[89] Shaw officials asked for a rehearing by the full sixteen-judge circuit court. On March 28, 1972, the full court upheld the ruling. Shaw officials opted not to appeal the case to the US Supreme Court.[90]

In the aftermath of the ruling, Shaw's police force stepped up its attacks of the Hawkins family. Officers repeatedly harassed Andrew and Mary Lou's daughter, Gloria Jean, and arrested their son, Andrew Jr., several times on bogus charges. On the night of April 29, 1972, the town's lone Black officer, Andrew Sharpe, arrested Andrew Jr. for disorderly conduct and resisting arrest. Disgusted, Mary Lou went to Sharpe's house the following morning, and made it known that she was "tired of the picking on [her] and her family." As she harangued the officer, residents came to watch. Sharpe reached for his gun and, as several witnesses testified, said, "God damn it, Mary, you got to go." Hawkins fled. Sharpe pursued. Neighbors screamed, "Don't shoot that woman." Sharpe eventually cornered Hawkins and shot her once in the chest. She died instantly. A large crowd amassed. Sharpe called in police reinforcements to escort him out safely. Back at the station, Sharpe claimed that Hawkins had threatened to kill him with a paring knife. Eyewitnesses testified that Hawkins was unarmed. A county judge dismissed the manslaughter charges against Sharpe.[91]

In the coming days, hundreds came out to mass meetings at local churches, where Black residents organized and demanded both Sharpe's firing and action by the town to equalize public services. "Whites in Shaw tried to intimidate the Hawkins family simply because Blacks were granted their constitutional rights. We see now that these threats should not have been ignored even though we are supposed to be living in a time of 'law and order.'"[92] Days after his wife's murder, a grieving Hawkins appeared in court to hear the reading of the final ruling in *Hawkins v. Town of Shaw*. The decision, many predicted, would spark a wave of similar suits seeking to force municipalities to equalize local services.[93]

Left undetermined, though, was the larger, and for Blacks in the hundreds of towns like Shaw across the South, more urgent question of service delivery in municipalities whose tax bases were so small that they could not meet basic needs for *any* of their residents, white or Black. That problem would require a political solution.[94]

8

BLACK POWER/LOCAL POWER

After graduating from Alcorn State in 1970, Evan Doss Jr. returned to his hometown of Port Gibson, Mississippi, and took a job teaching history in the public high school. At the time, Claiborne County's white families were pulling their children out of the public school system and enrolling them in a new, private segregated academy. Whites also pulled as many resources out of the public schools as they could. Doss scrambled to provide the barest education and enrichment for his Black students.

Whenever Doss pleaded with administrators for instructional materials, or for some funds for a field trip, he was told that the schools simply lacked the money. "That," as Doss put it, "got my attention." And it led him to ask "why the county was not generating more money from the taxpayers."[1] It was not for lack of support from the Black majority, who comprised over 70 percent of the county's population, even as their struggles to climb out of poverty had been consistently undermined by a local tax system that imposed heavy burdens on small farmers and low-income homeowners.

A year later, Doss challenged the county's tax assessor in the fall 1971 election. As he campaigned, Doss listened to Black voters describe their frustrations: at the county's pitifully small tax returns and the impoverishment of its public schools and local services, at the rumors of under-taxation of the county's largest landowners, and of their own struggles paying tax bills that seemed suspiciously high. He pledged to each of them that, if elected, he would assess property

Figure 8.1 Evan Doss, the first African American elected tax assessor of a county in Mississippi state history, speaking at his inauguration in Port Gibson, Claiborne County, January 1, 1972.

"without regard for race or wealth."[2] That fall, he became the first African American elected tax assessor in Mississippi's history.[3]

Doss's election marked a new phase in the struggle for tax justice in the South. Following passage of the 1965 Voting Rights Act (VRA), local organizers and movement activists moved to register Black voters and raise awareness of the powers of local offices.[4] Few powers were more tangible or more consequential than the power to tax and spend—especially in rural counties and small towns. "If a Negro is elected tax assessor, he will be able to tax equitably and channel funds for the building of better roads and schools serving Negroes," SNCC's Stokely Carmichael told audiences.[5] By electing candidates to offices like county boards of supervisors, Blacks would no longer have to "sit and beg for our roads to be graveled by a white man," another organizer noted. Instead, they could distribute public revenues more equitably, and add to the public coffers through targeted tax increases. "And," Carmichael added, "the handful of white land owners, if they don't pay the taxes, will have to forfeit their land, and the county will then redistribute it"—a power with which rural Blacks were all too familiar.[6]

By winning local offices, Blacks could also tap into the vast array of federal programs created during the War on Poverty that white officials had studiously avoided. Most immediately, Black participation and influence in local elections made those in power accountable to Black communities that, for generations, they had overtaxed and underserved with virtual impunity. As one researcher found, the extent of discrimination in property assessments and local tax policies "correlated directly with Negro registration. . . . When Negro voting in the county or city was higher, the assessors became less discriminatory in their assessment policies."[7]

Once in office, newly elected Black tax assessors and mayors learned the truth about racial discrimination in tax administration. They uncovered incontrovertible evidence of what many had long suspected: that for generations, whites had used these positions to relieve the wealthy of local tax obligations, quietly shift these burdens onto disfranchised Black populations, and force Black residents to go without when whites did not.[8] But they struggled to dismantle the Jim Crow fiscal order. Along with attempts to dilute Black voting power through gerrymandering and consolidating districts, conversion of elected positions into appointed ones, and other schemes to keep Blacks from occupying local offices, whites worked to constrain the powers of the offices that Black candidates won and to sabotage their attempts at reform. They did so not merely to keep their own taxes low but also to preserve a rural political economy predicated on Black poverty and dependency, one in which local government's point was enforcing hierarchy, not extending opportunity. For the post–Jim Crow generation of Black southerners, these local struggles to gain control over tax administration became a key battleground in the larger fight to dismantle white supremacy's fiscal structure.

* * *

In the wake of the Voting Rights Act, majority-Black counties and municipalities offered the earliest opportunities for African Americans to win local elections. At the time, African Americans constituted a majority in nearly one-fifth of all counties in the Deep South states of South Carolina, Georgia, Alabama, Mississippi, and Louisiana. Twenty-five of Mississippi's eighty-two counties were majority Black.[9] Well aware of Blacks' inherent electoral power across the Deep South, whites deployed every device available to prevent Black votes from resulting in Black officeholders. In Mississippi, lawmakers passed measures in 1966 that gerrymandered federal Congressional districts, created multi-member state legislative districts, permitted counties to elect members of county boards of supervisors and school boards at large rather than by district, imposed new requirements for running for office, and turned elected offices into appointed ones. Targeting majority-Black counties like Claiborne County, the legislature enacted an amendment to the state's constitution that allowed the legislature to consolidate counties. Civil rights groups, led by the Lawyers' Constitutional Defense Committee (LCDC), challenged these legislative maneuvers under section 5 of the Voting Rights Act. In its historic *Allen v. State Board of Elections* (1969) decision, the US Supreme Court ruled that such changes were subject to federal review under section 5, all of which the Justice Department subsequently rejected.[10]

But the fight over local power in the Deep South had only just begun. In cities and towns, whites worked to maintain voting majorities by annexing surrounding white residential areas while keeping

Black residents confined to unincorporated areas on the outskirts. Across the Deep South, it was common to find Black residential enclaves situated along the outer boundaries of municipalities and lacking in the services and amenities available to town residents. In the Delta town of Tunica, the population of the unincorporated "colored subdivision" North Tunica was roughly equal to the population of the town itself.[11] With the prospect of Blacks voting in local elections, some towns aggressively annexed white residential areas to maintain white electoral majorities.[12] As Blacks boycotted white-owned businesses in Edwards in 1966 and looked to run candidates in upcoming local elections, officials voted to annex an all-white subdivision to dilute Black voter strength.[13] In the two years following passage of the Voting Rights Act, the town of Indianola annexed four separate white residential areas, resulting in a 10.7 percent decrease in the town's voting-age Black population. These efforts continued up until 1971, when the US Supreme Court ruled that changes to voter rolls through annexation fell under the purview of the Voting Rights Act.[14]

The whites who wielded local power in these counties and towns did not fear Black faces in high (local) places so much as they feared Black candidates who promised to change local governing practices and priorities. Black schoolteacher Carver Randle, who ran for mayor of Indianola, Mississippi, in 1967, told voters he planned to "revise the city's tax system to place a heavier burden on the wealthiest (white) tax brackets" and then "use these increased revenues to provide municipal services to the poorest (black) parts of town."[15] In his campaign ads, Randle vowed he would create a "more equitable tax assessment," use "tax money to improve the entire city, not just sections of it," and provide "adequate sanitation and drainage systems" for all residents.[16] Upon being elected mayor of Fayette, Mississippi, in 1969, Charles Evers (brother of the slain civil rights leader Medgar Evers) promptly raised property tax rates to fund improvements in municipal services long denied to Black neighborhoods.[17]

Wherever Black people secured a measure of local political power, a fight over tax and spending practices and priorities ensued. In Bolton, Bennie Thompson secured a seat on the town's board of aldermen in 1969 and four years later was elected mayor along with a slate of Black candidates, running on the promise of equal services for Black residents. Thompson's white opponents challenged the results of both elections.[18] Soon after becoming mayor, Thompson was forced to deal with the costs of decades of neglect: a residential fire on the Black side of town that had consumed the house before a fire crew had even arrived. Lacking its own fire station, residents of Bolton had to wait upwards of a half hour for a truck to arrive from Jackson. And, as usual, fighters struggled to battle blazes with hoses that sputtered out from the 2-inch mains that the town had laid on the Black side of town.[19] With help from the Delta Ministry, Thompson secured a donated fire truck for the town.[20] But paying back the bonds needed to cover the costs for extending services and improving water and sewer lines for Black residents required tax revenues that the town lacked. Thompson quickly discovered how little he had to work with. The tax base was so small that it generated less than $8,000 per year. He also saw how grossly overtaxed Black residents were relative to whites. As Thompson described, "it became patently clear that the Black residents were paying a disproportionate part of the taxes compared to the whites." Scanning the tax rolls, Thompson zeroed in on his parents' small, wood-frame, two-bedroom home, which "was valued . . . more than [white-owned] homes with four or five bedrooms, all brick, all with more land."[21]

When he took the oath of office, Thompson had pledged to carry out his duties under state law—which included annually certifying that the tax rolls were "fair and equitable"—and that's exactly what he intended to do. "We put out the proper notice that we were going to do a reassessment of property pursuant to that statute. And all of a sudden, the white landowners in the community became upset." A group of white residents sued to prevent the reassessment. The parties ultimately reached a settlement requiring that the reassessment be carried out by a board-certified appraiser. But every single appraiser in the state (all of whom were white) refused to assist Thompson's office. In response, Thompson hired Rutledge Waker, a property appraisal specialist from Boston, Massachusetts, who was friends with Delta Ministry organizer Owen Brooks, to conduct the reassessment. Waker and Black officials discovered that not only were all the town's white homes undervalued relative to Blacks' but, as Brooks recalled, "much of [whites' property] wasn't even on the tax rolls."[22]After Bolton completed its reassessment and the new tax rolls were approved, the tax base ballooned from $400,000 to $1.4 million, and annual tax revenues grew from roughly $8,000 to $26,000.[23] In the years that followed, Thompson also worked to secure community-development block grants from the Department of Housing and Urban Development (HUD) as well as grants from the Environmental Protection Agency and Department of Transportation to improve water and sewer lines and paved streets in Bolton's Black neighborhoods.[24]

To the white minorities in towns and counties across the Deep South, these were the threats Black political power posed: of whites being taxed fairly and without favor, and of public bodies being responsive to the needs of the most disadvantaged and unbeholden to local ruling classes. They were determined to kill this new fiscal order in its infancy. As he packed up his belongings, Claiborne County's outgoing assessor gave Evan Doss a single piece of advice: don't "touch" the assessment rolls. If Doss stuck to that rule, the county's whites reasoned, things would be okay. But Doss had made it clear that he intended to do just that. "I can remember some of the larger white landowners trying to approach me," Doss recalled, "[saying,] 'You just need to understand that this is the way it has always been done and you need to continue this practice.' I'm thinking to myself, 'No, this ain't going to work here. . . . I am going to do something about this tax structure."[25]

As Doss's intentions became clear, Claiborne County's board of supervisors stepped in. Still firmly under white control, the board used its power over budgeting and hiring to constrain Doss's ability to perform his job. First, they slashed his office's budget down to $13,000 ($10,000 of which went toward Doss's salary), even as changes in state law had vastly expanded the duties of the assessor's office to include collecting tax payments and selling license plates, duties that had previously been performed by sheriffs' offices.[26] Next, they appointed as Doss's secretary a woman whose real job, he soon discovered, was to undermine the office's work and report on Doss's activities.[27] Doss remained unbowed. So far as the county's board of supervisors and white establishment were concerned, Doss remarked, "If they want to work with us, fine. We'll work with them." But make no mistake, he added, "We're here to see freedom, equality, and justice for all."[28]

His first day on the job, a cold chill hit Doss's face as he entered his new office downtown. His quisling secretary barely acknowledged him and avoided making eye contact. No one in the building would even give Doss the combination to the safe where the assessor's records were kept. But Doss remained unfazed, even giddy at the prospect of waging a fight for Black power in the rural South. Local organizer James Miller accompanied Doss and stood by his side as he prepared to do battle. Just so their intentions were clear, Miller hung a large poster of Malcolm X on the office wall.[29]

It quickly became clear to both men just how much help they were going to need. Days into his term, Doss dialed up Jesse Morris, a civil rights organizer in Jackson who had just been named director of the Mississippi branch of the Emergency Land Fund (ELF), a new organization under the Black Economic Research Center (BERC) in New York City (see chapter 9).[30] Doss told Morris that he actually had no idea how to do the job, but that he did have good reason to believe the existing assessments were unfair and had devised a plan for correcting them. As Morris wrote to his boss, Doss needed particular help in reclassifying the vast amount of white-owned acreage incorrectly listed as uncultivated "and to show cause and justification for doing so"—a massive undertaking.[31] Morris found Doss's plan both compelling and urgently needed. Morris requested funds to hire a full-time assistant to work with Doss for two to three months. Weeks later, Barbara Phillips arrived in Port Gibson.[32]

A recent graduate of Macalester College in Minnesota, Phillips also had little experience in tax matters. But she understood a grave injustice when she saw it. And from the moment she began flipping through the pages of the county assessment rolls, she knew something wasn't right. "It was astounding," she said. Antebellum-era mansions "were paying in dollars less than those little two- and three-bedroom brick shacks that Black people had. I mean they were paying, not in percentage, in dollars. Literally less. It was just mind blowing." Phillips had no idea "what the appropriate assessment should be, but," she added, "we certainly knew that what we were looking at was wrong."[33] When Phillips went in search of the formulas, she discovered there were none: no documentation of any assessments of individual properties or countywide reappraisals, no documents detailing how assessors determined property values, no explanation as to how any of the values in the assessment rolls had been established. There was also no help from other county administrators, who refused to provide Doss's office with maps showing property boundaries, townships, or taxing districts. As Doss wrote to the head of the State Tax Commission, "there are no records in this office or available in this county to indicate how and when the base values were determined from which the assessments which now appear on the tax rolls were figured."[34] Even so, it was plain that past assessors had followed a certain formula: "In most cases," Phillips and fellow researcher Joseph Huttie wrote, "the lowest percentages were being applied to the properties of the county's wealthiest citizens."[35]

Claiborne County's board of supervisors quickly caught wind of Doss's investigation and the outside assistance he was receiving. In March, the Board's president, M. R. Headley II, sent Doss what amounted to a cease-and-desist order. "We would expect," Headley told Doss, "that the assessment rolls be continued on approximately the same basis as before."[36] Doss, in turn, reached out to the State Tax Commission, sharing his initial findings and the board of supervisors' efforts to defund his office, and requesting that it provide staff to carry out a countywide reappraisal. The commission ignored him.[37] Next, he appealed to Governor William Waller, also newly elected on a platform that included property tax reform. Waller's office did not reply.[38] The county's white establishment, meanwhile, launched a campaign to arouse white hostility to the new assessor and demoralize his Black supporters. "The way we look at it," the editors of the *Port Gibson Reveille* said of Doss's plans, "the re-appraisal proposition is designed to . . . badger the board politically and to hand himself a salary raise." (Ironically, by state law, Doss's salary was the one budget item that the supervisors could not touch.) They assailed him as unqualified, ignorant, and incapable of "administer[ing] this important county office." The lone African American on the board of supervisors, Matt Ross, kept his silence.[39]

Jesse Morris worried that Doss would be run out of office or, worse yet, "turn 'Tom'" and "be very safe and secure in office," as other Black elected officials who "had no help with which to wage their battle" had. "The man desperately needs someone to go to bat for him," Morris told colleagues. "He needs outside assistance, publicity on his troubles and legal action taken immediately. Anything short of this will see him fail in office because he has too many things going against him." That summer, students from Harvard Law School and undergraduates from nearby Alcorn State assisted in reappraising and reclassifying properties.[40]

But Doss's troubles had only just begun. After firing the traitorous secretary, Doss relied entirely on the work of sympathetic volunteers to carry out his office's basic duties. It was not enough. That fall, his office struggled to issue new license tags to residents, generating a fresh round of attacks on Doss's competence and a court order to keep his office open for extended hours.[41] Despite it all, in November, the assessor's office submitted to the board of supervisors new assessment rolls with updated valuations for a portion of county properties. As with all local matters, the board of supervisors had the final say. It promptly sent the rolls to the chancery clerk with orders "to make sure that the '72 tax roll looked exactly like the 1971 roll." After the chancery clerk corrected Doss's "errors," the Board approved the assessments. Doss anticipated this turn of events and was already preparing to wage a wider campaign to reforms that would allow local assessors to do their jobs and ensure a degree of fairness and accuracy in property valuations. Later that month, Doss introduced resolutions at the state Tax Collectors and Assessors Association's annual meeting to establish a committee to examine assessment inequities in the state, limit interference by county boards of supervisors over the assessment process, and require county boards to provide up-to-date plat maps. Doss stressed to fellow assessors that these problems were not specific to Black taxpayers but affected all Mississippians and all assessors' offices. Doss's resolutions, as Phillips later wrote, "provoked a heated discussion." Many assessors "vent[ed] their anger at the treatment they also receive[d] at the hands of supervisors. A noon break, however, brought them to their senses." Fearing retaliation from their boards and voters for aligning themselves with the state's lone Black tax assessor, members voted down Doss's resolutions.[42]

Doss took his case directly to the people. Throughout 1974, Doss held mass meetings across the county, where he and local organizers attempted to counter the attacks, educate Black voters, and collect signatures to place a referendum on the ballot to force a countywide reassessment. The stakes were raised even higher when plans were announced for the construction of a nuclear power station—the state's first—at Grand Gulf in Claiborne County. The outcome of the conflict between Doss and the county supervisors would determine who, ultimately, would decide the property tax liability of a plant estimated to be worth hundreds of millions of dollars.[43]

Doss's team submitted the required signatures before the deadline for including it in the general election that fall. The board of supervisors, however, waited until after the deadline to call the referendum, ensuring that the vote would be held after the general election. In the weeks leading up to the vote, board members stepped up efforts to sabotage the assessor's office, smear Doss, and confuse and intimidate Black voters. First, they ordered the assessor's office closed for remodeling in October, forcing Doss to work out of a makeshift office during the busiest month of the year, when residents purchased automobile license tags. They enlisted one of the county's most prominent Black ministers to publicly denounce Doss and question his competency. They circulated rumors among Black voters that Doss intended to raise *their* taxes.[44]

On a Thursday afternoon in late October, two of the county's supervisors came to Doss's temporary office to get their license tags. They brought along a county district attorney to act as an "observer." A line of people waiting to renew their tags snaked out the door. The pair brushed past the line, marched to the front desk, and demanded to be served. Doss told them to get to the back of the line. For that, Doss was found in violation of the court order requiring him to issue license tags to the public. The following day, Judge Ben Guider ordered Doss be jailed, then gaveled his courtroom and drove to Baton Rouge to watch Ole Miss take on Louisiana State in that weekend's football game. Doss's attorneys were unable to reach the judge until he returned the following Monday, and Doss remained in jail all weekend. After his release, Doss told reporters, "I am the victim of two things[:] being black, and doing my job. My arrest and conviction are actions intended to stop me politically, stop me, a black official, from achieving equal taxation in Claiborne County." It was obvious, Doss later added, that the supervisors had "set me up for an arrest," and it was no coincidence that they had done so just as it had become "apparent we would win" the referendum vote.[45] Weeks later, the referendum passed anyway. The following year, Doss won reelection and gained a Black majority on the board of supervisors. Equal assessments came to Claiborne County, and as a result of the attention Doss's fight commanded, property tax assessment reform came to Mississippi.[46]

Doss was far from the only local Black official in 1970s Mississippi to face concerted attacks over tax and spending reforms. In Tchula, Mayor Eddie Carthan came into office in 1977 vowing to tax residents fairly and aggressively pursue federal dollars for desperately needed social services and infrastructure. At the time, most residents of Tchula's Black side of town, neatly separated by the Illinois-Central-Gulf railroad, lacked indoor plumbing; roughly 80 percent of its homes were severely deteriorated. A handful of white planters and area businessmen owned most of the property on the Black side of town, where the fear of evictions muffled complaints about unbearable conditions. Death, disease, and malnutrition stalked Black families, most of whom relied on food stamps, welfare checks, and the dwindling number of low-wage jobs on plantations to survive.[47]

When Carthan came into office promising to break those chains, Tchula's white establishment sprang into action. Carthan reported being approached by a man claiming to represent the "four most powerful men in the state." Their offer: $10,000 in cash if Carthan agreed to keep doing things "the way they had always been done." Carthan refused the bribe.[48] During his first three years in office, he secured over $3 million in federal and private support for the town, creating eighty new public-sector jobs and launching a new day care center, medical clinic, home rehabilitation project, and job training program, among others. Carthan secured federal grants to install new water mains in Black neighborhoods and hook all homes up to the sewerage system, as well as funds for acquisition of land and equipment for public recreation. He did so in the face of unremitting threats and attacks. Two years in, the white establishment had succeeded in pressuring the city's clerk and one of the aldermen who aligned with Carthan to resign. Both later said they did so out of fear for their family's safety.[49]

After Cathan's adversaries had secured a majority on the board of aldermen, a violent and deadly standoff ensued, as the aldermen worked to drive Carthan from office and cut off the federal funding spigot. Alleging corruption, the Board ordered Tchula's city hall locked and Carthan barred from entering. When Carthan's supporters protested, aldermen went through the assessment rolls and raised their taxes.[50] After the Black newspaper in Jackson published articles favorable to Carthan, the paper's offices were firebombed.

His opponents ultimately succeeded in removing Carthan from office and having him imprisoned on corruption charges. His case briefly attracted international attention and demands for his exoneration and release. But the coup ultimately succeeded. By the early 1980s, all the programs Carthan had launched had been ended, and the town's Black population slipped back into a state of endemic poverty and joblessness.[51]

* * *

Even after Black voters had secured fairer assessments for Claiborne County, their tax base—like that of many high-poverty, rural counties lacking in industry—remained pitifully small and incapable of generating the revenue to meet its population's needs. That was all poised to change, however, when the Grand Gulf Nuclear Station— located along the Mississippi River on the county's western edge— began operations in 1984. Constructed at a cost of $3.4 billion, it had promised to bring jobs and tax revenues.[52] Far fewer jobs came than promised, and of those, few went to local Blacks.[53] But residents still got to enjoy the benefits of a suddenly sizable tax base. When Grand Gulf began operations, Claiborne County's tax base ballooned from $20 million to $350 million. The county was poised to bring in over $15 million more in annual tax revenues. Residents had been planning for this day. Some had proposed providing a guaranteed annual income for all residents. Others called for a massive jobs program. Improving the county's schools and establishing health clinics was at the top of everyone's agenda.[54]

It was not to be. From the moment Grand Gulf began operations, Doss and the county supervisors battled over the plant's value, with the Board repeatedly reducing Doss's assessments. In the state legislature, lawmakers clamored for legal changes that would take the tax revenues the plant generated out of Claiborne County and its Black officials' hands. In the state capitol, civil rights activist Rims Barber overheard lawmakers openly remarking, "We don't want them n—— having that much money."[55] Multiple lawmakers went on

the record saying that the county's board of supervisors, now majority Black, "lacked the ability to tax and spend properly."[56] In 1985,
Mississippi lawmakers passed a bill that transferred taxing authority over the plant from the county to the state, contingent on voter
approval of a ballot measure to amend the constitution. Claiborne
County residents sued to stop the election, claiming that it violated
the Voting Rights Act. But the federal courts refused to intervene.
The amendment narrowly passed. One month later, the US Justice
Department cleared the results. Grand Gulf's tax revenues would be
shared among all the state's counties that received power from its
generators.[57]

Claiborne County appealed to the US Supreme Court, citing "over-
whelming direct and circumstantial evidence of racial motivation."
But the justices declined to hear the case.[58] "Unprecedented," Barber
said of this bald dispossession. "Never been done before. Or since. It
was only because it was going to be given to a Black-controlled government."[59] "We would have had the best schools," Evan Doss said.
"We could have had the highest paid teachers in the state. We could
have [been] a model of showing what Blacks could actually do" if
given the chance.[60]

* * *

In rural counties and small towns across the Deep South, control over
public dollars and decisions over public spending determined the
quality of the schools that Black children attended, the conditions of
the neighborhoods where Black people lived, and with it, the success
or failure of Blacks' struggles to climb out of poverty. In the town of
Tunica, Mississippi, the confinement of much of the local Black population to the unincorporated area known as North Tunica allowed its
white minority to maintain total control over municipal governance,
which they used to aggressively pursue federal grants for projects
mainly benefitting white residents. It secured a $750,000 federal
grant to construct landing strips for the private planes and jets owned
by the handful of wealthy families who lived in the county.[61] It secured

$1 million in federal funds for the construction of a new hospital, one that "routinely turn[ed] sick and injured black citizens away from its emergency room."[62] And in 1984, the town received a $500,000 grant from HUD for aesthetic improvements to its downtown.[63]

Mere blocks away from Tunica's downtown, impoverished Black families faced a public-health emergency. There, an open sewer known as Sugar Ditch ran past a row of dilapidated homes that lacked running water and flush toilets. Residents were forced to dispose of waste in the fetid stream that ran feet from their homes. After heavy rains, residents were forced to wade through pools of feces that formed in their yards and lapped against the sides of their homes. The stink was so unbearable, at times, that it awoke people from their sleep. Children suffered from liver tumors, abscesses, and parasitic and bacterial infections. The dozens of residents shared a single outdoor faucet for water.[64]

The town had secured over $1 million in federal funds to improve its water and sewer systems during the 1970s and, to comply with *Shaw* decision, had made these services available to homes in Sugar Ditch. But property owners had to pay a special assessment to have their homes connected. The white landlords who owned properties in Sugar Ditch declined to pay these expenses. Town officials didn't explore other options as they addressed other priorities.[65]

For Black civic leaders, the awarding of federal funds to beautify Tunica's commercial district while, mere blocks away, Black families were forced to live in filth and disease, was the last straw. When HUD officials came to Tunica in the summer of 1984 to present the award, state representative Clayton Henderson led the pool of reporters who covered the event on a detour through Sugar Ditch.[66] Tunica resident Nellie Johnson contacted the National Association of Health Service Executives (NAHSE), an organization for African Americans in medicine, which launched an investigation. NAHSE later released its findings on the dangerous and inhumane conditions Sugar Ditch residents were forced to endure and evidence of town officials' misappropriation of federal funds.[67] In March 1985, the Office of Revenue Sharing released a report finding Tunica's failure to ensure that Sugar Ditch properties received water and sewer services in violation of the State and Local Fiscal Assistance Act and ordered that it extend water and sewer lines into every home along the mile-and-a-half corridor. Town officials said that compliance would lead owners to evict tenants rather than absorb the extra fees and charges. A standoff ensued.[68]

By the summer of 1985, the conditions in Sugar Ditch had become national news. In July, civil rights leader Jesse Jackson led reporters and attendees at the annual meeting of Operation PUSH (People United to Serve Humanity), held that year in nearby Memphis, on a tour of the area. Jackson called Tunica "America's Ethiopia."[69] That fall, the CBS weekly news program *60 Minutes* ran a devastating feature on living conditions in the neighborhood and white officials' crass indifference to the public-health crisis. During one exchange, a Tunica official attempted to refute charges that the town had failed to deliver tax-funded services to its Black population by claiming that its public school system and swimming pool were "Black services," since the white population refused to use them.[70] By then, it was evident to all that the housing stock in Sugar Ditch had deteriorated to a level that precluded any attempts to rehabilitate. Town officials, in turn, used the crisis as an opportunity to relocate the area's residents— who comprised nearly all of the Black population residing in town— outside the municipality, securing a block grant from HUD and a $3 million loan from the Farmers Home Administration (FmHA) for the construction of eighty- and forty-unit apartment complexes for the relocation of Sugar Ditch residents. The site selected was, of course, located outside of town, and town officials refused to consider annexing the area.[71] "Blacks in Tunica," Jesse Jackson fumed, "are given the choice of living in the shacks of Sugar Ditch and keeping their right to vote in city elections or moving to better housing in the county" in exchange for having a voice in local government.[72] The United Voters' League of Tunica filed an objection under the Voting Rights Act, and the state's Civil Rights Commission held hearings, but the arrangement was ultimately upheld.[73]

Sugar Ditch was covered over and the houses that lined it torn down. But the struggle over race and local political power continued, at a time when Blacks across the rural South were fighting not just for an equal share of public goods and services but to hold onto what they had.

9

EMERGENCY

After deceiving Evelina Jenkins into failing to pay her property taxes and quietly taking ownership of her family's land on St. Helena Island at the 1932 tax sale in Beaufort County, South Carolina, William Levin waited for the right moment to sell. That moment came in 1961. The meteoric growth of leisure and vacationing across the coastal South had sent the value of quality undeveloped land soaring. Developers eyed places like Jenkins's secluded, undeveloped Horse Island for vacation-home developments. Looking to cash in, Levin sold the sixty-six acres that he had legally stolen from Jenkins decades earlier to local developers John and Hilda Gay.

Not long afterward, Jenkins went to hand Levin her property taxes, as she had done ever since he had befriended her. But this time Levin finally informed her that the property was no longer hers, and that it hadn't been for a while. All those property tax payments had been more like rent. And now that he had sold the property, Jenkins needed to leave. Jenkins returned home "just distraught, so upset," her grand-daughter recalled. "It crushed her." Neighbors helped move Jenkins's small wooden house to a piece of land one of her cousins deeded to her, just across from the entrance to Horse Island, where she watched as the Gays showed off lots to prospective buyers and construction crews began work on new homes.[1]

Owning land that had suddenly become valuable did not make rural Black landowners like Jenkins lucky; it made them vulnerable. Speculators and developers swarmed in search of land that could be

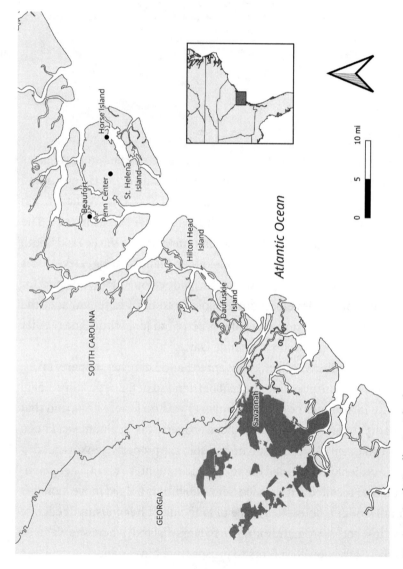

Figure 9.1 South Carolina Sea Islands.

acquired at low cost, from unsuspecting, financially distressed, or legally compromised families and individuals. Black property owners often checked one or more of those boxes, and thus became the juiciest of targets for predatory investors. And it wasn't just coastal land. In the rural counties of the Black Belt, agricultural mechanization, the rise of agribusiness, and the rampant discrimination of the USDA against Black farmers conspired to make Black-owned farmland ripe for the taking.[2]

During the decades when Black people were fighting to dismantle Jim Crow, a massive land grab was unfolding across the South.[3] Between 1950 and 1969, Blacks lost an average of 340,000 acres of land each year.[4] Black landownership plummeted most dramatically in South Carolina and Mississippi. Home to the highest concentrations of Black landowners in the early twentieth century, these two states also experienced the most extreme effects of agricultural mechanization, land consolidation, and the frenzy of real estate development gripping the Sunbelt. By one estimate, over fourteen thousand Black people in South Carolina and thirteen thousand in Mississippi were rendered landless between 1954 and 1969 alone.[5]

Across the South, local tax systems powered the engine of Black land dispossession. In booming real estate markets, soaring property taxes—made all the more burdensome by regressive and often-discriminatory assessment practices—forced untold numbers of Black families to sell their property under duress, at wildly discounted prices. Across the Black Belt, small-scale farmers and independent landowners struggled to make a living and meet expenses, none more consequential than their annual tax bills. During these years, growing numbers of farmers and small landowners fell into tax delinquency. As they did, a class of investors stood poised to take advantage of their hardships. By the early 1970s, tax buyers in Mississippi were claiming ownership of upwards of 1,600 separate parcels of Black-owned land each year.[6]

By then, a growing number of Black activists, organizers, and thinkers had begun to sound the alarm. Local and national organizations formed to arrest Black land losses and devise strategies for using the land that remained in Blacks' hands to aid and support Black rural economic development. On the Sea Islands, organizers at the Penn Center on St. Helena Island formed Black Land Services to identify and counteract the forces eroding Blacks' land base in the coastal South. In the Black Belt, the national Emergency Land Fund opened offices in Georgia, Alabama, and Mississippi and assembled teams of organizers, legal aides, and strategists to assist endangered Black farmers and rural landowners. Across the rural South, they found, as one state director put it, that "the problem is the same. . . . Racist and thieving white folks. Like a village in the grips of a plague, black people in the Black Belt are being held in an economic stranglehold by what in most cases is the white minority."[7] Instead of hooded nightriders and white mobs, rural Black landowners now faced "local tax, police, court and other officials [who] . . . [conspire] to deprive poor blacks of their land by illegal or 'barely legal' tactics."[8] A considerable amount of their time and energy was spent in county courthouses, sifting through delinquent tax rolls, contacting tax-delinquent land-owners, paying off late tax bills, competing with deep-pocketed and well-connected investors at tax sales, and attempting to throw sand in the gears of local tax-enforcement machinery. Fittingly, that struggle began in the place where Black people had first acquired land following emancipation: the South Carolina Sea Islands.

* * *

Joe McDomick had come to the Penn Center on St. Helena Island in 1964 to fight poverty, but what immediately stood out to him were the resources poor Black people possessed. Unlike the Black tenant farmers and sharecropping families among whom he'd grown up in north-central Louisiana in the 1940s, the rural Black poor of the Sea Islands owned the land under their feet. "The island Negroes of Beaufort," a writer remarked in 1935, "are probably the largest group of Negro landowners in the United States, each generation inherited from another its ten or twenty ancestral acres, first owned by former slaves and being tiny parts of once large and wealthy plantations."[9] Across the Sea Islands, Black families laid claim to thousands of small plots, with many of those holdings dating back to the dawn of freedom. Fewer than twelve percent of the region's Black landowners held plots greater than twenty acres; more than sixty percent possessed six or fewer acres. For McDomick, the Sea Islands offered a faint glimpse of what freedom following slavery could have been: a democracy of small freeholders, unchained from the tyranny of the plantation and the power of concentrated capital. To a fellow organizer, he remarked, "You know, all of the families up and down these Sea Islands [are] as fortunate as they could be, because they live on their own place."[10] But McDomick's awe soon turned to alarm, as scores of Black families streamed into the Penn Center's offices, seeking advice on paying property tax bills that had soared in recent years, or answers after losing their land under dubious circumstances.

Annual tax bills had long been a burden for rural Black landowners, but they had been, for most, a predictable, manageable one. By the 1950s, though, that was no longer the case. US agricultural policies and agencies created during the New Deal spurred large-scale farming operations to mechanize and dramatically decrease their reliance on labor, leading to a mass displacement of sharecroppers and tenant farmers and instigating the second wave of the Great Migration. At the same time, federal agencies created to assist small farmers worked, in practice, to hasten their demise. The Farm Security Administration and its successor, the Farmers' Home Administration, was established under the New Deal to assist struggling small farmers with loans and subsidies. But the local administrators of these federal programs routinely denied or provided much smaller loans to Black farmers. Rather than providing a lifeline, the 1965 US Commission on Civil Rights found that the FmHA had "served to accelerate the displacement and impoverishment of the Negro farmer."[11] In many parts of the coastal South, large-scale producers crowded out small farmers and devoured local markets.[12]

Changes to southern agriculture in the postwar era increased the odds of Black landowners falling delinquent on their taxes. It simply was harder for struggling landowners to make ends meet, as the prices they could command for their harvests went down, the costs of running small-scale operations went up, and many workers left to seek out wages in cities. Rising rates of tax delinquency among rural Blacks was, in this respect, a symptom of the larger forces conspiring to undermine small, independent farming, in general—the coda to a painful saga of desperation, dislocation, and abandonment.

Those rising rates also stemmed from the nature of their ownership arrangements. Throughout the Jim Crow era, few Blacks in the South wrote wills and fewer still had their wills probated. As a result, when the person listed on a property deed died, a cloud was placed on the title and ownership was passed down in the form of undivided shares. Many other Black-owned lands across the rural South had been acquired by adverse possession and never had clear title. These became known as heirs' properties. Because their property lacked clear title, heirs'-property owners often could not obtain mortgages to build or refurbish homes on their land, or use their property as collateral on a loan. They were also excluded from receiving many USDA benefits. Nor could they sell the land, or a portion of it, without first clearing the title, an expensive, time-consuming process that, first, requires the consent of all the heirs, and then requires a lawyer to make it work to the court's satisfaction. All these stipulations made restoring clear title difficult for most Black families in the mid-twentieth-century rural South. And, given the constant presence of predatory lenders lurking around Black communities—always willing to extend Blacks a loan to buy new farm equipment, a new car, or even a sack of groceries, if they agreed to put up their land as collateral—many Blacks saw these clouds on land titles as providing them a protective shield against predation. Which, for a time, and for some, they did.

But heirs' property did not shield its owners from taxes. Instead, it often prevented them from receiving tax abatements and exemptions or lower rates available to other small farmers. These collective ownership arrangements also left unresolved the question of who was responsible for paying the taxes. The responsible party might be the family members who lived on the land, or a relative who had moved up North. But whoever paid the taxes enjoyed no special benefit, nor gained any additional stake in its ownership, from doing so. Legally speaking, any direct descendant of the original owner had a claim on the land. Because the names listed on local records for heirs' properties did not match the names (or, as often, addresses) of the persons paying the bills, tax bills for heirs' properties were more prone to being sent to the wrong address; payments were more likely to be missed; and late notices and other important legal notices more often went unreceived.

Taxes became a major burden and increasingly a source of conflict for Black families in areas experiencing real estate development and rising land values, as subsequent heavier tax bills increased pressures within families to clear title and sell the land. This increased pressure was by design. In such areas, property assessments served not merely as a barometer of trends in housing and land markets but also as a means of bringing land *onto* the market. In South Carolina, local assessors valued property based on its market value, as opposed to the value of its current use—even if its use was limited by land-use restrictions. In practice, that meant that a modest home on a small plot of land near an exclusive resort could be assessed for taxes as if it, too, were an exclusive resort, even if it wasn't zoned for it. "Under market value assessment," a 1971 report concluded, if a farm had any of the attributes prized by real estate developers, such as "road frontage, marsh view, access to tidal estuaries . . . or access to the beach"—which most farmland in the low country did—"the county assessor has no alternative but to appraise many parcels of land at values far beyond what a farmer would be willing to pay for farmland."[13] Such an appraisal would be levied regardless of whether the owner wanted—or was legally able—to develop their property for such purposes. Property assessments became, as legal scholar Faith Rivers put it, "self-fulfilling prophecies," forcing land onto real estate markets and into capital-intensive uses by "forcing its current occupants to scramble to meet outrageous tax bills, sell under duress (invariably at below market value), or have a lien placed on their land."[14]

These pressures intensified as rural economies reoriented around real estate development. In South Carolina, the creation of the Sea

Pines Plantation Resort on Hilton Head Island and the completion of a toll bridge connecting the island to the mainland in the mid-1950s sparked a frenzy of real estate speculation across the Sea Islands.[15] At the time Sea Pines Plantation's developer Charles Fraser and his team of investors acquired twenty thousand acres of forests on Hilton Head Island's southern end in 1949, the island's population was nearly entirely Black. "When I was growing up, I must have seen one white man in my life," Alice Wine, who was born and raised there prior to its development, recalled.[16] Those lands that Black families did not own outright were undeveloped woodlands and forests and were treated as a commons.[17] "You could use pretty much any part of the island you wished," Emory Campbell, who grew up on the island in the 1940s, recalled.[18] Following completion of Sea Pines, fences went up across the island, white vacationers and second-home owners poured in, taxes soared, and Black families began to disappear. Speculators descended on families, exploiting their poverty and lack of knowledge to compel them to sell their properties drastically below market value. Those who refused to sell still struggled to pay taxes. During the 1960s, the number of properties that had tax liens auctioned at Beaufort County's annual tax sale ballooned, while the percentage of those properties that were ultimately redeemed by the owner fell.[19]

In counties across the postwar rural South, the annual lists of tax-delinquent properties that appeared in local newspapers or were posted on the walls of county courthouses told tales of economic distress and dislocation. But sprinkled throughout were also tales of greed, fraud, and deception, of people who fell into delinquency because someone conspired to put them there. The taking of Evelina Jenkins's lands on St. Helena Island sent shock waves across the insular Black communities on the Sea Islands, in part because many Black families had similar arrangements. This form of predation had been an ongoing problem and concern for decades. In 1932, the Penn School (as it was called) established a tax committee in response to a spike in tax delinquency in the wake of the first Great Migration and in the midst of the Great Depression. The committee held clinics to educate Black families on tax laws and warn them against land-grabbing tactics. They implored landowners to never trust someone else to pay their taxes for them.[20] But many continued to do so because, as Joe McDomick learned, "When the older people don't have no means of transportation, [and] can't read or write, . . . people will come and just prey on them. They'll say, 'Auntie, I'll go and pay your taxes for you. Give me your money, I'll go and pay it for you.'"[21]

Local white officials were often party to these schemes. As the postwar changes in agriculture pushed many Blacks to abandon farming, some began leasing their farmlands. Often, these arrangements stipulated that the leaseholder would be responsible for tax payments. In Bolivar County, Mississippi, investigators found, white leaseholders deliberately failed to pay taxes on land they were renting from Black farmers, then conspired with tax officials to keep the farmers in the dark by failing to send out late tax notices or notifications that their property had been sold at a tax sale. By the time victims uncovered the scheme, the redemption period had passed, a tax deed had been issued, and their property belonged to someone else.[22] There was no recourse.[23] Blacks owning property in cities and towns also faced this threat. Gladys Williams lost her 2.5-acre lot in Belzoni, Mississippi, over a $3.33 tax bill she claimed to have never received.[24] Cecil Taylor failed to pay taxes on three lots and a house he owned in Gulfport, Mississippi, in 1967. He paid the taxes in subsequent years but was never told what he still owed. That is, until he came to pay his taxes in 1973 and learned that the property had been sold at a tax sale three years earlier. It was no longer his.[25]

In county after county, local tax officials couldn't wait to put as much poor, underutilized land up for sale as possible. South Carolina's tax code, for instance, instructed local taxing authorities to only sell as much property as needed to satisfy the tax debt. But, as Faith Rivers found, "tax assessors in many coastal areas [sold] the entire parcel in order to satisfy the lien."[26] This behavior was the norm in virtually every state with such a limiting statute. "No matter how much land is involved, or how much money is owed for taxes, the practice . . . is to sell all of the property."[27]

Rising property values and rising taxes in Sunbelt markets divided families who owned heirs' properties and created an opening for land speculators, who inundated heirs'-property owners with offers to buy their land. Rarely did all family members agree on what to do. Legally, though, agreement wasn't required. Any heir could petition the local probate court for a partition action, essentially allowing them to claim their share of the land or its value. So, too, could any third party who managed to convince an heir to sell them their share. While judges could in theory order the physical partitioning of the property into separate units to be distributed to each descendant, in practice they simply ordered the sale of the entire property at what was known as a partition sale, with the proceeds distributed to all heirs. Exploiting this legal loophole, land speculators worked to convince individual heirs to file partition actions or sell them their share so that they could file such actions, often against the wishes of other family members who lived and paid taxes on the land. Black families in these circumstances rarely had an attorney they could turn to for legal advice or estate planning. The absence of trustworthy legal advice for Black property owners under Jim Crow was partly responsible for the prevalence of unclear titles, and also for the vulnerabilities of those same owners to partition actions.[28]

Once a judge ordered a partition sale, the property was as good as gone. Deep-pocketed land speculators and developers easily outbid family members whose only source of wealth, often, was the land they were bidding to buy back. Hastily arranged and poorly advertised, partition sales resulted in winning bids far below market value.[29] As a result, the family not only lost the land but received a mere fraction of its worth. After court costs and lawyers' fees, the check each family member received was a pittance. For those who had been living on the property, the amount was almost never enough to cover the cost of a new home.

Partition sales offered lucrative opportunities for land speculators, and they had devastating consequences for the families upon whom they preyed. They became one of the main instruments of Black land dispossession in the rural South throughout the second half of the twentieth century.[30] These were Jim Crow's spoils: property that was ripe for the taking because its owners were legally constrained, financially disadvantaged, more vulnerable to deception, and less able to defend themselves. By design, racist exclusion and subordination created the conditions for predation, loosened barriers to it, drove down its costs—and made the law and the state into accessories.

From his office at the Penn Center, Joe McDomick could see ample evidence of a lucrative business in Black land taking. "You could see just by being around in the communities," he recalled. "There was a place where Black folk used to live and you might find a golf course there. Or you might find a big nice house where Black folk used to live."[31] "We'll be back in slavery after a while if we keep going down this road," he thought. To his colleagues, he said, "We've got to do something."[32]

In 1970, the Penn Center's new executive director, John Gadson, formed a new initiative, Black Land Services, and appointed McDomick its first director. McDomick got to work compiling and investigating cases. He researched property records in the county courthouse in Beaufort. He attended the county's tax sale. His mere presence in these spaces raised alarms. "When I first started . . . going to the courthouse and . . . looking up records," McDomick recalled, the white staffers "would look at me and say, 'What are you doing in here?' 'What do you want?' 'What are you looking for?'" At the time, Black people simply did not "go in the courthouse looking through records" or attend tax sales. The "only time" we went to the courthouse, McDomick remarked, was "when [we got] arrested [or went on] trial." But McDomick persisted. "I let 'em know that that I was here to stay. I wasn't going anywhere. I was going to be there."[33]

McDomick began meeting with Charles Washington Jr., an African American attorney based in Charleston. Washington was one of the few Black attorneys in the state with expertise in property and real estate law. Washington, as McDomick described, "was really out front on all these issues. . . . He knew that in this area there wasn't anybody who was going to represent Blacks . . . and he was there to make sure people got justice, and he was there to help anybody he could." Together, they wrote and began distributing a manual for Black landowners.

Figure 9.2 Staff of the Penn Center's Black Land Services, standing outside the Treasurer's Office for Beaufort County, South Carolina. From left to right, Joe McDomick, Louis Dore, and Hugh Davis. *Penn Community Services*, October 1972.

Simply titled *Got Land Problems?*, it explained, in plain English, typical problems landowners might encounter and the legal options at their disposal. It worked to demystify the mechanics of local governance and property law, explaining, for instance, how tax assessments were determined and how a property owner could appeal theirs. At a time when Blacks were being deceived by white real estate investors and developers about the value of their land, the manual revealed just how much an acre of land in a place like Hilton Head was really worth, and it warned Black landowners about the deceptive tactics buyers were using. It explained the laws and procedures of tax sales, including those that local officials often failed to follow, and called attention to gray areas of the law that predatory investors often exploited. It provided a list of immediate actions that Black landowners could take to protect their land, such as getting it surveyed before a white neighbor tried to claim some of it as his own, a common occurrence. They wrote the manual so that a person lacking any formal education could, McDomick explained, "understand what was going on."[34]

Black Land Services began distributing thousands of copies of the manual and holding clinics and seminars in churches and community halls across the Sea Islands.[35] They held the clinics in the evenings, when people got off work, and they provided child care. McDomick and Washington got up and "explain[ed] what was going on with the land, why people left it, why we need to try to hold onto it, and what you need to do to secure it." They talked about the law, described some of the most common instruments of dispossession, and explained the stakes. Land, McDomick told audiences, is "the only economic resource that we have. You don't have money, but we got land. And that's just like gold." And, "once you get rid of your land, you might as well be back in slavery." Some attendees remained skeptical, unconvinced that they should hold onto land that wasn't generating income and that was, as taxes rose, becoming an increasingly heavier burden. McDomick recalled: "One fella told me one day, he said, 'What do I want to keep the land for. I can't eat no land.'" Raising an eyebrow, McDomick responded, "Oh really, you can't eat no land. I tell you what, if you can't eat no land, you sure can live on it. Your children [can, too. And they] are going to need somewhere to live, sooner or later."[36]

The one way Black Land Services could save considerable amounts of endangered property at relatively little expense, McDomick realized, was to keep as much of it from going to the tax sale as they could. But to do that, he needed time: to identify all of the Black-owned land on the tax-delinquency rolls, track down its owners, and get the debts paid before the tax sale was held. He needed the list as soon as it was prepared, not when it appeared in the local newspaper just prior to the tax sale. Most of all, he needed money to pay the taxes for those who couldn't do so themselves.

In 1972, McDomick convinced the Beaufort County treasurer's office to send him advance copies of delinquent tax lists. After identifying all the Black people on the list, he and his staff mailed out postcards informing them of the looming deadline, explaining the importance of paying before the tax sale in early October, and offering assistance. To every Black church in the county, they sent a list of the names of delinquent taxpayers in their district, asking them to post the list on their bulletin boards in hopes of catching people's attention. They checked in regularly with the treasurer's office to see who had paid. With whatever funds they could muster, they paid the taxes on those properties that were sure to be coveted by tax buyers. And with whatever they had left, McDomick tried to outbid tax buyers at the tax sale. In its first year, Black Land Services spent over $1,200 to save twenty-three parcels of land.[37]

Along with saving their property from the tax auction block, Black Land Services helped Black landowners lower their tax liabilities. As more Black families gave up farming and allowed acres to lie fallow, more of their land lost favorable tax rates for agricultural land. The families who were enjoying the least benefits from their land were being taxed at the heaviest rates, since they were assessed as if they were speculators. Many Black small farmers had never enjoyed these protections in the first place. South Carolina, like most states that provided tax exemptions on agricultural land, required owners to apply to receive them. Yet many Black farmers were not even aware that they could get their taxes lowered, and it was clear that local officials were in no rush to share this information, much less help with the forms. And, as some Black farmers who had applied learned, county officials were free to reject applications, and often did so on the narrowest technical grounds. McDomick stressed to families the critical importance of putting the land to use, if for no other reason than to lower their tax bills. "They will tax you to death if you just got it sitting out there doing nothing," he explained. If they couldn't farm it themselves, McDomick helped families find a farmer who could work it. They combed the state tax code for other available tax exemptions—like that for tree farms of five or more acres. "If [they] weren't going to farm it," McDomick explained, "we'd say, 'put some trees on it.'" Anything that would buy families, and Black Land Services, more time.[38]

* * *

During the same years when Black land loss was accelerating, a growing number of Black theorists, activists, and organizers placed the "land question" at the center of debates over Black liberation. "Black political preoccupation with land was pervasive" in the late 1960s and early 1970s, historian Russell Rickford notes. Schemes for securing a "land base" for Black liberation ranged from the "pragmatic" to the "quixotic."[39] In 1968, a collective of Black farmers under the leadership of Charles Prejean formed the Federation of Southern Cooperatives (FSC). Focused on making farming viable for small Black farmers, the FSC helped Black farmers form cooperatives and established research programs, methods of finance, and legal and technical expertise for them.[40] In 1968, Black nationalists formed the Republic of New Afrika and declared a large section of the Deep South from South Carolina to Louisiana a sovereign nation-state.[41] In southern Georgia, the Nation of Islam acquired 4,200 acres of farmland for growing the produce and supplying the fresh meats for its chain of urban supermarkets.[42] At the 1969 Black Economic Development Conference in Detroit, James Forman issued his Black Manifesto calling for white Christian denominations and Jewish synagogues to donate $500 million toward a southern land bank as reparations for their roles in the slave trade.[43]

For Robert S. Browne, the greater concern was less the land that Black people deserved to receive and more the land that they already held and were losing. The African American economist and project director for the Stokes-Phelps Fund delivered the keynote address at the 1969 conference in Detroit, where he called for more research into the causes of Black land loss and strategies for putting this valuable, and endangered, resource to use. He proposed setting up a fund for Black land acquisition and retention in the rural South. He called for more support for southern Black land-grant colleges and universities to establish programs for Black rural development.[44]

The following year, Browne received funding from the National Council of Churches and Ford Foundation to create the Black Economic Research Center (BERC). From its offices in Harlem, Browne directed a range of research projects on economic challenges and opportunities facing Black Americans and mapped out plans for a southern land bank.[45] On April 26, 1970, BERC ran a quarter-page ad in the *New York Times* aimed at soliciting support for a land-bank task force. Meant to look like a news article, it included the headline, "Must All Blacks Flee the South?" Next to it appeared a clipping from a recent article on the suspected poisoning of the livestock at the Nation of Islam's farm by white supremacists. BERC called attention to the sharp decrease in Black landownership in the South, which, it estimated, had dropped by 40 percent between 1950 and 1964. The recent wave of Black migrants pouring into northern cities, it told the mostly white, northern readership, should be treated as refugees forced into exile, the victims of a deliberate campaign "to drive black people off the land and out of the South."[46]

In 1971, BERC received a grant from the Rockefeller Brothers Fund to study the problem.[47] That summer, it convened a conference at Clark College in Atlanta. A foreboding atmosphere of crisis hung over the proceedings. Attendees offered personal testimonies of family members, friends, and acquaintances who had "lost sizable tracts of land against their will, often out of ignorance or poverty or sometimes as a result of cunning on the part of hostile or covetous whites." In his keynote address, Charles Washington singled out tax sales and partition sales as two of the main instruments of Black land dispossession. But, he stressed, these causes were symptomatic of deeper problems rural Black landowners faced: the dearth of Black lawyers, surveyors, appraisers, and real estate professionals in the South, which left them vulnerable to all manner of trickery, deception, and outright theft; the twin evils of financial exclusion and financial predation; systemic racial discrimination in the Farmers Home Administration and US Department of Agriculture (USDA), which kept Black farmers and rural landowners from being able to use their land effectively and profitably; and white-dominated local governments and courts structurally designed to protect and enhance white economic power.[48] Following the conference, BERC released the report *Only Six Million Acres: The Decline of Black-Owned Land in the Rural South*, which detailed, for the first time, the extent of Blacks' losses and the policies, practices, and forces driving rural Blacks from the land.[49]

The report received extensive coverage in the Black press and led to multiple printings. BERC's work also compelled white philanthropist Carol Bernstein Ferry, a generous supporter of progressive causes, to donate $1 million to Browne to establish the Emergency Land Fund (ELF), to be focused on protection, acquisition, and development of Black-owned land in the rural South.[50]

Browne tapped Joe Brooks, a young urban- and regional-planning scholar who had written on the centrality of land in Black struggles for economic sovereignty, to lead the organization. Browne and Brooks shared an understanding of the structural and political disadvantages Black landowners faced, a belief in the possibility of Black economic empowerment through agriculture and real estate development, and a strategically flexible and practical approach to advancing Black economic interests.[51] As historian Alec Hickmott has described, Browne's vision for unlocking the economic potential of Black-owned land in the South was "progressive, yet undeniably capitalist-oriented."[52] Like the Federation of Southern Cooperatives, the ELF aimed to work with Black farmers to preserve rural farmland and ensure the viability of family farms. But it also aimed to promote and implement alternatives to farming and find ways that rural Black landowners could capitalize on, rather than fall victim to, trends in the Sunbelt economy. "Black land," Brooks argued, "is tied to strategic points of development. . . . The South is growing fast [and] everything is up for grabs."[53] ELF set its sights on unlocking the potential of Black property. "I'm not tied to agriculture," Brooks made clear. "I'm for the best and highest use of land."[54]

Launched in 1972, ELF established state offices, first in Mississippi and Alabama, and later in Virginia, North Carolina, Georgia, and Louisiana. ELF also formally affiliated with Black Land Services in South Carolina.[55] In Mississippi, state director Jesse Morris soon identified tax delinquency, and manipulation and abuse of tax-sale proceedings, as one of the most immediate threats Black landowners faced. In 1971 alone, his staff found, over 1,400 parcels of Black-owned tax-delinquent land in the state went unredeemed and were claimed by tax buyers.[56] Moreover, they found that "a recurring complaint" in these cases "was that landowners were not aware that their land was

Figure 9.3 *Tax Sales: A Primer for Landowners*, the Emergency Land Fund's guide to Black landowners on how to protect their land from tax sales.

being sold or that they had a statutory right of redemption."[57] Before ELF arrived in Mississippi, there had been small-scale efforts to combat land predation through tax sales. In Bolivar County—where tax officials conspired with land grabbers to steer Black-owned land into tax delinquency and forfeiture—the Mound Bayou Development Corporation, a nonprofit group of Black farmers and business owners, bid on Black-owned land at the annual tax sale. In three years, the group had managed to save land valued around $361,715 for a total cost of $3,335.[58] That disparity underscored just how lucrative tax sales were.

Morris marveled at the returns on investment that tax buyers enjoyed. It was obvious to him why those in the business of acquiring and selling rural farmland would flock to tax sales, and why they would make a point of targeting Black-owned land. "When it comes to exploiting people, you exploit the most vulnerable."[59] But knowing why Blacks were being preyed on was one thing. Combatting it effectively was another matter. Morris studied the business and culture of tax buying. He attended tax sales, observed the different types of tax buyers, learned the lingo and the speculative strategies.[60] Morris taught what he learned to his staff and then sent them to tax sales, lists of Black-owned property in hand, with money to spend. He instructed them to participate and observe: the main buyers, their strategies and operations, their reputations and interactions with public officials. "We had to realize who we were dealing with," Morris explained. "We were dealing with cunning people so you have to be cunning, too. . . . They're not going away. And the only way you can combat them is to try to stay ahead of them."[61]

In the spring of 1973, Morris dispatched six ELF staffers to tax sales in Hinds, Clay, Leflore, Quitman, Panola, and Claiborne counties.[62] With the exception of a few Black landowners who came to pay their taxes at the last minute, in each county the ELF representative was the only Black person in the room. And, as was the case when McDomick began bidding in Beaufort County and Morris began observing tax sales in Hinds County, their mere presence was noteworthy and unsettling. When it became evident that the ELF staffers were there to bid, "the atmosphere immediately became tense, the consternation palpable."[63] ELF staffer William McGee, dispatched to Leflore County, described how, "after I picked over $900.00 worth of property," the tax sale's largest bidder, who had entered the room with the swagger of someone accustomed to dominating the proceedings, "became nervous and started walking around."[64] In one day, ELF recovered nearly 1,500 acres of Black-owned land valued

Figure 9.4 Emergency Land Fund agents bidding on Black-owned land at the West Point, Mississippi, tax sale. *West Point* [MS] *Times-Leader*, April 3, 1973.

at over $1 million at a cost of $5,390.[65] Morris was thrilled. "This was the first time a group of Blacks did anything like this on the scale that we did."[66]

But protecting rural landowners in remote counties required more than showing up at the courthouse one day a year. It required constant vigilance and local knowledge. For ELF's programs to be effective, it needed people who could monitor the legal notices in local newspapers, check public records, conduct title searches, and examine tax books. It needed locals who were "familiar with the economic, social, and political conditions of black landowners and farmers."[67] It needed "eyes and ears" on the ground. To that end, Morris began building a network of "county contacts" who reported developments, threats, and opportunities to the state director and represented ELF in communities.[68] By 1974, Morris had secured contacts in forty-four counties in Mississippi.[69] Many of these contacts were already active in civil rights and Black community organizing. "We had an orientation meeting with them, told them what they were supposed to do: . . . if [they] saw a foreclosure [notice in the newspaper], they would tell us. If they looked at the tax rolls and saw a name in the tax sale, they would tell us."[70] They learned how to run a land-education workshop. Mainly, their job was to become well known among their county's Black farmers and landowners, so that when problems arose, people knew where to turn.

County contacts also learned how to bid at tax sales. Morris budgeted $2,000 annually for each county.[71] Following the sales, contacts detailed the parcels purchased, providing a rare window into the local cultures of rural tax-sale investing, the landscape of racialized predation, and the persons and interests who profited from Black economic distress. In Clay County, contact Randolph Walker entered the tax auction and attempted to negotiate with the other bidders "by stating that I was interested in buying property owned by Black people. This did not work in that most of the people who came apparently came to buy property owned by Blacks. . . . The bidding on property thought to be owned by Black people," he reported, "was down right 'vicious.'"[72] In Lauderdale County, the local contact wrote, a white man named P. L. Parker was the largest bidder.[73] In Claiborne County, James Miller wrote, it was "the general rule . . . that James or George Hudson (white) would come to the sales, and purchase all black owned land."[74] Lowndes County's contact reported on Ralph Williamson, "a sleazy character who has been duping landowners and using partition sales and tax sales to gain land for years."[75]

ELF's methods for combatting tax delinquency had, by the mid-1970s, begun to slow the bureaucratic machinery of Black dispossession. Annual campaigns to help Black landowners pay their taxes protected untold amounts of land and saved Black families from paying the high interest and fees needed to redeem it. It also raised unprecedented awareness of the threat of predatory tax buying and put local white officials on notice. "Black people are beginning to come to the tax sales themselves," a 1976 ELF report noted, "demanding to see the tax record books and otherwise exercising rights which they have been intimidated from exercising in the past."[76] In Bolivar County, Mississippi, Black bidding at the tax sale compelled the assessor-collector to begin mailing notices to Black owners whose property taxes had been sold.[77] In South Carolina, Black Land Services forced the treasurer's office in Hampton County to postpone its tax sale after numerous Black families on the tax-delinquent list reported not receiving any notice.[78]

Before the 1977 Beaufort County tax sale, Black Land Services sent out a call to local Black residents to show up and bid against the speculators. "We had an ace in the hold for the speculators that prey on tax sales," one of the organizers said of that tax sale. That morning, outside the courthouse, "it looked as if some one [was] hav[ing] a field's day. Never in history had there been so many blacks to participate in a tax sale." Nearly one hundred Black people bid on properties that day. Black bidders outnumbered whites five to one. Previously, only "developers, lawyers and speculators [had been] the ones that partici-pate[d] [in the tax sale] and [bought] up all the land. . . . This time it was blacks that lined the courthouse galleries and bidded." ELF purchased roughly 80 percent of the taxes sold. "We were not to be denied."[79]

In counties where ELF and its affiliates became actively involved, both the number of properties removed from the tax-sale list prior to the sale as well as the number of properties that were later redeemed by their owners increased.[80] Joe Brooks phoned in to Black talk-radio shows in northern cities and spoke before large congregations in northern churches, describing the main threats to Black property and imploring audiences to make sure the taxes on family lands down South were paid. Brooks worked to get nationally circulated Black magazines and northern newspapers to write stories on the ELF and raise awareness of its work.[81] The files of state offices attested to their effectiveness. Numerous case files on Black land problems in Missis-sippi were first opened after a family member said they had read a newspaper or magazine article on the subject.[82]

* * *

Even as ELF directors and staffers worked to save Black property from tax sales, they knew this strategy was only a stop-gap measure. Ultimately, rural Blacks needed to be able to farm their land profitably or secure financing to develop it themselves. Throughout the 1970s, ELF ran a host of programs and services for helping Blacks put their land to use. "Idle land is likely to be lost," Joe Brooks preached. "If you don't use it, you lost it."[83] On his office wall, Brooks had a large map of the South marking areas of concentrated Black landownership. "Over each parcel of black-owned land," one reporter described, Brooks "superimpose[ed] a visionary development plan of what could be—from farm federations to playgrounds for the rich." "So when we get a call that 50 acres in Mississippi are about to be lost," Brooks explained, "we can act with intelligence overnight and know what to do with it."[84] After Black Land Services successfully prevented a partition sale of a fifty-acre parcel of heirs' property owned by an African American family on Hilton Head, ELF worked with the family to secure financing for a $25 million residential development. This, policy expert and former BERC researcher Lester Salamon argued, was how rural Blacks should be thinking about their future of their land: as potential sites for Black real estate and commercial development. In 1976, Salamon argued that the precipitous decline of Blacks' land base in the South should be understood as both a crisis *and* an opportunity. It was a crisis because these millions of acres of land constituted the bulk of Black wealth in America, and this equity base was disappearing fast. But these losses also pointed to the appreciating value of the lands Blacks held. "The frequent pattern is for land to remain in minority hands only so long as it is economically marginal, and then to be acquired by whites when its value begins to increase."[85]

Wherever Black land predation was on the rise, Salamon believed, the possibilities for Black economic development were greatest. To realize this potential, Salamon advised that rural Blacks look beyond farming. The size of most Black farmers' holdings, he concluded, were simply "not sufficient to generate an adequate income" at a time when southern agriculture was industrializing and consolidating. Persisting in farming only exposed more rural land to eventual loss. Salamon pointed to evidence that Black owners operating smaller, subsistence farms made up the bulk of Black land loss over the previous decades.

Many rural Blacks, he argued, should instead look to "generate capital [from] non-agricultural pursuits." Salomon called for a "concerted effort to identify areas of greatest potential for black landowners, to make black landowners aware of the capital leveraging power of the land, and to underwrite capital formation activities secured by this land through loan guarantees and interest subsidies."[86]

But to real estate capitalists in the Sunbelt South, Black people and their property remained strictly a resource to be plundered. What Salomon and other advocates of Black real estate development failed to appreciate was that Black-owned land held great value *because* it was Black-owned and, thanks to such legal tools as tax sales and partition sales, could be acquired cheaply. In this market, the value of Black people's land could only be fully realized once they had been pushed off it. And once they had been evicted, rural Blacks became the cheap labor that powered whatever was built on their former land.

On the Sea Islands, white real estate executives aimed to drum up support (or, at least, limit opposition) among Black populations by touting the jobs and shared benefits that economic growth promised. The banks financing these projects, meanwhile, summarily rejected Black business and development proposals. On Hilton Head, ELF abandoned its plans for a Black-owned development of the fifty-acre Washington estate after being unable to secure financing, and instead worked with the family members to ensure fair compensation in a sale to a white developer. Another Black family who owned five acres of beachfront property on Hilton Head struggled for years to obtain financing to develop it, until rising tax bills forced them to sell it to a white developer.[87] These doomed attempts to become partners in coastal capitalism fit into a broader pattern. Throughout the decade, Alec Hickmott observed, "black-initiated rural development efforts had, at almost every turn, been circumscribed by the organization of a rural economic landscape still hostile to black property rights or black enterprise."[88] On Hilton Head, Black enterprise remained confined to the ever-shrinking Black area on the island's northern half, and it consisted of only a few gas stations, groceries, and nightclubs that few whites ever patronized.

In Mississippi, ELF established a demonstration farm in Simpson County and helped promote farm cooperatives and community supported agricultural programs. Its Project LUBA (Land Utilization Benefitting Agriculture) promoted and provided markets for crops from small farming operations. It offered help for small farmers similar to that of county extension agents and agricultural experiment stations.[89] But it was forced to devote most of its time and energy toward helping Black people simply hold on to what they had. In 1973, ELF earmarked $200,000 for a revolving fund for small loans to Black farmers. The demand was so great, though, that ELF exhausted the fund faster than loan repayments could replenish it. By 1976, ELF's own deteriorating financial situation forced it to redirect loan repayments to operating expenses, preventing the loan program from becoming self-sustaining.

By the late 1970s, the Penn Center struggled to remain afloat as financial mismanagement nearly led to its closure.[90] In 1980, Emory Campbell came on board as executive director, determined to restore Penn Center as an "engine for bringing about equity in land ownership and . . . property tax reform." But he soon found himself consumed with the urgent task of "sav[ing] the Center itself" with fundraising. Unfortunately, "we never got back into the land program on the scale that I would have loved."[91] McDomick continued to fight to protect every acre of Black-owned land on the Sea Islands. But lacking the resources to compete with white bidders, McDomick could only try to appeal to them. Before each tax sale, he announced to the bidders that he was there on behalf of heirs'-property owners who sought to buy back their properties, and he asked the audience not to bid against them. "Even though we know you don't have to do it, we'd appreciate it."[92]

But as Hilton Head's popularity among middle-class white vacationers continued to grow, development spread, property assessments rose, and the number of Black-owned properties falling into tax delinquency soared. Between 1980 and 1984 alone, Beaufort County auctioned 236 parcels on Hilton Head for unpaid taxes; by compari-

Figure 9.5 Aerial shot of Sea Pines Plantation, Hilton Head Island, South Carolina (1976).

son, it auctioned a total of twenty-three parcels on the island between 1960 and 1970. On the first Monday in October, when the county held its annual tax sale, land speculators and investors (increasing numbers of them coming in from out of state for the occasion) sat, shoulder to shoulder, placards in hand, eager to bid on each one. Competition became fierce, with bidding wars over parcels as small as a few acres common.[93] "This island's black culture is an endangered species heading to extinction," Campbell lamented to a reporter.[94] Nationally, Hilton Head became a symbol of what one NAACP official described as "the ever-growing threat to Black lands."[95]

In 1983, Hilton Head's white residents—who, by then, vastly outnumbered Blacks—voted to incorporate the island as a "limited service" municipality, one that provided no services other than restricting land use. (White property was all covered by property owners' associations, which already provided services.) It was, writer Gunnar Hansen described, "an ingenuous way to limit the cost of owning recreational property on the island; wealthy neighborhoods would only pay for their needs, while poor neighborhoods still paid high taxes."[96] Black residents saw the move as clearly intended to limit their ability to make use of their land, raise their taxes, and hasten their removal. They sued to prevent the measure as a violation of the Voting Rights Act but lost.[97] "Hilton Head," Penn Center director Walter Mack bemoaned, "is a lost cause. All we can do . . . is look at it and try to let that serve as an example of what not to do . . . [or let] happen to the other sea islands."[98]

* * *

But to the architects of this New South, Hilton Head was a dream fulfilled. Resort developers and executives insisted that Black land dispossession was a positive development—for Blacks—and something for which they should be grateful. "I am jubilant, positively jubilant," Charles Fraser exclaimed, "when a black farm family that has held the land for five generations on Hilton Head Island, land that was worth $100 when we arrived here, sells it today for $50,000." (More jubilant, still, were those who had acquired land worth well over $50,000 for the price of a tax bill.) "I wish more of them would do that," Fraser added.[99]

Indeed, he did. Black land loss and dispossession were not just consequences of these emerging Sunbelt markets' growth and development. They were a rich source of the profits that flowed from it and the rising inequality that accompanied it. No matter what Blacks got in return for their land, the amount was only a fraction of what the land would ultimately prove to be worth; and yet, because of how race structured these markets and access to capital in them, that worth could never be realized so long as the land belonged to them.

PART IV

AGE OF REVOLTS

10

LOSING HANDS

On November 7, 1967, African American candidates won mayoral elections in Cleveland, Ohio, and Gary, Indiana, marking the first time in the nation's history that a Black person would hold the highest office of even a mid-sized city. But to get to his new office, Gary's new mayor, Richard Hatcher, had to enter City Hall through a basement entrance. The main entrance was closed due to crumbling mortar that the city couldn't afford to repair.[1] For Hatcher and his constituents, that closure was an ominous sign of the fiscal road ahead.

Founded in 1906 as a company town for US Steel, Gary was one of the many destinations for African American migrants seeking work in the first half of the twentieth century. Once there, corporate management and the white-controlled labor unions kept Black workers confined to the steel plant's dirtiest and most dangerous jobs. At the same time, the city's political machine denied Black neighborhoods the spoils of local tax revenues that it funneled to its friends and allies.[2] The city's schools, meanwhile, were, as NAACP lawyer Robert Carter put it, "as Jim Crow as Jackson, Miss.," formally or informally segregated by race, with the Black ones overcrowded to the point of running double shifts.[3]

Throughout the 1950s and early 1960s, Black parents, civil rights activists, and lawyers had fought to desegregate the city's schools and housing markets. Soon after earning his law degree, Hatcher joined the NAACP legal team that in 1962 filed a federal lawsuit against the school board, challenging the "neighborhood school" ruse that school officials used to prevent the transfer of Black students into predominantly white schools.[4] The following year, Hatcher beat the Democratic machine to win a seat on the city council.

Black Americans from across the ideological spectrum hailed Hatcher's 1967 election as mayor of the nation's seventieth-largest city as a watershed moment in the struggle for Black political empowerment. For mainstream voices in the civil rights movement, it was an indication of the turn "from protest to politics," as Bayard Rustin described. For more radical voices in the Black Power movement, cities like Gary provided a base of operations for the struggles to come. Winning political control of large and mid-sized municipalities offered a pathway toward liberating urban Black ghettos—America's "internal colonies"—from oppression and exploitation.

But as Blacks in Gary and other northern cities were assembling political power, these cities were being drained of their fiscal power. Facing the prospect of court-ordered school desegregation and pressured by blockbusting real estate speculators seeking to profit from white prejudice and Black demand, Gary's white middle class fled to surrounding suburbs. Retail and commerce followed white consumers there, further draining the city of tax revenue. Nationwide, the costs of running large cities and school districts rose sharply during these years, and far in excess of local tax revenues. The gap widened fastest in cities with the largest Black populations.[5] And in Gary the problem was even worse. The city's largest property owner—US Steel—enjoyed scandalously low tax assessments on its massive holdings thanks to the corrupt bargains it had struck with machine operatives in the assessor's office.

The fiscal structure of fragmented, rapidly suburbanizing postwar metropolises—and the ties that bound local tax revenues, household tax burdens, and local services to structurally racist housing markets—created the conditions for Blacks to gain political power in central cities. But it also limited the ability of Black elected officials to improve the lives of their constituents once they got there. By the early 1970s, property taxes were consuming an ever-greater share of household incomes at a time when, nationwide, wages were stagnating, the cost of living was rising, and the industries that had formed the backbone of mid-twentieth-urban economies were shedding jobs. Lower-income residents of the most fiscally disadvantaged cities felt the sharpest pinch, while the public goods and services they relied on suffered the most from mounting budgetary crises.[6] Disproportionately Black, brown, and poor, residents of these cities experienced the worst and most direct effects of broader structural inequities and regressive features of local tax administration. Here, in the cracked pavement of struggling cities at the bottom of the fiscal food chain, the seeds of a broader tax revolt against unfair and regressive local tax systems first sprouted. The twisted course of taxpayer unrest in the years that followed would transform American politics for decades to come.

* * *

By the mid-1960s, tensions and debates over the goals and objectives of Black freedom movements in northern cities split wide open. Few aroused greater division than the housing question. After decades of struggle, advocates for fair housing scored a landmark victory with the passage of the 1968 Fair Housing Act, which forbade many of the discriminatory practices that banks and realtors had used to keep the suburbs off-limits to Black homeseekers. But a large and growing segment of Black America expressed little interest in integrating into white neighborhoods and sharing in the purported benefits of suburban homeownership, or absorbing cities into new metropolitan governments.[7] At the moment when the white noose surrounding cities was loosening, Black nationalists argued for reclaiming the cities that whites were abandoning. They couched their political objectives in Black people's interests as local taxpayers. In their influential essay "The City is the Black Man's Land," Detroit radicals James and Grace Lee Boggs argued, "Negroes are the major source of pay that goes to the police, judges, mayors, common councilmen, and all city government employees taxed through traffic tickets, assessments, etc. Yet in every major city Negroes have little or no representation in city government. WE PAY FOR THESE OFFICIALS. WE SHOULD RUN THEM."[8]

Even as metropolitan consolidation promised to eliminate inequities in school funding and local services, urban Black activists and critics well understood that it weakened Black urban electoral strength—and that, they argued, was the point. Regional governance, Black studies scholar James Turner contended, "would effectively deprive the inner-city population from obtaining any meaningful political power and, most importantly, any control over significant land use with productive value." Its purpose, he concluded, "is to maintain the blacks' colonial status."[9] Under regional governance, Frances Fox Piven and Richard Cloward predicted, "white corporate control will be extended to the ghetto." Piven and Cloward, among others, contended that urban Blacks stood "to gain the most from localism," and lose the most from "consolidation and centralization."[10]

African Americans living in postwar cities had good reason to treat calls for metropolitan governance with suspicion. Throughout the 1950s and 1960s, white urban political coalitions sought to maintain their hold on power and dilute Black urban voting strength by absorbing surrounding suburbs. In 1952, the city of Atlanta annexed dozens of unincorporated white suburbs, tripling the city's physical footprint and adding nearly one hundred thousand new residents, nearly all of them white. The purpose of the annexations, Atlanta mayor William Hartsfield confided, was to prevent "hand[ing] . . . political control of Atlanta" over to the city's growing Black population. "Our Negro population is growing by leaps and bounds. They stay right in the city limits and grow by taking more white territory inside Atlanta. . . . With the federal government insisting on political recognition of Negroes in local affairs, the time is not far distant when they will become a potential political force."[11] During these decades, all the major cities that created metropolitan forms of government were Sunbelt cities seeking to prevent a Black takeover of city hall and maintain white political and economic control. In Jacksonville, Florida, African Americans constituted 41 percent of the population and with the passage of the 1965 Voting Rights Act were poised to make substantial political gains. That was, until the city consolidated with the surrounding Duval County in 1968. After consolidation, Blacks' share of the voting population was reduced to 20 percent. It would be nearly a half-century before the city would elect its first African American mayor.[12]

But even as they still embodied economic and industrial strength, many of America's cities—especially, the older, industrial cities to which Black migrants had flocked in large numbers—were, by the mid-1960s, in ill health. The publicly funded projects that urban growth coalitions had pitched to the public as self-supporting were instead becoming financial liabilities for cities. What had been touted as a means to spur economic investment and grow cities' tax bases was instead doing the opposite. By leveling entire working-class neighborhoods, eliminating scores of small businesses, and accelerating the out-migration of jobs from central cities, urban-renewal projects also compounded the problems facing the urban poor.[13] And the negative side effects of suburban separatism and exclusion, which made cities home to dense concentrations of people who relied heavily on public services but had limited capacity to contribute to public coffers, not only added to cities' costs but had set in motion a vicious cycle of rising needs and shrinking revenues. All the while, the costs of running big cities and school districts were exploding. The budgets of urban school systems were growing dramatically, partially as a result of teachers organizing and securing better salaries. Baltimore's annual school budget grew from $57 million in 1961 to $184 million in 1971, New Orleans's from $28.5 million to $73.9 million, and Boston's from $35.4 million to $95.7 million. Virtually every division of municipal government saw its costs increase sharply and far in excess of inflation during the decade. In some cities, total costs for public services, other than education, quadrupled. And as cities issued more bonds to pay those costs, debt servicing consumed an ever-greater portion of local budgets.[14]

Federal anti-poverty programs enacted under President Lyndon B. Johnson offered direct assistance to the urban poor: job training, assistance in securing welfare, and help in dealing with landlords, city officials, and school administrators. Federal grants-in-aid programs assisted local governments in providing new or enhanced social services. What none of these programs did, though, was help cities perform their core functions or alleviate their everyday costs. Instead, many of these programs wound up adding to those burdens, either by requiring cities to provide matching funds or by phasing out over time, in the expectation that cities could shoulder future costs. Added to these fiscal challenges and constraints were the self-inflicted costs resulting from decades of corrupt urban tax administration and the massive tax breaks big-city assessors had dispensed to large industries and campaign donors in the form of lower assessments.

By the time Richard Hatcher set his sights on the mayor's office in 1967, Gary already bore all the signs of a looming fiscal crisis. The city was hemorrhaging white homeowners and commercial and retail establishments to surrounding suburbs. As more Black families moved into what had been white neighborhoods, real estate values across the city plummeted. As they did, the city repeatedly raised its property tax rate to meet its budgetary needs. By 1967, that rate had soared to one of the highest in the nation, 50 percent above the statewide average and 15 percent above the national average for cities.[15] Between 1960 and 1969, the median property tax bill on a single-family home had jumped from $400 to $1,200.[16] And for that, residents—especially Black residents—saw little in return: The public school system was chronically underfunded and in disarray; the city struggled to perform basic services like garbage pickup and street cleaning. Even basic repairs to its crumbling city hall were too much to bear.[17]

By the 1960s, the tax breaks awarded to US Steel through fraudulently low assessments cost the city of Gary between $16 and $30 million in annual tax revenue.[18] For decades, Gary had managed small budgets by neglecting maintenance of public buildings and infrastructure, especially the streets, sewers, parks, and schools in Black neighborhoods. What services it did provide, city officials disproportionately devoted to the white middle- and working-class neighborhoods whose voters kept them in office, and whom they needed to remain in the city.

As a candidate, Hatcher vowed to reinvest in the beleaguered public schools and end decades of neglect toward Black neighborhoods. Blacks in Gary went to the polls in November 1967 expecting to elect a mayor who would, for once, provide Black people and neighborhoods services to which they were entitled and that whites had long enjoyed and taken for granted. Once in office, though, Hatcher confronted the fiscal limits of Black urban empowerment. The city's general revenues were so limited, the city stretched so thin, that any additional spending on neglected areas required either cuts elsewhere or an expansion in the tax base. Hatcher's first move was to attempt to annex the unincorporated, all-white suburb of Merrillville. Hatcher had barely finished unpacking his boxes, though, before state lawmakers blocked the move. The legislature quickly passed a law making it easier for unincorporated areas adjacent to cities to become municipalities, and for portions of existing cities to secede and form separate municipalities. Merrillville quickly incorporated as a municipality. In the years that followed, scores of businesses relocated from the city to there, further decimating Gary's tax base.[19]

Unable to grow the tax base, Hatcher aggressively pursued federal dollars. During his first three years in office, he reeled in over $106 million. But that money mostly went toward specific projects or new initiatives, a significant portion covered staffing and administrative expenses, and much of it required matching funds from the city. Many of these programs addressed the day-to-day needs of underserved neighborhoods but often did so indirectly. They did not provide relief to city agencies struggling under severe budget constraints. By requiring the city to dip into its general revenues for matching funds, the federal aid instead made those problems worse.[20]

When it came to the city's core functions, Hatcher had no choice but to reprioritize spending needs. White neighborhoods, long accustomed to being the first to have their streets repaved, their sidewalks fixed, their parks maintained, their snow plowed, now had to wait while the city attempted to make up for decades of neglect in

Figure 10.1 Gary, Indiana, Mayor Richard G. Hatcher.

Black neighborhoods. In order to "equalize services with the same resources," as Hatcher's executive secretary Don Leahy explained, "some [will get] less attention." In order to crack down on the city's slumlords, long accustomed to letting their properties deteriorate to the point of collapse with impunity, Hatcher sharply increased the budget of the city's housing division. During Hatcher's first year, the city inspected four thousand buildings a month, up from four hundred in the entire previous year.[21]

Gary's white minority was not content to wait at the back of the line, nor accept anything less than what they were accustomed to. "As far as we're concerned, Gary is dead," a steelworker from the all-white neighborhood of Glen Park fumed. Under Hatcher, he told a reporter, he and fellow white residents "don't benefit from being part of the city of Gary. We have no say in what the city does with our tax money." Whites' outrage was inflamed further still when the public-housing authority, with Hatcher's approval, slated a new project for the white neighborhood. Residents complained, "If we had a white mayor, we would have more response to our problems and complaints."[22]

In April 1969, a little over a year into Hatcher's first term, Glen Park announced plans to secede. At the time, the neighborhood constituted one-fourth of the city's population and one-fifth of its property tax base. While some Blacks in Gary saw the wholesale exodus of much of the city's remaining white population as an opportunity to entrench Black political power, Hatcher saw the threat. If Glen Park seceded, Hatcher explained, Gary "would face immediate and staggering revenue problems." More than that, if further balkanization was to be the response to Blacks' political empowerment, then "democracy as we know it doesn't work."[23]

Throughout the spring and summer of 1969, Hatcher went door to door in Glen Park, engaging with white voters. He held meetings in residents' homes, imploring them to remain. Gary needed Glen Park, he conceded, but Glen Park also needed Gary. Without each other, taxes for both would soar just to meet existing needs. That's because both localities depended on tax revenues from US Steel, whose property constituted 40 percent of the city's total tax base. Were Glen Park to secede, it would forgo that revenue source and be forced to raise tax rates on residential property exponentially in order to make up the difference. As residents stared at the numbers, Glen Park's secessionist movement quietly died. But the out-migration of individual white residents continued.[24]

The most pessimistic predicted that winning control of urban governments would prove, for urban Blacks, to be a "hollow prize."[25] But as Hatcher discovered, the prize was not hollow so much as it had been hollowed out: by fleeing white homeowners and industries, by decades of corrupt tax administration, and by federal and state government disinvestment and abandonment. From the mayor's office of one of the most hollowed-out of cities, Hatcher plotted road maps toward fiscal health that didn't compromise the political power and independence that Blacks in his and other cities had fought so hard to attain. In a 1970 essay for the journal *Black Scholar*, Hatcher outlined, in rough form, a model for doing so. Describing the fiscal straightjacket cities such as his faced, he proposed a form of metropolitan revenue sharing that preserved local political independence.

Treat "entire metropolitan areas as [single] taxing units," and then "allocate funds to municipalities on the basis of established formula of need for educational, social welfare, and other resources," while allowing them all to maintain their political independence. Revenue sharing, Hatcher argued, did not have to mean power sharing.[26]

But more than a share of white suburbs' tax revenues, what Gary needed, and needed urgently, was for US Steel to pay what it owed. The city's fiscal crisis, Hatcher's economic advisors concluded, was primarily the result of the under-taxation of the city's most valuable property. The year Hatcher entered office, Calumet Township tax assessor Tom Fadell assessed US Steel's property at $137 million. (Fadell's assessment, like those of all of his predecessors, was based entirely on what US Steel said the value of its property was. No assessor had ever inspected the company's records or conducted an independent appraisal.) The mandated assessment ratio for industrial property at the time was 33.3 percent, meaning that US Steel valued its property at $411 million. Outside estimates pegged its actual value as somewhere between $700 million and $1 billion. "[This] is one of the richest communities in the country in terms of heavy industry which are located in it," economic advisor Edward Greer observed, and yet, he said, "it's a poor man's town. . . . It is clear," Greer told Hatcher, "that the US Steel Corporation is grossly under-assessed, and that this fact is at the root of the fiscal difficulties of the city of Gary."

Greer pressed his case to Hatcher. *You want to address the needs of the city's poor and marginalized; you want to revitalize the city? Make US Steel pay. You want to find an issue that can bring the city's working-class white ethnics and Blacks together? Make US Steel pay.* Whites and Blacks, Greer wrote Hatcher, are "unhappy about high taxes and the inadequate level of municipal services (especially education and police protection), . . . and are looking for relief. . . . Conditions are presently uniquely auspicious for launching [a campaign] to demand reassessment for the Corporation."[27]

The under-assessment of US Steel's property was a tradition as old as the city itself. In 1907, the company assessed its land holdings at less than $2 million, even though it had paid over $7 million for that land years earlier. In 1908, US Steel paid $75,000 in property taxes, when it should have been paying over $600,000. But the company's tax avoidance had also been a source of conflict and contention. Citizens groups and the local business community had periodically railed against the company's under-taxation and the resulting impoverishment of the city.[28]

Hatcher needed to arouse the public's indignation because he could not simply order the tax assessor to do his job. In Indiana, tax assessors were elected at the township level, and Calumet Township covered both the city of Gary and outlying, predominantly white suburbs. It was an open secret that Tom Fadell was being lavishly compensated by US Steel for accepting its fraudulent valuations, but neither Hatcher nor Gary's Black voters could unseat him. Fadell answered only to his majority-white electorate, county government, and the state. But Hatcher's advisors uncovered an untested 1902 statute that allowed city governments to inspect the assessment records of their county governments. In July 1968, the city's controller contacted Fadell's office and requested records pertaining to US Steel's property assessment.[29]

In response, US Steel filed an injunction, which the circuit court granted. Publicly, it issued vague threats to downsize or relocate its operations if forced to pay more, using the city's daily *Gary Post-Tribune* as the company's mouthpiece. Days after Hatcher filed his request, it ran an editorial warning, "[If US Steel] were forced to pay a greater share of taxes than others, then it would be put at an obvious competitive disadvantage. In time that could lead to cuts in the use of production facilities and consequent cuts in both the tax base and jobs." Privately, the company tried to cajole Hatcher's administration into dropping the matter, at one point dangling the prospect of providing a corporate fund for low-income housing for the city in exchange. Hatcher pressed on.[30]

Next, US Steel enlisted Fadell to put the screws on Hatcher and make Gary's residents pay for their mayor's defiance. As in every city, Gary's mayor's office drew up an annual budget and set the tax rate based on an estimate of the tax base as supplied by the assessor's office. Seeking to sabotage Hatcher, Fadell overestimated the tax base for 1970 and 1971. On the basis of these projections, Hatcher's office lowered the property tax rate for the first time in years. But when tax returns failed to meet projections, Hatcher was forced to reduce operating expenses by $3.1 million. The schools, police, and fire departments saw their budgets slashed. Scores of workers were laid off. The recreation department was gutted, its summer youth programs shuttered, and twenty-nine full-time positions eliminated. Hatcher cut the health department budget in half. It was still not enough. Facing a $9.2 million budget shortfall in the fall of 1970, the schools eliminated music and physical education classes and laid off over two hundred teachers and staff.[31]

By then, Gary's fiscal crisis had become national news and, for tax reform activists, fit a pattern of corporate tax avoidance. In California, an investigative journalist's 1965 discovery of rampant corruption in San Francisco's assessor's office sparked public outcry and led the state to overhaul assessment procedures. In 1970, consumer advocate Ralph Nader and his growing army of law student volunteers (dubbed "Nader's raiders") launched investigations into the under-taxation of properties held by some of the nation's largest corporations, uncovering numerous examples of multi-million-dollar companies cheating local governments out of tax revenues through "grossly undervalued" assessments. In television and radio appearances, Nader made the case that America's public schools were broke and city services gutted because wealthy corporations were untaxed by crooked assessors. Nader implored lawmakers to address what he described as a "national scandal of corruption," which, he estimated, cost local governments over $6 billion annually.[32]

The same year Nader launched his national campaign, the US Justice Department indicted six subordinates of Cook County assessor P. J. "Parky" Cullerton over quid pro quo arrangements with wealthy property owners. Civil rights activist Jesse Jackson laid bare the scandal's implications for the city's Black poor. Not only are "the poor [forced to] pay more taxes" because "the rich are given tax breaks," Jackson argued, but thanks to the "subtracting machine [used] to figure the assessments of wealthy lake shore whites," critical public needs went unmet. In our schools, he continued, "millions which could go to improving the education of blacks and of poor people is squandered on the fraudulent pen of some assessor." What's more, "our health is jeopardized because [of] poor sanitation services and inadequate recreational facilities for our youth. Our neighborhoods are rundown because we have such poor city services[,] whether it is garbage collection, street repairs or tree removal."[33]

In Chicago, the grassroots Campaign Against Pollution (CAP), formed by community organizer Saul Alinsky, found that many of the largest polluters were being grossly under-taxed and costing the city upwards of $12 million in annual revenue. When the Cook County Board of Education announced in September 1971 that it would be forced to close schools for twelve days that fall due to a $26 million budget shortfall, CAP staged protests outside the assessor's office and called on school board members to demand that the assessor collect what it was due. The following year, Blacks in North Lawndale hung Cullerton in effigy during a protest. "If Cullerton can give special tax breaks to downtown interests and friends of City Hall," one of the organizers asked, "why can't he give them to this community?" "I wouldn't mind paying [taxes] if we got any kind of decent service from the city," one resident explained. "But there's poor police protection. The street lights don't work half the time. The streets never get repaired, and the garbage pickup is a laugh."[34]

In May 1972, Congress held hearings on corporate property tax avoidance. Speaking on the first day, Nader characterized the property tax, "as currently applied," as "rife with corruption, favoritism, antiquated laws, and secrecy." He characterized the actions of local assessors across the nation as an unreported "crime wave. . . . If what happens daily hundreds of times, in the administration of the property tax," he told Senators, "were to happen in plain view, on the street, we would call it unarmed robbery. It is literally pilfering billions of dollars out of school, out of streets and courts and parks and libraries and other services that civilized people need. It is taking billions of dollars from the pockets of the small taxpayers that have to make up the difference." Nader listed dozens of corporations that paid little or no property taxes, and he described how these companies used threats to relocate as a form of "tax blackmail." Nader assailed state and local governments for being unwilling to "stand up to corporate power." The situation in Gary, he told lawmakers, is an example of the costs of corporate tax avoidance. If US Steel were forced to pay its fair share, Nader explained, tax bills for the average homeowner would be reduced by 22 percent and the city would have the funds needed to pay its teachers a decent salary, keep its schools open, and maintain public services.[35]

* * *

In many cities and school districts across America, though, underassessing high-value properties was not the problem. The problem was the absence of high-value property in the first place. Only an overhaul of the fiscal structure could solve that.

In San Antonio, Texas, residents of the Edgewood School District had, by the spring of 1968, seemingly run out of options for addressing their schools' needs. There were no corporate tax evaders within their district. Everyone was paying *more* than their fair share. The school district's residents, in fact, paid the highest property tax rate in the metro area. And for that, their children attended the city's most overcrowded, underfunded schools. Fed up, in May 1968 over four hundred high school students walked out in protest over the poor quality of education and unbearable learning conditions. The protest was directed as much at the other school districts as their own. Edgewood's administrators were helpless because the overwhelmingly poor and Latino school district simply lacked the tax base. So long as public schools relied on property taxes for support, and so long as those property taxes were raised and distributed locally, that would remain the case.

The Elementary and Secondary Education Act of 1965 vastly expanded federal support for public schools across the nation and targeted resources toward children living in poverty. But the law did little to address the problems of poor schools, and many of its funds were allocated to all districts without regard to need. As a result, it did little to close funding disparities between school districts, or to counteract the incentive to hoard and exclude. Predominantly white school districts still enjoyed a fiscal advantage over those with larger non-white populations. And because they did, white parents still sought out white school districts *because* of the fiscal advantages of whiteness and resisted efforts to desegregate schools *and* housing markets. And as they did, the funding disparities between the fiscally advantaged and disadvantaged continued to widen, and resistance to change hardened.[36]

For this reason, growing numbers of legal experts, activists, and parents concluded, the fight to desegregate schools and close the funding gap between wealthy and poorer districts needed first to be understood as one. And like the fight to overturn "separate but equal," this "revolution in equality," legal scholar Arthur Wise argued, "cannot be consummated without aid from the judiciary." The fiscally advantaged simply would not relinquish their advantages willingly. They had to be made to do so. In 1967, Wise argued for the unconstitutionality of school-finance systems that, in effect, classified "students according to the tax base where they live." Using the precedents from recent Supreme Court rulings striking down segregation statutes, establishing the principle of "one person, one vote," and defining the rights of indigent defendants in the criminal justice system, Wise mapped out a legal argument for attacking inequitable school funding models.[37]

In 1968, attorneys representing a group of parents in the Los Angeles Unified School District filed a lawsuit charging that the system for financing public schools with local property taxes violated the state's constitution. That same year, parents in the Edgewood School District filed federal suit charging that Texas's school-funding system, which tied school funding to tax-base size, violated the equal protection clause of the Fourteenth Amendment of the US Constitution.

Both cases sought to dismantle the fiscal foundation of educational *and* residential segregation and its inequitable outcomes. And both came at a fluid political moment. As even privileged suburban school districts struggled to meet expenses, and as school administration increasingly centered on raising revenue over educating children, the supposed virtues of local taxation for local schools rang hollow—even for those whom it was designed to advantage. Funding local schools at the state and federal levels grew more appealing. Reformers argued that doing so would benefit all. "Liberated from the necessity of 'selling' bond issues and tax rate increases," a 1969 report envisioned, "school board members and superintendents could concentrate on their main concern—improving the quality of their children's education. The long tradition of local control of education and the keen concern of parents for the educational well-being of their children," it added, "would serve as sturdy defenses against any effort to short-change educational financial needs."[38] In the Black press, civil rights attorney Vernon Jordan made the case for structural reform, writing, "The use of the property tax to finance schools . . . encourages segregation. It leads to a mad scramble by suburban towns to land an office or factory that will increase the tax base, while at the same time discouraging towns from loosening zoning restrictions that would allow apartments and low-income housing for people to work in the new offices and plants. The reason: such changes mean more kids, which means higher school costs."[39]

When the California Supreme Court heard the arguments in *Serrano v. Priest* in the spring of 1971, the lawyers for the plaintiffs argued that, for the majority of California school children, local control was a cruel joke. The justices agreed. In finding the state's system of school finance unconstitutional, they wrote, "only a district with a large tax base will be truly able to decide how much it really cares about education. The poor district cannot choose to tax itself into excellence which its tax rolls cannot provide." Indeed, residents of poorer districts could—and did—tax themselves much more heavily than did residents of wealthy districts, who were able to "provide a high-quality education for their children while paying lower taxes."[40] The court ordered the state to come up with a new means of funding public schools that did not rely on local property taxes.

Later that year, a federal district court in Texas heard the arguments in *Rodriguez v. San Antonio*. Attorneys for the plaintiffs aimed to establish education as a constitutional right—indeed, a "preservative of other rights"—and one that the current funding structure denied to the poor *because* they were poor. This wealth-based discrimination, they argued, made the poor deserving of equal protection under the law, and it required the court to take action to ensure equal educational opportunity. In March 1972, the court agreed, ruling that Texas's school-financing system was unconstitutional.

The state would appeal, but these rulings emboldened school-finance reformers. Within weeks of the *Serrano* ruling, thirty similar cases were filed in state courts. In Illinois, state lawmakers hastily assembled a blue-ribbon citizens committee to explore reforms to an "inequitable and inadequate" funding system. President Richard Nixon ordered the Advisory Commission on Intergovernmental Relations to study school-finance problems, and he explored federal funding alternatives to local taxation. As Nixon cruised to victory in the fall of 1972, the US Supreme Court heard the case of *San Antonio v. Rodriguez*. The *Wall Street Journal* predicted that, if it was upheld, the decision "could reshape the face of America" and inspire "similar challenges to a host of vital public services, like housing, welfare and health care." At the very least, supporters predicted, it would remove the incentives for suburban governments to chase after industries and design exclusionary zoning laws.[41]

But the four conservative justices that Nixon had appointed to the Supreme Court during his first term had other ideas. In a five-to-four decision, the Court overruled the lower court and upheld the use of local property taxes to fund local schools, regardless of its inequitable outcomes. It rejected the argument that the right to an education was protected by the Constitution, or that poor people could be denied equal protection because they were poor. In his majority opinion, Justice Lewis Powell, who grew up attending whites-only schools in Jim Crow Virginia, extolled the virtues of leaving "each locality . . . free to tailor local programs to local needs."[42]

Justice Thurgood Marshall could only shake his head in disgust. In his dissent, Marshall characterized "local control" as a "myth," noting that "if Texas had a system truly dedicated to local fiscal control, one would expect the quality of the educational opportunity provided in each district to vary with the decision of the voters in that district as to the level of sacrifice they wish to make for public education. In fact, the Texas scheme produces precisely the opposite result." He concluded that the decision "can only be seen as a retreat from our historic commitment to equality of educational opportunity."[43]

The following year, the Court retreated further still, ruling in *Milliken v. Bradley* that federal courts could not dissolve school-district lines (no matter whom they were designed to exclude and at what cost) in order to achieve integration. "Given *Rodriguez*," Justice William O. Douglas wrote in dissent, the *Milliken* decision "means that there is no violation of the Equal Protection Clause though the schools are segregated by race and though the Black schools are not only 'separate' but 'inferior.'"[44] Indeed, the two decisions together closed the door on advancements in educational equality that the *Brown* decision had opened two decades earlier. They pushed the struggle for equitable funding down to state courts and legislatures, where, without the threat of federal intervention, pressure for change diminished significantly and the interests of white majorities regained command.[45]

The *Rodriguez* ruling also cast into doubt the federal court's ruling in *Hawkins v. Town of Shaw*.[46] In the wake of that decision, civil rights attorneys had been testing its broader applicability, with mixed results. In 1970, a federal district court in Alabama ruled against Black plaintiffs who sued the town of Prattville over its unequal provision of municipal services. The conditions in the town were virtually identical to those in Shaw, with the Black side of town lacking in paved streets, streetlights and signs, sidewalks or gutters, fire hydrants, and sewerage. The only difference (which made all the difference), was that Prattville officials provided these services by special assessments collected from the individuals receiving the services rather than from general tax revenues. Therefore, the court ruled, racial inequities were not the result of racial discrimination but rather were due to the "ability and willingness to pay for the property improvements" and thus permissible.[47] Municipal governments took note. Special assessments became the default mechanism for extending and improving municipal services.

The *Rodriguez* decision slammed the door on equal protection suits over municipal practices that underserved poor people and neighborhoods, regardless of race. It came on the heels of the Supreme Court's 1971 ruling in *Palmer v. Thompson* upholding the decision of the city of Jackson, Mississippi, to close its municipal swimming pools rather than abide by the 1964 Civil Rights Act ordering their desegregation. Deeming public recreation to be, in Justice Harry Blackmun's words, of the "nice-to-have but not essential variety [of] . . . service," the Court ruled it permissible for localities to simply withdraw services entirely rather than provide them on an equal basis.[48] Then in 1976, the Court ruled in *Washington v. Davis* that laws that had a discriminatory effect must also be proven to have had discriminatory motives to be overturned, singling out the *Shaw* decision as one that would not pass muster under the new standard.[49]

Neither poor people nor poor cities or school districts could find relief through the courts from a fiscal structure that seemed designed to disadvantage them. By the time Richard Hatcher testified before the Congressional committee investigating property taxation in 1972, he had given up trying. US Steel's repeated threats to downsize or relocate, and to lay off workers, had their effect. After the circuit court upheld the injunction against the city's attempts to inspect the township's assessment records, Hatcher briefly engaged with attorneys from the Lawyers' Committee for Civil Rights under Law and considered filing a lawsuit against the corporation and township assessor in federal court. But the legal argument was novel and untested, and he saw little to gain from "engag[ing] in an all-out struggle against" the city's dominant industry and largest employer at a time when it was already shedding jobs and downsizing production.[50]

The Nixon administration ended or phased out many of the grants-in-aid programs and forms of direct assistance for cities. Under the New Federalism scheme, the Nixon and Ford administrations replaced targeted aid with block grants. But many of these funds were routed through state governments and did not require distribution based on need. As a result, already-advantaged suburbs received a disproportionate share, and the neediest cities saw their federal funding cut significantly.[51] Hatcher and other leaders of fiscally dis-advantaged cities became increasingly beholden to the demands of corporate taxpayers and bondholders, who ordered cities to prioritize subsidizing downtown redevelopment and increasing police budgets, while cutting social welfare, schools, recreation programs, and other public goods and services that benefitted those most in need.[52] As the first Black mayor of a major city, Hatcher was also the first to learn, as two reporters wrote, "that black power at the lowest tier of a federal system doesn't amount to much unless the white majorities at the higher tiers are willing to help."[53]

11

ON OUR OWN

George Wiley was worried. After a decade of remarkable victories for poor people's rights, the founding director of the National Welfare Rights Organization (NWRO) feared it was all slipping away. By the early 1970s, old myths and old lies about race, poverty, and public spending were creeping back into national politics. As wages stagnated, the cost of living rose, and taxes (especially state and local taxes) consumed an ever-greater share of household incomes, opponents of progressive taxation and public spending on the poor sensed an opportunity. Rising stars on the Right, like California governor Ronald Reagan, seized on taxpayer unrest and sought to direct it at the most visible recipients of public support: the Black poor. Within a few years, the former actor would be regaling audiences on the presidential campaign trail with outlandish and racially laden stories of "welfare queens" amassing small fortunes at taxpayers' expense and of "strapping young bucks" buying T-bone steaks with taxpayers' dollars while hard-working (white) Americans made do with hamburger meat.[1] This "ingenious con game," Wiley lamented, had taught "the average worker . . . to despise the impoverished welfare recipient . . . when in fact their economic interests coincide far more than they conflict."[2]

The time had come, Wiley concluded, to adopt new strategies and new approaches to combatting inequality. In January 1973, Wiley resigned as NWRO's director. "Welfare rights," he said at the time, "was a minority strategy" and "minority movements can only succeed if the majority is either sympathetic or passive."[3] To counter this rising "hostil[ity] toward welfare recipients as well as toward blacks and other minority groups" among white Americans, he believed, the Left needed to build a "broad-based movement aimed at the economic interests of the majority of Americans."[4] It needed to focus on issues that affected the poor and middle class alike, and through them, make the case to those white Americans being seduced by the Right that "it is in their interest to unite with poor blacks and Chicanos and Indians, to unite with women, to unite with people who are in motion for social and economic change."[5]

"I believe today we need a taxpayer's revolt," Wiley said in announcing the formation of the Movement for Economic Justice (MEJ) in March 1973.[6] A taxpayer's revolt among the working poor and middle class, one that would be directed, as he put it, at "the real chiselers": the "multi-billion dollar corporations and very wealthy individuals [who] do not pay their fair share of the tax [burden]" and who raise the tax burdens for everyone else.[7] The Movement for Economic Justice would aim to educate taxpayers on how the system worked for the few at the expense of the many. It would give people the tools to lower their taxes. And it would work to build the organizational capacity and sense of purpose needed to change the system, as NWRO had done with remarkable success for welfare recipients.[8] "There is probably no more potent issue . . . for forging a majority coalition of poor-to-middle-income Americans," Wiley concluded, "than taxes."[9]

Indeed, few political issues in early 1970s America were more volatile or seemed better suited to uniting poor and middle-class Americans in common cause than unfairness and inequity in state and local taxation. Between 1962 and 1972, per-capita state and local taxes more than doubled nationwide, with low- and middle-income Americans experiencing the sharpest increases. People in the lowest income brackets were already paying a higher percentage of their income in taxes than the wealthiest Americans, and middle-income earners were closing in fast. Nationwide, property taxes consumed—

Figure 11.1 Civil rights activist George Wiley, Central Park, New York, April 15, 1969. In 1973, the founder and former executive director of the National Welfare Rights Organization formed the Movement for Economic Justice, dedicated to uniting a broad cross-section of Americans against regressive taxation and tax avoidance among the wealthy.

directly or indirectly—eight times more of poorer families' incomes than those of middle- and upper-income families. A 1973 poll found that 88 percent of Americans felt that "the big tax burden falls on the little man in this country today." It fell hardest on Black Americans. Among demographic groups, Blacks devoted the highest percentage of their incomes to taxes. And because of a fiscal structure that kept the places where they lived perpetually short of tax revenues, Blacks were constantly being asked to pay more still.[10]

During these years, taxes moved to the center of Black pocketbook politics and seemed poised to become a vehicle for class-based coalition building. Activist groups and grassroots organizations fought to secure tax relief for the poor and force the wealthy to pay their fair share. White and Black homeowners joined together in protest against unfair assessment practices. Black candidates for local offices put property tax relief and reform at the top of their agendas. But as Blacks fought for taxpayer justice, and to be recognized *as taxpayers*, their greatest adversary was local tax structures. Nothing was a more powerful instrument of racial division than the zero-sum game people and municipalities forced each other to play.

* * *

The reasons why property taxes were consuming an ever greater proportion of household incomes in the early 1970s were many. In addition to the exploding local budgets discussed in the previous chapter, there was a pronounced shift in property taxation, from commercial and industrial to residential. Residential properties were being taxed more because nonresidential properties were being taxed less. There were two main causes of this development. The first, ironically, stemmed from some of the reforms adopted in response to public outrage over corruption and favoritism in assessor offices in the 1960s. California lawmakers in 1967 established a single, uniform assessment ratio on all property and created a computerized system for tracking property values and updating assessments. These changes came in response to revelations that businesses had received assessment reductions in exchange for bribes. But as middle-class white homeowners across the state soon discovered, the new system also eliminated the informal but pervasive underassessment of *their* properties. Before, nonresidential properties had been assessed at higher effective rates and paid a larger overall share of the property tax. After, residential taxes soared.[11]

Other states that adopted similar reforms also saw the tax burden shift decisively onto residential properties. After Michigan wrote a 50 percent assessment ratio for all properties into its constitution in 1963, owners of business and commercial properties saw their tax bills plummet in direct proportion to tax increases for homeowners. In Wayne County, the total assessed value of residential property increased by $14.5 million, while that of its commercial and industrial property decreased by $14.2 million.[12] With the exception of five states that enacted circuit-breaker laws limiting property taxes for low-income homeowners, none of these reforms relieved the tax burdens of lower-income homeowners; indeed, they often made those burdens worse.[13]

Alongside these reduced assessments on nonresidential properties was the growing use of incentives by localities to attract or retain businesses. US Steel's threat to leave Gary, Indiana, if it forced the company to pay more taxes was a harbinger of things to come. As cities lost revenue in the wake of deindustrialization, corporations wielded the threat of relocation to secure tax reductions. Rather than being brokered in smoke-filled rooms, these reductions were negotiated out in the open. Growing Sunbelt cities, especially, dangled property tax exemptions to lure industries to relocate.[14] Several southern states enacted constitutional provisions authorizing localities to provide property tax exemptions and five- to ten-year property tax moratoriums to recruit new industries.[15] Desperate Rust Belt cities, in turn, scrambled to offer the same. The race to the bottom had begun. With each property tax abatement and exemption, local tax bases shrank, tax rates on everyone else rose, and the burden shifted further onto residential properties.

But these factors alone cannot explain why so many Americans were mad as hell. As historian Josh Mound points out, taxpayer unrest was just as great in states that did not adopt reforms and among those groups who had never been favored by assessors.[16] Like Black people. "Every day in the week," a white Virginia newspaper columnist wrote, "I receive shocking and appalling letters and telephone calls from poor old desperate souls . . . who tell me their agonizing experiences of the tax assessor riding up the alley and ruthlessly increasing the assessments on their humble little hovels. . . . There are no racial connotations to these cries of calamity," he added. "They come from the desperately poor; they come from the black and the white. They are all being robbed of their last mundane symbol of security by [a] bureaucracy that perpetually caters to the monstrous greed of the multi-millionaire."[17] Wielding one of the few direct tools for reducing taxes at their disposal, Blacks took the lead in voting down school-bond levies, voting "no" at higher rates than white voters during these years.[18]

Grassroots community organizers took note. In 1972, the Alinsky-formed Campaign Against Pollution renamed itself the Citizens'

Action Program (CAP) and broadened its efforts in Chicago's Black and working-class neighborhoods. CAP organizers met longtime white homeowners and newer Black homeowners struggling in the face of crippling property tax bills. By the early 1970s, property tax bills on homes in working-class white ethnic neighborhoods like Beverly and racially transitioning neighborhoods like South Shore had nearly doubled in five years. Many white homeowners believed the high taxes were intentional, meant to drive them out so that real estate speculators could profit from Black demand. "Rather than stabilize the community, the assessor is trying to run us out with high taxes," said white South Shore resident Edna Vaughn. "The real estate people are just sitting there waiting for us to abandon our building so they can pick it up for taxes."[19]

These were the city's most racially volatile neighborhoods, where, so often, working-class white ethnics projected their anger at banks and realtors onto the Black families moving in next door. But CAP organizers saw something else, a possible unifying issue. In South Shore, older white property owners and newer Black ones were both getting slammed with taxes, the former being pushed to sell or abandon their homes, the latter struggling to hold onto what they had recently obtained.

The year before, CAP had hired a young economist named Arthur Lyons to investigate whether the assessor's office was undervaluing the properties of major industries and political donors. Now, it wanted to know whether it was also overassessing properties in neighborhoods like Beverly and South Shore. Lyons got to work. He found that both neighborhoods were grossly overassessed, each roughly 33 percent above the official ratio.[20] CAP organizers spread the news across both neighborhoods. Over four hundred Beverly residents packed a school auditorium to discuss the findings and organize the group Fair Assessments for Beverly. In South Shore, a group of white and Black residents formed a new CAP chapter, dedicated "to combat[ting] rising property taxes and declining services." "Taxes," Black member Cecil Howell predicted, could be "an issue on which blacks and whites can unite."[21]

In December 1972, white and Black residents from both neighborhoods marched on the Cook County Assessor's Office. Carrying a black coffin filled with hundreds of tax protest forms, they demanded Cullerton offer them immediate tax relief. Already under siege and facing the prospect of being dropped from the party ticket in the next election, the scandal-plagued assessor quickly complied, issuing certificates of error and assessment reductions for any resident of either neighborhood who applied. CAP declared it "a complete and total victory for the taxpayers." Public outcry also compelled Cook County to adopt a new, computerized system for valuing properties.[22] These changes, county officials insisted, would ensure that all neighborhoods would be taxed fairly in the future. Reflecting on the unlikely racial alliance, CAP chairman Paul Booth exclaimed, "[We] finally hit the mass organizing issue." Tax reform, he predicted, is the issue on which we "can build mass organization."[23]

Black Americans were ready to fight. Tax reform emerged as a major issue at the National Black Political Convention, held in Gary in 1972. The National Black Political Agenda, a product of the convention, called for the elimination of income taxes for low-income families, a 50 percent federal tax on corporate profits, and closure of tax loopholes for upper-bracket taxpayers and corporations.[24] During his insurgent campaign for mayor of Oakland, California, in the spring of 1973, Black Panther Bobby Seale vowed to temporarily freeze property taxes, raise assessment levels on downtown properties and reduce taxes on small businesses, and introduce a 1 percent local tax on privately owned stocks and bonds if elected.[25]

That same year, the Department of Housing and Urban Development (HUD) published a lengthy study of property tax inequities in urban America. In every city studied, it found that properties in the poorest neighborhoods were taxed at the highest effective rates, while those in neighborhoods where property values were high or on the rise were taxed at the lowest. The evidence undercut the standard excuse tax administrators offered for these disparities, that assessments inherently lagged market values. The highest effective tax rates were not in those areas where property values were falling;

they were in those neighborhoods where property values had already bottomed out. This finding suggested something else was going on. Interviews with local tax administrators offered clues. They conceded to being "reluctant to impose full tax burdens on higher income residential property because they knew that the consequence would be to drive households into the suburbs." Presumably, they felt no such reluctance toward poorer residents. Regardless of their motives, the result was the same. "All evidence indicates," the study concluded, "that the poorer neighborhoods of many cities are being forced to subsidize heavily, through tax payments, the special tax concessions granted to residents of upward transitional neighborhoods where revitalization is strongest, capital appreciation most likely, and residents most affluent."[26]

* * *

As director of the National Welfare Rights Organization, George Wiley had organized welfare recipients to demand from agencies all that they were entitled to receive, and nothing less.[27] Now, he aimed to do the same for poor and lower-income taxpayers: to educate them on their rights and provide them with the resources needed to secure the reductions they deserved—not in order to starve the state, but to force it to go after "the real chiselers" at the top and ultimately, to "change the basic tax structure" in America.[28]

The path toward a movement for structural change began, Wiley believed, with addressing people's most immediate needs. As its first initiative, the Movement for Economic Justice partnered with organizers in cities across the country in opening free tax clinics in lower-income neighborhoods. Staffed with trained accountants and tax preparers, these clinics offered for free what for-profit companies did for a fee: help average taxpayers prepare and submit their federal and state tax returns. These clinics also aimed to educate taxpayers on their rights. As Wiley explained, "It is primarily a service, but if properly done, it can be the first step in an organizing strategy to involve low and moderate income people in the struggle against the injustices of the entire system of income and property taxation. . . . The tax clinic will provide an opportunity to talk to people about tax injustice." In a matter of weeks, the MEJ had opened free tax clinics in twenty-two cities.[29]

As organizers in newly formed MEJ chapters were rallying citizens to fight for change, scores of Ralph Nader–inspired public interest groups were uncovering and exposing tax breaks and benefits enjoyed by the wealthy and well-connected. In the summer of 1973, organizers and activists began making plans to gather in Philadelphia in December for the first meeting of the Tax Equity for America (TEA) Party, on the bicentennial of the original Boston Tea Party. A cross-section of groups and organizations representing the interests of poor working people, women, and racial minorities was slated to come: chapters of the NWRO, groups fighting for child care for working families, representatives from various labor unions, groups dedicated to consumer rights and protections, faith-based organizations, tenants' organizations, and civil rights groups. Sessions and workshops would focus on developing strategies for reducing property assessments in low-income neighborhoods and on combatting "the racist burden that taxes impose on Black and poor communities."[30]

The groups gathering for the TEA Party convention embodied Wiley's vision of a "majority making" movement. But he would not be there to see it. Less than six months after launching his initiative, on August 8, 1973, Wiley tragically drowned in a boating accident in the Chesapeake Bay. At the time, Wiley's biographers wrote, "the Movement for Economic Justice was little more than a grand vision."[31]

Tax justice organizers and activists soldiered on. But when they turned to problems with the property tax, movements for tax reform entered into a zero-sum game that racialized tax advantages and undermined efforts at coalition building. In 1975, the group Research Atlanta released a study showing wide disparities in assessment ratios among neighborhoods, with lower-income, predominantly Black neighborhoods assessed at higher rates than higher-income, predominantly white neighborhoods. Following the report's release, the

Figure 11.2 Welfare recipients speak at a tax-reform rally in Chicago, Illinois, May 30, 1974.

NAACP sued the Fulton County Board of Tax Assessors. In response, the county agreed to reassess properties in three of the most under-assessed neighborhoods identified by the study.[32]

White homeowners in the affected neighborhoods went ballistic. Angry phone calls from enraged suburban homeowners rained down on the office of the Joint City-County Board of Tax Assessors. Fulton County superior court judge Phillips McKenzie issued an injunction ordering that the previous assessments remain in place. The NAACP sued to have the injunction lifted. But the following year, superior court judge Joel Fryer sided with the white homeowners, ruling that the county could not reassess some neighborhoods without simultaneously reassessing all property in the county, a practical impossibility. White homeowners' tax advantages were restored. Atlanta NAACP executive director Jondell Johnson said she was "outraged and appalled" by the ruling.[33]

Taxpayers—white and Black—wanted relief. But for African Americans, property tax relief was inseparable from the broader struggle for tax equity and justice. As the decade wore on, though, white taxpayers' frustrations over the persistence of high tax bills mounted, with neither of the major political parties offering any substantive solutions to working families' pocketbook concerns. At the national level, a new generation of post-Watergate Democrats shunned redistributionist politics and instead maintained a singular focus on, and blind faith in, promoting economic growth.[34] Lacking institutional support, growing numbers of white Americans turned away from the hard work of structural reforms that would force the wealthy to shoulder a heavier burden and instead grabbed for tax cuts wherever they could find them. At the same time, they jealously guarded their existing advantages.

In 1978, California voters marked this decisive shift in taxpayer politics in America, from tax justice to tax cuts. Exorbitant and ever-escalating property taxes (the result of an overheated housing market and flaws emerging from the 1967 assessment reforms) led two-thirds of voters to favor a ballot initiative promising immediate relief. Proposition 13 rolled back assessments on all properties, placed strict limits on future assessment and tax-rate increases, and required a two-thirds majority in both legislative chambers for any future tax increases. Supported by a broad cross-section of white homeowners, Prop 13 was written with the interests of the business class in mind. Over half of the total tax relief went to corporations and owners of commercial properties. Black Californians—whether property owners or renters—enjoyed far less relief, while their communities experienced the heaviest cuts to public services. Not coincidentally, African Americans were the only demographic who opposed the measure.[35]

Even as pocketbook concerns, more than racial animus or political ideology, drove many white voters to embrace tax and spending cuts, white supporters of Prop 13 and similar measures in other states ultimately sought to restore racialized tax advantages. Recognizing that less revenue would require local governments to cut or scale back programs or services, they tended to favor cutting those that were perceived as benefitting Blacks: 62 percent of Prop 13 supporters suggested "welfare" and 41 percent named "public housing" for the chopping block. Ronald Reagan and other prominent figures of the New Right actively sought to stigmatize such programs as wasteful and its racially coded recipients as undeserving. As Stanford professor Clayborne Carson remarked followed Prop 13's passage, "such a sweeping change indicates that many property owners—a large proportion of whom live in the suburbs—were less interested in tax and government reform than in declaring their unwillingness to pay for public facilities and services that are needed for central cities." Paul Cobb of the Oakland Citizens Committee for Urban Renewal was more blunt: "Prop 13 was white folks message to us that we are going to have to do it ourselves."[36]

* * *

By the late 1970s, Black taxpayers were indeed on their own. In Chicago, the Citizens' Action Program struggled to build a multi-racial organization. CAP's college-educated, white leadership were, as one member recounted, "simply unprepared to organize poor blacks" and unwilling "to devote the time and resources to making this vision a reality." Struggling in the neighborhoods most adversely affected by the issues it aimed to address, CAP quietly folded in the fall of 1976.[37] The previous year, Arthur Lyons had joined the faculty at the University of Illinois at Chicago Circle, where he taught urban fiscal policy and researched property tax assessment inequities in the city. In 1978, he published a study that showed that the assessment reforms enacted earlier in the decade had failed.[38] Because of how race affected market values, disparities in assessment ratios disproportionately harmed Black neighborhoods. One of the graduate students who assisted Lyons in his research, Toni Mahan, wanted to know more: was race a factor in determining assessment levels, regardless of property value? She wanted to know, in other words, how an assessment for a property in a Black neighborhood with a market value of $50,000 compared to, say, the assessment for a property in a white neighborhood with the exact same market value. Along with four of her peers, Mahan set out to answer that question.

With Lyons supervising, the team focused on six predominantly Black and six predominantly white neighborhoods across Cook County, all carefully chosen. Included among the white neighborhoods was Bridgeport, the nucleus of the late Mayor Richard J. Daley's political machine, "because," as Lyons put it, "that was where all the politicians lived [and] was notorious." They selected Marquette Park (white) and West Englewood (Black) because they were adjacent to each other, had relatively similar housing stock, and had been the site of extreme racial tension over blockbusting and Black attempts to breach color lines. The team began pulling assessment records and comparing them to home sale prices. The work was tedious, time consuming, and endlessly frustrating. Staffers in the assessor's office were "openly hostile" to the researchers. They refused to accommodate large data requests and instead made them "go through the process that any individual would have to go through to get information on their property." That meant no more than ten records requests per day, even if (as often was the case), five of those records came up missing. It meant that researchers "had to stand at the counter, literally stand at a counter" all day placing requests and transcribing information by hand.[39] In total, the students spent over 1,250 hours comparing assessments and home sale prices for nearly four thousand properties.[40]

Then they ran the numbers. They discovered that, almost without exception, properties in Black neighborhoods were assessed higher than similar properties in white neighborhoods. They found that, in some cases, homes in Black neighborhoods paid three times the amount in property taxes as comparably valued homes in white neighborhoods. And, while poorer white neighborhoods were overtaxed relative to middle- and upper-middle-class white neighborhoods, they were all under-taxed compared to Black neighborhoods. The annual property tax bill for a $20,000 home in Black North Lawndale, for example, was $411 higher than the bill for a $20,000 home in white Bridgeport. A $50,000 home in increasingly Black South Shore paid $295 more in taxes than a home worth the same amount in white Portage Park. "We expected a hint of it," Mahan remarked, "but this is a lot more than a hint."[41]

Lyons asked the assessor's office to respond to their findings. A staff member curtly responded, "No, there can't be a problem. There's

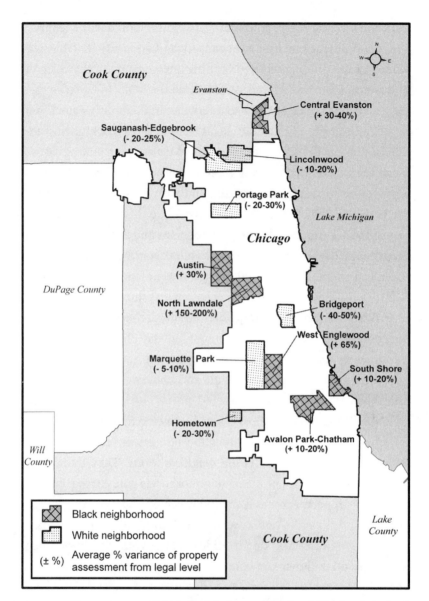

Figure 11.3 The percentage of deviation of white and Black neighborhoods in Cook County, Illinois, from the county's official assessment ratio, as found in "Relative Tax Burdens in Black and White Neighborhoods of Cook County," the 1979 study conducted by a team of graduate students under the supervision of Arthur Lyons at the University of Illinois at Chicago Circle's School of Urban Sciences.

nothing racist [about our assessments]. We're not interested [in your study]." Lyons asked, "Do you want to look [at it], let me come in and present?" "No, we don't. We're not interested in looking at some student report." And hung up.[42] Lyons shared the findings with *Chicago Tribune* reporter Ed McManus. After poring over the data and verifying their accuracy, in April 1979 the paper published the study's findings on the front page of a Sunday edition: "Property tax rate higher in black areas, study says."[43]

For many Black Chicagoans, the study offered proof of what they already knew. "We were not totally shocked to hear this," state senator Harold Washington told reporters. "It's something that's been known on the South and West sides for a long time." "The black community . . . has long suspected that we pay a color tax for our property," Evanston alderman Edna Summers commented. "I've known for a long time that blacks get the short end of both sticks," NAACP South Side chapter president Frank Williams added.[44] But whereas numerous recent studies in Chicago and other cities had offered definitive proof that property tax assessments were regressive, with lower-valued properties taxed at higher rates than higher-valued ones, this was the first study to show that they were racist.

South Side community organizer Arvis Averette immediately sensed the report's explosiveness. Black neighborhoods were suffering the worst effects of the city's deindustrialization and the nationwide economic downturn. "Inflation was double digits. Everything was out of whack. The economy [on the South and West sides] was horrible," Averette recalled. The vast majority of Black homeowners in Averette's South Shore neighborhood had owned their homes for less than five years. Imagine this: "You just bought this overpriced house" that you are struggling to pay the mortgage on because "prices are going out the window." Because of the enduring color line, Black people's homes did not appreciate in value like white houses in the suburbs did. And now "we find out they're cheating us [on our taxes]."[45]

Averette began to spread the word. He printed out thousands of copies of the study and spread them across Black neighborhoods.

Within days, "all the Black community was incensed." "Everybody was circulating them," Averette recalled. "And walking around like it was a newspaper, [saying to each other] 'See? I told you so,' [and] 'Look at this. This is terrible.' . . . 'All these other things are happening [to us and] now they gonna charge us more?!?' . . . There was so much outrage."[46]

Harold Washington also sensed an opportunity to bridge long-standing divisions that had undermined Black political power in the city and to topple its weakened political machine. In 1972, Congressman Ralph Metcalfe, a loyal Daley lieutenant and anointed successor to William Dawson as "boss" of its Black sub-machine, famously broke ranks with the mayor over his indifference to police brutality. Deadpanning that "it is never too late to be black," Metcalfe held Congressional hearings on the criminal actions of Chicago's police force, became a "persistent thorn" in Daley's side right up until the mayor's death in 1976, and helped to launch what the Black *Tribune* columnist Vernon Jarret called a "plantation revolt" in Black Chicago politics.[47] Washington was among those leading the charge off the plantation. By the early 1970s, he had emerged as an independent and uncompromising voice for civil rights and a champion of progressive causes in Springfield. As a legislator, Washington took a special interest in combatting financial predation against Black and low-income communities, introducing bills that targeted some of the exploitative practices that haunted his Black constituents.[48]

As a rising Black politician with his eyes set on City Hall, Washington saw the implications of the study's findings for bridging class and geographical divisions that had long stymied broad-based Black political mobilization in the city. Weeks after the study's release, over one hundred people from eleven community groups protested outside the Cook County Assessor's Office, where Washington called on the governor to order a reassessment of the county's Black neighborhoods.[49] In June, Averette, Washington, and a group of Black lawmakers announced the formation of the Black Taxpayers' Federation (BTF), an umbrella organization that aimed to educate and empower Black Chicagoans to fight for equitable taxation. The group chose

Washington as its chairperson and Averette as its executive director. "Black taxpayers in Cook County," Washington told reporters,
"have lost tens of millions of dollars through discriminatory taxes.
We intend to stop this practice." The BTF would embed itself into
the existing fabric of neighborhood organizations and incorporate
taxpayer issues into group agendas. The BTF "didn't do the typical
organizing where we got the people together and we marched and so
forth," Averette explained. "We went to existing structures and [tried
to get the BTF placed] on their agenda [and make taxpayer issues and
organizing] a part of what they were going to do. . . . We were like a
holding company."[50]

Throughout the spring and summer, the BTF held workshops in
Black churches and before block clubs and other groups across the
city. Lyons accompanied them. Standing before a blackboard or a
rolled-out sheet of butcher paper, the soft-spoken professor explained
how property taxes worked, how Black neighborhoods were being
unfairly taxed, and why it mattered. "I would always come and try
to explain the system, and the broader issues and how the property
tax is important [and why] we need to fix" it, Lyons recalled. Lyons
worked to dispel many of the myths and misconceptions surrounding property taxes. He made a point of drawing taxpayers' attention
away from the tax rate—which many erroneously assumed was the
source of their high tax bills—and toward the assessment. "We['d]
develop the whole presentation around that, how we have to be aware
of the relative assessments." To do that, Lyons would compare two
homes, showing how a decrease in the assessment on one increased
the tax bill on the other, even if its assessment remained the same.
"Just keep it simple," as Lyons put it. "And once people got that," he
expanded it out to the neighborhood level. At that point, audiences
understood, "I do have to be concerned about my assessment, and
not just my assessment here in [Black] Chatham, but criminy sakes,
I have to worry about [white] Sauganash, because if they're too low
up in Sauganash, then I'm paying more, even if I'm exactly right in
Chatham."[51] Averette marveled at Lyons's ability to make taxation

Figure 11.4 Arthur Lyons at the blackboard conducting a tutorial on property tax assessments to residents of West Englewood at an informational session organized by the Black Taxpayers' Federation (BTF) in May 1979. Illinois state senator and BTF founder Harold Washington watches. *Chicago Defender*, May 10, 1979.

and public finance "user friendly," in ways that "the common person could look at it and understand."[52]

On Sundays, BTF organizers sat in the pews of Black congregations, waiting for services to end. Averette recalled, "We'd [schedule] a one o'clock [meeting] right after the services and we would come and make a presentation." On weeknights, they sat through interminable block-club meetings, waiting patiently while residents aired complaints and concerns and discussed various plans. "And then we [got up there and] talk[ed] about taxation." Attendees never expressed any surprise at being overtaxed. "Nobody said, 'really? We are being cheated?'" Instead, they "wanted to know how they were doing it." And as the speakers explained, "They would sit there, saying, 'oh my God' and they'd get angry because now they could see for the first time what they've known the whole time." Then, BTF organizers walked audiences through the steps for filing an appeal.

Within months, the county's Board of Tax Appeals found itself inundated with thousands of appeals from homeowners in Black neighborhoods. In addition to securing tax reductions for individuals, the unprecedented volume of appeals from areas of the city where assessments had long gone uncontested forced the assessor's office to readjust valuations across entire neighborhoods. The office reduced assessments on residential properties in the Woodlawn neighborhood by 50 percent. It also empowered countless numbers of Black citizens. "When they won, when they got [their taxes] lowered," they felt as if systemic change was possible. They began to ask, "What else can we do?" They began to scrutinize other taxes that disproportionately overburdened the poor. They began to ask, for instance, "why . . . we have a tax on food and medicine" in Illinois. They began to question the entire system of taxation.[53]

With Washington at its helm, the BTF also worked to break down long-standing tensions between working-class neighborhoods on the West Side and the more established, middle-class Black communities on the South Side. For years, divisions among Black Chicagoans had limited their ability to build political power. South Side Black neighborhoods looked down on the poorer residents on the West Side, while the latter eyed the Black establishment on the South Side with distrust. The city's political machine had actively worked to cultivate these tensions and keep Black Chicagoans internally divided. That the Black tax study revealed that both affluent and poor Black neighborhoods, both the West and the South Side, suffered from overtaxation made it, in Washington's mind, a catalyst for building Black political power.

Washington played a central role in shaping BTF's political and legal strategies. In Springfield, Washington implored fellow state lawmakers to take action. "We, in my community, have been ripped to the tune of tens of millions of dollars," he said. He called on US attorney Thomas Sullivan to launch an investigation into possible civil rights violations by the assessor's office, proposed that the Department of Local Government Affairs investigate and hold hearings, and co-sponsored a Senate bill that would give the state the authority to order, supervise, and direct a countywide reassessment if it determined that assessments did not comply with state law. "The beauty of [having] Harold Washington [involved]," Averette remarked, "was that he was a member of the Democratic Party." He "knew the inner workings of the machine."

Washington also knew the source of white lawmakers' reluctance to act. During one floor debate, Washington acknowledged the zero-sum nature of property assessments, and that the heavy burden imposed on Blacks ultimately served to lower taxes for whites. To a colleague's comment that his bill threatened to raise taxes on other homeowners, Washington responded, "All you're saying is that you've been unjustly enriched with our money, and you don't want to put it back. . . . In plain simple English[,] if your taxes are lower, because mine are higher, then you are unjustly enriched. I don't expect you to give it up willingly, no I expect you to go kicking, screaming and yelling, into the twentieth century, but you're going there one way or the other."[54]

In August, over three hundred protesters gathered in Daley Plaza for a rally, where they delivered a list of nine demands to Hynes's office.[55] Under pressure, Hynes agreed to form a commission to investigate racial bias in property assessments. He named Leon Finney, an African American community organizer-turned-businessman and Democratic Party insider, as the chairman. Loyola law professor Richard Michael was placed in charge of the investigation. BTF leaders scoffed at Finney, given his extensive real estate holdings, which posed a glaring conflict of interest, and knew that a whitewash was in the works. And indeed, six months later the commission found "no evidence of racial discrimination" in the assessment process. Whatever racial disparities Lyons's students found were, it concluded, due to "bugs" in the system. Finney stated unequivocally that there was "no discrimination against black homeowners." The following day, the front page of the *Chicago Sun-Times* read, "No Racial Bias in Tax Process." Press coverage carried pictures of Finney, supplying all the ammunition the assessor's office, and for that matter, most white taxpayers, needed to dismiss Black taxpayers' charges. Hynes and his staffers trashed Lyons as a "rabble-rouser" and "activist" academic and dismissed the study as a frivolous student paper.[56]

Few in the media, of course, bothered to read the report written by

Michael and endorsed by Finney. But Lyons did, and he was amazed at its crass cynicism. He searched in vain for any evidence to support their conclusions or refute his students' findings. Incredibly, the commission "never looked at any actual assessments." Instead, it generated hypothetical assessments on a handful of properties in white and Black neighborhoods chosen by staffers in the assessor's office. In essence, as Lyons described, the investigators said, "Okay, assessor, what would you assess these properties at if you were doing an assessment?" Staff members, knowing full well the purpose of the exercise, generated figures that, "lo and behold, c[ame] out similar in the white and Black neighborhoods." Were they his students, Lyons would have flunked the commission for its shoddy methodology.[57]

Instead, Lyons and the BTF were forced to call out the fraudulence of the report to a press that had already started treating the Black tax issue as a "he said, she said" debate. The assessor's office's report, Lyons told reporters, "does not in any way whatsoever address the problem of differences in actual assessment levels." It "contains not one single shard of evidence which in any way calls into question, or can call into question, our finding that homes in black neighborhoods are actually assessed higher than homes in white neighborhoods." Said Washington, of the report: "I reject it totally. . . . [It's] a phony. It does not deal with the questions Lyons raises." He called out Hynes's cynical enlistment of Finney as the face of the report. And he questioned Finney's own ability to remain objective, given his "extensive real estate holdings subject to assessment by Mr. Hynes' office." But the assessor's office knew that the whitewash had worked.[58]

It worked, in part, because the white majority in Cook County was in no mood to fix structurally racist features of tax administration from which they ultimately benefitted. Black Chicagoans' revolt against inequitable tax assessments came in the midst of white homeowners' own tax revolt. As the county reassessed properties following reforms earlier in the decade—including a confusing and ultimately ineffective formula meant to equalize county contributions to state educational funds—many suburban white homeowners saw their tax bills soar. So, too, did owners of older properties in upper-income, exclusive neighborhoods that had benefitted from the previous assessment model. On Chicago's North Shore, white homeowners formed taxpayers' groups with the Gadsden flag's coiled snake and slogan, "Don't tread on me," adorning their letterhead. At meetings, angry homeowners likened their condition to living under fascism. "This is a Nazi method, not an American one," one protester yelled. Following California voters' passage of Prop 13, Illinois's Republican governor James Thompson placed a non-binding referendum on the 1978 ballot to cap state and local tax increases. It received the support of 82 percent of voters. As Harold Washington struggled to find co-sponsors for his bill to tackle uneven assessments, 80 members of the state's general assembly joined a newly formed Tax Limitation Committee and introduced an amendment to the state's constitution that would limit property tax increases and state revenues. That, in practice, would lock in assessment inequities and exacerbate them over time.[59] It was a sign of things to come.

* * *

The age of revolts grew out of widespread unrest over a tax system that punished the poor, rewarded the wealthy, and left those in the middle gasping for air and fearing for their future. Middle- and lower-income whites and Blacks alike shared a belief that the system—especially the property tax—was broken. The moment was ripe, in ways never seen before or since, for structural change. But when those changes failed to materialize—when the hard work of overhauling a fragmented fiscal system proved too much for the most visionary reformer to fathom—white voters embraced across-the-board tax cuts in the hope that some of their benefits would eventually trickle down to them. They resisted race-conscious corrections to tax inequities that, in the zero-sum game of local property taxation, would shift the burden onto them.

When he first began to study and speak out against property tax inequalities in the early 1970s, Art Lyons believed in the power of taxpayer politics to bring disparate and adversarial groups together and allow them to see common interests. "I thought that if I could get them thinking of themselves as taxpayers, then then they would see what they're putting into the system, their responsibility for that system and responsibility for making it work."[60] He was not alone. During the early 1970s, left-leaning and progressive groups employed the language of taxpayer citizenship and taxpayer rights to demand that the wealthy pay their fair share in supporting the social programs and public services necessary for building a more equal society. They also used inequities in local tax burdens to highlight the ties that bound whites and Blacks together in a shared fight.

What Lyons and others failed to account for, and what the Right would deftly exploit, was the possibility that white taxpayers' frustrations could lead them to reject the social compact entirely and embrace tax cuts, rather than tax redistribution, as their salvation. In the years to come, this choice turned Blacks' struggle for tax justice into a defensive battle against an austere and increasingly predatory local state.

12

HORROR STORIES

David Balin entered into the family business at the ground level. Each fall, the Cook County Treasurer's Office published a list of every tax-delinquent parcel in the county. "So, I would get this list of ten thousand properties," Balin recalled, "and drive out and look at the properties." Balin's uncle, Gilbert Balin, who ran the family's tax-buying operation, wanted to know "whether or not there was a building [on the lot], whether or not [it was] vacant." He also wanted to know if there was a home on the lot and, best of all, a person living inside.[1]

Balin spent most of his time driving the streets of Chicago's south and west sides, where in the 1970s tax-delinquency rates had soared. Most of the parcels were vacant and abandoned—some smoldering shells, burned down for insurance—whose owners had stopped paying taxes years earlier, and who had no intention of doing so again. These, Balin immediately crossed off. But amid the detritus from decades of predation and extraction, Balin might find a single-family home with flowers planted in the front yard and a car in the driveway. Or a three-story walk-up with kids playing on the front stoop. Or a storefront housing a small, struggling, family-owned business. These were the ones Balin's uncle, like all of the city's other professional tax buyers, placed stars next to on the lists they brought to the tax sale the following spring. It was these owners' hardships that provided the source of their profits.

Rising tax bills, made all the more burdensome by the higher effective tax rates imposed on their neighborhoods by racist assessments, compounded the financial distress many Black homeowners in cities like Chicago experienced in the 1970s. Each year, many of them missed a tax payment. Many of those who fell delinquent were elderly and on fixed incomes, or were experiencing a medical issue, or had recently lost their job or income, or suffered the death of a family breadwinner or bill-payer. Most had paid too much for their home but had already sunk so much into it they feared the consequences of missing a monthly mortgage payment, or sending their children to bed hungry, more than they feared the consequences of falling behind on their taxes. Many had to make tough, impossible, choices like these every day. Many didn't know the devastating consequences of tax delinquency until it was too late. In this and other severely disinvested urban housing markets, the people most likely to fall delinquent on their property taxes were also less likely to be able to quickly settle their debts with a loan from a bank or family member. They were also less likely to have a clear understanding of their legal rights, less capable of hiring a lawyer, and more susceptible to deception and intimidation. And the longer it took them to pay their delinquent taxes, the more it cost to redeem their property, and the greater the likelihood they would miss the final deadline and lose their home altogether. For these reasons and more, urban Black neighborhoods supplied not only greater volume for tax buyers but greater return on their investments.

But as tax buyers amassed fortunes exploiting people's mistakes and hardships, some Black victims of predatory tax buying fought back. In Chicago, that fight commenced when, in 1969, Louis and Doretta Balthazar decided not to quietly comply with tax buyer Allan Blair's demands. He wanted them to give up the deed to the three-flat apartment building they owned on the West Side and begin paying him rent for *their* property. Instead, they sought out legal counsel. That decision led to the filing of a federal lawsuit challenging the constitutionality of the entire tax-buying enterprise as practiced in Illinois and other states. It brought the business of tax buying out into the open and subjected its practitioners to unprecedented public outrage and opprobrium. Throughout the decade, activist and public-interest attorneys, lawmakers, muckraking journalists, community organizations, and appalled individuals attacked the machinery of tax buying and worked to defend those who had been caught in its grasp. Invariably, it was hearing one of the litany of horror stories of homeowners—often poor and elderly, disproportionately Black—facing the threat of being evicted, being stripped of their wealth and dignity, or being forced to buy or rent their property back that spurred them to action.

Yet no matter how disreputable the business of tax buying became, wherever demands for reforms arose, whenever public outcry reached a fevered pitch, tax buyers always had an ace in the hole. Their ruthless pursuit of profits, they insisted, kept *all* taxpayers in compliance, and kept revenues pouring into local coffers. In a literal sense, tax buyers paid other people's tax bills and removed properties from the tax-delinquency list. They were performing a public service. Governments and taxpayers *needed* them. Without these extreme consequences in place, they warned, tax delinquency would spread like a cancer. Without the high interest rates and opportunities for windfall profits that tax sales offered, tax buyers would invest elsewhere. Without their capital, municipal and public school budgets would suffer, and everyone's tax bills would go up. And besides, people actually losing their home to tax delinquency was rare and never tax buyers' intention. Or so they claimed.

When they weren't searching for new veins to extract wealth from poorer neighborhoods, tax buyers worked to embed themselves in the machinery of tax enforcement. They made their financial interests synonymous with those of local governments. The horror stories told by tax-sale victims aroused the compassion and indignation of the public and led to outpourings of support. But the biggest challenge reformers faced was local governments' belief that their solvency depended on predation.

* * *

By 1968, Allan Blair had built a small fortune through his partnership with Interstate Bond Company and had become Chicago's leading tax buyer. Like the contract sellers and slumlords he worked with and sold his properties to, he remained in constant search of ways to squeeze more profits from Black neighborhoods. With the passage of the HUD Act that year, which vastly expanded the availability of federal mortgage insurance in poor Black urban areas, he applied for a line of credit to open his own mortgage-banking firm.[2] The future could not have been brighter.

But as Louis and Doretta Balthazar sat in Blair's well-appointed downtown office in March 1969, they smelled something rotten. As Blair explained the arrangement—if Balthazar would agree not to contest Blair's tax deed to his home, he could remain there at a reduced rent if he agreed to manage the other units and collect rent for Blair—Balthazar kept shaking his head and asking if there was some other way. He didn't understand how he could lose a property he had invested over $16,000 in just over a single missed tax bill. Blair eventually gave him the phone number and address of the Chicago Bar Association (CBA). "You go over there and talk to some lawyers," Blair advised, confident that Balthazar would then learn, in no uncertain terms, that there was nothing he could do except comply.

After they left Blair, Louis said to Doretta, "There is something wrong. This doesn't sound right." Louis wanted to pay the taxes he owed, but with what Blair was proposing, there was no end in sight. "This will go on forever," he exclaimed.

"Well, what are you going to do?" Doretta asked. Louis resolved to "find out really what was happening."[3]

The Balthazars contacted the CBA, which referred them to Marshall Patner, a staff attorney at the public interest, research, and legal watchdog organization Businessmen for the Professional Interest (BPI).[4] The year before, Patner had represented pro bono a retired African American factory worker, William Parks. Blair had acquired a tax deed to Parks's South Side home. At trial, Patner compelled Blair to give a sworn deposition in which he revealed his professional procedures.[5] Patner was horrified. Further, he argued that Blair's deceptive tactics rendered the deed void. The jury upheld Blair's deed, though, and Parks was forced to buy his home back from him for $13,000 on an installment contract. The experience left Patner shaken and disgusted. It revealed to him, as he wrote, that "the law was the oppressor."[6] Patner resolved to defend victims of predatory tax buying and challenge Illinois's tax-sale law. Soon after, he reached out to the CBA's Legal Aid division and volunteered to take all tax-deed cases that came their way.[7]

Meeting with the Balthazars that spring, Patner explained what, exactly, the couple had agreed to when they signed those papers in Blair's office. Shocked and dismayed, the Balthazars decided they would try to renegotiate with Blair. But Blair made it clear that he would only negotiate over the cost to buy the building back. Paying the taxes owed, plus interest and fees, was no longer an option. The property was now his. And to prove it, Blair told the couple that he would evict them on Saturday, April 26. "He told me that I no longer had a place to live."[8] At the time, the Balthazars had nine children between the ages of seventeen and one.

Having previously battled with Blair, Patner knew that Blair's petition for deed was, under state law, airtight. The Balthazars' only hope was to challenge the law itself in federal court. And so, on Friday, April 25, with eviction imminent, the Balthazars became the named plaintiffs in a class-action federal lawsuit challenging the constitutionality of Illinois's tax-sale law. The suit singled out Illinois's lack of any provision for former owners to recover the equity from their property. Selling it for taxes and awarding the "surplus value" (the market value minus outstanding debts) to a real estate speculator had "no rational connection to a legitimate governmental purpose," the suit argued. Therefore, the practice was a violation of due process and just compensation as required under the US Constitution's Fourteenth and Fifth Amendments.[9] Ten days later, US District Judge Bernard M. Decker issued a restraining order preventing Blair from carrying out eviction. He also agreed to convene a three-judge panel to determine the constitutionality of the tax-sale law.[10]

What Patner and other critics saw as so abusive about Illinois's tax-sale law was not just that it allowed for the loss of equity when a property owner failed to redeem. There were several states that allowed local governments to auction tax-delinquent property at public sales and pocket some or all of the proceeds. But these sales came only after a long redemption period and were coupled with moderate interest rates. There were many states that allowed private investors to purchase and earn interest from others' tax debts, but if the property remained unredeemed it was sold at a public sale—like a mortgage or equity foreclosure—with the net proceeds going to the former owner. Similarly, some states ordered local governments to sell the deed at a public auction but then gave the owner one last opportunity to redeem; if they failed to do so, owners still received the net proceeds. These arrangements rarely resulted in former owners receiving anything close to the full value of their properties, but they offered some narrow measure of restitution.

But Illinois, along with a handful of other states, offered the worst of both worlds. It unleashed private investors who sought only the profits from outrageous interest rates and fees, *and* it automatically granted free and clear ownership to those same predators if the property owner failed to redeem in time.

To Patner, Allan Blair personified this predatory system, and his victims embodied its costs. As he prepared his case, he made sure the public came to know who Blair was and how he made his living. He began feeding stories about Blair's tax-buying operation to news reporters and columnists, none more prominent than *Chicago Daily News* columnist Mike Royko. Beginning that spring and continuing for the next several years, Royko told readers about how Blair amassed a fortune by preying on the city's most vulnerable. People like Wilhelmina Schutty, an elderly recluse who owned a two-flat two blocks from the Maxwell Street market, who had accumulated $893 in back taxes. Blair had acquired a tax deed to Schutty's property and was trying to sell it back to her for $7,500. And people like Bob Rosborough, a man suffering from schizophrenia who had failed to pay $1,200 in taxes. When he refused to pay $12,000 to buy his house back, Blair had him evicted. Rosborough, Royko wrote, now lived in a seedy motel on North Clark Street. In contrast, Royko detailed, Blair and his wife lived in a luxurious apartment on Lake Shore Drive and regularly rubbed shoulders with the city's most prominent socialites.[11] More damning, Royko told of Blair's high standing in Chicago's legal community—he was the chairman of the CBA's ethics committee, no less!—and how he and other tax lawyers and tax-buying specialists wrote the law from which they were now profiting.[12]

As he brought readers' blood to a boil, Royko also explained, in plain English, how Illinois's tax-sale law worked. Echoing the argument Patner planned to make in court, Royko explained how the law allowed tax buyers to claim ownership of a home for the cost of a single tax bill, leaving the delinquent taxpayer with nothing. This allowance, Royko stressed, was not a mere hypothetical. Indeed, "men like Blair have become rich doing it."[13]

Royko's columns brought the shadowy world of tax buying into the open as never before, and soon other reporters were scrambling to find more of Blair's victims. A reporter for the *Sun-Times* covered Blair's eviction of Veronica Micetich, an eighty-three-year-old widow from Yugoslavia, from her home in West Englewood. Micetich had failed to pay the property taxes following her husband's death and failed to respond to Blair's letters after he obtained the deed. When the sheriff arrived to evict her, one neighbor said, Micetich ran "out in the backyard screaming . . . 'Save my house, save my house.'" When her son frantically arrived moments later, Blair quoted him the cost to buy it back. Unable to pay it, the mother and son begged Blair to allow them to rent it back until they could properly move out. He agreed and charged them $500 in rent and $500 for the eviction costs.[14] Other reporters dug into the tax-deed petitions filed in the Circuit Court and found that Blair's law firm was filing upwards of fifty of them each month, more than half the total.[15]

All told, over sixty stories on Blair and other tax buyers' activities appeared in Chicago newspapers for thirty-five consecutive days in the spring of 1969. As they did, letters poured into Royko's office and area newsrooms from tax buyers' victims. "My home was completely taken away from me," one widow wrote. "They came out to my house. Furniture and all out on the sidewalk in the rain and snow." Some struggled to understand what had happened to them, and what they

Mike Royko

Allan Blair

strikes again!

When times were hard, and Carlee Robinson was a young man with a strong back, he dug ditches in Tennessee for $15 a week, and he was glad to get it.

Now he is 53 and he's doing better. He works for a tire company in Freeport and every Friday he takes home $116.

That's not a lot of money, but Carlee and his wife Beatrice are very careful with a dollar.

So, over the years, they have managed to acquire the one thing most working men can point to as material wealth. A house.

It wasn't much when they bought it 10 years ago in Lockport for $4,700. Frame, six creaking rooms, worn out wiring. But Carlee is handy. They've put in good hardwood floors, made repairs, painted, carpeted. The back yard has a pleasant garden.

Figure 12.1 One of several columns written between 1969 and 1974 by the syndicated columnist Mike Royko on the practices of Chicago tax buyer Allan Blair and his victims. *Chicago Daily News*, February 27, 1973.

could do. One asked Royko, "Is there anything I can do to get my house back?"

Lawmakers were similarly inundated. State senator Richard Newhouse, who represented a heavily Black district on the South Side, said his office heard numerous "horror stories" from constituents who had lost, or nearly lost, their homes to tax buyers. "Half the lawyers I see on LaSalle Street," he added, "also have similar stories to tell."[16] The CBA pressured Blair to resign as ethics committee chairman and announced that it had opened an investigation into his conduct. Weeks later, the CBA announced that Blair had "acted within existing laws in the conduct of his tax business" and committed "no violation" of the profession's "code of ethics." When a reporter asked CBA president John L. Sullivan if Blair had violated a more general human code of ethics, Sullivan responded, "No comment."[17]

The following month, the federal district court of northern Illinois convened a three-judge panel to hear arguments in *Balthazar v. Mari, Ltd.* Patner's case for overturning the law rested on its lack of a procedure for providing the former owner the remaining proceeds of a forced sale. This, he argued, "constitute[d] a deprivation of property without due process of law and without just compensation" as required by the Fifth and Fourteenth Amendments of the US Constitution.[18] The defense countered that the two-year redemption period afforded delinquent taxpayers time to sell their property and recover its equity; therefore, there was no unconstitutional taking.[19] Patner tried to steer the court back toward reality by pointing to his client's circumstances. "Being black, and without advice or credit," he argued, "Mr. Balthazar was not able to sell his property to pay his taxes, or to redeem his property." The defendants, Patner added, produced no evidence that Balthazar "was even able to sell" his property during the two-year window, and there was considerable evidence that the law's statutory notifications did more to confuse Balthazar than inform him of his impending loss. Even if Balthazar had fully understood the law and the consequences of nonpayment, Patner argued, the penalty far exceeded the crime. Patner likened the situation to "sentenc[ing] a man to death for stealing a loaf of bread as long as the man was given adequate procedural safeguards."

Ultimately, the court deemed such an outcome acceptable, upholding Illinois's tax-sale law on the grounds that the two-year redemption period afforded delinquent taxpayers the opportunity to recover their equity. (The US Supreme Court upheld this decision on appeal.) The three-judge panel condemned Illinois's tax-sale law as exceedingly harsh but concluded that "oppressive statutes must be tempered by the legislature, not the courts."[20]

But Illinois's legislature, like many others, was littered with lawmakers with personal and professional relationships with tax buyers and their lobbyists. Attorneys like Interstate Bond Company's general counsel Robert Cushman were already working to quell any talk of an overhaul to the state's Revenue Act when the state constitutional convention convened in 1970.[21] After the *Balthazar* decision, South Side state senator Richard Newhouse drafted a bill that would require that unredeemed properties be sold at a public auction, with the net proceeds awarded to the former owner. In the State House, Representative Harold Washington introduced a similar bill.[22] The State Senate Judiciary Committee held hearings on the tax-sale law. They heard testimony for several of Blair's victims, including Louis Balthazar and William Parks, as well as legal experts and advocates for the poor, who called the present law a "horror" that made it "too easy for the uneducated and the incompetent to lose their property without getting their day in court."[23]

But lobbyists for the tax-lien industry furiously counterattacked. Cushman told lawmakers that the statutory notifications and protections offered more than enough security. He assured lawmakers that only "the dumb and dim-witted" could ever lose their homes to tax delinquency. Cook County Circuit Court judge Robert J. Dempsey said the current law wasn't tough enough and argued for "a harsher law" that would bring more finality to tax-deed proceedings. Maurice Scott, head of the Taxpayers Federation of Illinois, stoked fears of possible repercussions from Newhouse's bill, arguing in the *Chicago Tribune* that by removing the prospect of windfall profits, the reform threatened to depress turnout at county tax sales and would ultimately result in more properties remaining delinquent. Without harsh laws, Scott argued, taxpayers would shirk their obligations "and 'good old John Doe Taxpayer' would pay more than his share." Neither bill made it out of committee. The following year, Illinois's tax-sale law emerged from the overhaul of the state's constitution unscathed. The only reform to emerge was a bill passed in 1970 that required counties to create an indemnity fund to compensate victims of tax foreclosures who could prove that they were "without fault or negligence," supported by a fee attached to every tax-lien certificate purchase.

The Balthazars, meanwhile, were forced to buy their three-flat apartment back from Blair for $7,000.[24]

* * *

Blair got his money, and the state's tax buyers had successfully fended off threats from lawmakers. But the rest of Blair's plans were in tatters. The bank that was backing Blair's plan for a mortgage-banking firm pulled out, citing "newspaper stories." He lost several clients. His nomination to the board of directors of one of the city's largest, most prominent charities was withdrawn, as was his nomination as vice chairman of the Chicago Bar Association's state and municipal tax committee. The Union League Club asked that he withdraw his application for membership. His and his wife's application to join a Lake Shore Drive co-op was rejected because the members deemed Blair "too controversial." The prospects of a judgeship, or an invitation to teach at a prestigious law school, went out the window.[25]

But while the press coverage of his exploits made Blair a pariah among Chicago high society, it only enhanced his reputation and standing among the slumlords, contract sellers, and other real estate speculators with whom he did business. Up-and-comers looking to break into the business and old hands in search of the latest scheme sought out his expertise. Where others saw unconscionable predation, they saw savvy investing.

Like the business of slumlording and contract selling, tax buying was a world of masters and apprentices, teachers and proteges. Experienced tax buyers found business partners with whom they shared their secrets and strategies. In 1967, a young real estate attorney named David R. Gray caught Blair's attention after purchasing nearly half the properties sold at a county sheriff's auction. Gray, Blair learned, was trading on insider knowledge to acquire properties near future highway and urban-renewal sites, speculating on future condemnation payouts. Impressed, Blair took him under his wing.[26]

Tax buying was also often a family business. Tax buyers sent their wives and daughters downtown to pull court records and tax filings. Sons got their first taste of the trade when they were handed a list of addresses and sent out to inspect their condition. David Gray groomed his sons, Timothy and David Jr., in the trade. "I attended my first auction when I was a teenager," Timothy recalled, "and was instantly hooked."[27] Inside the tax sale, it was rare to see an unfamiliar face. "It was a good old boys club. We all knew each other. We all knew who all the players were," David Balin said of the tax sales he attended with his uncle. And they all knew the rules of the game and ruthlessly took advantage of those who didn't. As Timothy Gray described, during a tax sale, "there is no such thing as an intelligent question. You either know what you are doing or not, and any sign of weakness will be used against you."[28]

Tax buying could also be a dangerous business. Taking people's homes, even if under the color of law, carried inherent risks. John Rasch worked for his father, Howard Rasch, one of the largest tax buyers in Wayne County, Michigan, in the early 1960s. After foreclosing on a tax-delinquent home owned by sixty-one-year-old Claire Hammond in the Detroit suburb of Ferndale in 1963, Howard Rasch dispatched his son to the property to inform Hammond that the house he had owned for decades was no longer his, and that to remain in it, he would need to begin paying his father monthly rent. A distraught Hammond listened in disbelief, then grabbed his 12-gauge shotgun and shot and killed Rasch on his front porch.[29] Along with fear, some people tasked with carrying out evictions felt guilt and shame. After he had graduated from inspecting properties to carrying out evictions, David Balin decided to get out of the family business and pursue a career in education, where, as he put it, he could "help people . . . instead of taking [advantage of] people." Despite the riches he earned acquiring properties sometimes worth tens of thousands of dollars for as little as $50, Detroit real estate broker Robert Davis got out of the tax buying business because "[I] began to have a problem looking at my face in the mirror every morning."[30] To succeed in tax buying, it was best not to dwell on the nature of one's earnings or its collateral effects.

By the late 1960s, Chicago's major slumlords were extracting the last bits of profit from their holdings. Decades of packing as many families into aged buildings as they could and neglecting repairs had taken their toll on the housing stock of Chicago's Black ghettos. And increased code enforcement by the city's buildings department, payment and rent strikes by contract buyers and tenants, and the looming threat of lawsuits from both threatened their bottom line. Chicago's slumlords and real estate speculators were, by 1968, in search of an off-ramp and a new hustle.

A new federal program designed to facilitate homeownership among low-income urban minorities offered one. The 1968 HUD Act made FHA-insured mortgages available to low-income Black homeseekers in severely depressed urban areas. This program provided Blair and other real estate speculators an opportunity to unload crumbling, dilapidated properties onto a new raft of buyers. Contract sellers partnered with corrupt appraisers to inflate the value of properties that were often unfit for habitation. They also colluded with mortgage brokers to falsify loan applications for the mostly poor, single Black women and young families seeking homes.[31] As a result, people bought properties they couldn't afford and that would never be worth what they paid for them. Waves of foreclosures soon followed. Nationwide, real estate speculators and mortgage banks pocketed hundreds of millions of dollars in FHA insurance claims before HUD shut the program down in 1973.[32] Many of the foreclosed properties were deemed uninhabitable and demolished.

In Illinois, a state fire-insurance program created in the aftermath of the urban uprisings opened up another vein of extraction. Slumlords took out massive policies on what remained of their decaying, often-uninhabitable holdings, lit a match, and then collected their insurance. By the early 1970s, many of the city's most notorious slumlords, like Gilbert Balin, had collected hundreds of thousands of dollars in insurance claims and been linked to arson investigations.[33] Blair's protégé David Gray took out policies on the severely dilapidated properties to which he had gained tax deeds on the West Side. One was a barely habitable building on West Maypole Avenue. After evicting the eighty-year-old woman who had owned it, Gray sold it on contract to a Black couple for $12,500 and took out a $20,000 fire-insurance policy under the state program. The couple lasted less than a year, unable to bear the deplorable conditions. Days after they moved out, the house went up in flames, and Gray filed his insurance claim.[34]

By the early 1970s, Chicago's West Side was a sea of empty shells and piles of rubble. Once again, the slumlords and contract sellers who had amassed millions preying on Black Chicagoans for decades were looking for the next opportunity. Gilbert Balin, listed by the *Chicago Tribune* in 1973 as one of the city's ten worst slumlords, dove headfirst into tax buying. So, too, did notorious contract seller and slumlord Moe Forman.[35] But because of their decimation of the city's housing stock, the nature of tax-lien predation had changed.

Throughout the 1950s and 1960s, there was money to be made from any tax-delinquent property in Black Chicago and in every other major city where racist real estate practices restricted Blacks' housing options and drove up demand. Property owners had good reason to pay delinquent tax bills before the deadline, and tax buyers could always find a buyer for properties to which they had acquired deeds. But once properties had become empty lots or uninhabitable, the process of extraction had reached its end stage. The owners no longer wanted them and neither did anyone else. Tax-delinquency rates in Cook County soared to levels not seen since the Great Depression. Between 1971 and 1976, the number of properties on Cook County's tax-delinquency rolls rose from eighteen thousand per year to nearly seventy-seven thousand. By 1975, Chicago's tax-delinquency rate was 13.92 percent, the highest among the nation's major cities. In these markets, tax delinquency was a telling indicator of future abandonment; owners scaled back on all expenses as they prepared to walk away.[36]

Where abandonment spread, tax buyers knew to avoid. Where the number of tax-delinquent parcels skyrocketed, the number of tax certificates sold plummeted. At the 1974 tax sale, 3,100 parcels in Hyde Park township, 4,888 parcels in Lake township, and 3,356 parcels in

West Chicago went unsold. By the mid-1970s, Cook County's tax-sale ledgers were filled with pages and pages and pages of unsold taxes on properties in the city's most severely depressed housing markets.[37]

But across these pages of vacant and abandoned lots, the experienced tax buyer could still find lucrative opportunities. National tax-lien investment firms like Atlantic Municipal Corporation began vacuuming up tax liens on properties in areas that were being eyed for condemnation or redevelopment and could fetch a government payout. In 1973, the Miami-based company hired David Gray to act as its local agent, purchasing tax liens at such strategic locations in the Woodlawn, Kenwood, Oakland, Hyde Park, and South Shore neighborhoods.[38] And then there were those properties that were still occupied, in good condition, whose owners had likely missed a tax payment by mistake or due to financial hardship, not intentionally. These were the properties—and the property owners—that offered the surest, and often greatest, return on investment.

In Chicago, Allan Blair and his new business partner, David Gray, showed the way. With Blair acting as his attorney, Gray's firm, DRG Inc., targeted owner-occupied homes in poorer, working-class neighborhoods, speculating on owners' desire to remain in their homes at any cost. One of Gray's specialties was buying liens on properties whose owners had failed to pay a special assessment. These were the extra taxes that homeowners had to pay for specific projects, such as the laying of new water or sewer lines, or the paving or repaving of a sidewalk, curb, or back alley. The bills arrived separately from property tax bills. They came in various installments that could last for years. They imposed an added burden on a homeowner living on a fixed income. They were also easy to overlook. When African American couple Carlee and Beatrice Robinson missed a $22.21 special-assessment payment for a sewer line to their modest home in Freeport, Illinois, Gray bought it at the 1970 Stephenson County special-assessment tax sale. Then, when the couple failed to redeem, he sold it to one of Blair's LLCs, which promptly filed for a tax deed. After gaining ownership, Blair sold it back to the couple for $1,750.[39]

Even better than the home whose owners would buy it back were

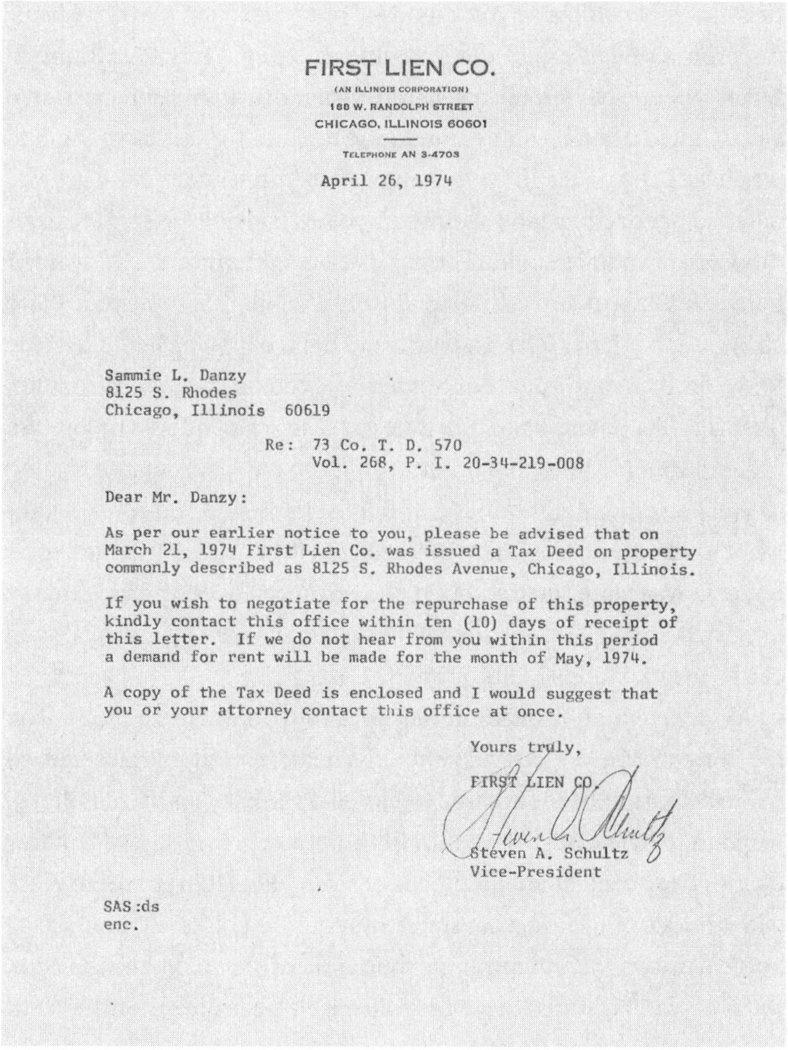

FIRST LIEN CO.

(AN ILLINOIS CORPORATION)
188 W. RANDOLPH STREET
CHICAGO, ILLINOIS 60601

TELEPHONE AN 3-4703

April 26, 1974

Sammie L. Danzy
8125 S. Rhodes
Chicago, Illinois 60619

Re: 73 Co. T. D. 570
Vol. 268, P. I. 20-34-219-008

Dear Mr. Danzy:

As per our earlier notice to you, please be advised that on March 21, 1974 First Lien Co. was issued a Tax Deed on property commonly described as 8125 S. Rhodes Avenue, Chicago, Illinois.

If you wish to negotiate for the repurchase of this property, kindly contact this office within ten (10) days of receipt of this letter. If we do not hear from you within this period a demand for rent will be made for the month of May, 1974.

A copy of the Tax Deed is enclosed and I would suggest that you or your attorney contact this office at once.

Yours truly,

FIRST LIEN CO.

Steven A. Schultz
Vice-President

SAS:ds
enc.

Figure 12.2 In 1969, tax buyer Allan Blair's LLC, First Lien Co., purchased a tax-lien certificate to a house owned by Sammie L. Danzy, a retired African American World War II veteran, in Chicago. Danzy paid the first installment to Blair but died before settling his debts. First Lien Co. subsequently petitioned for the deed to Danzy's house, at the time owned and occupied by Danzy's widow, Josperl Danzy. This is the letter First Lien sent to Danzy following the issuing of a tax deed, in which it inquires as to whether the former owner would be interested in repurchasing their home.

the ones that could also command value on the open market, ensuring profits regardless of the outcome. In 1969, Gray found one in Evanston. The owner, Lillian Ware, was an African American woman who worked as an in-home nurse. She and her former husband had purchased the house in 1940 using a land-installment contract and had managed to pay it off within ten years. The house—in good condition and in a stable, middle-class Black neighborhood—was valued between $17,500 and $20,000. Though regularly employed, Ware struggled to pay her bills, and got into a habit of paying her taxes late. Between 1960 and 1972, her home appeared on the tax-sale list ten times for late payments. Each time, she settled her debts before the redemption deadline. In January 1968, the city of Evanston mailed to Ware and her neighbors a $59 bill for the tenth and final installment of a special assessment for repairs to the back alley behind their houses. Ware later claimed that she never received the bill. In any event, it went unpaid, and the following spring, Gray bought a tax-lien certificate on Ware's home.[40] Then he waited.

As the redemption deadline neared, Gray could sense a windfall on the horizon. Ware, who had suffered a heart condition that required her to be hospitalized for three weeks near the deadline, had failed to respond to his notices. Two months before the redemption window closed, Gray dispatched his process server, Juan Huey, to serve Ware with a notice of sale, another statutory requirement for obtaining a tax deed. Ware was bedridden at the time and unable to come to the door. But Huey later testified that he served her with the notice. Subsequent statements revealed he had likely served the notice to Ware's neighbor. Regardless, the deadline passed, Ware had failed to redeem, and on March 7, 1972, Gray received a tax deed to Ware's home. In April, Ware took a job as a long-term live-in nurse and rented her house to her grand-nephew Patrick Francellno. She was completely unaware that her house belonged to someone else.[41]

Soon after beginning her new job, Ware received a call from Francellno. Several people had been knocking on her door, interested in buying the house. Ware told him to, first, tell them it's not for sale and, second, find out who had sent them. Francellno passed along the number of Gray's office. Ware spoke to Gray, who informed her that she no longer owned the house and that it would cost her $17,000 to buy it back. Gray told Ware that she could either pay up, or he would have her evicted, and hung up.[42] Gray moved forward with evicting Francellno and taking possession of Ware's home. Ware's nephew arrived to find Ware's "possessions . . . scattered around on the street, many of them were destroyed." Boards were nailed across the windows.[43]

Ware turned to Robert Pool, an officer at a local bank where she had obtained a second mortgage on her home, for help. Pool reached out to the downtown white-shoe law firm Sidley and Austin, which agreed to take Ware's case pro bono. In July 1973, Ware's new attorney, Gerald Ambrose, filed a motion for preliminary injunction and a temporary restraining order against Gray's attempts to take possession of the home. He also began mapping a different kind of strategy. As Patner learned years earlier, tax buyers meticulously adhered to every legal procedure. To save Ware's home, they needed to take her case to the public.[44]

Ware's legal team flooded the press with details on the case of a Black woman who lost her home over a $59 tax bill to "two unscrupulous tax buyers." Public outcry was immediate. In Evanston, the NAACP launched a fundraising campaign to help Ware buy back her home, raising over $10,000 in one weekend. Evanston NAACP president Carl Davis promised to make it hard for Gray and Blair to ever attempt to sell Ware's home.[45] Ware's story was picked up by the Associated Press and United Press International and went pointed toward. Articles, accompanied by a picture of Ware in front of her modest home, appeared in over one hundred newspapers across the country. Donations to the NAACP's campaign poured in.[46] Illinois's bombastic governor, Dan Walker, lambasted Blair and Gray as "unscrupulous men" who "prey[ed] on a helpless woman in pursuit of the almighty dollar"[47] and later attempted to have their real estate licenses revoked.[48] But Blair and Gray had the law on their side, and they won on every appeal. Ware was forced to negotiate with Gray to repurchase her home, using the funds raised by the NAACP.[49]

Going where there was money to be made, Gray and Blair continued to target owner-occupied properties in poorer, predominantly
Black neighborhoods. In 1973, DRG Inc. purchased a tax lien on a
house in the southwest neighborhood of Roseland owned by Warren and Mattie Hardie. The Hardies had purchased the empty lot on
South Princeton Avenue in 1954. Between shifts as a stock chaser at
the Southside Ford motor plant, Hardie built a brick bungalow house
there himself. Like Ware, Hardie was chronically delinquent on his
property taxes and in 1971 overlooked a $130 special assessment bill.
Soon after Gray bought the tax lien to Hardie's home, tragedy struck.
Warren Hardie's mother and sister burned to death at their home in
Michigan. Distraught, Hardie overlooked the first notice. Finally, on
the last day to redeem, Hardie went to Gray's office and attempted to
pay his bill. The receptionist told him he had come to the wrong place;
payments had to be made to the county clerk's office. Hardie placed
his payment in the mail, postmarked November 7, 1975, the last day
to redeem. The payment did not arrive until November 10, but the
clerk's office nevertheless processed the payment and sent Hardie a
receipt.[50]

Hardie assumed he was in the clear. He was wrong. As the clerk's
office was processing Hardie's payment, Blair was in circuit court
filing an application for a tax deed to Hardie's home. After he was
awarded the deed, Gray mailed Hardie a letter informing him that
the house he had built was no longer his, but that he could buy it back
for $25,000. Hardie could not believe it. "I did pay the tax I owed to
the county clerk's office. They accepted it and even cashed my check."
He refused to accept that his home was gone and refused to negotiate with Gray. A standoff ensued. Blair advised his partner to "throw
the guy out. Hardie had his chance and he blew it." Gray summoned
the sheriff's office to carry out an eviction. When the deputy sheriff
arrived, Hardie refused to budge. "I dug the sewers around here,"
Hardie shouted. "[I] layed or supervised the placement of almost
every brick in this building; I know it's not much, but it's all I have
and I'm not going to get kicked around and give it up to anyone."[51]

Hardie took his story to the press. "$30,000 Home Lost in Tax

Trap," the headline in the *Chicago Defender* read, next to a photo of Warren and Mattie in their living room, angry and defiant. Black Chicagoans mobilized in their defense. Operation PUSH announced that its members would physically block any attempts to evict the Hardies. "We are prepared to give the family physical as well as spiritual aid," Jesse Jackson told reporters. "We will stand with them, and the authorities will have to move the furniture out over us." Hardie's neighbors stared in disbelief. "I just want to cry," one neighbor remarked. "They've been here 23 years and they're a credit to the community." Days later, guards were stationed about the courthouse where circuit court judge Cornelius Collins heard Hardie's request for a hearing to contest the tax deed, prepared for a confrontation with protesters. Inside, Judge Collins dismissed Hardie's request. "It has to be that way," Collins explained to the distraught Hardie, "because if nobody pays their taxes there won't be a county." Blair turned to Hardie and again offered to sell him back his home for $25,000. Hardie had to be restrained from assaulting Blair.[52]

Following the circuit court's rejection, over two hundred Black Chicagoans met at Operation PUSH's headquarters. Dozens of community leaders, ministers, and elected officials heard residents share their harrowing experiences of tax delinquency and dealings with Gray and Blair. "The only way we can really help people like Warren Hardie is by getting a new law," Operation PUSH's national housing director, Bill Thurston, told attendees. A new organization, the Coalition Against Tax Scavengers (CATS), formed and announced plans for a citywide campaign against predatory tax buying. They lobbied lawmakers to adopt immediate reforms that would put people like Gray out of business. Neighborhood groups began taking direct action to prevent other tax-sale evictions.[53]

Public outrage forced Illinois lawmakers to respond. In 1976, the legislature formed a commission to study problems with the tax-sale laws and recommend reforms. As before, tax buyers and their lobbyists read from a well-rehearsed script. They reminded lawmakers that tax buyers directly placed an estimated $11 million annually in local coffers, which would accordingly be threatened by any reforms that diminished tax buying's profitability. They warned that, without harsh penalties, people would stop paying their taxes. "A main objective of the law," Blair repeated, "is to deter people from failing to pay their taxes." They reminded lawmakers of the state's fiscal conditions in the decade prior to the 1951 reforms, when "only two-thirds of taxes were collected. But today, 96 per cent are collected."[54] Maurice Scott of the Taxpayers' Federation of Illinois argued that the threat of "total loss of deed" explained these high collection rates, while expressing his fear that "tax buyers would show no interest in tax-sale proceedings if there was no possibility of a parcel of property going to deed."[55]

The facts said otherwise. On Chicago's South and West Sides, tax-delinquency rates were soaring, as they were in disinvested, fully plundered housing markets across urban America. They soared in states with the harshest penalties, and they soared in states with the weakest. As in the 1930s, rates of tax delinquency bore no relation to the laws governing tax enforcement; they were entirely a reflection of broader economic conditions and, in particular, changes in housing and real estate markets.[56] Moreover, tax buyers in Illinois and elsewhere did not step in to save local governments from fiscal insolvency during these crises. Rather, whenever tax-delinquency rates soared, wherever the problems of vacancy, abandonment, and tax delinquency were most severe, tax buyers were nowhere to be found. Like parasites, tax buyers died with their hosts.

For cities and urban Black populations alike, tax delinquency was a major problem at the end of the 1970s. For older cities experiencing economic contraction and population loss, the proliferation of abandoned properties deprived them of tax revenue while adding significant costs to already-stressed budgets. After extracting the last payments from tenants and after milking the equity dry by not paying taxes, slumlords set fire to scores of buildings.[57] Those they simply walked away from were more prone to catching fire or becoming havens for crime, which cost cities money to combat. At the same time, rising rates of tax delinquency reduced cities' bond ratings, making it costlier to borrow for immediate needs and future projects.[58] For African Americans in disinvested urban neighborhoods, vacant and abandoned housing posed a threat to safety and well-being, making neighborhoods more dangerous, accelerating disinvestment and abandonment, and driving property values down further still. Tax buyers didn't only fail to help properties in the most distressed areas get back on the tax rolls, or to solve the underlying causes of tax delinquency. They made the situation much worse. By design, their strategies compounded the financial struggles and distress of low-income homeowners and injected more volatility into already-reeling housing markets.

The state commission's final report, issued in the fall of 1976, was unsparing in its criticism of tax buyers and damning in its conclusions about the tax law, calling it unjust and "crude, even primitive." It exploded many of the myths surrounding the tax-sale law and its role in tax enforcement. Contrary to tax buyers' claims, the commission reported, the 1951 Revenue Act did not compel taxpayer compliance. In truth, tax-delinquency rates had already been falling before the law was enacted, as a result of economic growth and housing-market demand following World War II. Property owners paid their taxes because they had the resources to do so, not because they feared losing their home to a tax buyer. Indeed, the commissioners added, many property owners were unaware of the consequences of tax delinquency—a general ignorance that tax buyers shrewdly exploited. They concluded that there was "no relation between the threat of total forfeiture and the rate of tax collection."[59]

What purpose, then, did the tax-sale law serve? "If there is no causal relation between this threat and the collection rate," the commission wrote, "then the only function of total forfeiture is the enrichment of tax buyers." Turning to Allan Blair and David Gray, in particular, the commission noted that the two "claim their work is ultimately a benefit to the people of the State but in fact their work largely benefits only themselves." They and other tax buyers "use the law like a trap for their own personal enrichment." And to those who warned about the dangers of reforms that might "curtail the interest and participation of professional tax buyers," the commission responded, "The truth is that their interest and participation has already dwindled significantly over the past few years. They are interested in only the very best property—the kind of property the state would generally have no difficulty disposing of itself."[60]

But even as it castigated tax buyers and cast doubt on the tax sale's ostensive purpose, the commission remained circumspect in its recommendations for fixing it. It singled out the need to repeal some of the reforms that Blair had convinced lawmakers in the 1960s to enact—such as allowing tax buyers to pay additional taxes after the final notice had been sent out. It called for a stronger notification system that required property owners to appear in court to hear the seriousness of the consequences spelled out, and to allow the court the opportunity to determine owners' capacity to handle their own affairs. It offered vague recommendations for opening up the tax sale to "people other than professional investors"—such as civic groups, churches, and community organizations—but provided no guidance on how to do so. It recommended adding a second sale for unredeemed properties, with net proceeds awarded to the former owner, as in other states. But the proposed method for doing so, the commission acknowledged, would require lawmakers to engage in a high-wire balancing act to keep it from running afoul of state constitutional proscriptions against double sales.[61]

Lawmakers took no action. A tax-enforcement machinery powered by predation, and a rich vein of real estate speculation, remained operational. In Chicago, Allan Blair remained at the top of it all, revered by his peers, reviled by his critics, despised by his victims.

In January 1979, having recently returned to Chicago after several years teaching law in California, Marshall Patner resumed his fight against Blair. He took on the case of Willie Henry Moore, a Black man who had lost his home to Blair, then bought it back using a land contract. But Moore lost it again when the seller (one of Blair's LLCs) failed to pay property taxes, as it had agreed to in the contract. Patner alleged that Blair's firm was engaged in a complex scheme to steer properties into tax delinquency, then evict the tenants and pocket the payments. Rinse and repeat. As he dug into the case, Patner expressed cautious optimism that this might be the one that could bring Blair—and his tax-buying enterprise—down.

Just before leaving his office on Friday, January 26, Blair phoned Patner. They had some matter involving Moore's case to discuss. If he was nervous, Blair didn't show it, promising that he would, as always, beat Patner in court. Blair mentioned that he would be flying his twin-engine Beechcraft Baron up to Wisconsin the following morning to visit his daughter, outside Milwaukee. A massive blizzard had blanketed the Midwest. The forecast for Saturday called for cloudy skies and an additional one to two inches. Patner cautioned Blair about flying in bad weather. "Marsh, I'm invincible," Blair replied, and hung up. Early the following morning, Blair flew out of Chicago Midway airport. His daughter, Jan, pulled into General Mitchell Airport in Milwaukee and awaited his arrival. At 9:21 a.m., radar lost contact with Blair's aircraft. Moments later, reports came in of a crash near Pewaukee. Blair was pronounced dead at the scene.[62]

Blair's protégé, David Gray, was devastated. As press reports on Blair's death made sure to mention the controversies surrounding his tax buying enterprise, Gray came to his mentor's defense. Gray scolded the *Chicago Tribune* for "rehash[ing] a five-year old story" in its obituary and recounted Blair's long list of achievements—the number of cases he argued before state and federal courts, the number of committees he chaired or was a member of. Blair's "integrity," Gray claimed, was "above reproach."[63]

* * *

Gray and other tax buyers had good reason to want to keep their names out of the news. Whenever the public learned about the business of tax buying, calls to reform or abolish the practice soon followed. In Florida, public outrage ensued after news spread of an elderly African American couple who lost their home to tax buyer John Barrow in 1979 over a $3.05 unpaid special assessment. As the story garnered national headlines, a circuit judge voided the deed, citing the doctrine of unconscionability, while the state legislature rushed to enact a reform forbidding the sale of tax liens on debts of $100 or less.[64] In New York, the case of Annie Kennedy, the elderly Black woman mentioned in the book's introduction who lost her home to a tax buyer over a $92.07 missed tax bill in 1986, renewed calls to reform Nassau County's tax-lien sale law, which, like Illinois's, automatically awarded a deed to the tax buyer at the end of the redemption period, leaving the homeowner with nothing. "The system is outdated, inequitable, and wrong," an editorial in *Newsday* argued. "It should be changed without further delay."[65] Public outrage forced county officials to reform the law to require tax buyers to file for foreclosure, and that the property then be sold, with the homeowner receiving the proceeds minus taxes, interest, and court costs.[66]

But such reforms ultimately did little to cut into tax buyers' profits. And in those cities where tax sales had become a vital source of revenue, tax buyers remained virtually immune to public outrage. In Illinois's state legislature, tax attorneys and tax-lien lobbyists continued to quietly wield extraordinary influence. In 1983, they succeeded in getting lawmakers to make a seemingly small tweak to the "sale in error" statute that would reap rich rewards for tax buyers, this time at the expense of local governments. This provision had been meant to ensure that if a property landed on the tax-delinquent rolls by accident, the tax buyer would be refunded the amount they paid for the tax-lien certificate plus interest. For years, tax buyers had exploited this provision by bidding on properties that they knew were tax exempt in order to accumulate modest, but guaranteed, profits from the interest. The refunds and interest payments came out of the treasuries of the local tax jurisdiction of the property. As this practice grew, tax buyers pushed to expand the possible "errors" eligible for compensation. The reform enacted in 1983 expanded the scope of what constituted an error to encompass virtually any incorrect information on a property's listing—from a street listed as an avenue, to a minor spelling error—and opened up a new source of profits. (David Gray Jr.'s tax buying firm, Wheeler Dealer, would later become a prolific user of the "sale in error" loophole, amassing over $3.5 million in profits at local governments' expense during one seven-year stretch.)[67]

In the course of exploiting Illinois's "sale in error" loophole, one tax buyer, Tony Bryant, discovered that many of the Black churches that were landing on the tax-delinquency rolls were not, in fact, tax exempt, because their owners had failed to submit paperwork to the assessor's office each year. Bryant subsequently began filing for tax deeds on scores of churches across Chicago's south and west sides, then attempted to sell them back at exorbitant prices. Blindsided ministers scrambled to round up the cash; many were so embarrassed by their carelessness they tried to hide the ordeal from their congregations. Bryant made a killing. After buying the deed to the House of Blessing Christian Church on South Halsted for $800, he sold it back to the Reverend Robert L. Evans for $20,000. He bought the Sunlight UMB Church on South Prairie Avenue for $400 and sold it back to Reverend L. J. McSwain for $13,000. The Reverend Bessie Jones was forced to take out a $16,000 loan to buy back the Mt. Sinai Apostolic Church from Bryant. For years afterward, her congregation's Sunday donations went toward paying off the loan. He demanded the outrageous sum of $337,000 from a church in Austin to which had acquired a tax deed for $1,100. Bryant perpetuated this legal extortion against more than 250 Black churches in Cook County. When his scheme came to light, Bryant expressed no remorse. "It's just business," he repeated. "I buy any lien on a property that I think can make me money."[68]

True to form, lawmakers rushed to denounce Bryant and close the loophole he exploited. The public reacted in horror and rallied to aid and offer sympathy to the victims. But demands for structural reforms that would put tax buyers out of business remained muted. As local governments and schools strained to balance budgets and address mounting funding needs—none greater than in those cities where tax buying thrived—calls for reform grew quieter still, while tax buyers' leverage remained as strong as ever.

PART V

NEOLIBERALISM AT HOME

13

STARVED

The parks and playgrounds where John Singleton grew up in 1970s South Los Angeles were built by demand. For decades, Blacks had fought to force cities to provide the same level and quality of public services and amenities they had provided to others. Born three years after the 1965 Watts uprising, Singleton grew up at a moment when cities like Los Angeles were investing, many for the first time, in neglected Black neighborhoods. Singleton recalled "being able to go to the park when I was a kid, and there would always be a park supervisor there."[1] Local tax dollars paid for these city employees to organize games and activities, to engage with underprivileged youth, and to build and maintain social infrastructure. Free public recreational facilities and programs made a profound difference in the lives of children whose parents worked long hours for low pay, couldn't be home when kids got out of school, and couldn't afford to send them to camps during the summer, or buy them a new basketball or baseball glove. The staffers, coaches, lifeguards, and other employees at the neighborhood parks had them covered.

That all ended abruptly after California voters passed Proposition 13 in 1978. The ballot referendum dramatically reduced the size of local tax bases and forced cities to slash their budgets. Programs and services for the poor experienced the heaviest cuts. Cities cut funding for public recreation, welfare and jobs programs, and other services for lower-income minority populations. Los Angeles's city council slashed annual appropriations for public recreation by $7.5 million, reducing the city's Recreation and Parks Department budget by over 15 percent. Public parks and recreational programs that had offered summer day camps, organized sports, swimming lessons, and other activities in many of the city's Black and brown neighborhoods were shuttered or forced to charge fees that poor families could not afford. Public spaces that had once nurtured a vibrant civic life fell into disrepair.[2]

As a teenager, Singleton experienced this public disinvestment firsthand. As an adult, his iconic films like *Boyz n the Hood* would depict its aftermath. Reflecting on the upsurge in gang violence in 1980s Los Angeles, Singleton pointed to the erosion of the manufacturing base that had sustained the city's Black working class, a postindustrial urban economy that enhanced elite power, and a militarized police force that kept the poor and marginalized contained. But compounding all these challenges was the rapid public disinvestment in programs and services for poorer neighborhoods and at-risk youth. "After Proposition 13, tax money didn't go towards park supervisors or anything [like that]," Singleton recalled. And without public investment, "what does a park [in a low-income neighborhood] become then? The park becomes a turf [for gangs]."[3]

Los Angeles's "dead parks," as they became known, were a sign of things to come for the nation. Following passage of Prop 13, the thrust of taxpayer unrest in America shifted decisively from demands that the rich pay their fair share and the poor be relieved of undue burdens, toward calls for across-the-board tax and spending cuts. These cuts disproportionately benefited the wealthy and harmed the poor. In addition, they constrained the ability of states and local governments to raise taxes, tax property fairly and accurately, or increase spending to meet needs. In the immediate aftermath of Prop 13's resounding passage, anti-tax groups rushed to place similar measures on other state ballots. Similarly, lawmakers advanced a host of proposals aimed at handcuffing governments' revenue-raising capacities and forcing cuts to social services and programs serving lower-income communities and people.[4]

After spending the past decade stoking white resentment over

Figure 13.1 Teachers, parents, and schoolchildren march in Los Angeles, California, on June 19, 1978, to protest cuts to public education threatened by the passage of Proposition 13.

social spending on racial minorities and the poor—most infamously, his thinly veiled racist attacks on Black welfare recipients—in 1980 former California governor Ronald Reagan rode to a landslide victory in the Presidential election. In office, Reagan enacted massive federal tax cuts for the wealthy and worked to slash federal spending on programs and services for the poor. These efforts included slashing federal support and phasing out revenue-sharing programs for the neediest cities and school districts. Washington and state governments alike signaled to local governments and school districts that they needed to fend for themselves. As they did so, states and localities engaged in an ever-more-cutthroat competition to attract and retain employers and promote economic development by offering various tax breaks, concessions, and direct subsidies to those who needed them the least. As revenues decreased, public spending on programs and services for the poor suffered the heaviest cuts.

The most fiscally disadvantaged cities—those that had lost middle-class whites, manufacturing industries, and commercial retailers to the suburbs and beyond, and those where Blacks had gained a measure of political power—joined this race to the bottom. But they remained at the back of the pack, scrambling to catch up, and compelled to inflict a death by a thousand cuts to the social services and safety nets that the previous generation had struggled to build.

* * *

In the wake of the passage of Prop 13, lawmakers across the country tried to make sense of its message. Exit polls and voter surveys made it clear that the white voters who poured out in support of Prop 13 did not want to shrink the size of government or enact draconian cuts to all public programs. They did not share an ideological commitment to "small" government. What they wanted was relief—relief from soaring property tax bills; relief from footing any share of public spending on others. On both counts, Prop 13 was remarkably effective. The measure not only dramatically reduced property assessments for existing homeowners, with the greatest reductions going to those who had benefited most from rising property values over the previous decades. It also allowed for only minuscule increases in a property's assessed value so long as the property wasn't sold.[5] Prop 13 also hastened local governments' move toward funding public services and programs through user fees. That was just fine with wealthier communities, whose formerly tax-funded programs and services continued without any disruption; over time, their budgets even improved. In contrast, parks, swimming pools, and other public amenities in low-income areas struggled to remain open. In many cases they dramatically scaled back services.

Limits on assessments and future increases afforded the greatest tax advantages to longer-tenured owners, who tended to be white. They also benefited residents of places where real estate values were most rapidly appreciating, which—because of how race informed property values—were overwhelmingly white. In contrast, Black neighborhoods experienced greater turnover. Since assessments could be significantly raised only when properties changed hands, assessments in Black neighborhoods soared relative to those in white neighborhoods. This same dynamic disincentivized local governments from accurately assessing property in stagnant or downwardly transitional areas: any reductions in assessed values, and resulting shrinkage of the tax base, would remain locked in.[6]

During these years when white California homeowners were beginning to enjoy the benefits of this structurally racist assessment formula, white homeowners on Long Island, New York, were waging a fight to the death to preserve their own version of it. In 1975, the state's Supreme Court ruled in *Hellerstein v. Assessor of Islip* that all local tax jurisdictions must assess properties at their full market value.[7] At the time, Nassau County assessed properties using a combination of construction costs in 1938 and land values in 1964. Like California's, this system inherently advantaged owners of older homes and residents of appreciating housing markets. It also disadvantaged residents of communities with large and growing Black and Latino populations, where values remained stagnant or depreciated.[8] Countywide, the relative tax burdens of residential areas with the lowest property values were two times greater than those of the wealthiest ones. By the early 1980s, assessments on homes in the largely Black city of Roosevelt were 66 percent higher than the countywide average. The assessment-to-market-value ratio of residential properties in Black and Hispanic neighborhoods were, on average, 40 percent higher than those in white neighborhoods.[9]

The *Hellerstein* ruling threatened to dramatically shift the property tax burden onto residential properties, which assessors had invariably assessed at a lower ratio than commercial and industrial properties. It also promised to defrost the "frozen" assessments on homes in Nassau County and remove the structural advantages white homeowners in predominantly white housing markets enjoyed. Long Island's tax revolt was thus aimed at preserving this existing system. Following the ruling, taxpayer groups led by white women like Valley Stream's Rose Eisner applied relentless pressure to state lawmakers to enact constitutional reforms that would nullify its effects. Groups like Eisner's Civic Action Council of Nassau County and the State Coalition Against 100% Re-Assessment (SCAR) organized marches, staged protests, conducted letter-writing campaigns, and chartered buses for trips to Albany, where they flooded the hallways of the state legislature, blocking doors and screaming at lawmakers. "They'd have beat your brains in" if you crossed them, one lawmaker later remarked.[10]

In 1981, they got what they demanded. Led by Nassau County representatives, the state legislature overrode a veto from Governor Hugh Carey to repeal the provision in the state's constitution requiring full-value assessments. They replaced it with one that allowed for fractional assessments; locked in the percentage of total tax shares collected from residential, commercial, industrial, and corporate properties at the time; and capped annual assessment increases on residential properties at 6 percent, and 20 percent over five years. While the new law specified how much local governments could collect from each class of property owners, and how much it could raise taxes each year, it remained silent on how local assessors were to determine assessed values in the first place. It also did not require local governments to conduct full reassessments, thus preserving existing inequities.[11]

By the early 1980s, lawmakers and voters across the country were rushing to adopt versions of California's radical reforms. Between 1978 and 1983 alone, twenty states enacted limits on property-assessment increases, tax-rate increases, spending increases, or some combination of them.[12] By 1995, forty-six states had some law limiting local governments' ability to raise tax rates, upwardly adjust assessments, or increase local budgets.[13] In 1978, voters in Michigan approved an amendment to the state's constitution requiring local governments to seek voter approval of any new property taxes or increases in property tax rates. In 1994, they followed up with an amendment preventing local assessors from imposing annual increases exceeding inflation or 5 percent, whichever was less.[14] In 1980, voters in Missouri amended their constitution to require that any increase in local taxes be approved by a citywide referendum.[15]

By design, tax and expenditure limits (TELs) imposed a form of shock therapy on local governments, forcing dramatic reductions in budgets and severely restricting their ability to raise revenue. Wherever they were adopted, public spending on education, services, programs, and institutions suffered, as did the people who relied on them.[16] Over time, TELs made fiscal systems more regressive, both because of their structural features that benefited owners of properties that appreciated more rapidly, and by compelling governments to adopt user fees to support programs and services once funded by taxes. By design, TELs compelled local governments to embrace progrowth policies, reject tax fairness, and privatize public functions.

Along with political movements to handcuff local government came constraints imposed by bondholders. Municipal bond servicers and buyers emerged from the urban fiscal crises of the 1970s with even greater leverage over the tax policies and spending priorities of local governments. They used this power to suffocate projects that would benefit the urban poor, inflict more punitive terms for cities with large minority populations, and push cities to become more reliant on regressive sales and use taxes, fines, and user fees. By the 1980s, cities could turn to bond markets only to finance projects that benefitted the private sector or promised to generate enough revenue pay off cities' debts directly from its users.[17]

Cities with the greatest spending needs could not look to the federal government for assistance. Throughout the 1960s and 1970s, America's largest cities had derived ever-greater amounts of their municipal budgets from federal sources, peaking at 25 percent in 1978. That figure fell dramatically after Reagan entered the White House in 1981. His message to revenue-starved cities was the same he delivered to the nation's poor: you're on your own. In his first year, Reagan cut federal aid to cities by 46 percent, a $26 billion reduction. He dramatically scaled back revenue sharing before eliminating the program entirely in 1986. He also redirected other funds and programs targeted for cities through state governments, while relaxing or eliminating entirely requirements on how they were spent. Between 1980 and 1985, the overall amount of federal support to state and local governments fell by 23.5 percent, with the heaviest cuts applied to community and regional development (-39.8 percent); education, training, and social services (-33.4 percent), and general purpose assistance (-45.1 percent).[18]

Under Reagan, federal programs that primarily served underprivileged urban populations were always first on the chopping block. Like the Neighborhood Self-Help and Planning Assistance program, which Reagan eliminated. And the Urban Development Action Grant program, which saw its budget reduced from $675 million in 1981 to $216 million by 1988. And HUD's housing programs, whose budget was reduced from $55.7 to $15.2 billion over the course of the decade. Reagan also sharply reduced federal support for public transit, urban infrastructure needs, job training, and urban economic development programs. These cuts not only eliminated or drastically scaled back programs and assistance that helped Blacks; they also decimated public-sector workforces that had formed the backbone of the Black middle class in most cities. They also reversed the trend toward greater federal support for public schools that had begun with the Elementary and Secondary Education Act of 1965. Public schools with the largest numbers of low-income and minority students derived the largest portion of their budgets from federal dollars and, as a result, now suffered the most.[19]

* * *

After serving one term in Congress, Harold Washington returned home to Chicago in 1983 to run for mayor. As a candidate, Washington assailed the regressive tax policies of his opponent, incumbent mayor Jane Byrne—whose administration had supported an increase in the state sales tax, fought to preserve sales taxes on food and medicine, and had sharply increased user charges and fees. He attacked budgeting practices that funneled public dollars to the city's predominantly white neighborhoods and delivered services based on political loyalty. He vowed to "improve services and increase citizen input into resource allocation decisions and service delivery."[20] And he promised an "equitable distribution of the tax burden."[21]

Washington scored an upset victory in the 1983 Democratic primary over Byrne and Richard M. Daley. Later that spring, he withstood a nakedly racist campaign by Republican challenger Bernard Epton that had the backing of many prominent white Democrats and became the city's first African American mayor.[22]

But from the moment he entered office, Washington encountered mounting fiscal challenges. The city's tax base continued to suffer from the loss of residents and commerce to the suburbs. The schools were sinking deeper into debt, forced to continually issue tax-anticipation bonds to meet payroll and keep the lights on. The manufacturing employment base was evaporating. Between 1967 and 1982, the city lost over 250,000 manufacturing jobs, nearly half of its total manufacturing workforce. And it was reeling from severe reductions in federal aid for urban job and training programs, public transit, public schools, social welfare, and economic development.[23]

In order for cities like Chicago to grow again, they were told, they had to compete harder. "State and local governments," the Department of Housing and Urban Development counseled in 1982, "will find it is in their interests to concentrate on increasing their attractiveness to potential investors, residents, and visitors."[24] In order to compete, they were told, they had to placate wealthy residents and cater to the interests of capital.[25] They had to forget about distributing tax burdens equitably and instead aggressively do the opposite.

Chicago already had a head start. More than many cities, Chicago pioneered neoliberal urban governance. Former Mayor Richard J. Daley had molded the city's institutions and policy approaches to serve private interests and follow a market logic.[26] As its manufacturing base eroded, Chicago planned a postindustrial future centered on real estate and commercial development and executed through the use of tax cuts and tax-funded subsidies. Beginning in the late 1970s, the city began granting massive property tax reductions (up to 60 percent over 13 years) to real estate developers in areas deemed to be "blighted." Yet this practice did not benefit disinvested and distressed neighborhoods; rather, it targeted areas that real estate and commercial interests saw as worthy of investment. The city's first use of this ordinance for a commercial development was for a luxury hotel and convention center.[27]

Chicago was also an early adopter of tax increment financing (TIF) as a tool of real estate development.[28] Under this scheme, the city would issue a bond to develop a district, which could be anywhere from a single lot to several city blocks. After a TIF bond was issued, revenue from any subsequent increase in property taxes within that area over a predetermined number of years would not go into the city's general revenues but instead be set aside to pay off the bondholders. In essence, this practice kept the district's assessed value for general tax purposes artificially low, in the expectation that at a later date its enhanced value would be released. With each new TIF, more of the tax base was diverted, unavailable to meet a city's core obligations.

Pitched as a way to attract and retain corporate investment and stimulate economic growth, tax abatements and TIFs became, in practice, tax breaks and tax-funded subsidies to real estate developments that, many analysts found, would have occurred anyway. They made little to no difference in the locational decisions of the businesses and industries they benefitted.[29] But as federal aid disappeared, and state limits constrained cities' powers to raise revenue, few cities were in the mood to test this theory. Instead, local officials thought these fiscal inducements could demonstrate their commitment to delivering jobs and opportunities at whatever cost. That these tax breaks tended to be seen by the public as cost-free made them all the more attractive. For the beneficiaries, tax breaks served, above all, as a demonstration of public officials' fealty to the market, a sign of a city's overall "business climate," and a form of tribute that, over time, became a "political precondition for investment." Scholars observed that tax incentives functioned as a "potent symbolic weapon," signifying politicians' capitulation to the desires of capitalists.[30] For state and local tax systems, and for individual taxpayers, though, the cumulative effects of capital's demands were profound. Whereas in

Figure 13.2 Chicago Mayor Harold Washington at a press conference on December 22, 1986, announcing the sale of $58 million in tax increment financing (TIF) bonds for the redevelopment of the city's North Loop.

1950, over 20 percent of all state and local property tax receipts came from businesses, by 1983 that figure had plummeted to 8 percent.[31]

As mayor, Harold Washington struggled to break from these fiscal logics. His calls for a more equitable distribution of local tax burdens quickly took a back seat to the more pressing need to staunch the bleeding of the tax base, tap new revenue sources in the wake of federal and state funding cuts, and appease Wall Street bond-rating agencies.[32] Until his untimely death in 1987, Washington struggled to disentangle the private interests that had been guiding fiscal policy from those of the neighborhoods that had vaulted him to office.[33] In this respect, Washington's administration was typical of many Black mayors in major cities during these years.[34]

Many Black mayors embraced pro-growth politics reluctantly, but embraced it nonetheless. In Detroit, Mayor Coleman Young—a former Marxist labor organizer—aggressively pursued corporate investment through tax abatements and subsidies, but he did so under no illusions. "This suicidal outthrust competition . . . has got to stop,"

Young vented, "but until it does, I mean to compete. It's too bad we have a system where dog eats dog and the devil takes the hindmost. But I'm tired of taking the hindmost."[35] Cities like Detroit still got stuck being the hindmost, and its poorest residents got left with the bill. The larger a city's Black population, the less likely they were to realize broad-based economic benefits from the prevailing fiscal strategies, and the more likely they were to experience deepening inequality.

Supply-side fiscal policies not only drained cities of tax revenues, they increased the relative tax burdens of unfavored local populations. The remaking of Jersey City, New Jersey, into an "entrepreneurial city" demonstrated these dynamics and their tax implications for Black residents. By the early 1980s, decades of capital flight, manufacturing losses, and disinvestment had decimated the city's tax base. Over the previous decade, rates of joblessness and poverty had risen sharply among the Black population. The city's public housing had suffered from years of neglect. Its public schools were among the lowest performing in the state. Jersey City residents needed help. The city responded by throwing public dollars at the feet of luxury housing and commercial developers, whom it showered with subsidies, tax breaks, abatements, zoning variances, and low-cost public land, all aimed at growing the city's moribund economy from the top down. "Here there is no city income tax, no corporate tax, no payroll tax and no commercial rent tax," promotional materials read.[36]

This was the kind of urban renewal that the Reagan administration could get behind. In 1983, Jersey City received a $40 million federal urban-development grant, at the time the largest ever awarded. The bulk of the funds went toward laying sewer lines and streets and clearing sites for new office buildings and luxury condominiums along the riverfront. The largest of the new developments, the Newport project, received a fifteen-year tax abatement from the city along with tens of millions of dollars in tax breaks from the state. In exchange for generous public support, luxury apartment developers could choose to either designate a number of units for affordable housing or pay into the city's affordable-housing trust fund. Nearly all of them chose the latter.[37]

In the years that followed, Jersey City's waterfront boomed, real estate values and rents soared, and developers reaped the rewards of taxpayers' support. But even that was not enough. For along with tax abatements, owners of downtown and waterfront real estate demanded that the city keep property assessments frozen at their 1988 levels. For the next three decades, that's where they stood. New Jersey lacked any law mandating periodic reassessments.[38] No matter how much the market changed, property assessments remained the same. They did so even as property values in Jersey City's downtown and waterfront districts rose more than tenfold, while those in disinvested Black and brown neighborhoods remained stagnant or even decreased in value. Assessment ratios began to vary dramatically, from 10 to 70 percent of market value, always to the disadvantage of Black and brown neighborhoods. With every passing year, the gap grew wider, and, for Black taxpayers, the burden grew heavier.[39]

As neoliberal urbanism reduced local taxes on the wealthy and cut public spending, movement conservatives in Washington aimed to force progressive states to do the same. Since the introduction of the federal income tax in the early twentieth century, taxpayers had been able to deduct the state and local taxes they paid from their federal income taxes. This deduction chiefly benefitted high-income earners, who paid more of those taxes and were more likely to itemize. Specifically, it benefitted high-income earners in states with more progressive tax policies that spent more on public services and education. For residents of states that taxed high-income earners lightly, spent less, and relied more on sales taxes and user fees, the state and local tax deduction (SALT) was a negligible benefit.

For that reason, the political Right believed that removing SALT from the federal tax code would increase pressure on states to reduce or eliminate income taxes and cut social spending. In 1985, future Reagan administration advisor Bruce Bartlett described SALT's elimination as "one of the most important provisions" in Reagan's proposed overhaul of the federal tax code, not because it would bring more revenue, but because it would force progressive states to tax the rich less and spend less on services and programs for the poor. Eliminating SALT "could trigger the most powerful tax revolt since . . . Proposition 13," Bartlett predicted. It would force states with more progressive tax policies to join the fiscal race to the bottom in order to prevent rich people from "'vot[ing] with their feet' and mov[ing] to states with less tax bite." Without the SALT deduction, high-income earners would demand that states cut spending and replace progressive income taxes with flat-rate income taxes; or, better yet, eliminate the income tax entirely and rely instead on user fees and sales taxes that imposed their heaviest costs on the poor. With less revenue, states and local governments would be compelled to privatize "police and fire protection, trash collection, education, parks, and similar services."[40] Another policy expert predicted that eliminating SALT would compel local governments to become more like the private homeowners' associations proliferating across suburban America, where members paid only for services they used and not a dime on those for the poor.[41] This change, they said, would be a good thing.

Liberals in Congress fought to preserve the SALT deduction, and they did so less by defending the policy itself and more by calling attention to the Reagan administration's cynical motives. New York senator Jacob Javits characterized the anti-SALT effort as a "Trojan Horse" aimed at triggering "a tax migration by businesses and better-off families."[42] The Congressional Research Service predicted that older, industrial cities with large Black populations would suffer the greatest harm from the removal of the SALT deduction, as in these places "any decline in State and local government revenues that might be stimulated by a decrease in their deductibility would soon present serious problems." The impact on Blacks, it predicted, "would be severe," leading to decreased funding for public services, programs, and schools; wage freezes and job cuts in the public sector that formed the bedrock of the urban Black middle class; and diminished political influence of Black mayors and urban regimes.[43]

The Right's gambit failed in 1986, and the SALT deduction survived for another three decades before being sharply reduced by the Trump administration in 2017.[44] But the targeting of SALT underscored the advantages that fiscal federalism afforded a political party oriented around tax cuts for the wealthy and spending cuts for the poor, as well as the structural and political disadvantages this system imposed on those seeking to protect, much less strengthen, the social safety net at the state and local levels. Because fiscal federalism promoted tax competition, and because Sunbelt states were actively competing to attract people and capital with low taxes, and because of the tax revolts of the late 1970s, liberal lawmakers increasingly embraced strategies to placate those taxpayers best positioned, and most inclined, to stage a revolt or vote with their feet. It placed liberal lawmakers in states with progressive taxes and significant social-spending programs in the contradictory position of advocating for a federal tax policy that cut taxes on the wealthy at the federal level in the hopes that it could forestall those same taxpayers' demands for tax cuts at the state and local level. It was a losing proposition, but this fiscal structure offered them few alternatives.

In high- and low-tax states alike, residents of wealthier municipalities and school districts pressed their advantage. More than merely hoarding local tax dollars, well-resourced school districts engaged in what historian Esther Cyna described as an "active process of resource diversion" that siphoned off resources from poorer schools.[45] They did so by redrawing school-district boundaries to bring in wealthier areas and push out poorer ones, by manipulating state aid formulas to claim a disproportionate share, and by working to undermine judicial decisions and legislative actions aimed at ensuring greater funding equity.

Following the Supreme Court's 1973 decision in *San Antonio v. Rodriguez*, the fight to correct school funding imbalances moved down to the state courts. In the thirty years following that decision, thirty-six state supreme courts heard challenges to their state's school-funding system, and of those, fifteen found the system under review unconstitutional. These rulings laid bare the woeful insufficiency of local funding models in serving children in the poorest districts, but they were limited in generating solutions to funding gaps. Many of the legal challenges filed in state courts centered on the failure of local funding models to meet state constitutional requirements for providing an adequate education. In response, lawmakers increased state funding for local school districts to ensure that all met a minimum threshold, but in the face of intense opposition from voters in wealthier school districts, resisted measures that equalized school funding across districts. School funding reforms instead often allocated aid to local school districts on a need-blind basis, preserving the positional advantages enjoyed by parents and schoolchildren in wealthier, whiter districts and incentivizing their perpetuation.[46]

* * *

During the 1980s, the reorientation of governance around market principles extended into local fiscal politics and administration, turning what just a decade earlier had been widely seen as bugs in America's federated fiscal structure into features. Competition for the people and businesses who grew tax bases became, in Reagan's America, something to celebrate, even as the winners and losers were easy to predict. Governing by market fundamentals not only fueled inequities in public expenditures across jurisdictions and led winners and losers alike to sharply reduce public spending on goods and services for the poor. As we'll see in the next chapter, it also gave local governments even more incentive to utilize local tax administration to shape and enhance area real estate markets, and to off-load neoliberalism's costs onto those who could afford it least.

14

CHARGED

Beaufort County's council members could barely contain their excitement. After a year of waiting, in early December 1988 the day had finally come when residents would receive their updated property assessments following a countywide reappraisal. "We're going to bring Beaufort County into the twenty-first century even if we have to bring the taxpayers kicking and screaming," one councilman reportedly boasted.[1]

Black landowners on Daufuskie Island soon discovered what that meant, as they received their tax notices. Bertha Stafford opened hers to discover that her bill was six times greater than before. Ella Mae Stevens' tiny home on a one-acre lot, previously valued at $11,000, was now deemed to be worth nearly $100,000 and taxed accordingly. Geneva Wiley's acreage was now being assessed at over $112,000, up from $10,000 a few years before. A disabled widow living on social security, who sold homemade crab cakes to make ends meet, saw the assessed value of her land nearly quadruple.[2]

None of them had the money to pay these exploding tax bills, and that was the point. For years, real estate developers had their eyes on this picturesque barrier island next to Hilton Head. The only thing that had been standing in the way were the dozens of Black families there, still stubbornly holding onto their land, some of which had been in their family's possession for over a century. The developers and their allies in county government hoped that these updated tax assessments, based on projected values in a hot market, would take care of the holdouts.

Beaufort County was aggressively pro-growth. And this was how they measured growth: by each family-owned farm, each acre of undeveloped forest land, and each small plot of land that had been turned into a golf course fairway, or a seaside vacation home, or a luxury hotel meant to resemble an old plantation estate, replete with Black cooks, maids, and groundskeepers. Other cities and counties looked to different metrics to gauge progress: formerly disinvested urban neighborhoods and depressed real estate markets teeming with new restaurants, coffee shops, and young professionals. But no matter what they envisioned growth to be, by the 1980s, local governments big and small understood that enabling growth was their chief function. They saw tax assessments as both a barometer and instrument for their success. Rising tax assessments fattened local tax bases. They were a sign of a healthy real estate market. And, in some places, they could be a means to an end.

As the federal government beat a hasty retreat from revenue sharing and fiscal equalization in the 1980s, as cities deindustrialized, and as states told local governments to compete for the people and businesses that generated tax revenue, real estate interests assumed an ever-greater role in shaping public policy and fiscal strategies.[3] Property taxes not only remained the lifeblood of local government, but local tax administration became a powerful tool for bolstering, protecting, and transforming housing and real estate markets. The manner in which public authorities administered tax policies to serve the interests of real estate capital varied by markets and by the political and financial stakeholders involved. Given the dizzying complexity and diversity of laws, regulations, and structures governing property tax administration, it never conformed to a standard model or formula. But regardless of the form it assumed, local fiscal policies and practices in the age of neoliberalism tended to share similar aims: to attract and retain the types of residents and businesses that drove up real estate values and to minimize threats to those values. And it tended to produce similar results: sharp escalations in housing costs, upward redistributions of wealth in real estate, and downward redistributions of local tax burdens.[4] Police departments and municipal courts assumed a crucial role in these processes. They protected and enhanced capital investments in urban real estate through aggressive policing practices targeted at the poor and socially deviant. And through those same aggressive enforcement strategies and the tickets, fines, and court costs they yielded, police served as key generators revenue for local governments.

These trends and phenomena, commonly grouped under the term "gentrification," emerged in cities or rural areas alike: wherever the gaps between acquisition costs and speculative values were widest and wherever public officials were most eager to use their public powers to facilitate real estate investment and development.[5] Because the places where Black people lived and owned property in larger numbers had suffered from underdevelopment and disinvestment in the past, and because they continued to experience the negative fiscal effects of real estate market–driven racism, they became the places where these practices, and this mode of governing, flourished.

* * *

Real estate development had transformed Sunbelt counties like Beaufort County, South Carolina, from some of the poorest into some of the fastest-growing, most prosperous in the nation. But its benefits remained highly concentrated and came directly at the expense of rural, landowning populations, who became targets of land speculators seeking to exploit their financial precarity and susceptibility to deception. The combination of poor people holding valuable property fueled this and other counties' growth and provided the foundation for capital gains from real estate investment and development. In these booming markets, property taxes not only captured a portion of the value from rising demand, they fueled market expansion.[6] During these decades, rising property taxes had forced untold numbers of acres onto the market, and forced poor Black people out of areas targeted for development.

All of this displacement and dispossession was done, strictly speaking, by the book, and according to the routine formulas and procedures used to assess property values. By the 1970s, most states had enacted laws requiring property assessments to be based, at least in part, on market values, defined by recent sales of comparable properties. These reforms aimed to make assessments fairer, to correct inequities that disadvantaged residents of lower-value properties, and to prevent land speculators from holding valuable land off the market at minimal cost. But too often, these assessments were self-fulfilling prophecies in service of market consolidation. By valuing rural people's family homesteads, small farms, and undeveloped acres based on what they could be worth, tax assessors played a crucial role in making them so.

Throughout the 1970s, demand for coastal real estate in South Carolina remained insatiable and policymakers prioritized bringing more of it onto the market. In 1980, Beaufort County was poised to take its next great leap forward. That year, a consortium of investors led by Hilton Head developer Charles Cauthen purchased nearly five thousand acres on Daufuskie Island—one half of the entire island— for $4.5 million. In 1982, it announced development plans.[7] At the time, the remote barrier island was home to a poor but resourceful and fiercely independent community of Black landowners. Aside from an elementary school, church, and general store, it remained free of development. Many families' land claims dated back to the dawn of emancipation. The land that the developers had purchased had been held by absentee whites who used it for hunting expeditions. Functionally, that land had served as the island's commons, a place where Black families' cattle and hogs roamed and grazed freely, where men and women hunted wildlife and fished, and where children played and explored. The only fences on the island protected small garden plots from foraging animals.[8]

As he surveyed the land and walked along its white sand beaches, Cauthen envisioned Daufuskie as something entirely different: an exclusive destination and high-end real estate market, a place where wealthy families could escape without hordes of middle-class vacationers following them. In 1984, the Cauthen-led land trust sold one thousand acres to International Paper, which began work on the Haig Point Plantation. At the same time, Cauthen and a team of local investors began developing and marketing the Melrose Plantation Resort. They got to work marking boundaries, designating land uses, and removing liabilities that threatened to limit the island's appeal to investors. The Melrose Company fenced and cleared four hundred acres of forest land for a golf course designed by Jack Nicklaus. Doing so eliminated much of the island's commons. It shipped away all the island's cattle. It drove and killed off as much of the island's wildlife as it could. What they deemed nuisances were the basis of Black islanders' way of life.[9]

State and local officials worked with Daufuskie's developers every step of the way. Every permit, they approved. Every request, they worked to fulfill. Every barrier to growth, they worked to remove. Such barriers included the Black families, whose continued presence on the island as independent, self-sufficient landowners was considered an obstacle to future development and market appreciation. Through their routine actions, public officials steadily made it harder for poor Black families to remain. The state's Coastal Council (of which Melrose's CEO and attorney were both members) closed off access to public roads leading to the shore, ensuring that the beach could be exclusive to homeowners and club members and inaccessible to the public. This restriction, in turn, prevented islanders from accessing the places where they had fished and harvested shellfish.[10] As the county paved roads to the new resorts, assisted in water and sewerage infrastructure, expended millions of dollars on beach renourishment projects, it denied requests and petitions from residents for the extension of water and sewer lines and garbage service to the Black side of the island. After the resort owners began operating a ferry for its members, Beaufort County discontinued its daily public ferry, claiming it could no longer afford the $48,000 annual expense. (In that same budget, the county allocated over $200,000 to improvements at the airports on Hilton Head and Lady's Islands.) Beaufort County thus not only made it impossible for Blacks who lived on the island to work on the mainland; they also made it impossible for children in grades eight and above to get to school. Their parents had to decide between moving off the island or placing their child in a home on the mainland.[11]

With each year, the number of Black people living on Daufuskie dwindled, and the footprint of future development spread. As had been the case across the coastal South over the previous decades, and in spite of the efforts of the Penn Center's Black Land Services and other campaigns to preserve and protect Black landownership, those families who sold their land invariably got much less than it was worth.

Many, though, resisted offers to sell and defiantly held onto their land. After Beaufort County completed the reassessment of property values in 1988, though, many of them no longer had a choice. Using recent sale prices of lots in the private resorts as the baseline, the tax assessors increased valuations of the small homes and undeveloped acres on the Black side of the island by as much as 700 percent. Residents who had paid less than $20 a year received $130 bills; a family that had previously paid $130 annually received a $2,800 bill. Those who could tried to sell a few acres to meet the expense. But the lack of clear title to heirs' properties made that option impossible for many. Others saw no other choice but to sell and leave. After the new assessments were mailed out, one realtor reported at least twelve Black landowners on Daufuskie had come into his office looking to sell. Many others never got the chance. Between 1986 and 1991, the number of properties that had tax liens sold at the county's annual tax sale tripled.[12]

Blacks decried the new tax bills as a deliberate attempt to force them out. "It is crystal clear that . . . the county has a sophisticated, legally knotted noose around [Black Daufuskians'] necks and . . . are using the tax machinery to force blacks off their land," the island's African American postmaster and civil rights veteran, Henrietta Canty, fumed. Canty penned an op-ed in the Hilton Head *Island Packet* denouncing the new assessments as "exorbitant [and] absurd." "Where on God's earth," she asked, "can the current Daufuskie Island population, mostly more than 60 years old and living on the lowest level of fixed income, find $7,000 to pay as taxes on 40 acres of non-income producing land?" They couldn't, and that was the point. "Just as the atomic bomb cleared Hiroshima, Beaufort County taxes will clear blacks from" Daufuskie, she predicted. The tax bills were all the more outrageous given the county's refusal to extend public services to the Black side of the island and its removal of ones that Blacks relied on. For these high tax bills, Canty fumed, Blacks received "no city water, no paved streets, no garbage collection, no fire service . . . no police services, no health services, not one street sign, no elected officers, no sewage system, no street lights, and no jobs paying $15,000 a year."[13] Nothing.

As Canty and others looked closer at the county's assessment rolls, they also began to notice glaring disparities between how Black people's modest dwellings were valued and what some of the island's well-heeled newcomers paid. A wealthy white retiree was taxed $395 on his vacation home and ten-acre lot, while an elderly Black woman received a tax bill for $674 on her modest home and six acres of woodland. A white-owned beachfront house on an eight-acre lot received a $171 tax bill, while an African American widow was forced to pay $443 for her two-acre tract. One sampling found that Black-owned land on the island was being assessed at an average of $119.50 per acre, versus $16.77 for white-owned land. Canty filed a formal complaint with the office of the state attorney general, which ordered the State Tax Commission to investigate the county's assessment practices.[14]

But Beaufort County tax assessor Ed Gay had nothing to hide. He had performed his duties as required under the law. The assessments Black people received accorded with the market-valuation model required under state law. "Each property is taken on its own individual merits," fellow tax assessor Leslie Smith insisted. The lower tax bills some white property owners enjoyed were due to their own savviness and ingenuity, or, more precisely, to their ability to hire a tax attorney who could find every possible exemption buried in the tax code. Some had received agricultural exemptions that dramatically lowered their tax liabilities simply by planting a tree. That Black people failed to avail themselves of these opportunities was their own fault. "You're dealing with a very uneducated population," Gay said, dismissing charges of intentional discrimination. "It was confusing to them." But the state's exemptions were so vague that the local assessor still had great discretion. They could allow favored property owners to receive such exemptions no matter how shaky their claims, and they could put the squeeze on property owners they considered undesirable. Indeed, several Black landowners had applied for agricultural exemptions only to be denied, as happened to Louise Wilson's family for their thirteen acres. Her son Christopher Holmes recounted that the county offered no explanation. "All it said was that I was ineligible." The family's tax bill jumped from $500 to $2,315. This instance typified how exemptions were handled for landowners in the path of future development. Some were even denied at the behest of land speculators who made a habit of reporting to county officials exempted land that was not being farmed.[15]

County and state officials insisted there was nothing wrong with the reassessments. Rather, they saw them as helping the market to grow to its fullest potential, and thus as a benefit to all. Higher tax bills ensured that property was in the hands of those who deserved it and who could maximize its value, county council chairman Bill Bowen claimed. "If someone can't afford to own property because they cannot pay taxes then they shouldn't own the property." The State Tax Commission found no evidence of racial discrimination. "What we see now are very poor people who cannot afford to pay the property taxes," spokeswoman Vicki Jinnette-Ringer remarked. "That's not discrimination, that's just the way it goes."[16]

Yvonne Wilson wasn't buying it. A fifth-generation islander, Wilson had moved back to Daufuskie in the early 1980s. Like many others, she was initially excited about the jobs and opportunities that resort developers promised. But after several years of working for low pay and being bypassed for management positions at Haig Point, she grew disillusioned. After learning that the Melrose Company was actively digging up a cemetery on the island to build a real estate office, Wilson spoke out. These developers, she warned, "want to tear

Black landowners of Daufuskie, S.C., fight to hold on against inequitable taxes

AN ISLAND'S DOUBLE STANDARD

Figure 14.1 Fifth-generation Daufuskie Island, South Carolina, resident Yvonne Wilson (center), with daughters Javonne (left) and LaKesha (right). Wilson led the fight against the overtaxation of Black-owned land by Beaufort County officials and resulting displacement of Black families from the island in the late 1980s and early 1990s. *Atlanta Constitution*, June 3, 1990.

up the island, push us off of it and do what they want to do." As president of the island's informal governing body, Wilson tried to rally opposition among the island's Black population. Resort executives struck back, sowing divisions among Black residents, stoking fears of retaliation and job loss, and ostracizing Wilson, blacklisting her from employment in the resorts and barring her from the company-owned ferries that provided the only transportation to and from the island. But Wilson refused to back down, and she became a leading critic of developers and their allies in local government and a tireless defender of islanders' land claims and way of life.[17]

In the spring of 1990, the National Council of Churches' Racial Justice Working Group sent a twenty-person delegation to the Sea

Islands, and afterward condemned the "greed [that was] destroying the unique sea-island culture and environment." It described the new plantation economy as "the latest form of segregation extolled, packaged, and sold by corporate giants."[18] The Christic Institute South, an activist law firm, dispatched a team of lawyers and organizers to investigate and soon began building a case charging collusion between public officials and private developers to hasten the removal of Black landowners. In 1992, the NAACP's Legal Defense Fund (LDF) dispatched its own lawyers to investigate the exorbitant tax increases, land seizures, and uneven distribution of public services on Daufuskie.

One thing none of these organizations did was contest the legality of the assessments. That approach, they all concluded, was a loser. Christic Institute attorney Lewis Pitts dismissed the chance of proving in court that the higher assessments were racially motivated. Their legal team instead challenged one of the Melrose Company's more appalling actions: the placement of a real estate office on top of a cemetery. They charged the company, county officials, and the coastal commission with "economic racism and cultural genocide."[19] Similarly, the NAACP LDF concluded that it would be, as attorney Alan Jenkins described, "very difficult to prove that there was any actionable discrimination" by county officials.[20] Instead, it charged that the county had violated Title VI of the 1964 Civil Rights Act by using federal community-development and block grants to pay for infrastructure development and service extensions to new, predominantly white residential developments. They also sued over the resorts' advertising and promotional practices, which had entirely privileged white audiences.[21] The developers ultimately settled both suits, agreeing to move the real estate office and place advertisements in Black publications. The county agreed to apply for federal grants for low-income housing, build a new school, and secure an agreement to allow island residents to use the developers' private ferry service. But these measures did little to reverse the decline of the island's Black population, which continued to shrink throughout the 1990s, or the concentration of wealth generated on the island, which remained behind gated walls.[22]

* * *

The same interests, priorities, and fundamental dynamics that were undermining Black land retention and economic opportunity in gentrifying rural counties in the Sunbelt South were doing the same in urban housing markets during these years. In Philadelphia, Pennsylvania, residents of predominantly Black neighborhoods near the city's center began experiencing the telltale signs of gentrification in the early 1980s: for renters, sharp spikes in monthly rents, and for homeowners, soaring property tax bills coupled with a barrage of letters, flyers, business cards, and phone calls from developers and real estate agents pressuring them to sell. And in response to their concerns over the displacement of longtime residents and disappearance of small Black-owned businesses, they heard the same rosy predictions from city officials: of the beneficial trickle-down effects of rising property values on the city's tax base and its public schools and city services, and of the jobs that new establishments catering to young, white urban professionals would bring to their neighborhoods. Protests and organized attempts to counteract what some Black Philadelphians labeled "recycling" of Black neighborhoods and the city's Black newspaper the *Philadelphia Tribune* called "the big land grab" formed. "It's like a war, man," community advocate Ralph Wynder said of the public-private forces aligned against Black neighborhoods in the path of development. "First they attack our weakest points and then they get our stronger, more stable areas."[23] Scholar and writer Gerald Horne cited the city's tax assessment office as a key facilitator of urban real estate profiteering. "It has been an open scandal for some time now," Horne charged, "that the Board of Revision of Taxes (BRT) tends to tax property in 'certain neighborhoods' higher than others." They did so, he added, to induce property owners to "sell their homes for a song often to those with close connections to the BRT, who then re-sell it at a dramatic profit."[24]

Tax assessors didn't need to actively collude with land speculators in order to advance their interests and facilitate their investments. They just needed to do their jobs, as they understood them, using the increasingly standardized models and formulas for assessing property being adopted by tax-assessment offices across the nation during these years. As discussed in chapter 11, many cities and counties adopted computerized assessment systems during the 1970s, often in response to revelations of rank corruption and favoritism among local tax assessors. Many others contracted with private firms like Cole-Layer-Trumble to conduct mass appraisals of area real estate. Whether done in-house or outsourced, the computer models used to determine tax assessments, critics pointed out, structurally disadvantaged longtime residents of gentrifying markets. The problem with these models, Arthur Lyons and Jason Hardy of the Center for Economic Policy Analysis argued in a 1999 report for the Chicago Rehab Network, is that they treated two distinct real estate markets—the "gentrifying" market of developers, rehabbers, and flippers, and the "traditional" market of longtime homeowners and tenants, and small businesses—as a single market, and they used sales data from recent property transactions as the basis for valuation across both markets. Since all the sales activity took place in the gentrifying market, these valuations became the basis for property valuations and, with them, tax assessments across both markets. In the course of doing so, these assessment formulas facilitated the gradual merging of both markets into a single, gentrified one.[25]

In response to widespread taxpayer unrest and fears, especially among the elderly, of being taxed out of their homes in the 1970s, states adopted or expanded property tax relief programs.[26] The two most common were programs that allowed homeowners to seek tax relief when property taxes on a primary residence exceeded a certain percentage of a household's income (known as circuit breakers) and exemptions on a certain amount or percentage of the assessed value of a primary place of residence from taxation (known as homestead exemptions). (These were coupled with many states placing statutory limits on annual increases in property assessments, which, as discussed in the previous chapter, proliferated in the wake of California voter's passage of Prop. 13 in 1978.)[27] By 2002, thirty-five states plus the District of Columbia had adopted some circuit breaker program. Most of these programs offered tax relief to renters as well as homeowners. Circuit breaker programs were also funded at the state level and thus had no impact on the size of local tax bases and local property tax revenues. All but eleven of these states plus the District of Columbia restricted eligibility for circuit breakers to elderly or disabled homeowners, though. Forty states plus the District of Columbia offered homestead exemptions. Eligibility for these exemptions varied considerably. In some states, they were only available to veterans or the disabled. In others, any person could claim one on their primary place of residence. In still others, different exemptions were available to different groups.[28] Some cities or counties adopted their own homestead exemptions on top of what their states provided. In response to mounting concerns and protests against gentrification in Chicago, in 2004 Cook County allowed all homeowners to exempt from taxation up to $20,000 (later increased to $33,000) of the assessed value of their primary place of residence.[29]

Most of these measures fell short, though, in providing sufficient tax relief to those most in need. State-funded circuit breakers offered the most efficient and effective means of protecting vulnerable homeowners from being taxed out of their homes, and they did so without negatively impacting local budgets. But in addition to restricting eligibility to the elderly and disabled, most states placed a low ceiling on income levels and capped benefits at low amounts. Homestead exemptions offered even more of a mixed bag. Many states, for example, exempted a uniform percentage of an eligible property's assessed values from taxation, providing the greatest tax breaks to the wealthiest homeowners.[30] Assessment caps and other limits on annual increases, as well, tended to greatly advantage the already-advantaged and, in practice, shift the incidence of local property taxation further onto lower-income and minority neighborhoods.[31]

A key factor shaping the impact of these exemptions and other protections were the state and local offices entrusted to administer them. Most of the tax exemptions, circuit breakers, and preferential rates that states created to protect low-income property owners required those who were eligible to apply for them, and they placed responsibility for evaluating applications in the hands of local tax administrators. Advertisement of these programs to eligible taxpayers was also often left to local tax authorities. Studies consistently found low participation rates among eligible homeowners, especially in those programs designated for low-income homeowners and that required annual reapplications. One study found that, in some states, less than one-third of eligible homeowners applied for circuit breaker rebates. Few participated in these programs because few knew they existed. One survey conducted by the American Association of Retired Persons (AARP) found that many homeowners who were eligible for tax exemptions were not aware of their existence. The lowest levels of public awareness were for those programs designated for low-income homeowners.[32]

As the Black landowning families on Daufuskie Island denied tax exemptions for dubious reason could attest, tax exemptions were, in practice, only as effective in preventing home and land loss among vulnerable populations as the public officials charged with administering them allowed them to be. When it was not in those officials' fiscal and political interests to advertise these programs, assist homeowners in completing applications, or approve them, they didn't. This trend was most apparent with state-run circuit breaker programs. In addition to providing miserly rebates to eligible homeowners, most states put little effort into notifying the public of their availability or providing assistance to those seeking to apply.[33] Michigan's Poverty Tax Exemption (PTE) program, created in 1980, allowed eligible homeowners to claim up to a full exemption on their property taxes due to poverty. But few of those who were eligible took advantage of it. In Detroit, where, in the mid-2010s, 28 percent of all homeowners in the city were eligible for full exemptions on their property taxes, fewer than 12 percent of eligible homeowners applied for and received any exemption under the program.[34] Management of the program helps explain why. As a team of researchers at the University of Michigan that studied the PTE program during these years found, many poor homeowners in the city did not know about the program, and those who did often struggled to successfully complete an application that, the plaintiffs in one lawsuit against Michigan's PTE program described, was "needlessly complex and impenetrable" and "unduly burdensome."[35] Eligible participants described having their applications rejected without explanation, of having exemptions rescinded for no discernible reason, of help lines where no one answered and messages that were never returned, and of trying to apply repeatedly and unsuccessfully before giving up. "It's like they make it difficult for you on purpose," one exasperated Detroit homeowner put it.[36]

Given Detroit's fiscal circumstances at the time, such suspicions were warranted. In the wake of the housing foreclosure crisis of 2008, few cities had more homeowners deserving of property tax relief, and few cities were more disincentivized to grant it, than Detroit. Between 2008 and 2010, home values in the Motor City plummeted from an average of $80,000 to $25,000. The city was facing massive erosion of its tax base at the very moment when it was drowning in debt and staring into the fiscal abyss. Under Michigan law, assessments could not be greater than 50 percent of a property's market value, and local assessors were required to reassess properties annually. But budget cuts had reduced the city's assessment office's workforce by nearly one-third since the 1990s. At the time of the crash, the number of parcels assigned to each of the appraisers was nearly double the recommended ratio. An audit of the assessment division found employees fatigued and demoralized by lack of staffing and support. That state of affairs, combined with a botched transition to a new assessment system in 2003 that had resulted in a massive loss of data, had severely constrained the office's ability to carry out its most basic functions. The assessments it rendered had been highly inaccurate and regressive even before the market collapsed. Moreover, Michigan's constitutional limits on property tax increases discouraged local assessors from valuing property accurately in the wake of a market downturn, since downward adjustments and shrinking of the tax base would be locked in place even if the market recovered and property values rebounded. The laws themselves, and the lawmakers who passed them, were guided by the assumption that property values could only rise.[37]

Lacking the personnel to do its job and disincentivized from doing so anyway, Detroit's assessment office opted to ride out the crash. It did not adjust assessments downward and hoped that home prices would rebound. By 2010, homes that sold for $2,300 and $12,500 were being assessed at $42,000 and $62,000. The lower the property's value, the greater the gap. Assessments on upwards of 84 percent of homes in Detroit exceeded the state's 50 percent constitutional limit, with the vast majority of those homes, and the greatest excesses, found in the poorest neighborhoods. The lowest-value residential properties were overassessed at 4.8 times the legal limit. Conversely, nearly all residential properties in the highest-value markets received assessments below 50 percent.[38]

The city's failure to reassess properties following the housing-market crash forced its poorest and most vulnerable homeowners to assume crushing tax burdens. Between 2010 and 2017, Detroit overtaxed homeowners by over $600 million. During these same years, property tax-delinquency rates soared to levels not seen since the Great Depression. As they did, the Wayne County Treasurer's Office aggressively foreclosed on tax-delinquent homes. Between 2011 and 2015, the county tax foreclosed one out of every four properties in Detroit. Over thirty thousand of those properties were occupied at the time. Most of these properties were sold to professional real estate investors who, using dozens of different limited liability companies (LLCs), bought hundreds of tax deeds in bulk each year. After flipping the most valuable properties, bulk buyers of tax-foreclosed properties tried to rent the rest of their acquisitions back to dispossessed former owners, sell to low-income homeseekers using an installment contract, or keep as a speculative investment. Rarely did these new owners improve, maintain, or even pay subsequent tax obligations on the properties they had acquired.[39]

* * *

While fiscally distressed cities like Detroit resisted reassessing properties downward, cities experiencing intensive real estate development and sharp, but uneven, spikes in real estate values were also reluctant to conduct reassessments, out of fear of cooling the market and in deference to powerful constituents. By 2011, it had been twenty-three years since Jersey City's last reassessment. That year, it began one. But in 2013, new Mayor Steven Fulop halted the process, allegedly at the behest of one of the largest investors in downtown real estate and major contributors to his political action committee. By then, residents of the poorest and most overtaxed neighborhoods were paying tens of millions of extra dollars in taxes each year.[40]

In the summer of 2015, local Black congregations and nonprofit groups formed Jersey City Together and began inviting residents of low-income neighborhoods to share their challenges and concerns. One issue rose above the rest: the crushing burden of high property taxes. The organization hired Arthur Lyons's Center for Economic Policy Analysis and researchers at the Philadelphia-based Reinvestment Fund to study assessment levels across the city. They found that, along the waterfront and downtown, areas that had seen massive public investment in private development, properties were assessed at as little as 10 percent of market value. In Black neighborhoods, assessment ratios exceeded 70 percent. A home in the predominantly Black Greenville neighborhood that sold for $175,000 and one downtown that sold for $530,000 received the exact same assessment ($90,000) and same tax bill ($6,733). The city's assessments were so biased in favor of white and higher-income households that it risked a federal civil rights lawsuit. The researchers urged city officials to act. "Every year Jersey City waits to conduct a revaluation," they warned, "the burden on largely low- and moderate-income neighborhoods and communities of color increases, and the impact on everyone of the eventual revaluation becomes more difficult to manage."[41]

Black residents knew they were being gouged and underserved, and now they had the proof. Jersey City Together called for a full revaluation of all city properties. State officials agreed, finding that the city's assessment ratios were so inequitable that they violated the state's constitution. Fulop alleged that the state's order was politically motivated, intended to embarrass him. Privately, city officials begged

Jersey City Together to not publicly release its findings. They did so anyway.[42]

In April 2016, Jersey City Together demanded Fulop and other officials appear at a community forum. That evening, nine hundred people crammed into pews in the Old Bergen Church. Fulop sat, stone-faced, as the Reverend Alonzo Perry lambasted the city for its deliberate inaction. Standing next to images of two properties, Perry pointed to the overtaxed, Black-owned home and said, "This person is a law-abiding, loving citizen of Jersey City, who just happens to pay three times more taxes than this loving, law-abiding citizen. I'm ashamed." Anticipating public officials' response, Perry continued, "They will tell you, . . . 'we have different calculations, it's hard, it's complex.' Is it?" The audience responded with shouts of "No!" Perry concluded, "This isn't a political issue. This isn't about politicians fighting. This is about people having to decide whether they can afford to stay in their homes. So, it's about fairness. . . . We've got one side of the city that's overtaxed, and we got another side of the city that's over-developed. . . . All I want is a level playing field. No matter where you live in this city, you're paying your fair share." As Perry took his seat, the crowd erupted in cheers and applause.[43]

Fulop struggled to respond. He claimed that a revaluation would hurt low-income homeowners, and he insisted that it would force some poor elderly people to lose their homes. Audience members scoffed and jeered. Perry interrupted, "People are losing their homes now, Mr. Mayor." Fulop attempted to dismiss residents' claims that the city had intentionally kept assessments frozen at the behest of wealthy property owners and downtown and waterfront developers. Listing off all of the mayors during the three decades when the city had failed to update its assessments, he asked the crowd, "Now do you think all those individuals have some conspiracy to suppress a certain community?" Numerous people shouted back, "Yes!"[44]

Days after his disastrous performance, Fulop agreed to proceed with a full revaluation of the city's property assessments. Thus, in February 2018, owners of downtown properties saw massive tax hikes, while residents of the predominantly Black neighborhoods

Greenville, the West Side, and the Heights saw their tax bills fall by 60 percent or more. Perry and Jersey City Together claimed vindication. "We've seen that a lot of the development Downtown was being subsidized by people in the poor areas of the community," he said. "The numbers bear that."[45]

* * *

Indeed, the numbers told the story. Whenever some investigative reporter or researcher peeked under the hood of local property tax systems, they found evidence of structural racism. In Pittsburgh, Pennsylvania, a 2002 study found, homes in heavily Black neighborhoods were assessed at a ratio two times greater than homes in white neighborhoods.[46] In New Haven, Connecticut, residents of majority-Black and majority-Latino neighborhoods were assessed at a rate 75 percent greater than residents of majority-white neighborhoods.[47] In Baltimore, Maryland, the assessment ratio in heavily Black census tracts was 28.8 to 34.4 percent higher than the citywide average. Similarly, in Washington, DC, Black census tracts had assessment ratios between 37.1 and 64.6 percent higher than the rest of the city.[48]

What was a revelation in some cities was an all-too-familiar set of numbers in others. In the summer of 2017, the *Chicago Tribune* and ProPublica revealed that the city's Black and brown neighborhoods continued to suffer from overtaxation while the wealthiest, whitest areas enjoyed generous tax breaks. Owners of the most valuable properties downtown received the biggest breaks of all. The effective tax rate in the severely depressed North Lawndale neighborhood was two times that in Gold Coast and Lincoln Park, two of the more exclusive neighborhoods. Homes in Black neighborhoods received assessments that were, in some cases, twice the property's market value, while homes that sold for $1.5 million were assessed at nearly half that amount.[49] "It's a textbook example of institutional racism," property tax policy expert Christopher Berry said.[50]

And yet the available solution—the appeals process—in practice made the problem worse. Assessments were consistently more regressive *after* appeals had been heard. That's because, for all intents and purposes, only owners of higher-value (and, often, under-assessed) properties could file a successful appeal. As was the case across the nation, in Chicago specialized law firms, such as the one led by state Speaker of the House Michael Madigan, annually filed thousands of appeals, earning their clients significant reductions in their property tax obligations. Between 2011 and 2016, Madigan's firm—which generally worked with commercial and industrial landowners—alone reduced the overall assessed value of property in Cook County by $1.7 billion, a 20 percent reduction.[51] Alongside such law firms were those that handled appeals on residential properties. Most of the city's major firms charged clients on a contingency-fee basis, meaning that they got paid only if their clients won. As such, they only took on cases involving properties whose tax bills were so large that any reduction would be substantial. Others charged a flat fee that was, for many poorer homeowners (those most likely in need of relief), often greater than the tax bill itself.

The tax appeal industry grew rapidly in the wake of the Great Recession. By 2015, tax appeal lawyers in Cook County annually collected $35 million in fees from residential property appeals alone, triple the amount they had collected in 2003. On residential blocks in North Center, one of the city's most expensive neighborhoods, nearly half of all homeowners filed appeals on homes that were, in all cases, either fairly assessed or already under-assessed. Over 95 percent of those cases resulted in further reductions. But tax appeals remained functionally unavailable to those most deserving of reductions. In North Lawndale, where homes were overassessed on average by 40 percent, few homeowners had ever filed an appeal. Many indicated that they did not know about this option. Others were treated rudely or given false information when they had tried. "They're short and nasty when you call," one homeowner said of the appeals office. "They're not willing to do anything to help us."[52]

Even among those who did appeal, Black homeowners in the poorest neighborhoods—the most overassessed homeowners—were also the least likely to win a reduction.[53] On one block in North Lawndale, only a single homeowner filed an appeal on a property that was grossly overassessed. The reduction that Rozalyn Shelton received failed to fully correct for the initial overvaluation, and her effective tax rate remained 60 percent higher than what homeowners in North Center paid. Shelton had inherited her home from parents and worked hard to "honor [them] by keeping up the property." "But," as she told a reporter, "the taxes are killing us."[54]

Two years earlier, Cook County assessor Joseph Berrios had announced his office's adoption of a new "state of the art" computer program that promised to cut down on inaccuracies and unfairness.[55] But that was all for show. Berrios's office never implemented the new system, and instead continued to reward major developers and corporate interests, placate white middle- and upper-class homeowners, and stick it to the urban poor.

Under fire, Berrios stonewalled FOIA requests for his office's valuation methods. He claimed his Latino heritage and childhood spent in the Cabrini-Green housing project as defenses against charges of racism. But community organizers and activists rejected these empty appeals to identity politics. Multiracial groups protested outside Berrios's office, demanding that it issue refunds to residents of Black and Latino neighborhoods and calling for fundamental changes to a system that, as one organizer described, functioned to "[transfer] money from poor and minority communities into the hands of the wealthy."[56] The following spring, voters rallied behind reform candidate Fritz Kaegi, who soundly defeated Berrios.[57]

After Detroiters weathered the city's housing foreclosure crisis—what one besieged residents described as a "hurricane without water"—they demanded justice and reparations for victims of illegal overtaxation and resulting foreclosures. In 2016, the ACLU and NAACP-LDF sued the county to halt tax auctions, alleging violation of the Fair Housing Act, and sued the city over its failure to make the state's poverty tax exemption accessible to the poor.[58] The following year, law professor Bernadette Atuahene, who had been instrumental in uncovering the causes and extent of overtaxation, founded the Coalition for Property Tax Justice. That group brought together over a dozen grassroots organizations to fight to end the illegal overassessment of lower-valued and predominantly Black-owned homes in Detroit, halt the Wayne County tax auction, and compensate homeowners who had been overtaxed and/or lost their home to tax foreclosure. Activists flooded public meetings, demanding the city correct unfair assessments and offer restitution to its victims. They fought for a moratorium on tax auctions, foreclosures, and evictions. The Coalition offered pro bono tax-appeal services.[59] In 2020, a group of Detroit homeowners filed a federal lawsuit against the city, alleging that the city had sent updated assessments after the deadline for residents to file appeals. The suit attempted to bring the protections of the 1968 Fair Housing Act to bear on local property tax administration and circumvent the barriers established by the 1937 Tax Injunction Act.[60]

In the decades since the US Supreme Court declined to hear the lawsuit filed by Black residents of Edwards, Mississippi, in 1972, there had been several attempts to convince the federal courts to relax the Tax Injunction Act's restrictions.[61] In 1976, a group of Black homeowners in Berks County, Pennsylvania, filed a lawsuit in federal court alleging that, by intentionally neglecting to conduct reassessments at a time when property values were sharply rising in white housing markets and falling in Black ones, the county had violated Black taxpayers' rights under section 1341 of the Civil Rights Act. It further charged that, because it did not allow for class-action lawsuits over local tax matters, the state of Pennsylvania had failed to meet the Tax Injunction Act's "plain, speedy, and efficient" threshold. A federal appeals court agreed with the plaintiffs on the latter charge, but when Pennsylvania lawmakers responded by amending state law to allow for class litigation, the federal court found the state in compliance and dismissed the case.[62] In 1981, the US Supreme Court heard a challenge to Illinois's tax assessment and appeal procedures filed by an African American property owner who argued that the state's tax appeals law failed to meet the Tax Injunction Act's standard for barring federal claims. In a 5–4 decision, the high court deemed the state minimally, but sufficiently, in compliance.[63] In 1999, the US Justice Department filed a federal lawsuit against Nassau County, New York, alleging that the county's structurally racist assessment formula, which resulted in homes in predominantly Black residential districts being grossly overtaxed relative to white areas, violated the Fair Housing Act. But a federal district court refused to hear the case while a separate lawsuit filed by a group of Black residents was pending in state court. To avoid having either case go to trial, county officials agreed to conduct a full-scale reassessment of properties based on market values.[64]

Detroit homeowners were also unable to convince the federal courts to consider suits alleging discrimination in local tax administration. The cases against the city for violating the Fair Housing Act were dismissed in both state and federal courts, while the federal lawsuit alleging that the city had failed to provide a "plain, speedy, and efficient" method of correcting inaccurate assessments was dismissed in the district court.[65]

* * *

On August 9, 2014, Ferguson, Missouri, police officer Darren Wilson stopped eighteen-year-old African American resident Michael Brown and his friend Dorian Johnson for walking in the street. It was one of numerous minor violations of local ordinances that officers were trained to aggressively enforce. That's because Wilson's job was not to protect public safety so much as to collect revenue. Fines for violations such as Brown's constituted one-fifth of the city's overall budget. How Wilson was trained to do his job, where he was assigned to work and when, how he won the favor of his bosses, and how he secured pay raises and promotions were all geared toward that one overriding goal. The best officers in the Ferguson police department were those who could "issue the largest number of citations during a single stop."[66] But Wilson did not get the chance to slap Brown with multiple citations and demonstrate his "productivity." Instead, when Brown resisted Wilson's commands and following a brief pursuit, Wilson fired six shots into his chest, killing him.[67]

The uprising that followed cast unprecedented attention on the role of police departments as revenue collectors, in addition to being one of the most voracious consumers of local tax dollars. Ferguson was far from an outlier in its reliance on fines and tickets, or in its incentive structure that trained officers to act more as tax collectors than as protectors of public safety. In the years leading up to Brown's killing, tickets and fines constituted a significant, and growing, portion of local government budgets in cities and towns across the US, including several others in the St. Louis metro area.[68]

Sharp decreases in federal and state funding and support for local governments and public schools, structural limits on localities' ability to raise revenue, and the subordination of fiscal policies to market imperatives—all of which began in the 1980s—resulted in more than sharp cuts to services for the poor and disadvantaged. They also compelled local governments—especially the most fiscally disadvantaged—to rely even more heavily on regressive sales taxes, fines, and fees extracted disproportionately from the poor. The effects were most evident in smaller, inner-ring suburbs, where growing numbers of Black Americans had flocked during these decades in search of better schools and greater opportunities.

By the 1990s, majority-Black suburbs dotted the landscape of most American metropolitan regions. But few of these Black enclaves enjoyed the tax advantages that had helped to fuel the postwar suburban boom. One study of over one thousand suburbs in thirty-one metro areas found that residents of majority-Black suburbs paid "substantially . . . higher taxes" than residents of predominantly white suburbs. Effective tax rates on residential properties in Black suburbs were $1.16 per $100 of market value, in comparison to 82 cents per $100 in white suburbs.[69] There were wide disparities in effective tax rates for Black homeowners in most major metro areas in the US. In 58 percent of suburban housing markets, a home in the hands of a Black person was assessed as being worth more than a comparable home owned by a white person.[70] All the while, majority-Black suburbs suffered from stagnant home prices that made a mockery of homeownership's touted wealth-building benefits.

In addition, Black suburbs struggled to attract and retain commercial retailers and major employers, which limited the size and growth of their tax bases. This limitation, in turn, also made it more expensive for Black cities and suburbs to borrow. In the first decade of the 2000s, majority-Black municipalities were consistently rated lower and forced to pay higher interest on bonded debt than predominantly white cities.[71] As a result, majority-Black suburbs were forced to tax property heavily. In the Chicago region, the three suburbs with the highest tax rates (Ford Heights, Park Forest, and Riverdale) all had Black populations over 60 percent, while the three suburbs with the lowest tax rates (Hinsdale, Burr Ridge, and Barrington) all had white populations over 80 percent.[72] Between 1998 and 2016, the per-capita property tax obligations of residents of majority-Black suburbs around Chicago rose from $184 (in 2016 dollars) to $690, while payments in predominantly white, middle-class suburbs rose from $175 to $400.[73] In suburban Pittsburgh, the place with the highest tax rate was the low-income, majority-Black town of Wilkinsburg.[74] By the early years of the first decade of the 2000s, residents of cities with small tax bases paid more than twice the local taxes and fees per $1,000 of income than residents of affluent municipalities.[75]

Even the most prosperous Black suburbs were not immune. Outside Washington, DC, Prince George's County, Maryland, became home to a large Black middle class in the 1990s. But here, too, officials struggled to attract the kind of commercial development that generated sales and property tax revenue and grew tax bases. Commercial retailers opted instead for the whiter Montgomery County in Maryland and Fairfax County in Virginia. As a result, property tax rates in Prince George's County remained consistently higher than rates in those neighboring counties. Black consumers' sales tax dollars went to enhance the budgets of their white neighbors. At the same time, per-pupil spending in the county's schools remained lower. Writing about Prince George's County, the legal scholar Sheryll Cashin observed that "external prejudice against black neighborhoods ma[de] it virtually impossible for the black middle class to form havens of their own that approximate the economic or opportunity benefits of a white enclave."[76]

It was not for lack of trying. During these years, majority-Black suburbs became the most aggressive adopters of neoliberal fiscal strategies to attract and retain businesses, employers, and commercial retailers. In suburban Chicago, majority-Black suburbs tended to award more generous tax abatements and use TIFs more aggressively than white suburbs did. These strategies not only deprived localities of tax revenue but often led to disastrous outcomes.[77] As Ferguson, Missouri, saw its Black population rise and property values flatline early in the first decade of the 2000s, it offered businesses major tax concessions. It used TIFs to attract commercial development, but the bonds issued failed to cover development costs. The Great Recession sent sales tax revenues from the retailers in TIF districts plummeting. In 2009, Ferguson officials struck a deal with Fortune 500 company Emerson Electric to build its flagship data center there. In return, Ferguson assessed Emerson Electric's 152-acre property at rock-bottom levels, generating minimal revenue for the fiscally belea-guered city.[78] Between 2009 and 2014, Ferguson's public debt soared from $14.2 million to $25.9 million.[79] Limited in its ability to tax by Missouri law, Ferguson turned to tickets and fines. By 2014, fines in Ferguson generated $2.5 million in annual revenue, one-fifth of the overall annual budget. Ferguson was not unique among mid-sized cities and suburbs.[80] Indeed, eleven municipalities in suburban Chicago collected more in fines and forfeits per capita than did Ferguson.[81] It was not even the most reliant on fines among municipalities in metro St. Louis. St. Ann and St. John derived 39.6 percent and 29.4 percent of their budgets, respectively, from fines.[82]

These fines targeted poorer populations. Municipalities enforced ordinances against wearing saggy pants, playing loud music, leaving toys in a front yard, placing a basketball hoop or grill in a front yard, having mismatched curtains, or loitering in a park.[83] They placed cameras on traffic signals, ticketing every car caught in an intersection when the light turned red. In Ferguson, three cameras resulted in 5,318 traffic tickets in 2013 alone.[84] This tactic proved so lucrative that some cities manipulated traffic signals to generate more tickets. In the St. Louis suburb Belt-Ridge, law enforcement were credibly accused of manually switching a traffic signal from green to red, then issuing citations to unwitting offenders.[85] In 2014, Chicago placed hundreds of cameras on traffic lights, disproportionately in neighborhoods with larger Black and Latino populations. It also shortened the duration of yellow lights by 0.1 second after projecting that the measures could generate up to $300 million more in annual revenue.[86]

Black-governed cities and cities with large Black populations were among the most aggressive pursuers of fine-generated revenue. Many of these municipalities had tried to follow the neoliberal playbook for achieving fiscal health—tax abatements, TIFs, and the like—and lost. Yet Black public officials did not indict a system that systematically funneled tax revenue and concentrated growth in white spaces. Instead, drawing on an older and perhaps more familiar playbook, they blamed the Black poor. In metro St. Louis, Black officials of some of the most predatory cities blamed depressed housing markets and small tax bases on the cultural deviancy of the Black poor. Internalizing the racist logic that had been used to justify the overtaxation and under-servicing of Black people for generations, Black suburban officials rationalized their excessive fines for minor quality-of-life violations as a means of both disciplining poor Blacks and ensuring they paid their "fair share."[87]

* * *

It was that same contempt for the poor and disadvantaged, that same instinct to ascribe social inequalities to individual failures and deviant cultures, and that same faith in the efficiencies of the market—the core features of the neoliberal era—that would come to inform how local governments enforced tax payments during these decades, the subject of the final chapter.

15

DEBT PAYS

Attendees at the 2016 annual meeting of the National Tax Lien Association (NTLA) in Fort Lauderdale, Florida, were in a festive mood. In the years since the mortgage foreclosure crisis and throughout the Great Recession, property tax–delinquency rates across the country had soared while local governments' tax revenues and support from federal and state governments plummeted. These conditions offered tax-lien investors greater volume and the industry more favorable terrain for advancing its political agenda. So, it was fitting that the O'Jays' hit song "For the Love of Money" introduced executive director Brad Westover's annual state of the industry address. Attendees, some still nursing hangovers from the open bar and casino tables the previous night, clapped and cheered as Westover strode onstage. Westover smiled sheepishly as the music died down and joked that, after what he had seen the night before, the NTLA would refrain from holding any future meetings in Las Vegas. Then, snapping back into his role as the tax-lien industry's chief spokesman and defender, Westover pointed toward his assistant and her infant child, who was resting comfortably in a stroller. "This is what we're about," Westover soberly told the audience: making America a better place for future generations by funding local governments and schools. "Without the funds that we contribute to America—that's about $4 billion a year—education would be in a world of hurt." "So," he continued, "we're in the business of funding education and other stuff that local governments use with our funds."[1]

It was a fittingly awkward moment for an industry whose earnings grew in proportion to household financial distress and overall economic inequality, but that framed its work as a service, and itself as a benefactor, to local governments and taxpayers alike. Since its founding in 1997, the NTLA had worked to mold the local practice of tax-lien speculation into a national industry and advance the interests of the institutional investors, private-equity firms, financial servicers, consultants and financial advisors, lawyers, and government officials who held stakes in it. It pushed states to adopt legislation favorable to tax buyers' bottom line. It argued that private investors, motivated solely by the prospect of personal financial gain, were better capable of collecting delinquent taxes than sclerotic and incompetent bureaucrats, and better able to force recalcitrant taxpayers into compliance. By partnering with tax-lien investors, it argued, cities could not only receive an annual infusion of revenue that would go toward keeping schools funded, parks open, streetlights on, and sidewalks repaired; they could solve the problem of vacant and abandoned homes, spur neighborhood revitalization and investment, and, ultimately, serve the public.

Figure 15.1 National Tax Lien Association promotional flyer, stressing that tax buyers' investments help fund local governments, 2016.

From the early 1990s to the Great Recession, tax-lien investing grew into a multibillion-dollar industry financed by global investment banks and wielding considerable influence over state and local governments. Its growth came to embody American culture, society, and governance in the neoliberal age: the financialization of public institutions and government functions; the growing faith that the market could solve whatever ailed cities and communities; the reorientation of public policy and administration around market principles and mechanisms; and an increasingly punitive political culture that exacted harsh punishments for the most minor infractions and ascribed economic inequality to individuals' failures and shortcomings.[2]

But even as the investors changed and strategies evolved, the game remained the same. Tax buyers preyed on financially distressed and vulnerable homeowners. They harvested the bulk of their profits from low-income and minority neighborhoods, with devastating effects for individuals, families, and communities.

* * *

In the early 1980s, the actions by Federal Reserve chairman Paul Volcker to curb inflation sent interest rates soaring to record levels, nearly reaching 20 percent in 1981. The statutory interest rates on tax liens, which had once made them so attractive to investors, suddenly seemed less attractive, as tax buyers had any number of investment options that generated a greater return. In Cook County, the percentage of tax liens auctioned plummeted in 1980 and 1981. States that conducted bid-down auctions responded by hastily raising the maximum interest rate. In 1982, New Jersey raised its interest rate cap from 8 to 18 percent, while Illinois raised its from 12 to 18 percent. The following year, the number of tax liens sold at Cook County's auction doubled and the amount of revenue it generated quadrupled.[3]

By the early 1990s, the federal interest rate had fallen back below 4 percent, but the adjusted interest rates on tax liens remained. High interest rates, combined with the growth of secondary markets in various forms of asset-backed securities, made local governments' tax debts an attractive investment option. Because of the way states structured tax-lien sales and the various profit streams flowing from a single tax lien, investors with enough capital could not lose. You did not need an intimate knowledge of local real estate markets. You did not need to send your son or nephew out, delinquent tax list in hand, to cruise through neighborhoods inspecting each property prior to a tax sale. In many states, you didn't even need to secure a high interest rate on the initial tax debt. You just needed to flood the market and buy in bulk.

Richard Heitmeyer showed the way. In the early 1990s, the Florida accountant built a database of tax-sale listings in states, like Florida, that awarded tax buyers the right to pay subsequent late taxes on properties at a statutory interest rate. He then identified properties that had been late in consecutive years. By zeroing in on these properties, Heitmeyer could accumulate massive volumes of tax liens by simply outbidding all competitors, agreeing to collect as little as zero-percent interest on the original tax debt if need be, while being assured of profits from the high interest he could charge on subsequent tax debts.[4] In 1992, Heitmeyer founded the Capital Asset Research Corporation (CARC) and shopped his plan to private-equity firms and investment banks. Lehman Brothers dove in headfirst, giving Capital Asset a $500 million revolving line of credit. CARC was soon dominating tax sales across Florida. In 1994, the company purchased 30 percent of all tax liens sold there, spending over $200 million on tax liens that, in almost all cases, Heitmeyer purchased at zero percent interest.[5]

Even as Heitmeyer replaced the tedious process of inspecting individual properties with computer-generated spreadsheets, he still had to travel to county courthouses across the state and sit through endless hours of bidding. The time, expense, and complexity of conducting tax sales and working with dozens of individual tax buyers was costly for local governments, as well. So, Heitmeyer came up with a solution: local governments would sell their entire delinquent tax digest to a single buyer at a discount and clear their books. The investor would handle the rest. In 1994, CARC pitched the idea of a bulk tax-lien sale to the commissioners of Fulton County, Georgia, home of the city of Atlanta. At the time, Fulton County had over $155 million in unpaid taxes, and the city government and public schools were facing severe budget shortfalls. The chairman of the county commission, Mitch Skandalakis, was a childhood friend and former associate of the tax-lien investor's vice president, John "Buddy" Ramsey. He sold the idea to Atlanta's school board president, Aaron Watson, and mayor, Bill Campbell, who characterized the bulk sale "a win-win situation for all of us."[6]

Groups and organizations dedicated to revitalizing disinvested neighborhoods in Atlanta immediately noticed a problem with this plan.[7] For years, neighborhood associations, Habitat for Humanity, the Carter Center, and the city's newly created Land Bank Authority had been working to clean up and rehabilitate vacant, abandoned, and chronically tax-delinquent properties in poorer neighborhoods. Their efforts were continually frustrated by tax-delinquency laws that fattened tax buyers' return on investment the longer a property remained tax delinquent. Exploiting this feature of tax delinquency proceedings was the entire basis of CARC's profit model for bulk sales. Their interest was not to quickly restore properties to taxpaying status, but the opposite. Moreover, this plan sold tax liens on vacant and abandoned properties on which the tax buyer had no hope of collecting or paying taxes themselves, but that would nevertheless remain in limbo, with neither the city's land bank nor a local nonprofit able to take any action toward rehabilitation in the interim. Emory law professor Frank Alexander, who had spearheaded the creation of the Land Bank Authority, expressed alarm. "While this could provide a short term cash advance to the County, and the City, it could potentially have a devastating impact on the functions of the Land Bank Authority, and on neighborhood redevelopment," he said.[8] These warnings went unheeded, and in 1994 Fulton County completed its first bulk tax-lien sale.

Wall Street investors took notice of the lucrative potential of local governments' unpaid taxes. In 1993, Bret Schundler, the mayor of Jersey City, New Jersey, and former Wall Street bond broker, convinced state lawmakers to enable local governments to securitize and market their tax debts. That year, Jersey City bundled its $44 million in uncollected property taxes and transferred the money into a trust managed by Breen Capital, which issued $31 million in bonds. Jersey City received $25 million in cash, along with the prospect of more after the bondholders had been paid off. Breen Capital received $6 million in cash and additional profits from interest, fees, and foreclosures.[9]

Following that groundbreaking deal, large financial firms and institutional investors began lobbying legislatures to authorize negotiated bulk sales and tax-lien securitization. New investment groups, backed by massive amounts of money, fanned out across compliant states, seeking to broker deals with local governments. Invariably, they went after the most fiscally distressed and desperate cities first. They pitched their financial products as a miracle drug, allowing ailing cities to "transform a non-performing asset"—unpaid tax bills—into cash. The wonders of financialization, promoters breathlessly announced, now allowed cities to bring in revenue without raising taxes or selling tax liens one at a time at cumbersome auctions or, even worse, pursuing delinquent taxpayers themselves. Let us handle it.[10]

It didn't take much convincing. For years, local governments had groaned under the weight of uncollected taxes. Sharp cuts in federal and state funding under Reagan had decimated municipal budgets, while tax and expenditure limits (TELs), combined with the era's anti-tax politics and businesses' veto power over local tax increases, had severely restrained cities' revenue-raising capacities. Government austerity had forced numerous counties and municipalities to cut staff and delay software upgrades and equipment repairs that treasurer's offices needed to enforce tax payments. During these years, many cities and counties cut funding for programs for assisting homeowners in avoiding tax delinquency and foreclosure. Local governments had also spent the previous decade selling off numerous assets—from vehicle fleets and recreational facilities to public buildings and lands—and outsourcing all manner of public responsibilities to private vendors and contractors. Local governments had strong material incentives to hear tax-lien investors' pitch. The growing consensus over the efficiencies of the market and the relentless drive to apply market principles to governance made them ideologically predisposed to listen, as well.

As they vowed to crack down on tax scofflaws, tax-lien investors and proselytizers of financialization promoted tax enforcement as good for distressed neighborhoods. "We will work to revitalize the blighted areas," CARC's executive vice president of acquisitions, Joseph Whelihan, promised.[11] "We're basically a financial partner of the revitalization needs of your community," Roger Finnegan of the investment group GLS assured local officials.[12] A trio of influential law professors touted tax-lien privatization as a means of neighborhood revitalization, claiming that private investors would have "a financial incentive to revitalize not only the specific propert[ies]" on which they acquired tax liens, "but also to invest in the surrounding properties" and "engage in community redevelopment."[13]

Throughout the 1990s, scores of states enabled bulk tax-lien sales and tax-lien securitization or adjusted existing laws to enhance investors' profits. In 1993, lawmakers in Connecticut allowed cities to sell their tax debts in bulk to investors. In 1995, California—where Prop 13 had blasted a hole in local-government budgets—authorized counties to conduct tax-lien sales and negotiate bulk sales. In New York City, Mayor Rudy Giuliani convinced the city council in 1996 to create a public authority to securitize the city's tax liens on an ongoing basis, fully and permanently privatizing the collection of delinquent taxes in the nation's largest city. It jumped right in, packaging and securitizing $300 million in tax liens (25 percent of all its tax debts). That same year, Massachusetts allowed local governments to sell tax liens in bulk to third parties.[14] As states enacted reforms, local governments brokered deals. In 1994, Waterbury, Connecticut, signed a three-year contract with CARC for its tax liens, while Bridgeport sold $20 million in tax liens to CARC, getting $10 million in return.[15] In 1996, the District of Columbia completed a $24.6 million securitization deal.[16] Pittsburgh, Pennsylvania, sold $22 million in tax liens to CARC for $16 million, the first of three bulk sales with the company between

1996 and 1998.[17] In 1997, Philadelphia created a public authority to issue bonds backed by $106.3 million in tax liens.[18]

By the late 1990s, tax liens had mushroomed into a $2 billion market dominated by a handful of major investment firms. Between 1992 and 1997, CARC alone had purchased over $1.3 billion worth of tax liens from 512 cities and counties. In 1996, the financial services company MBIA acquired a controlling interest in CARC; two years later, it acquired the remaining shares.[19]

In 1997, institutional tax-lien investors and servicers formed the National Tax Lien Association, a centralized voice for promotion and lobbying.[20] Along with new financing schemes, NTLA and other lobbyists pushed states to raise statutory interest rates, increase the number and amounts of penalties, lengthen the time that investors could collect interest on tax debts, and allow tax buyers to tack attorney fees onto delinquent taxpayers' bills or remove caps on legal fees.[21] In Kentucky, lobbyists pushed through a bill in 1998 that doubled the redemption period from five to ten years. Supporters framed it as helping struggling taxpayers settle their debts without losing their property, but its true purpose was to allow tax-lien investors to accumulate even more profits from interest.[22] In 2004, Kentucky's legislature further permitted tax-lien buyers to add legal fees to redemption costs, at the behest of lobbyists for American Tax Funding.[23] Other states did the same.[24]

In negotiating deals, investment firms demanded clauses allowing tax-lien servicers to tack on fees and charge interest above the maximum rate. As part of its negotiated bulk sale, Allegheny County and the city of Pittsburgh allowed CARC to add a $60 fee for unspecified "costs" for each year it held a lien, as well as an additional 1 percent monthly interest on top of the statutory interest rate.[25] In Lucas County, Ohio, the firm Plymouth Park (founded by former New Jersey governor Jim Florio) slapped delinquent taxpayers with a $1,500 upfront fee in addition to the standard 18 percent interest as part of its 2006 deal to purchase the county's outstanding tax debts.[26]

As local governments consummated deals with private investors, tax officials came to share the spirit of punitive entrepreneurialism.

MARILYN F HARTLEY
ATTORNEY AT LAW
P. O. BOX 32
GLENVIEW, KY 40025
PHONE: 502-551-1155
FAX: 502-897-6464
E-MAIL: mfh5213@aol.com

July 9, 2012

Please be advised that we have not received your payment regarding the delinquent property tax lien that our client, DETCO, holds on your property located at:

Kentucky law allows foreclosure one (1) year after the lien has become delinquent. We are attempting to give you adequate notice that foreclosure action will be taken against your property at the earliest date allowed by law. This could result in the sale of your property by the Jefferson County Commissioner to satisfy the tax lien.

Interest on the lien will accrue at 12% per year and fees will accumulate until the lien is paid in full.

In order to avoid further costs and litigation, please remit your certified check, cashier's check or money order in the amount of **$1,116.77 by July 31, 2012** to:

DETCO
P. O. Box 31
Glenview, KY 40025

Sincerely,

Marilyn F Hartley
Attorney at Law

NOTICE: THE UNDERSIGNED COUNSEL IS ATTEMPTING TO COLLECT A DEBT. ANY INFORMATION OBTAINED BY UNDERSIGNED COUNSEL WILL BE USED FOR THE PURPOSE OF COLLECTING A DEBT.

THIS IS A COMMUNICATION FROM A DEBT COLLECTOR.

Figure 15.2 Letter sent to an elderly woman in Louisville, Kentucky, who had missed payment of a $91.71 property tax on her home. By the time the tax lien investment firm Detco filed for tax foreclosure, the debt had ballooned to $1,116.77.

Soon after completing its first bulk sale of tax liens, Fulton County appointed Arthur Ferdinand as tax commissioner. A retired IBM executive, the Trinidad-born Ferdinand held a doctorate in mathematical physics from the University of London and a belief that tax delinquency was a matter of choice—a byproduct of government leniency and a culture of irresponsibility—that could only be addressed through tough, uncompromising measures. He vowed to erase the county's $155 million in unpaid taxes and ensure total taxpayer compliance. He believed that siccing ruthless debt collectors motivated solely by profit on delinquent taxpayers was the way to do it. "The promise of significant profit from the purchase of tax liens motivates investors," Ferdinand said. Further sales of tax liens to CARC "should provide strong incentive for taxpayers to keep their tax status current."[27]

But once a taxpayer fell behind, tax-lien servicers like CARC had one overriding goal: maximizing the amount of debt added to a single tax lien. Debt was maximized by lengthening the amount of time it took for a delinquent taxpayer to redeem their property, thereby allowing interest to accumulate and, in some states, for interest rates to climb to astronomical levels and for additional fines and fees to be tacked on. Soon after Fulton County completed its first deal with CARC, the tax commissioner's office was inundated with calls from scared and bewildered homeowners. They complained about receiving letters from a company whose name they didn't recognize and that were written in a way that seemed designed to confuse. Some said the letters "looked like junk mail or some kind of scam." It was as if the tax-lien servicer was inviting them to toss it in the trash and forget about it.[28] When they called the phone number listed, no one answered. When they left a message, no one ever called back. They said they wanted to pay their late taxes, but they didn't know how to do it, or whom to pay. Others called in months later, frantic, saying they had just received a purported second notice but had never received the first. Now they were being forced to pay hefty penalties and interest. The vast majority of complaints came from homeowners in low-income and predominantly Black areas.[29]

Tax-lien servicers pushed delinquent taxpayers to enroll in monthly installment plans that significantly increased total repayment costs. In Jersey City, Breen Capital "strongly recommend[ed]" delinquent taxpayers enroll in its plan.[30] Those who did struggled to climb out from under crushing and ever-growing, debt. In 1990, Black resident Ruth Fails missed a property tax payment on the home her family had owned since 1977 and where she had raised her six children. After it purchased her debt in 1993, Breen Capital aggressively steered Fails into its installment plan. Fails signed up, hoping that it would make the repayments manageable as she worked toward financial stability. But instead, the bills became another unsurmountable burden. Enrollees were charged 18.25 percent annual interest (.25 above the state limit) and charged extravagant penalties and fees. After Fails missed a couple payments, Breen Capital moved to foreclose and eventually took ownership of her home, which it subsequently rented back to her. In total, Breen Capital foreclosed on 20 percent of the homes whose owners signed up for the plan.[31] In both Jersey City and Pittsburgh, tax-delinquent homeowners filed class-action lawsuits against tax-lien servicers over excessive interest rates.[32]

Bulk sales and securitization deals not only subjected tax-delinquent homeowners to devious forms of predation. They left cities and poorer neighborhoods handcuffed, unable to address the problems stemming from vacant and abandoned properties. In selling tax liens on vacant and abandoned properties, cities were placing the fate of entire neighborhoods in the hands of an industry for whom these parcels were numbers on a spreadsheet, uncollected debts accumulating interest, baked into future earnings projections. After a servicer had collected debts and foreclosed on all the properties in a portfolio holding any value, it was left with thousands of parcels whose owners had no intention of paying and whose tax debts far exceeded their properties' market value. In Pittsburgh, CARC held tax liens on over eleven thousand properties, the vast majority in low-income minority neighborhoods. "I just keep the shades shut and don't look at it," Black homeowner Imogene Boyd said of the decaying three-story Victorian house across the street from her residence in Pittsburgh's Hill District. Since CARC had acquired the property's tax lien, it had fallen into dangerous disrepair, becoming infested with rats and raccoons, a haven for illicit drug use and trafficking, with a collapsing roof that dumped rainwater onto neighboring houses.[33]

Throughout this and other Black neighborhoods in Pittsburgh, churches, community groups, and nonprofits implored the city to do something about vacant and abandoned properties that attracted crime and vandalism, posed safety hazards, drove down property values, and drove away businesses and outside investment. But the city had forfeited its ability to do anything about the problem when it sold its tax liens to CARC. And the servicer refused to sell the properties for anything less than the full cost of redemption. MBIA had factored those amounts into its future earnings projections, after all: collateral on the nearly $200 million in bonds it had issued over the course of its relationship with the city.

When one of Boyd's neighbors, Wilbert Washington, attempted to buy the abandoned Victorian to tear it down, MBIA demanded no less than the full amount of tax liens, interest, and penalties: $4,987.27. Washington could not afford that, on top of the cost of demolition, and instead was left to hope that the house would collapse on its own.[34] When Reverend Charles Davis, a pastor in the Beltzhoover neighborhood, attempted to buy three vacant lots adjacent to his church that had become "overgrown with weeds, full of garbage and obvious health and safety hazards," the city told him to take it up with MBIA. Their price: over $10,000 each. "It makes no sense that something can't be done to get these properties into the hands of regular people," Davis lamented. "No one else is going to do anything with that land."[35]

Tax-lien investors tended to not only have no interest in community redevelopment, as its proponents had claimed. They often had no interest in maintaining the properties. By 2006, community organizers and advocacy groups stepped up demands for the city of Pittsburgh to negotiate a settlement with MBIA that would allow it to regain control over the remaining tax-laden properties, nearly all of which were in majority-Black neighborhoods. MBIA finally agreed to sell back its remaining tax liens to the city, school district, and water and sewer authority for pennies on the dollar. "It was a short-term solution that created a very long-term problem for everybody," one city official said afterward.[36] This was the story in many of the fiscally distressed cities that had sold off their tax debts. In Connecticut, the city of Waterbury's deal with CARC similarly left its lower-income

Black neighborhoods pockmarked with hundreds of distressed properties carrying tax debts and other encumbrances that scared off nonprofit and for-profit developers alike. The deal also did nothing to ease the budget crisis that had precipitated the initial deal. In 2001, the state stepped in and assumed control over the city's finances.[37]

More so than any other deal, Philadelphia's failed attempt to sell tax-lien securities in 1997 revealed the nature of the game. Philadelphia's city council structured the deal to exclude as many owner-occupied homes from the tax-lien pool as possible. After the city issued the bonds and signed contracts with companies to service the debt, it implored tax-delinquent city residents to pay up before private collectors arrived. It established a $1 million fund to assist poorer homeowners in making payments, and its Legal Services Department set up an assistance program, too.[38] In addition, the city allowed each council member to remove properties in their districts from the list; council president John Street removed over a thousand properties in his district alone.[39] In the months leading up to the deal, residents flooded the Revenue Department to set up repayment plans that would save their homes from being included in the tax-lien package.[40]

Philadelphia's efforts to protect homeowners from private collectors reduced the number of tax-delinquent properties in the deal from over eighty-eight thousand to 33,591. It also reduced the dollar amount of the tax liens in the deal from $190 million to $106 million.[41] But even that amount grossly overestimated the value of the package for servicers and investors, for the city had effectively removed the main source of investors' profits: homeowners who had fallen behind on their taxes but wanted to remain in their homes. All that was left was "the junk": mostly vacant and abandoned properties, and other parcels whose tax debts far exceeded their value. Nevertheless, Moody's still gave the bonds an AAA rating. From the outset, payments trickled in far below initial projections. Though the deal had been initially promoted as bringing revenue to the city on both front and back ends, the city instead fell $42 million short of the minimum needed to pay off the bondholders. In 2004, Philadelphia defaulted on $46.3 million in tax-lien bonds, the victim of its attempt to both harness the power of finance and protect its citizens from financial predation.[42]

Even cities that did not deal with investors became more dependent on the proceeds from tax sales and more inclined to see their interests and those of tax buyers as one and the same. In Baltimore, Maryland, decades of economic contraction, population loss, and chronic budget crises left public officials scrambling for revenue. The city's tax sale provided an annual burst of revenue that officials were keen to exploit. They sold liens on homes over unpaid water and sewer bills, as allowed under state law. And they supported a 2003 bill that removed the $400 cap on legal fees on tax-lien foreclosures, a change that industry lobbyists had been demanding.[43]

Tax-lien sale reforms that removed or raised caps on legal fees would have severe repercussions for delinquent taxpayers and create a bonanza for tax buyers. Under Maryland's reform, if a property owner failed to pay their debts within six months following the tax sale, the lien holder could initiate a foreclosure and begin adding seemingly unlimited legal fees to the final bill. As one tax buyer put it, "Once you file suit, the sky's the limit." Overnight, the number of foreclosure filings skyrocketed. In 2002, the year before the reform was enacted, the Baltimore Circuit Court handled four hundred tax-lien foreclosure filings in the entire year. By 2007, the court was processing upwards of three thousand foreclosure filings every two weeks. In the six years after Maryland removed the legal fee cap, the state's two biggest tax buyers, Harvey Nusbaum and Steve Berman, earned $6 million and $4 million, respectively, in legal fees from delinquent taxpayers. One of Nusbaum's business partner's daughters earned over $2.5 million in title-search fees on those same tax liens.[44] In filing for foreclosure, Baltimore tax buyers never sought to actually gain ownership. The filing was simply a means of accumulating more profits.

The amounts that Baltimore tax buyers charged in legal fees could have been numbers pulled out of the sky. Judges rarely reduced the fees that attorneys demanded and never asked for documentation of work performed. One tax-sale victim failed to pay a $272 water bill. By the time she received notice of a foreclosure action, the redemption costs had soared to $6,414. Of that, nearly $5,000 were for legal fees. Another homeowner had overlooked a $298 water bill. When they learned of the foreclosure suit, the bill had risen to over $3,000. Nusbaum bought a lien on a home whose owner had failed to pay a $283 business-license bill after the city discovered that a relative was cutting hair in the basement. The cost of redemption soared to $4,600. When angry and bewildered homeowners called Nusbaum's office, he simply replied, "You will pay, everybody does."[45]

But many simply could not. The *Baltimore Sun* found that, between 2005 and 2007 alone, over four hundred homes in the city were lost to foreclosure over non-property tax debts, with over half those properties taken for debts of $500 or under.[46] Among the impacted homeowners was Vicki Valentine. An African American mental health counselor and mother of four, Valentine had moved back into the two-story brick row house in West Baltimore where she grew up in the mid-1990s to care for her father, who suffered from Alzheimer's disease. The family had called the house their home for over three decades; her father paid off the mortgage in 1984. After he died in 2003, Valentine inherited the house and continued to live there with her teenage son. But after her father's death, Valentine fell into depression. She struggled to find steady employment and pay the bills on time. In 2005, Valentine missed paying a $362 water bill. The following May, the city auctioned a lien on the house. Sunrise Atlantic LLC snatched it up. In 2008, when Sunrise Atlantic filed for foreclosure, the redemption costs had ballooned to over $3,600, including $305.91 in interest, $1,500 in legal fees, $1,000 in unspecified expenses, $325 for a title search, and $79 for photocopies. A judge approved all of the expenses. Valentine didn't have the money and didn't have anyone she could turn to for help. Sunrise Atlantic didn't want to take ownership of her property. It was in a poor neighborhood pockmarked with vacant and abandoned homes. The one person it held real value to was Valentine. "We bent over backwards for her [trying to] work something out," an exasperated lawyer for the tax-lien firm later said. But Valentine simply could not meet their demands. So the firm moved to evict. On a snowy day in February 2010, sheriff's deputies escorted Valentine and her son to the curb while a crew punched out the lock on the front door and boarded up the windows. Valentine and her son sought shelter with a family member but within a year were homeless. The home remained vacant for years afterward.[47]

Even as tax buyers preyed on their most vulnerable constituents, the Black elected officials who ran Baltimore clung to the revenues from tax sales and embraced punitive entrepreneurialism. As neighborhood groups and community activists lambasted the city's sale of tax liens on unpaid water bills as unconscionable, multiple Black mayors and majority-Black city councils remained convinced that, without these extreme penalties, their mostly Black and poor constituents would simply stop paying their bills. "Without the tax sale," the head of the Bureau of Treasury Management repeated, "we'd have to raise rates unconscionably."[48] After Valentine's story attracted national headlines and scorn, in 2010 the city council voted overwhelmingly to raise the minimum amount of debt eligible for the tax sale to $750. New mayor Stephanie Rawlings-Blake came out in opposition, announcing that her administration "does not support an amnesty for property owners that failed to pay taxes and fees."[49] The measure died.

That same year, Baltimore auctioned liens on 12,689 properties totaling $203 million in debts (13 percent of which were for debts less than $750). It set a record for the number of liens auctioned in one year and was twice the number sold just four years earlier.[50] America had entered the Great Recession, and tax-lien investors were ready to clean up.

* * *

Just as tax-lien securities magically turned cities' uncollected taxes into assets, the advent of mortgage-backed securities and market deregulation in the 1980s and 1990s turned Black homes from liabilities into goldmines for mortgage lenders. Mortgage-backed securities vastly expanded the market for home mortgages, and they turned potential borrowers and housing markets that lenders had once shunned into people and places to target. So long as there remained a market for these products, mortgage banks no longer needed to worry about borrowers' qualifications or the risk of default. The riskier the mortgage—the higher the fees, the higher the interest rate, the greater amount of wealth that could be extracted from its borrower—the better.[51]

Mortgage lenders sought out homeowners who had been left behind in the new economy, those who were struggling in the face of flatlining wages and rising expenses for working families. In place of their fully amortized mortgage with defined payments and fixed interest, they offered to help them refinance into one that was more *dynamic*, that purported to lower their monthly payments (at least initially) and free up more of their earnings for other expenses, but that came with much higher and variable interest rates and sharp escalation clauses. Mortgage lenders went in search of new, untapped markets, people and places that had historically been denied access to home financing, who longed for the financial security and wealth-building capacity of homeownership that they, their families, and their communities had long been denied. Lenders wagered that these borrowers were less likely to grasp the risks that came with adjustable rates, more susceptible to deception; in other words, easy marks.[52]

Beginning in the 1990s, the market in subprime mortgages grew exponentially. During that time, African American borrowers were nearly four times more likely to have a subprime mortgage than whites. By 2005, more than half of all mortgages held by African Americans were subprime, at a time when the subprime market constituted less than 20 percent of the overall market. These disparities were not a reflection of the greater risk Black borrowers posed but rather of the greater extractive possibilities lenders saw in a specific class of homeowners. Blacks had been historically excluded from mortgage markets and were more likely to be experiencing wage stagnation and mounting household debt. Blacks were less likely to have access to generational wealth and thus were more susceptible to lending terms that required smaller down payments and purported to offer lower monthly payments. Lenders thus steered Black borrowers, no matter their credit score, into subprime deals. By 2005, 55 percent of all subprime borrowers qualified for a conventional mortgage.[53]

Property tax payments were woven into mortgage lenders' web of deceit. Among the ways that peddlers of subprime mortgages convinced people to finance or refinance was by stealthily removing the property tax escrow accounts that had become a standard feature of home mortgages. Doing so lowered borrowers' monthly payments but left them on the hook for paying property taxes themselves in lump sums. Rarely if ever did a lender volunteer this detail. Instead, most subprime borrowers discovered this trick of the trade when they received a bill from their local government demanding a payment that few had been expecting and fewer still had saved for. This shock was especially jarring for homeowners who had been on conventional mortgages and were accustomed to having the bank handle property tax payments. At the height of the market, three out of four subprime mortgages did not carry an escrow account for property taxes.[54] The day those bills came due was, for many, the day they began their descent into default and foreclosure. The Federal Reserve found that property tax liabilities were the proximate cause of 12 percent of all subprime mortgage defaults.[55] As early as 2006, one out of every seven low-income borrowers struggling to meet their monthly mortgage payments cited property tax payments as a contributing factor.[56]

Even when lenders included an escrow account, first-time African American homeowners reported not being made aware of this detail (and the added monthly costs that it entailed) prior to closing. In Baltimore, high school teacher Denzel Mitchell and his wife closed on a modest two-story house in the Belair-Edison neighborhood. They looked forward to decorating their son's bedroom, filling the living room with books and toys, planting a garden, and raising a family. "But then we got the first bill, and it was $300 more than what they had told it was going to be when we closed," Mitchell recounted. The paperwork the lender had shown Mitchell did not include monthly payments toward property taxes. The young family struggled to keep up and soon fell behind on payments. In 2008, the bank foreclosed and repossessed their home.[57]

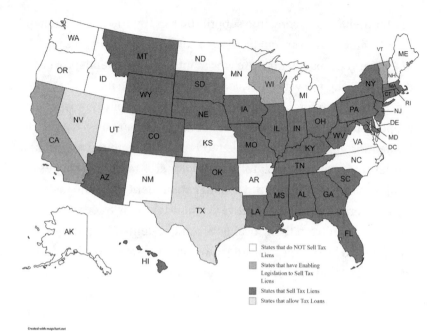

Figure 15.3 Map of US states by tax-sale laws, as categorized by the National Tax Lien Association (NTLA), circa 2023. As the leading trade organization for tax buyers, NTLA works to bring more tax liens onto the market by lobbying state governments that currently prohibit tax-lien sales to change or amend laws to permit them, and for local governments in states that permit the sale of tax liens to do so.

The cities and neighborhoods that had been prime hunting grounds for predatory lenders in the years leading up to the crash experienced the sharpest spike in tax-delinquency rates in the aftermath. One of the cities hardest hit by housing foreclosures, Cleveland, Ohio, saw its tax-delinquency rate jump from 13 percent to 20.2 percent between 2006 and 2011. From 2009 to 2014, the average amount of property tax debt on delinquent properties in the city grew from $3,064 to $5,734.[58]

As tax-delinquency rates soared, the tax-lien industry licked its chops. "Florida is probably the most popular state for tax investment," NTLA executive director Howard Liggett remarked in May 2007, as the state's housing markets began to implode. "There's a lot of volume here." Indeed, there was. Between 2004 and 2007, the number of tax delinquencies quadrupled in Florida counties that would become the epicenter of the state's—and the nation's—foreclosure crisis.[59] Given local governments' reliance on property taxes, the housing market's collapse inevitably spawned a fiscal crisis and, with it, an unprecedented opportunity for the tax-lien industry to further exert its influence over revenue-starved states and cities. As Liggett put it, "states are starved for cash, the cutbacks have been Draconian and the reliance on local property taxes hasn't subsided." Now was the time for the investors to lean in, and for the industry to press its advantage.[60]

They did. In 2009, local governments sold a record $30 billion in property tax debt to investors, more than twice the amount sold the previous year. The spike in tax buying was greatest in those cities hardest hit by the subprime crisis. Miami-Dade County sold over sixty thousand property tax liens at its 2009 auction, depositing over $374 million into its depleted coffers.[61] Baltimore's record sale in 2010 came on the heels of a three-year period in which the number of liens purchased at its annual auction doubled. As a 2014 report found, most of the liens sold were on homes owned by African Americans "living below the poverty line. Nearly half," it added, "were elderly." Every one of them had either owned their home outright or been the victim of a subprime or reverse mortgage. Rather than being taken from a sea of new homeowners who had gotten in over their heads, the properties sold at Baltimore's tax-lien sales in this time had belonged to their owners for an average of twenty-one years.[62]

Desperate for revenue, many local governments moved their tax-lien sales online to lower administrative costs and drive up sales. Some of the heaviest investors in online sales were the same banks that were responsible for the foreclosure crisis. JPMorgan Chase and Bank of America formed numerous LLCs and flooded online tax-lien auctions around the country. Wells Fargo and US Bank set up private trusts for hedge-fund clients to invest in tax liens. At the depth of the foreclosure crisis in 2010, Bank of America's securities division packaged $301 million worth of tax liens acquired through online sales into bonds that carried a 7–10 percent estimated return. The move to online auctions, as one reporter remarked, "put the whole process on steroids." It also fueled a "gold rush" among hedge funds, who, by 2013, controlled an estimated 40 percent of the tax-lien market.[63]

Tax-lien investors continued to press their leverage on desperate local governments. In 2008, Aeon Financial bought a package of tax liens from Cuyahoga County, Ohio, for $25 million. Nearly one-third of the liens were on properties in neighborhoods that were over 90 percent non-white, and another 50 percent in neighborhoods that were more than 60 percent non-white. The county treasurer secured a judge's approval for Aeon to charge up to $6,650 in legal fees for any foreclosure actions. (State law required that any fees above $2,500 needed to be approved by a court first.) Accordingly, Aeon began aggressively foreclosing. Within the first year of the deal, it had filed over four hundred foreclosure actions, each of which allowed it to add legal fees onto the final bill.[64]

But what Aeon intended as a profit-enhancing measure on the road toward eventual redemption instead pushed thousands of desperate homeowners over the edge, and it left the investment firm with thousands of properties scattered across Cleveland's Black neighborhoods that it had no desire to own and no intention of maintaining. In 2013, the city cited over one hundred Aeon-owned properties for code violations and condemned another forty. Local activists begged the city to do something. "The houses are stripped to the bone—no windows, no doors, no walls, no pipes. This is what I'm screaming about," activist Anita Garner told a reporter.[65] "Aeon has an extra-vicious business model," Cleveland city councilman Jay Westbrook fumed. "Take no prisoners, take no responsibility."[66]

But in this and other counties hardest hit by the foreclosure crisis, local officials saw little choice but to continue cutting deals with private investors and outsourcing delinquent tax collection. In Cuyahoga County, the treasurer's office had had to eliminate sixteen full-time positions dedicated to outreach and communication with taxpayers, as well as a six-person unit focused on assisting tax-delinquent homeowners and managing tax payment plans. In total, that office shrank from eighty-three to thirty-seven employees, including all positions in customer service and taxpayer outreach.[67]

Unable to do the job itself, in 2011 Cuyahoga County sold another package of tax liens to Woods Cove LLC for $14 million. By 2015, the shadowy firm had foreclosed and taken possession of 223 properties on the heavily Black east side and in inner-ring suburbs. And, like Aeon Financial, it let the properties rot. Neither company ever inspected, secured, or boarded up any of its properties. In 2014, the NAACP LDF demanded that the county issue a moratorium on future tax sales.[68]

* * *

In this and other severely depressed neighborhoods in post-recession cities, real estate capitalism completed another cycle of extraction.[69] But out of capitalism's calamities, new opportunities for profit always arose. And in housing markets across the country, tax-lien investors were poised to take advantage. Wherever they saw signs of gentrification, tax buyers pounced, vacuuming up tax liens in the hopes of scoring deeds to valuable properties. Their victims remained the same. They were people like Bennie Coleman, a seventy-six-year-old African American former Marine sergeant and Vietnam veteran who owned a duplex in a section of northeast Washington, DC, that was in the early stages of gentrification. In 2006, Coleman, who had begun to show signs of dementia, failed to pay his property tax bill. The following year, Steve Berman, one of the city's largest tax buyers, bought it at DC's tax sale. Like many others, Washington had redesigned its tax-delinquency laws to maximize tax-lien investors' profits. In 2001, the city council permitted tax buyers to tack on unlimited legal fees as well as court costs.[70] Berman began tallying the fees and in 2010 filed for foreclosure. But unlike in Baltimore, Berman was not filing for foreclosure just so he could tack on the additional fees. In this and other gentrifying cities, he and other tax buyers did actually want the property. The exorbitant fees increased the likelihood that they would get it.

Between 2007 and 2013, as the district gentrified, its tax foreclosure rate doubled. Tax buyers acquired over two hundred homes valued at an estimated $39 million. More than half of all tax foreclosures

Figure 15.4 DC Office of Tax and Revenue real property tax sale, July 15, 2013. *Washington Post*, September 8, 2013.

were in the seventh and eighth wards, both of which were over 90 percent Black. Seventy-two percent were in neighborhoods with less than a 20 percent white population.[71] Tax-lien investors strategically bought liens on distressed homes in gentrifying areas. Among those was Coleman's.

By the time Coleman's son caught wind of his father's predicament, the $134 missed tax payment had ballooned to $4,999. He drained his savings but could muster only $700. Berman demanded no less than the full amount. The Colemans watched helplessly as Berman obtained the deed in 2011, evicted Coleman, and quickly resold the property. Coleman, meanwhile, was forced to move into a group home. For months afterward, he returned to his former home, believing it was still his, sleeping on its porch, flagging down police cruisers and firetrucks asking for their help, telling them he had locked himself out.

In September 2013, the *Washington Post* published an investigation of the city's tax sales and the predatory practices it spawned. It explained how tax buyers were taking advantage of vulnerable homeowners in order to profit from its gentrifying real estate market and, spotlighting Coleman, their victims. The mayor, Vincent Gray, expressed shock and outrage at the findings, calling the situation "absolutely unconscionable." He vowed, "We're going to stop this." Gray insisted that, prior to opening the Sunday newspaper, he "didn't even know this was taking place."

But he had known. Sixteen months earlier, the Alliance to Help Owners Maintain Equity (AT HOME), a coalition of community advocates and law firms, had alerted the mayor, all council members, and the tax office of abuses of tax sales mainly affecting elderly and economically disadvantaged homeowners. It had warned that "the current tax sale system deprives affected homeowners ... of fair treatment [and] constitutional protections." The tax office said it would step up notifications to endangered homeowners. Neither the mayor's office nor the council responded.[72] City officials had plenty of reasons to look the other way. Because of the high demand and the way the tax sale was structured, annual revenues from it were often double the amount of the outstanding tax debt.[73] Washington's economy and its fiscal health were being powered by gentrification, and tax buyers were advancing those interests.[74]

In the weeks that followed, anger and condemnation rained down on DC officials and the tax-lien industry. The NAACP LDF urged officials to overhaul an "unfair and predatory debt collection system" that allowed private investors to operate without "any meaningful government oversight." A group of US senators called for the Justice Department and the Consumer Financial Protection Bureau to investigate the industry. And lawyers announced plans to file a class-action lawsuit against the district on behalf of Bennie Coleman and other victims of tax-lien predation. Reeling, the city's chief financial officer, Natwar M. Gandhi, ordered all residential properties be removed from the upcoming tax sale. Councilman Jack Evans, who had recently announced plans to run for mayor, introduced emergency legislation barring the sale of liens on homes owned by seniors, military veterans, and disabled persons, raising the minimum amount of tax debt for a lien to be sold to $2,000, and placing a $1,500 cap on legal fees.

Alarmed, NTLA executive director Brad Westover rushed to meet with Evans and the head of the city's tax office in an attempt to calm the waters and protect tax-lien investors' interests and prerogatives.[75]

District officials curbed the most predatory abuses. They placed a $1,500 cap on attorney fees, lowered the interest rate from 18 to 12 percent, forbade the sale of liens below $2,500, banned companies or individuals with checkered backgrounds (including persons convicted of fraud or other deceitful practices) from participating in the tax sale, and gave all the equity to owners who had lost their property to tax foreclosure. In 2017, the district reached a $1 million settlement with Coleman and other victims and their families, agreeing to pay up to 65 percent of the assessed value of each property lost to tax foreclosure after the 2001 reforms to the tax-sale law.[76] But it left the machinery of tax buying, and its gentrifying effects, in place.[77]

* * *

As its members accumulated riches from others' misfortunes, the NTLA doggedly fended off political threats. "Tax lien sales do not create injustice," Brad Westover insisted. "The reality is the entire community benefits from the tax sale process."[78] He was quick to respond to every negative story in the media, scathing editorial, or study revealing all of the damage tax-lien sales inflicted. Whenever a state or city announced plans to form a study group or task force to look at tax sales, Westover fought his way onto the committee. In state houses and city halls, he worked to convince lawmakers to protect and expand the reach of an inherently predatory practice. "Our members have no interest in stripping property from people," he assured them. "We generate income by helping communities fund short-term cash shortages at market determined rates."[79] He took his message to cities that had the legal authority to sell tax liens but chose not to, rattling off the number of police officers and teachers it could hire, and programs it could support, if it just played ball. He pressed state lawmakers to "make minor tweaks in the legislation to make it more attractive to the private sector." When he spoke at the NTLA's annual convention and other industry gatherings, Westover promised to continue to push forward their mission "to bring more liens into the marketplace . . . because of my belief in what we do."[80] Scattered throughout those audiences were numerous public officials representing city and county governments across the US, nodding in agreement, ready to do their part.[81]

CONCLUSION

On August 30, 2022, the aging water system that served the entire city of Jackson, Mississippi, collapsed, cutting off water to all 164,000 residents of the state's largest city. On that same day in Philadelphia, Pennsylvania, the state's largest school district was forced to send many of its more than 115,000 students home due to excessive heat in the city's school buildings, most of which were over seventy-five years old and lacked air conditioning.[1]

In both cases, the majority-Black city and school district lacked the resources needed to make the necessary repairs and upgrades on their own. Over the previous four decades, Jackson's local tax base had shrunk by 20 percent, as first whites and then middle-class Blacks fled to surrounding suburbs. During that time, a succession of Republican governors and state legislatures slashed taxes on the state's businesses and highest earners, raised taxes on the state's poor, and starved the state capital and its 82 percent Black population of revenue. For years, Jackson's mayor, Chokwe Antar Lumumba, pleaded with state officials to help fund the more than $2 billion needed to fix the city's severely compromised water infrastructure, to no avail. Instead, state lawmakers rejected two separate bills to increase taxes and issue bonds to assist the city, and they took whatever money the state received from the federal government for infrastructure and gave it to predominantly white, conservative localities—anywhere but the city and people who needed it the most.[2] In Philadelphia, the city's public school system faced massive budget shortfalls that, in previous years, had forced it to shutter many schools, lay off thousands of employees, cut arts and music programs, and cram more children into overcrowded classrooms. As in Jackson, Philadelphia's public schools lacked the funds needed to build new schools and upgrade older ones in this, the fifth-most-fragmented metropolitan area in the US, where per-pupil spending in affluent, predominantly white suburban school districts was more than two times greater than in the city.[3]

Providing clean water and educating children are two of the many duties of a functional, advanced nation that the United States has placed in the hands of local units of government and made contingent on local tax revenues. And because of this fiscal structure, thousands of municipalities and school districts across the US today struggle to meet these most basic human needs. The more dire and uncertain their fiscal situation becomes, the greater the yield institutional investors on whom these cities depend can command, the greater the leverage that financial institutions and capital markets wield over their budgets and priorities, and the more susceptible local governments become to the allure of harvesting revenue, by predatory means, from their poorest and most vulnerable citizens.

The siren song of the tax buyers still rings loudest in the ears of the fiscally famished. As fiscal inequities between rich and poor localities continue to widen, and as fiscal competition and neoliberal logics foreclose more progressive tax-revenue-generating options, this predatory industry's profit margins and political influence continue to grow. Take Baltimore, Maryland, a city whose residents have been a rich vein of extraction for tax buyers for generations. Between 2016 and 2022, tax lien speculators harvested over $10 million in profits just from the interest payments made by desperate Baltimore homeowners. They made an additional $27 million during those years from foreclosing and flipping tax-delinquent properties. They extracted the vast majority of those interest payments from Black homeowners, and they made all—literally all—of their profits from foreclosing and flipping properties in Black neighborhoods. A 2023 investigation by reporters at the *Baltimore Banner* found that every single one of the 1,763 homes on which tax buyers completed the foreclosure process during those years were located in one of the city's majority-Black neighborhoods. In some of the city's majority-Black neighborhoods, nearly one out of every two properties had been sold for taxes at least once since 2016. Not coincidentally, these same neighborhoods are also the city's most overtaxed, with assessments upwards of 164 percent of market values, as contrasted with the city's wealthier neighborhoods, where assessments hover around 68 percent of market values.[4]

Those who fall victim to tax-lien predation in cities like Baltimore remain, overwhelmingly, Black and elderly longtime homeowners on low, often fixed, incomes. Legal aid groups who held tax-sale clinics during these years reported that 72 percent of their clients were seniors and 85 percent identified as Black. Their household incomes were well below the poverty line, and they had owned their homes on average for twenty-seven years. A significant percentage of tax-sale victims did not hold clear title to their homes, having inherited them from the original deed holder. These Baltimore homes were, like the millions of acres of land Black people held—and were dispossessed of—across the rural South, heirs' properties. As a result, these properties were more prone to becoming tax delinquent, and once they did, their owners faced higher odds—and greater costs—in saving them from tax foreclosure. Because the person named on each deed was deceased, the city's finance department listed these properties as non-owner-occupied, which increased the statutory interest rate from 12 to 18 percent, shortened the redemption period from nine to six months, and lowered the minimum debt for landing in the tax sale from $750 to $250.[5]

As the plague of tax-lien predation enveloped Black neighborhoods in the city, groups formed to assist Baltimore homeowners at risk of losing their homes and to press lawmakers to suspend tax sales and enact reforms. As president of Baltimore's city council and candidate for mayor in 2020, Brandon Scott supported the suspension of the city's tax sale during the pandemic and called for overhauling the system. In his first state of the city address as mayor in 2021, Scott vowed to protect "vulnerable legacy homeowners" from the threat of tax foreclosure. "Make no mistake, we will not go back to the systems and practices that have historically failed our residents," he said. Scott created a tax-sale work group and directed its members to develop a set of comprehensive reforms. The group recommended that the city create an office to assist tax-delinquent homeowners in remaining in their homes and to make it easier for the city to foreclose on vacant and abandoned properties—those that tax buyers shunned—and place them in a land bank. In the meantime, reformers called on Scott to maintain the pandemic-induced moratorium on tax sales.[6]

But as it stared at budget deficits, the city could not resist the temptation of the tax sale. In 2021, the city council voted to resume holding tax sales after the city's finance director said that the city "desperately need[ed]" the revenue. Scott supported the measure, while promising to personally remove all owner-occupied homes from the sale and assuring reformers that comprehensive changes were forthcoming. At the start of the 2023 state legislative session, the Baltimore city delegation advanced legislation that would give cities broad discretionary powers to remove owner-occupied homes from tax sales and enter into payment plans for municipal debt. As lawmakers debated the bill, spokespersons for the tax-lien industry lobbied hard against its passage, warning that such protections would cripple the city's revenue-collection system because they would signal to all the city's property owners that there were no consequences for nonpayment. Their message was tailored to lawmakers conditioned to see poor people, especially poor Blacks, as shirkers of their tax obligations who were only responsive to punitive measures, and to city officials in perpetual fear of further revenue losses. And the tactic worked. In spring 2023, Scott withdrew his support for the reform bill after the city's finance department and the chief of its bureau of revenue collections warned that the legislation would negatively affect the city's budget and undermine its ability to enforce tax payments. Scott vowed to protect the most vulnerable homeowners from the tax sale. But the machinery of tax-lien speculation remained in place.[7]

That poor cities will prey on their poorest citizens for revenue is the predictable end result of decades of neoliberal fiscal policies that, starting at the federal level, slashed taxes on wealthy individuals and corporations and forced lower units of government to fend for themselves. It is the product of a fiscal structure that encourages local governments and school systems to be attentive, solicitous, and indulgent toward some, while contemptuous, parsimonious, and predatory toward others. By design, this structure works to isolate and contain those seen as fiscal liabilities in under-resourced cities, towns, and unincorporated areas, and it makes those fiscally disadvantaged localities prone to relying on regressive taxes on consumption and basic necessities, ticketing, fines, fees, and tax-lien sales to meet budgetary needs. And it compels any city or town seeking to grow their local economy and improve their fiscal position to pursue high-end development and generous subsidies for the rich while enacting policies of austerity, overtaxation, and dispossession for the poor.[8] Because of the way race structures housing markets and, through the property tax, local tax revenues, this dynamic compels local governments to treat African Americans, especially low-income Blacks, in Colin Gordon's words, as "targets of public policy rather than its beneficiaries, a problem to be solved rather than a population to be served, subjects rather than citizens."[9]

African Americans' experiences as local taxpayers—the history told in these pages—not only reveals a litany of injustices that have been hiding in plain sight. It casts into doubt all of the supposed virtues of the federated fiscal structure that Americans live under today. Proponents of this system claim that competition among local governments improves quality and efficiency and lowers costs, that it promotes civic engagement and brings people closer to government, and that it makes government more responsive to its constituents. They argue that an ever-expanding galaxy of small, independent local governments, each attentive to the material interests of homeowners (or, as one proponent of this view labels them, "homevoters"), achieves an optimal balance of taxes and services for all and produces socially desirable outcomes.[10]

The truth is, localizing tax raising and spending does not encourage localities to govern well nor promote efficiency. It does not drive down the collective costs of running a functional society. It does not improve the overall quality of schools and public education. On all of these counts, it does the exact opposite. What proponents label as efficiency and cost reduction are in fact mere instances of tax shifting and cost offloading. The benefits enjoyed by the advantaged under this fragmented system, and the measures taken to secure and defend these advantages, impose significant and lasting costs on everyone else, while undermining our capacity to think and act collectively. The forms of civic engagement such a system promotes are often oriented toward exclusionary and undemocratic ends. In short, reliance on local taxes does not make localities and their citizens stronger. It makes all of us weaker.

It doesn't have to be this way. The United States stands alone among federated nations in lacking any permanent measures for reducing fiscal inequalities between lower units of government.[11] We can combat the place-based inequalities our current system generates by creating a federal fiscal-equity program, like those found in Canada, Australia, and Germany, that allocates funds to cities and school districts according to need.[12] We can provide tax relief to the poor and end the racist overtaxation of Black-owned homes and neighborhoods by adopting a universal home tax exemption, one that every person (owners and renters alike) could claim on their primary place of residence (and only that), set at the median home value within the metro housing market where a person resides. And we can pay for both (and more) by enacting a federal wealth tax targeted at the nation's top one percent.

Such broadly egalitarian, downwardly redistributional reforms attack the root causes of racial discrimination in local taxation, and the particular disadvantages Black people face. A universal home tax exemption would transform the property tax from being what it has become—a tax on housing—to what it should be: a tax on wealth. By pegging the exemption to median home values and rents within a broader housing market, all residents of areas that had suffered from disinvestment and extraction in the past would be virtually exempt from taxes on their homes, while homeowners in areas that benefitted the most from past and current housing policies and real estate industry practices would pay some, and residents of the most prosperous and advantaged areas would pay the most. In other words, the property tax would work in the exact opposite way that it currently works.

By relieving all poorer and working-class and most middle-class homeowners of local property tax obligations, a universal home tax exemption would drastically reduce the size of local tax bases and require massive federal support for all local units of government that rely on taxes from low- and middle-income homeowners, which a fiscal-equity program funded by a federal wealth tax would do. A home tax exemption would also render low-, moderate-, and fixed-income homeowners immune to financial predation by tax buyers, eliminating such buyers' main profit source and hastening this predatory industry's demise. It would also compel states and local governments to adopt effective solutions to the problem of vacant and abandoned properties, such as the creation of land banks. A federally managed fiscal-equity program for cities and school districts would also diminish the power of state governments—an urgent necessity in itself—and limit their ability to control the fiscal capacities and spending decisions of local governments.[13]

With public expenditures decoupled from local fiscal capacity, local governments and school districts would no longer be compelled to cater to wealthy residents or overtax and drive out poorer ones in order to better their fiscal fortunes. A federal system for funding local governments based on need removes the fiscal penalties incurred by cities with poorer populations and depressed housing markets, and by those that are home to large numbers of tax-exempt properties and institutions. It accomplishes all these ends while preserving and improving the best aspects of local governance, freeing public officials from the fiscal factors and revenue pressures that currently consume their energies and distort their priorities.

To be sure, such reforms won't solve all the problems that contribute to the inequitable distribution of public goods and services, especially public education. But they will counteract the ever-widening funding disparities between wealthy and poor places in America, and greatly diminish the structural disadvantages for Black Americans, that the current system of fiscal federalism generates. They won't ensure that local governments and school districts prioritize the needs of the most disadvantaged nor allocate public services and resources equitably. But they will remove fiscal incentives for undertaxing and overserving the most advantaged. They won't stop local governments from overtaxing the poor and people of color by other means, but they will diminish the incentives for doing so. They won't solve structural racism in US housing markets. But they will help to erode its foundation.

Reparations for the untold billions of dollars in wages and property stolen from Black Americans in the past begins with dismantling systems of racial stratification, exploitation, and dispossession in the present. A federal fiscal-equity program, when combined with a universal home tax exemption, would work to dismantle one such system that has quietly drained Black Americans of income, wealth, and property for generations, and that continues to do so to this day. More importantly, it would do so through comprehensive, universal reforms whose benefits and protections would be broadly shared.

We can do this if we want to. We can tax the nation's immense— and extremely concentrated—wealth and generate enough revenue to ensure that every city, town, and school district in America has the resources to provide the goods and services that its constituents need. As economists Emmanuel Saez and Gabriel Zucman point out, there is no law of nature that prevents us from enacting and effectively enforcing a federal wealth tax targeted at the nation's top 1 percent, from sharply raising corporate taxes on the nation's most profitable companies, or from coordinating with other nations to prevent tax avoidance.[14] We can do that and more. We can make the massive public investments necessary to meet the challenges of a warming planet, repair the damage from neoliberalism, and build a more just and equitable future for all.

But in order to do this, we need a tax system that doesn't reinforce the very problems, inequities, and injustices that these public investments aim to combat. Until we do that, America's local tax systems will continue to fuel—rather than counteract—inequality and division. They will continue to ensure that those wielding the most power will enjoy the greatest benefits and protections, and that those with the least power will be left with the heaviest burdens, fewest benefits, and greatest vulnerabilities.

This is what a history of taxation as seen through the lives and experiences of Black Americans teaches us. This is the past that we live with today. But it does not have to be our future.

ACKNOWLEDGMENTS

This book took shape over the course of a decade and was made possible by the assistance, support, inspiration, and insights of numerous people I worked with and met at various stages of that journey.

First and foremost, I am grateful for the unwavering support of my superb editor at the University of Chicago Press, Tim Mennel, and for all the time and thought he has devoted to this project over the past several years. Throughout the long and arduous writing process, Tim provided the kind of substantive and critical feedback and guidance that any author dreams of. I could not have completed this book without him. Special thanks to my copyeditor Jessica Wilson, and to Kristen Raddatz and Caterina MacLean and the marketing and production teams at the Press. I also wish to thank my agent, Wendy Strothman, for her encouragement and advice throughout the entire process.

I am so grateful to the many friends and colleagues who took the time to read and comment on chapter drafts, conference papers, and article manuscripts, especially Brian Balogh, Stephen Berrey, Brent Cebul, Nathan Connolly, Melissa Cooper, Andrew Diamond, Lily Geismer, Brian Highsmith, the late Gordon Hylton, Destin Jenkins, Talitha LeFlouria, George Lipsitz, Mike McCarthy, Sarah Milov, Sarah Mullen, Kali Murray, Rourke O'Brien, Barbara Phillips, Justin Randolph, Beryl Satter, Amanda Seligman, Shirley Thompson, Mason Williams, LaDale Winling, and the anonymous readers for the *Journal of Urban History*, *Critical Sociology*, *Transatlantica*, the

Journal of Southern History, and the *Law and History Review*. I am especially grateful to those who read and commented on the entire manuscript: my brilliant colleagues and friends Lawrie Balfour, Kevin Gaines, Grace Hale, Claudrena Harold, Justene Hill-Edwards, and Rich Schragger; and Colin Gordon and the anonymous reader for the University of Chicago Press. Their insights and feedback were indispensable and deeply appreciated. I wish to give special thanks to Frank Alexander, who, in addition to reading and commenting on several chapters of the book, generously shared his expertise with me on numerous occasions, and to Art Lyons, with whom I spent many hours in deep and rich conversations about his life and career, the history this book tells, and the underlying issues it unpacks. I appreciate the time they shared with me and the friendships we made along the way. I am also thankful for the support I received from Melody Barnes and Laurent DuBois and the staff of the Karsh Institute of Democracy, fellow Repair Lab co-directors Sally Pusede, Sarah Milov, and Kim Fields, and lab managers Chrissy Linsinbigler and Jane Kulow.

I benefitted immeasurably from the many opportunities I had to share my research and receive feedback at conferences, seminars, workshops, and symposia over the past decade. For inviting me to share my work, I wish to thank the Mississippi Center for Justice, the University of Georgia's Odum School of Ecology, the Fair Housing Council of San Diego, Boston University Law School's Elizabeth Battelle Clark Legal History Series, the UCLA School of Law's Colloquium on Tax Policy and Public Finance, the Chicago-Kent School of Law, Columbia University's Seminar on the City, the Virginia Tech history department, Johns Hopkins University's history seminar, the Urban History Association's workshop series, the Chicago Historical Society's Urban History Seminar, Bates College, the South Carolina Law Review's symposium on Taxation, Finance, and Racial (In)Justice, Maryland Legal Aid, the Mattress Factory in Pittsburgh, the Virginia Law Foundation, the Center on Budget and Policy Priorities, the Center for Community Progress, the Thurgood Marshall Institute and NAACP Legal Defense and Educational Fund, the Virginia Office of the Governor's Commission to Examine Racial and Economic Inequity, the Cook County (Illinois) Office of the Assessor, Georgetown University Law Center's Racial Wealth Gap Workshop, and the Law and Humanities Interdisciplinary Workshop for Junior Scholars. I received valuable insights into my research, timely assistance, and the kind of encouragement that I needed to keep pushing forward from numerous people. I wish to particularly thank Bernadette Atuahene, Mary Battle, Jeffrey Beauvais, Sarah Bond, Dorothy Brown, Michael Carriere, Stephen Engel, Devin Fergus, Donna Genzmer, Mike Glass, Risa Goluboff, Kim Graziani, Tom Guglielmo, Owen Gutfreund, Cheryl Harris, Alec Hickmott, Mel Leffler, Todd Lighty, the late Jim Loewen, Ken Mack, Aims McGuinness, Guian McKee, Ajay Mehrotra, Todd Michney, Thomas Mitchell, Josh Mound, Margaret Newkirk, John Rao, Mildred Robinson, Rob Sevier, Harrison Smith, Rob Smith, Andrew Sandoval-Strausz, Mark Schultz, and June Manning Thomas.

This book was made possible by generous financial support from the American Council of Learned Societies; the National Endowment for the Humanities; Marquette University's College of Arts and Sciences; and the University of Virginia's Corcoran Department of History, Carter G. Woodson Institute for African American and African Studies, College of Arts and Sciences, and Karsh Institute of Democracy. A research affiliation with Harvard University's Hutchins Center for African and African American Research also provided access to crucial source materials used in this study.

In conducting research, I relied on the assistance and expertise of many librarians and archivists. I am especially grateful for the help I received from the research librarians and interlibrary loan department at the University of Virginia, and the archivists at the Mississippi Department of Archives and History, Amistad Research Center, Avery Research Center, the University of North Carolina at Chapel Hill's Southern Historical Collection, the Special Collections and Preservation Division of the Chicago Public Library, the Chicago History Museum's Archives and Manuscripts division, Special Collections at the University of Illinois at Chicago, the Wisconsin Historical Society, Archives and Special Collections at Mississippi State

University, the South Caroliniana Library at the University of South Carolina, and the Library of Virginia. I am also grateful to the staff at the Penn Center, the Cook County (Illinois) Treasurer's Office, the Cook County (Illinois) Office of the Assessor, and the Beaufort County (South Carolina) Office of the Register of Deeds.

My warmest gratitude goes to those who welcomed me into their homes and places of work, shared their stories, facilitated contacts and connections, and helped me gain a deeper understanding and appreciation of the people, places, and practices described in this book: David Balin, Darelene Balthazar, Rims Barber, Thomas Barnwell, Czerny Brasuell, Joe Brooks, the late Owen Brooks, Emory Campbell, Emilye Crosby, Lakesha Daley, Evan Doss, Kelwin Harris, Fritz Kaegi, Joe McDomick, James Miller, the late Jesse Morris, Tiyi Morris, K. C. Morrison, the late Andrew Patner, Barbara Phillips, Lewis Pitts, Sallie Ann Robinson, Kenneth Ross, Connie Thompson, Timla Washington, Jean White, and Yvonne Wilson.

My students inspire and motivate me every day, and over the course of writing this book, they helped me immensely. I am grateful for the research assistance of Malcolm Cammeron, Sara Dunklee, Gramond McPherson, and Thomas Storrs. Thomas read and provided feedback on the entire manuscript in addition to tracking down source material, designing maps, crunching numbers, securing permissions, and helping me get this manuscript across the finish line. I could not have done it without him.

No matter where my research interests take me, so many of them can be traced back to my experiences as an undergraduate student learning under the mentorship of Will Scott and Peter Rutkoff. Words cannot adequately express my appreciation and gratitude for all that they taught me and how much their friendship means to me.

Writing a book, especially one that posed as many challenges as this one, can be a lonely experience. I am grateful for the time that I did get to spend, whether at home or during my travels, with dear friends Karl and Amy, Kevin and Penny, Sameena and Tipan, Billy and Meade, Morgan and Keelan, Gabe and Liz.

My family made innumerable sacrifices to make this book happen. My mother-in-law, Cindy Sevier, opened her home to me on my numerous trips to Chicago and cared for our children while I was in the archives. My mother, Susan Kahrl, also cared for our children and allowed me to retreat to our family's lake house in Ohio on several occasions for distraction-free writing.

The greatest sacrifices of all were made by my wife, Aileen, and our daughters, Elodie and Muriel, who endured the long and grueling process of my work on this book and provided me with the love and support that I needed at every step along the way. I dedicate this book to them, with all my love.

NOTES

INTRODUCTION

1　"Penalties for Those Who Struggle," *New York Newsday*, May 13, 1985.

2　"Property Taxes: The Unbalanced Burden," *New York Newsday*, May 12, 1985; "Penalties for Those Who Struggle."

3　Alan Singer, "American Apartheid: Race and the Politics of School Finance on Long Island, NY," *Equity and Excellence in Education* 32, no. 3 (1999): 25–36; Martin Buskin, "A Suburban Dream Turned Sour," *New York Newsday*, November 13, 1972. See also Thomas J. Sugrue, *Sweet Land of Liberty: The Forgotten Struggle for Civil Rights in the North* (New York: Random House, 2008), 513.

4　"A House Lost for $92.07," *New York Newsday*, June 29, 1986.

5　Beryl Satter, *Family Properties: Race, Estate, and the Exploitation of Black Urban America* (New York: Metropolitan Books, 2009); N. D. B. Connolly, *A World More Concrete: Real Estate and the Remaking of Jim Crow South Florida* (Chicago: University of Chicago Press, 2014); Ta-Nehisi Coates, "The Case for Reparations," *Atlantic* (June 2014), http://www.theatlantic.com/features/archive/2014/05/the-case-for-reparations/361631/; University of Richmond Digital Scholars Lab, "Mapping Inequality: Redlining in New Deal America," accessed July 21, 2020, https://dsl.richmond.edu/panorama/redlining/; Richard Rothstein, *The Color of Law: A Forgotten History of How Our Government Segregated America* (New York: Liveright Publishing Corporation, 2017); Leif Michael Fredrickson, "The Age of Lead: Metropolitan Change, Environmental Health and Inner City Underdevelopment in Baltimore" (PhD diss., University of Virginia, 2017); Chloe N. Thurston, *At the Boundaries of Homeownership: Credit, Discrimination, and the American State* (New York: Cambridge University Press, 2018); Jessica Trounstine, *Segregation by Design: Local Politics and Inequality in American Cities* (New York: Cambridge University Press, 2018); Andre M. Perry, Jonathan Rothwell, and David Harshbarger, "The Devaluation of Assets in Black Neighborhoods: The Case of Residential Property," Brookings Institution, November 27, 2018, https://www.brookings.edu/research/devaluation-of-assets-in-black-neighborhoods/; Keeanga-Yamahtta Taylor, *Race for Profit: How Banks and the Real Estate Industry Undermined Black Homeownership* (Chapel Hill: University of North Carolina Press, 2019); LaDale C. Winling and Todd M. Michney, "The

Roots of Redlining: Academic, Governmental, and Professional Networks in the Making of the New Deal Lending Regime," *Journal of American History* 108 (June 2021): 42–69; Gene Slater, *Freedom to Discriminate: How Realtors Conspired to Segregate Housing and Divide America* (Berkeley, CA: Heyday, 2021).

6 James E. Ryan, *Five Miles Apart, A World Away: One City, Two Schools, and the Story of Educational Opportunity in Modern America* (New York: Oxford University Press, 2010); Pauline Lipman, *The New Political Economy of Urban Education: Neoliberalism, Race, and the Right to the City* (New York: Routledge, 2011); Noliwe Rooks, *Cutting School: Privatization, Segregation, and the End of Public Education* (New York: New Press, 2017); Nancy MacLean, *Democracy in Chains: The Deep History of the Radical Right's Stealth Plan for America* (New York: Viking, 2017); Eric Klinenberg, *Palaces for the People: How Social Infrastructure Can Help Fight Inequality, Polarization, and the Decline of Civic Life* (New York: Broadway, 2018); Heather McGhee, *The Sum of Us: What Racism Costs Everyone and How We Can Prosper Together* (New York: One World, 2021).

7 In 1900, local taxes and fees generated 48.4 percent of all government revenue in the US. Local revenue as a proportion of total government revenue fell sharply between 1933 and 1945, from 47.9 percent to 11.9 percent. As of 2023, local revenue makes up 17.7 percent of all government revenue, state revenue 31.9 percent, and federal revenue 50.3 percent. See https://www.usgovernmentrevenue.com/. A 2020 study by the University of Chicago's Harris School for Public Policy found that property assessments were regressive in 97.7 percent of all US counties. See University of Chicago Harris School of Public Policy, "Property Taxes and Equity," 2020, https://harris.uchicago.edu/research-impact/centers-institutes/center-municipal-finance/research-projects/property-tax.

8 Camille Walsh, *Racial Taxation: Schools, Segregation, and Taxpayer Citizenship, 1869–1973* (Chapel Hill: University of North Carolina Press, 2018); Camille Walsh, "White Backlash, the 'Taxpaying' Public, and Educational Citizenship," *Critical Sociology* 43, no. 2 (2017): 237–47; Vanessa Williamson, "The Austerity Politics of White Supremacy," *Dissent Magazine* 68 (Winter 2021): 106–14. On pervasive myths and misperceptions among the American public about who pays taxes, see also Vanessa Williamson, *Read My Lips: Why Americans Are Proud to Pay Taxes* (Princeton, NJ: Princeton University Press, 2017), 46–78; Ian Haney Lopez, *Dog Whistle Politics: How Coded Racial Appeals Have Reinvented Racism and Wrecked the Middle Class* (New York: Oxford University Press, 2015); Mildred Wigfall Robinson, "'Skin in the Tax Game': Invisible Taxpayers? Invisible Citizens?" *Villanova Law Review* 59, no. 4 (2014): 729–52. On the racialized disadvantages embedded within the federal tax code, see Dorothy A. Brown, *The Whiteness of Wealth: How the Tax System Impoverishes Black Americans—and How We Can Fix It* (New York: Crown, 2021).

9 On the historic and enduring ties that bound struggles for civil and economic rights and contests over federal authority and local power together, see Jefferson Cowie, *Freedom's Dominion: A Saga of White Resistance to Federal Power* (New York: Basic, 2022). As William J. Novak notes, a pragmatic approach to American state development reveals the vast infrastructural powers (among others, property tax administration) wielded by "relatively autonomous sub-units of government." See Novak, "The Myth of the 'Weak' American State," *American Historical Review* 113 (June 2008): 766.

10   For details on property tax structures in each state, see Lincoln Institute of
     Land Policy's Property Tax Database, available at https://www.lincolninst.edu/
     research-data/data-toolkits/significant-features-property-tax/access-property
     -tax-database. For a summary of each state's property tax system and history, see
     Lincoln Institute of Land Policy, *State-by-State Property Tax at a Glance* (Wash-
     ington, DC: Lincoln Institute of Land Policy, 2022), https://www.lincolninst.edu/
     sites/default/files/ptaag_full_2022.pdf.

11   The variety and complexity of states' tax-sale laws and procedures defy easy cat-
     egorization. While all states allow some form of tax sale to settle unpaid property
     taxes, what is sold at a tax sale, the manner in which the sale is conducted, the
     statutory rights and requirements of the property owner and tax buyer subse-
     quent to the sale, and the sale's final resolution differ by state and locality. In
     some states, localities have the option of conducting tax sales to recoup unpaid
     taxes but can choose to do so at their discretion; in other states, localities con-
     duct tax sales according to state guidelines on a set schedule.
         In general, state tax-sale laws fall into two categories: states where localities
     auction tax-lien certificates on tax-delinquent properties (tax-lien states), and
     those that auction tax deeds to tax-delinquent properties (tax-deed states). In
     tax-lien states, local taxing authorities hold auctions where the liens to tax-
     delinquent properties are sold to private bidders, who in turn obtain the right to
     collect interest and penalties, which the property owner must pay within a cer-
     tain time frame (known as the redemption period) to remove the cloud, typically
     between one and two years. In some of these states, the interest rate remains
     the same over the course of the redemption period; in others, the interest rate
     increases at certain intervals. At the close of the redemption period, if the debt
     remains unpaid, the tax buyer can initiate a tax foreclosure. Some states allow
     tax buyers to automatically obtain ownership of an unredeemed property at the
     close of the redemption period. Other states conduct a second public auction
     following the redemption period, where the unredeemed property is then sold.
     In tax-deed states, local jurisdictions auction the deeds to tax-delinquent prop-
     erties. Though like a tax-lien sale, tax-deed sales often provide tax-delinquent
     property owners the ability to redeem their property by paying back taxes,
     interest, and penalties by a certain date subsequent to the sale. In addition to
     property tax liens, many states also authorize local authorities to sell liens for
     unpaid water and sewer bills, special assessments, or building-code violations at
     tax sales.
         The bidding procedures at tax sales also vary by state. In some states, bidding
     begins at the highest rate of interest a tax buyer can charge under state law,
     with the winning bidder being the one who is willing to accept the lowest rate of
     interest from the property owner to redeem (known as the interest rate or bid-
     down method). In other states, the auctioning of a tax-lien certificate or tax deed
     begins at the amount of taxes owed plus costs, with the winning bidder the one
     willing to pay the highest additional amount (known as the overbid method).
         Tax lien sales typically attract bidders seeking to profit from the interest and
     fees that can be charged on a tax debt, while tax-deed sales attract bidders
     seeking to acquire properties at low cost, though both types of sales can allow
     for both kinds of investing. A general characteristic of tax-deed states, though, is
     the handling of delinquent tax collection and enforcement by public authorities,
     with the tax-deed sale an instrument of last resort meant to transfer ownership

of a property to someone willing to pay taxes on it. In contrast, tax-lien states outsource the process of enforcing delinquent tax payments to private investors.

Prior to 1993, public tax sales or auctions were the only method used by local taxing authorities for recouping unpaid taxes and disposing of tax liens. Since then, growing numbers of local governments have conducted negotiated bulk sales of tax liens to private investors or packaged and sold them as securitized bonds, as discussed in chapter 15.

For an accurate general summary of state laws, see John Rao, *The Other Foreclosure Crisis: Property Tax Lien Sales* (Boston, MA: National Consumer Law Center, July 2012), https://www.nclc.org/resources/the-other-foreclosure -crisis-property-tax-lien-sales/, appendix A. See also "State Laws on Property Tax Sales," nolo.com, accessed July 21, 2023, https://www.nolo.com/legal -encyclopedia/state-laws-property-tax-sales. For a critical assessment of tax-lien sales, see Cameron M. Baskett and Christopher G. Bradley, "Property Tax Privateers," *Virginia Tax Review* 41 (2021): 89-135.

12 Thurgood Marshall, "Cold, Cold Ground," *New Republic*, August 12, 1940.

13 Interview with Maurice Lucas (btvct03107), interviewed by Mausiki S. Scales, Renova (MS), August 7, 1995, *Behind the Veil: Documenting African-American Life in the Jim Crow South*, digital collection, John Hope Franklin Research Center, Duke University Libraries, Durham, NC, https://repository.duke.edu/dc/behindtheveil/btvct03107.

14 Robert Samuels and Toluse Olorunnipa, *His Name Is George Floyd: One Man's Life and the Struggle for Racial Justice* (New York: Viking, 2022), 39-44.

15 Jon C. Teaford, *The Rise of the States: Evolution of American State Government* (Baltimore, MD: Johns Hopkins University Press, 2002), 55-58; Ajay K. Mehrotra, *Making the Modern American Fiscal State: Law, Politics, and the Rise of Progressive Taxation, 1877-1929* (New York: Cambridge University Press, 2013), 214-21, 222-41.

16 Charles Abrams, *Forbidden Neighbors: A Study of Prejudice in Housing* (New York: Harper, 1955), 158. See also David M. P. Freund, *Colored Property: State Policy and White Racial Politics in Suburban America* (Chicago: University of Chicago Press, 2007); Carl H. Nightingale, *Segregation: A Global History of Divided Cities* (Chicago: University of Chicago Press, 2012), 295-332; David Imbroscio, "Race Matters (Even More than You Already Think): Racism, Housing, and the Limits of the Color of Law," *Journal of Race, Ethnicity and the City* 2, no. 1 (2021): 29-53.

17 On suburban tax-base formation as a stratifying process, see John R. Logan and Harvey L. Molotch, *Urban Fortunes: The Political Economy of Place* (Berkeley: University of California Press, 1987), 195-99. Cities' fiscal constraints enhanced the power of municipal bond markets over public spending priorities and the distribution of public goods and services. See Destin Jenkins, *The Bonds of Inequality: Debt and the Making of the American City* (Chicago: University of Chicago Press, 2021).

18 Isaac William Martin, *The Permanent Tax Revolt: How the Property Tax Transformed American Politics* (Stanford, CA: Stanford University Press, 2008).

19 John Young, telephone interview by Andrew Kahrl, July 14, 2022.

20 David Balin, telephone interview by Andrew Kahrl, June 16, 2021.

21 On the "economic incentives for predatory and financially exploitative relationships with African American communities" that housing segregation created, see Keeanga-Yamahtta Taylor, "Backstory to the Neoliberal Moment," *Souls: A*

Critical Journal of Black Politics, Culture, and Society 14, no. 3–4 (2012): 187. See also Connolly, *World More Concrete*; Satter, *Family Properties*; Taylor, *Race for Profit*.

22 "College Students and Others Needed for CORE Summer Program," CORE summer program brochure, n.d., in the Congress of Racial Equality Papers, Martin Luther King, Jr. Center for Nonviolent Social Change, Inc., Atlanta, GA.

23 Janelle Jones, "The Racial Wealth Gap: How African-Americans Have Been Shortchanged out of the Materials to Build Wealth," *Working Economics* (blog), February 13, 2017, https://www.epi.org/blog/the-racial-wealth-gap-how -african-americans-have-been-shortchanged-out-of-the-materials-to-build -wealth/; Vanessa Williamson, "Closing the Racial Wealth Gap Requires Heavy, Progressive Taxation of Wealth," *Brookings* (blog), December 9, 2020, https:// www.brookings.edu/research/closing-the-racial-wealth-gap-requires-heavy -progressive-taxation-of-wealth/.

In recent years, scholarship and commentary on the racial wealth gap has proliferated and become a popular metric for gauging racial inequality, in general, and identifying the historic forces fueling it. This focus on wealth disparities between white and Black Americans as racial groups, Walter Benn Michaels and Adolph Reed Jr. argue, works to obscure the vast and growing wealth gap between the top 10 percent of Americans and everyone else, the fact that, among Black Americans, wealth is as equally concentrated at the top as it is among white Americans. By implication, calls to close this racial wealth gap (which, as Reed and others note, is largely due to wealth disparities between the wealthiest 10 percent of white and Black Americans) avoid addressing the underlying causes of the wealth gap between the rich and the poor, or operate from the premise that ensuring wealth equality among different racial groups is a prerequisite to combating wealth inequality, more broadly. This book, and the history it tells, speaks more to the absence of wealth among the bottom 90 percent Black Americans (and its extraction in the service of capital accumulation and wealth concentration at the top) than the overall wealth gap between white and Black Americans. See Walter Benn Michaels and Adolph Reed Jr., "The Trouble with Disparity," *Nonsite.Org*, September 10, 2020, https://nonsite.org/the-trouble -with-disparity/. See also Adolph Reed Jr. and Merlin Chowkwanyun, "Race, Class, Crisis: The Discourse of Racial Disparity and Its Analytical Discontents," *Socialist Register* 48 (2012): 149–75.

24 Trymaine Lee, "How America's Vast Racial Wealth Gap Grew: By Plunder," *New York Times*, August 18, 2019, https://www.nytimes.com/interactive/2019/08/14/ magazine/racial-wealth-gap.html.

25 On racial exploitation as a "multiply interacting" system, see Charles W. Mills, *Black Rights/White Wrongs: The Critique of Racial Liberalism* (New York: Oxford University Press, 2017). See also Cheryl Harris, "Whiteness as Property," *Harvard Law Review* 106 (June 1993): 1707–91.

26 On racial capitalism as concept and methodological practice, see Destin Jenkins and Justin Leroy, eds., *Histories of Racial Capitalism* (New York: Columbia University Press, 2021). On the historic relationship between social inequality, racial categorization, and capital accumulation, this study draws in particular on Jodi Melamed's observation, "Capital can only be capital when it is accumulating, and it can only accumulate by producing and moving through relations of severe inequality among human groups—capitalists with the means of production/

workers without the means of subsistence, creditors/debtors, conquerors of land made property/the dispossessed and removed. These antinomies of accumulation require loss, disposability, and the unequal differentiation of human value, and racism enshrines the inequalities that capitalism requires." See Jodi Melamed, "Racial Capitalism," *Critical Ethnic Studies* 1, no. 1 (2015): 76-85. On the racialized processes of Black underdevelopment, devaluation, extraction, and dispossession through which white space and white property accrue value, see Danielle M. Purifoy and Louise Seamster, "Creative Extraction: Black Towns in White Space," *EPD: Society and Space* 39, no. 1 (2021): 47-66. On the concept of accumulation by dispossession, see David Harvey, *The New Imperialism* (New York: Oxford University Press, 2003).

27 Carlos Avenancio-León and Troup Howard, "The Assessment Gap: Racial Inequalities in Property Taxation" (working paper, Washington Center for Equitable Growth, Washington, DC, July 10, 2020), http://www.equitablegrowth.org/working-papers/the-assessment-gap-racial-inequalities-in-property-taxation/.

28 Dania V. Francis, Darrick Hamilton, Thomas W. Mitchell, Nathan A. Rosenberg, and Bryce Wilson Stucki, "Black Land Loss: 1920–1997," *AEA Papers and Proceedings* 112 (2022): 38-42.

CHAPTER ONE

1 Steven Hahn, Steven F. Miller, Susan E. O'Donovan, John C. Rodrigue, and Leslie S. Rowland, eds., *Land and Labor, 1865*, series 3, vol. 1 in *Freedom: A Documentary History of Emancipation, 1861-1867* (Chapel Hill: University of North Carolina Press, 2008), 396.

2 Committee of Freedmen on Edisto Island, South Carolina, to the President, October 28, 1865, in Hahn et al., *Land and Labor, 1865*, 443.

3 W. E. B. Du Bois, "The Negro Farmer" (Washington, DC: Government Printing Office, 1906), 523. See also Loren Schweninger, *Black Property Owners in the South, 1790-1915* (Urbana: University of Illinois Press, 1990).

4 On Black visions of "progress through property" in post-Reconstruction America, see especially N. D. B. Connolly, *A World More Concrete: Real Estate and the Remaking of Jim Crow South Florida* (Chicago: University of Chicago Press, 2014), 28-30.

5 Hahn et al., *Land and Labor, 1865*, 554, 613; René Hayden, Anthony E. Kaye, Kate Masur, Steven F. Miller, Susan E. O'Donovan, Leslie S. Rowland, and Stephen A. West, eds., *Land and Labor, 1866-1867*, series 3, vol. 2 in *Freedom: A Documentary History of Emancipation, 1861-1867* (Chapel Hill: University of North Carolina Press, 2013), 32, 147–48, 502.

6 W. E. B. Du Bois, *Black Reconstruction in America, 1860-1880* (New York: Harcourt, Brace, 1935), 361, 440, 468.

7 See Robin L. Einhorn, *American Taxation, American Slavery* (Chicago: University of Chicago Press, 2006); Katherine S. Newman and Rourke L. O'Brien, *Taxing the Poor: Doing Damage to the Truly Disadvantaged* (Berkeley: University of California Press, 2011), 1–30.

8 Jack M. Bloom, *Class, Race, and the Civil Rights Movement* (Bloomington: Indiana University Press, 1987), 21; Lawyers' Committee for Civil Rights under Law, "Board of Supervisors Handbook," June 1967, box 1, folder 23, Charles Horwitz Papers, Tougaloo College Civil Rights Collection, housed at the Mississippi

Department of Archives and History, Jackson; John C. Willis, *Forgotten Time: The Yazoo-Mississippi Delta after the Civil War* (Charlottesville: University Press of Virginia, 2000), 45-46, 48; Williamson, *After Slavery*, 155.

9   J. Mills Thornton, "Fiscal Policy and the Failure of Radical Reconstruction in the Lower South," in *Region, Race, and Reconstruction: Essays in Honor of C. Vann Woodward*, eds. J. Morgan Kousser and James M. McPherson (New York: Oxford University Press, 1982), 351; Eric Foner, *Nothing but Freedom: Emancipation and Its Legacy* (Baton Rouge: Louisiana State University Press, 1983), 68.

10   Clyde Woods, *Development Arrested: The Blues and Plantation Power in the Mississippi Delta* (London: Verso, 1998), 73; Charles Hillman Brough, "Taxation in Mississippi," in *Studies in State Taxation: With Particular Reference to the Southern States*, ed. J. H. Hollander (Baltimore, MD: Johns Hopkins University Press, 1900), 193; Willis, *Forgotten Time*, 45; Carol K. Rothrock Bleser, *The Promised Land: The History of the South Carolina Land Commission, 1869-1890* (Columbia: University of South Carolina Press, 1969), 67; Eric Foner, *Reconstruction: America's Unfinished Revolution, 1863-1877* (New York: Harper and Row, 1988), 415-16; John Hope Franklin, *Reconstruction after the Civil War* (Chicago: University of Chicago Press, 1961), 143; W. Scott Poole, *Never Surrender: Confederate Memory and Conservatism in the South Carolina Upcountry* (Athens: University of Georgia Press, 2004), 78.

11   Vanessa Williamson, "The Austerity Politics of White Supremacy," *Dissent* (Winter 2021), https://www.dissentmagazine.org/article/the-austerity-politics -of-white-supremacy.

12   Brough, "Taxation in Mississippi," 193; Bleser, *Promised Land*, 67; Williamson, *After Slavery*, 155.

13   Foner, *Reconstruction*, 416; Thomas Holt, *Black over White: Negro Political Leadership in South Carolina during Reconstruction* (Urbana: University of Illinois Press, 1977), 141.

14   C. Vann Woodward, *Origins of the New South, 1877-1913* (Baton Rouge: Louisiana State University Press, 1951), 59. See also Judith Stein, "'Of Booker T. Washington and Others': The Political Economy of Racism in the United States," in *Renewing Black Intellectual History: The Ideological and Material Foundations of African American Thought*, eds. Adolph Reed Jr. and Kenneth W. Warren (Boulder, CO: Paradigm Publishers, 2010), 19-50.

15   Thornton, "Fiscal Policy and the Failure of Radical Reconstruction," 368.

16   Newman and O'Brien, *Taxing the Poor*, 35-39.

17   Foner, *Nothing but Freedom*, 70-71.

18   Laurence Frederick Schmeckebier, "Taxation in Georgia," in *Studies in State Taxation*, ed. Hollander, 223-34; Harley Leist Lutz, *The State Tax Commission: A Study of the Development and Results of State Control over the Assessment of Property for Taxation* (Cambridge, MA: Harvard University Press, 1918), 576. On the low pay and low regard for local tax assessors, see Edwards Echols, *Report of the Joint Committee on Tax Revision* (Richmond: Commonwealth of Virginia, 1914), 14.

19   J. Morgan Kousser, *The Shaping of Southern Politics: Suffrage Restriction and the Establishment of the One-Party South, 1880-1910* (New Haven, CT: Yale University Press, 1974), 18.

20   Daniel Farbman, "Redemption Localism," *North Carolina Law Review* 100 (2022): 1530.

21   Manning Marable, "The Land Question in Historical Perspective: The Econom-

ics of Poverty in the Blackbelt South, 1865-1920," in *The Black Rural Landowner—Endangered Species: Social, Political, and Economic Implications*, eds. Leo McGee and Robert L. Boone (Westport, CT: Greenwood Press, 1979), 12.

22 Schweninger, *Black Property Owners in the South, 1790-1915*, 173-75. See also Tipton Ray Snavely, *The Taxation of Negroes in Virginia* (Charlottesville: University of Virginia Press, 1916), 48. On the formation of Black mutual benefit and insurance societies and Black-owned banks and their role in facilitating Black land acquisitions, see Schweninger, *Black Property Owners*, 173; Mehrsa Baradaran, *The Color of Money: Black Banks and the Racial Wealth Gap* (Cambridge, MA: Harvard University Press, 2017), 43-44.

23 Du Bois, "Negro Farmer," 517; Carter G. Woodson, *The Rural Negro* (Washington, DC: Association for the Study of Negro Life and History, 1930), 34. See also Neil R. McMillen, *Dark Journey: Black Mississippians in the Age of Jim Crow* (Urbana: University of Illinois Press, 1989), 119.

24 Woodson, *Rural Negro*, 35-36.

25 Du Bois, "Negro Farmer," 517; Arthur Raper, *Preface to Peasantry: A Tale of Two Black Belt Counties* (Columbia: University of South Carolina Press, 1936), 129, 132; Du Bois, "Negro Farmer," 526.

26 Conversely, in Georgia, Raper observed, "there are scarcely any Negro owners in the vicinity of the white churches and schools, near the railroads, on the leading highways, or on the most fertile soil" (*Preface to Peasantry*, 125-126).

27 Samuel Tilden Bitting, *Rural Land Ownership among the Negroes of Virginia with Special Reference to Albemarle County* (Charlottesville, VA: Michie Co., 1915), 37.

28 William Taylor Thom, *The Negroes of Litwalton, Virginia: A Social Study of the 'Oyster Negro,'* bulletin of the US Department of Labor (Washington, DC: Department of Labor, 1901), 1121.

29 Figures calculated from table LXIII in Du Bois, "Negro Farmer," 578.

30 Snavely, *Taxation of Negroes in Virginia*, table XVI, p. 50.

31 Snavely, *Taxation of Negroes in Virginia*, 54.

32 Black-owned land was valued more highly by tax assessors in ninety-eight of the 191 tax districts in Virginia where Black people owned land in 1901.

33 Snavely, *Taxation of Negroes in Virginia*, table XXVI, 75.

34 Figures derived from listings of total number of acres of land and value of land for landowners categorized respectively as "White" or "Colored," by county in Virginia. See *Recapitulation of Land Book* (for each county), in the Virginia Land Tax Records, 1782-1927, available on microfilm at the Library of Virginia (Richmond). See also Snavely, *Taxation of Negroes in Virginia*, 75-76.

35 W. E. B. Du Bois, "The Negro Landholder of Georgia," *Bulletin of the Department of Labor* 35 (1901): 647-777.

36 T. J. Woofter, *Black Yeomanry: Life on St. Helena Island* (New York: H. Holt and Company, 1930), 160.

37 Hugh Stephen Whitaker, "A New Day: The Effects of Negro Enfranchisement in Selected Mississippi Counties" (PhD diss., Florida State University, 1965), ProQuest dissertation no. 6602102, 147-50.

38 Neil Canaday, "The Accumulation of Property by Southern Blacks and Whites: Individual-Level Evidence from a South Carolina Cotton County, 1910-1919," *Explorations in Economic History* 45, no. 1 (January 2008): 51-75.

39 Robert Higgs, "Accumulation of Property by Southern Blacks Before World

War I," *American Economic Review* 72, no. 4 (1982): 726. See also Echols, *Report of the Joint Committee on Tax Revision*, 10.

40 Schmeckebier, "Taxation in Georgia," 234, 229.

41 As late as 1973, eighteen counties in Mississippi had never conducted a full appraisal of all their property; only nine had conducted appraisals since 1960, and only six of those had done so since 1965. See Barbara Phillips and Joseph Huttie Jr., *Mississippi Property Tax: Special Burden for the Poor* (Jackson, MS: Black Economic Research Center, 1973), 15.

42 "Our $7,000 Tax Raise (Editorial)," *Norfolk Journal and Guide*, February 6, 1932; "Norfolk Increases Tax Assessments on Us," *Baltimore Afro-American*, February 13, 1932.

43 Figures derived from Virginia county tax-assessment rolls in the Library of Virginia, Richmond.

44 Raper, *Preface to Peasantry*, 135–36.

45 Clyde Vernon Kiser, *Sea Island to City: A Study of St. Helena Islanders in Harlem and Other Urban Centers* (New York: Atheneum, 1932), 217.

46 William Pickens, *The New Negro: His Political, Civil and Mental Status and Related Essays* (New York: Neale Publishing Company, 1916), 164.

47 Evalyn W. Shaed, "Negroes' Contributions to the Economy Cited," *Richmond Times-Dispatch*, July 20, 1958.

48 P. Bernard Young Jr., "Slums and Taxes," *Norfolk Journal and Guide*, February 22, 1936.

49 "Protest Tax Raise in Prince Georges," *Baltimore Afro-American*, February 11, 1928.

50 Charles S. Johnson, *Negro Housing: Report of the Committee on Negro Housing, Nannie H. Burroughs, Chairman*, eds. John M. Gries and James Ford (New York: Negro Universities Press, 1969 [1932]), 31–32.

51 W. E. B. Du Bois, *The Souls of Black Folk* (New York: Penguin, 1903).

52 "Wins Tax Exemptions," *Associated Negro Press*, August 10, 1932.

53 Woofter, *Black Yeomanry*, 184.

54 Raper, *Preface to Peasantry*, 136.

55 Michael J. Bednarz, "Comity Bars Federal Damages for Section 1984 Discriminatory State Tax Assessments," *Boston University Journal of Tax Law* 1 (1983): 152–53.

56 28 USC 1341; see also Frederick C. Lowinger, "The Tax Injunction Act and Suits for Monetary Relief," *University of Chicago Law Review* 46 (1979): 736–66.

57 Lowinger, "Tax Injunction Act," 741.

CHAPTER TWO

1 Hortense Powdermaker, *After Freedom: A Cultural Study in the Deep South* (New York: Russell and Russell, 1939), 11; Charles Louis Knight, *Negro Housing in Certain Virginia Cities* (Richmond, VA: William Byrd Press, Inc., 1927), 53; Craig E. Colten, *An Unnatural Metropolis: Wresting New Orleans from Nature* (Baton Rouge: Louisiana State University Press, 2005), 80; "Where a Minority Drags Its White Feet," *Boston Globe*, July 30, 1972. See also Steven T. Moga, *Urban Lowlands: A History of Neighborhoods, Poverty, and Planning* (Chicago: University of Chicago Press, 2020).

2 Jay Winston Driskell, *Schooling Jim Crow: The Fight for Atlanta's Booker T. Wash-*

ington High School and the Roots of Black Protest Politics (Charlottesville: University of Virginia Press, 2014).

3   As historian Jay Winston Driskell Jr. observed, "Progressive Era development had not simply been restricted to 'whites only.' It depended upon a subject, voteless population to serve as a tax base to sustain the development of public education and . . . infrastructural improvements" (*Schooling Jim Crow*, 47).

4   Booker T. Washington, "My View of Segregation Laws," *New Republic*, December 4, 1915, 113-14.

5   William Pickens, *The New Negro: His Political, Civil and Mental Status and Related Essays* (New York: Neale Publishing Company, 1916), 212.

6   Powdermaker, *After Freedom*, 130.

7   Steven Hahn, Steven F. Miller, Susan E. O'Donovan, John C. Rodrigue, and Leslie S. Rowland, eds., *Land and Labor, 1865*, series 3, vol. 1, in *Freedom: A Documentary History of Emancipation, 1861-1867* (Chapel Hill: University of North Carolina Press, 2008), 613.

8   Hahn et al., *Land and Labor, 1865*, 612.

9   Hahn et al., *Land and Labor, 1865*, 818; René Hayden, Anthony E. Kaye, Kate Masur, Steven F. Miller, Susan E. O'Donovan, Leslie S. Rowland, and Stephen A. West, eds., *Land and Labor, 1866-1867*, series 3, vol. 2, in *Freedom: A Documentary History of Emancipation, 1861-1867* (Chapel Hill: University of North Carolina Press, 2013), 17.

10 Rebekah Barber and Billy Corriher, "Honoring Reconstruction's Legacy: Educating the South's Children," *Facing South*, October 11, 2018, https://www.facingsouth.org/2018/10/honoring-reconstructions-legacy-educating-souths-children.

11 W. E. B. Du Bois, *Black Reconstruction in America, 1860-1880* (New York: Harcourt, Brace, 1935), 664-65. On the shifting strategies and approaches white redeemers took toward local government power and their underlying objectives, see Daniel Farbman, "Redemption Localism," *North Carolina Law Review* 100 (2022): 1527-56.

12 Zachary L. Guyse, "Alabama's Original Sin: Property Taxes, Racism, and Constitutional Reform in Alabama," *Alabama Law Review* 65 (2013): 526.

13 Horace Mann Bond, *The Education of the Negro in the American Social Order* (New York: Octagon Books, 1934), 104.

14 Hayden et al., *Land and Labor, 1866-1867*, 716; Camille Walsh, *Racial Taxation: Schools, Segregation, and Taxpayer Citizenship, 1869-1973* (Chapel Hill: University of North Carolina Press, 2018), 50; Farbman, "Redemption Localism."

15 Horace Mann Bond, *The Education of the Negro in the American Social Order* (New York: Octagon Books, 1934), 99. On the political economy of taxation and public spending in the 1880s and 1890s South and the rise and fall of southern populism, see also Judith Stein, "'Of Booker T. Washington and Others': The Political Economy of Racism in the United States," in *Renewing Black Intellectual History: The Ideological and Material Foundations of African American Thought*, eds. Adolph Reed Jr. and Kenneth W. Warren (Boulder, CO: Paradigm Publishers, 2010), 19-50.

16 "Letter from Colonel Ruffin," *Richmond Dispatch*, February 25, 1890, https://chroniclingamerica.loc.gov/lccn/sn85038614/1890-02-25/ed-1/seq-4/.

17 "To Discover the Negro Taxpayer," *Hazleton [PA] Plain Speaker*, February 24, 1890.

18 "Race Issue Again: Maj. Vardaman More Radical Than Anybody," *St. Louis Post-Dispatch*, July 16, 1899; "Vardaman the Nominee," *Baltimore Sun*, August 29,

1903; see also William F. Holmes, "Whitecapping: Agrarian Violence in Missis-
sippi, 1902-1906," *Journal of Southern History* 35, no. 2 (1969): 165-85; Neil R.
McMillen, *Dark Journey: Black Mississippians in the Age of Jim Crow* (Urbana:
University of Illinois Press, 1989), 76.

19   "Mrs. W. H. Felton Attacks Georgia's School System," *Atlanta Constitution*,
November 15, 1901.

20   On the appropriation of state and local tax revenues earmarked for Black schools
by white school administrators in the post-Reconstruction South, see Robert A.
Margo, "Race Differences in Public School Expenditures: Disfranchisement and
School Finance in Louisiana, 1890-1910," *Social Science History* 6, no. 1 (1982):
9-33; Walsh, *Racial Taxation*, 18.

21   Westin, "State and Segregated Schools," 192. See also Walsh, *Racial Taxation*,
50-53.

22   "Alabama's New Constitution," *Nashville Tennessean*, May 12, 1901; Katherine S.
Newman and Rourke L. O'Brien, *Taxing the Poor: Doing Damage to the Truly
Disadvantaged* (Berkeley: University of California Press, 2011), 35-39.

23   "Will Cause Delay: New Constitution May Not Be Voted On in November,"
Baltimore Sun, August 5, 1901.

24   J. Morgan Kousser, *The Shaping of Southern Politics: Suffrage Restriction and the
Establishment of the One-Party South, 1880-1910* (New Haven, CT: Yale University Press, 1974), 229.

25   See Charles S. Johnson and Lewis W. Jones, *Statistical Atlas of Southern Counties:
Listing and Analysis of Socio-Economic Indices of 1104 Southern Counties* (Chapel
Hill: University of North Carolina Press, 1941), table 3, 13.

26   "Inequalities of Educational Opportunities in Brunswick County," *Norfolk Journal and Guide*, March 12, 1927.

27   Driskell, *Schooling Jim Crow*, 47.

28   Charles L. Coon, *Public Taxation and Negro Schools* (Cheyney, PA: Committee of Twelve for the Advancement of the Interests of the Negro Race,
1909), 6-8.

29   "Negro Education," *Bulletin of Atlanta University*, May 1909, folder 149,
Charles L. Coon Papers, 1775-1931, Southern Historical Collection, University of
North Carolina, Chapel Hill.

30   Richard Kent Smith, "The Economics of Education and Discrimination in the
U.S. South: 1870-1910" (PhD diss., University of Wisconsin, 1973), ProQuest
dissertation no. 7410269, 92. See also McMillen, *Dark Journey*, 79.

31   "Negro Education."

32   "Mr. Coon's Mare's Nest," *Raleigh News and Observer*, September 28, 1909,
folder 149, Charles L. Coon Papers, 1775-1931, Southern Historical Collection,
University of North Carolina, Chapel Hill.

33   J. D. Eggleston, quoted in Charles L. Coon to J. D. Eggleston, October 15, 1909,
folder 28, Charles L. Coon Papers, 1775-1931, Southern Historical Collection,
University of North Carolina, Chapel Hill.

34   Coon to Eggleston.

35   "Mr. Coon's Mare's Nest."

36   Thomas B. Gregory, "A New Yorker on Coon: A Native North Carolinian Is
Shocked at His Remarkable Document," *unknown newspaper*, October 11, 1909,
folder 149, Charles L. Coon Papers, 1775-1931, Southern Historical Collection,
University of North Carolina, Chapel Hill.

37 James D. Anderson, *The Education of Blacks in the South, 1860-1935* (Chapel Hill: University of North Carolina Press, 1988), 156.

38 Booker T. Washington, "Is the Negro Having a Fair Chance?" *Century*, November 1912, 54.

39 Washington, "My View of Segregation Laws," 114; William Pickens, *The New Negro: His Political, Civil and Mental Status and Related Essays* (New York: Neale Publishing Company, 1916), 165; James Weldon Johnson, "The Apportionment of Public School Funds in the South" (New York: Oxford University Press, 1915), 112-13.

40 David R. Goldfield, *Cotton Fields and Skyscrapers: Southern City and Region, 1607-1980* (Baton Rouge: Louisiana State University Press, 1982), 97.

41 Edward L. Ayers, *The Promise of the New South: Life after Reconstruction* (New York: Oxford University Press, 1992), 55-76.

42 W. E. B. Du Bois, "Violations of Property Rights," *Crisis*, May 1, 1911, 32.

43 Ayers, *Promise of the New South*, 67.

44 Paige Glotzer, *How the Suburbs Were Segregated: Developers and the Business of Exclusionary Housing, 1890-1960* (New York: Columbia University Press, 2020), 84-99; Buchanan v. Warley, 245 U.S. 60 (1917).

45 Charles S. Johnson, *Negro Housing: Report of the Committee on Negro Housing, Nannie H. Burroughs, Chairman*, eds. John M. Gries and James Ford (New York: Negro Universities Press, 1969), 24-25.

46 Johnson, *Negro Housing*, 23.

47 Knight, "Negro Housing in Certain Virginia Cities," 63.

48 T. J. Woofter, *The Negroes of Athens, Georgia* (Athens: Bulletin of the University of Georgia, 1913), 13.

49 "Martinsville Is Guilty!" *Pittsburgh Courier*, May 21, 1949.

50 Knight, "Negro Housing in Certain Virginia Cities," 53.

51 "The Dirt Roads of Norfolk," *Norfolk Journal and Guide*, August 11, 1917.

52 Driskell, *Schooling Jim Crow*, 71.

53 "Buchanan v. Warley U.S. Supreme Court Transcript of Record with Supporting Pleadings," US Supreme Court transcript of record, October term, 1917, 72-73. See *Buchanan v. Warley*, 245 U.S.

54 Charles E. Connerly, *"The Most Segregated City in America": City Planning and Civil Rights in Birmingham, 1920-1980* (Charlottesville: University of Virginia Press, 2013), 44.

55 Knight, "Negro Housing in Certain Virginia Cities," 53.

56 "Are Rebuked for Showing Bad Housing," *Norfolk Journal and Guide*, May 14, 1921. See also J. Douglas Smith, *Managing White Supremacy: Race, Politics, and Citizenship in Jim Crow Virginia* (Chapel Hill: University of North Carolina Press, 2002), 71.

57 Driskell, *Schooling Jim Crow*, 156. See also "Statement by Atlanta Branch of NAACP on Bond Issue" (February 26, 1919), in part 12: Selected Branch Files, 1913-1939, series A: The South, Papers of the NAACP, Library of Congress, Washington, DC, available in the ProQuest History Vault; "Will Carry Vote for Higher Taxes to the Assembly," *Atlanta Constitution*, March 8, 1919; "Negroes Are Told of Revenue Needs," *Atlanta Constitution*, April 9, 1919; E. Bernard West, "Black Atlanta—Struggle for Development, 1915-1925" (MA thesis, Atlanta University, 1976), 13-19.

58 "Bonds of Atlanta to Be Sold Soon," *Atlanta Constitution*, March 7, 1919; Driskell, *Schooling Jim Crow*, 233-42.

59 "Bond Issues and New NAACP Program to Be Discussed Tonight," *Atlanta Daily World*, July 24, 1935; "Plans Underway to Eliminate Double Sessions," *Atlanta Daily World*, December 23, 1942; "Demand Better Atlanta School Aid for Negroes," *Chicago Defender*, December 23, 1944.

60 "WPA Projects Given Approval," *Jackson Clarion-Ledger*, July 27, 1935; "Administrator Alliston to Go to Washington with Two Millions in Projects," *Jackson Clarion-Ledger*, August 4, 1935; "$47,929,944 Filed in State Projects by PWA Deadline," *McComb Semi-Weekly Journal*, September 10, 1935; United States Works Progress Administration and Harry L. (Harry Lloyd) Hopkins, *Inventory: An Appraisal of the Results of the Works Progress Administration* (Washington, DC: Works Progress Administration, 1938), https://hdl.handle.net/2027/mdp .39015008626007; United States Federal Works Agency, *Final Report on the WPA Program, 1935-43* (Washington, DC: Government Printing Office, 1947); Emilye Crosby, *A Little Taste of Freedom: The Black Freedom Struggle in Claiborne County, Mississippi* (Chapel Hill: University of North Carolina Press, 2005), 41.

61 On public works programs under the New Deal, see Jason Scott Smith, *Building New Deal Liberalism: The Political Economy of Public Works, 1933-1956* (New York: Cambridge University Press, 2006). On the administrative structure of New Deal programs and the discretionary powers local administrators wielded, see Ira Katznelson, *When Affirmative Action Was White: An Untold History of Racial Inequality in Twentieth-Century America* (New York: W. W. Norton, 2005).

62 Others sought out opportunities to acquire cheap farmland in some of the less prosperous agricultural regions. In Claiborne County, Mississippi, in the state's southwest corner, the number of Black farm owners nearly tripled in the years between 1930 and 1945.

63 On race and municipal annexation decisions in mid-twentieth-century southern cities and towns, see Charles S. Aiken, "Race as a Factor in Municipal Underbounding," *Annals of the Association of American Geographers* 77, no. 4 (1987): 564-79. See also Michelle Wilde Anderson, "Mapped Out of Democracy," *Stanford Law Review* 62, no. 4 (2010): 931-1003.

64 Clyde Woods, *Development Arrested: The Blues and Plantation Power in the Mississippi Delta* (London: Verso, 1998), 225.

65 "Showdown Comes to Shaw, Miss.," *Cleveland Call and Post*, January 16, 1971; "Meaning of the Shaw Case," *Baltimore Afro-American*, April 10, 1971; R. Dennis Anderson, "Toward an Equalization of Municipal Services: Variations on a Theme by Hawkins," *Journal of Urban Law* 50 (November 1972): 177-97.

66 Kenneth Lambright, untitled summary of interviews with residents of Port Gibson, Mississippi, box E76, folder Analysis, Claiborne County Property Tax Study, 5-29-74, Emergency Land Fund Records, Amistad Research Center, New Orleans, LA.

67 Bennie Thompson, telephone interview by Andrew Kahrl, May 12, 2022.

68 Jean White, interview by Andrew Kahrl, Edwards, MS, July 10, 2013; K. C. Morrison, interview by Andrew Kahrl, Starkville, MS, July 8, 2013.

CHAPTER THREE

1 "Tax Sales Book, Beaufort Township," December 5, 1932, Beaufort County Register of Deeds, Beaufort, SC.

2 Margaret Newkirk, "How Generations of Black Americans Lost Their Land to

Tax Liens," *Bloomberg.com*, June 29, 2022. See also Roy Reed, "Blacks in South Struggle to Keep the Little Land They Have Left," *New York Times*, December 7, 1972.

3 W. E. B. Du Bois, "Georgia Negroes and Their Fifty Millions of Savings," *World's Work* 18 (May 1909): 11551.

4 William F. Holmes, "Whitecapping in Georgia: Carroll and Houston Counties, 1893," *Georgia Historical Quarterly* 64, no. 4 (1980): 388–404; William F. Holmes, "Whitecapping: Agrarian Violence in Mississippi, 1902-1906," *Journal of Southern History* 35, no. 2 (1969): 165–85; Ida B. Wells, *Southern Horrors: Lynch Law in All Its Phases*, pamphlet, 1892. See also Megan Ming Francis, "Ida B. Wells and the Economics of Racial Violence," *Reading Racial Conflict (Items* blog series), January 31, 2017, http://items.ssrc.org/ida-b-wells-and-the-economics-of-racial-violence/.

5 Thurgood Marshall, "Cold, Cold Ground," *New Republic*, August 12, 1940.

6 Frank S. Alexander, "Tax Liens, Tax Sales, and Due Process," *Indiana Law Journal* 75, no. 3 (2000): 747–807, at 758.

7 Robert P. Swierenga, "The 'Odious Tax Title': A Study of Nineteenth Century Legal History," *American Journal of Legal History* 15 (1971): 138–39.

8 Willie Lee Rose, *Rehearsal for Reconstruction: The Port Royal Experiment* (Indianapolis, IN: Bobbs-Merrill, 1964); Joel Williamson, *After Slavery: The Negro in South Carolina during Reconstruction, 1861-1877* (Chapel Hill: University of North Carolina Press, 1965), 149–55.

9 Eric Foner, *Nothing but Freedom: Emancipation and Its Legacy* (Baton Rouge: Louisiana State University Press, 1983), 69.

10 Faith R. Rivers, "Restoring the Bundle of Rights: Preserving Heirs' Property in Coastal South Carolina," paper presented at the Property Preservation Task Force Program: Preservation and Development of Tenancy in Common Property—Societal, Real Estate and Tax Considerations, San Diego, CA, 2006, p. 7. Copy in author's possession.

11 Carter G. Woodson, *The Rural Negro* (Washington, DC: Association for the Study of Negro Life and History, 1930), 36.

12 Samuel Tilden Biting, *Rural Land Ownership among the Negroes of Virginia with Special Reference to Albemarle County* (Ithaca, NY: Cornell University Library, 1915); Carl Kelsey, *The Negro Farmer* (Chicago: Jennings and Pye, 1903), 35.

13 Thomas Barnwell, video oral history interview with the HistoryMakers, January 30, 2007, Hilton Head, SC, https://www.thehistorymakers.org/sites/default/files/A2007_034_EAD.pdf.

14 Skip Rozin, "Daufuskie Island: The Next Hilton Head?" *Historic Preservation* 35, no. 2 (March/April 1983); Joe McDomick, interview by Andrew Kahrl, St. Helena Island, SC, April 17, 2014.

15 Ann S. Pointer, interview by Paul Ortiz, July 22, 1994, *Behind the Veil: Documenting African-American Life in the Jim Crow South*, digital collection, John Hope Franklin Research Center, Duke University Libraries, Durham, NC, https://repository.duke.edu/dc/behindtheveil/btvct10098.

16 Money Alan Kirby and Anne Oda Kirby, interview by Mausiki S. Scales, July 13, 1995, *Behind the Veil: Documenting African-American Life in the Jim Crow South*, digital collection, John Hope Franklin Research Center, Duke University Libraries, Durham, NC, https://repository.duke.edu/dc/behindtheveil/btvct02018.

17 Milton Douglas Quigless, interview by Paul Ortiz, October 12, 1993, *Behind the*

Veil: Documenting African-American Life in the Jim Crow South, digital collection, John Hope Franklin Research Center, Duke University Libraries, Durham, NC, https://repository.duke.edu/dc/behindtheveil/btvnc03030.

18   Mehrsa Baradaran, *The Color of Money: Black Banks and the Racial Wealth Gap* (Cambridge, MA: Harvard University Press, 2017), 45.

19   See Du Bois, "Georgia Negroes and Their Fifty Millions of Savings," 11554.

20   Tipton Ray Snavely, *The Taxation of Negroes in Virginia* (Charlottesville: University of Virginia, 1916), 55.

21   Arthur Raper, *Preface to Peasantry: A Tale of Two Black Belt Counties* (Columbia: University of South Carolina Press, 1936), 213.

22   H. K. Allen, "Collection of Delinquent Taxes by Recourse to the Taxed Property," *Law and Contemporary Problems* 3 (1936): 405.

23   William H. Chafe, Raymond Gavins, and Robert Korstad, eds., *Remembering Jim Crow: African Americans Tell about Life in the Segregated South* (New York: New Press, 2001), 16.

24   Armstrong Edward Manuel, interview by Felix Armfield, August 11, 1994, *Behind the Veil: Documenting African-American Life in the Jim Crow South*, digital collection, John Hope Franklin Research Center, Duke University Libraries, Durham, NC, https://repository.duke.edu/dc/behindtheveil/btvct06054.

25   Robert Georgia and Abraham Smith, interview by Mary Hebert and Blair Murphy, June 14, 1995, *Behind the Veil: Documenting African-American Life in the Jim Crow South*, digital collection, John Hope Franklin Research Center, Duke University Libraries, Durham, NC, https://repository.duke.edu/dc/behindtheveil/btvct09090.

26   Lillie Pierce Fenner, interview by Chris Stewart, June 26, 1993, *Behind the Veil: Documenting African-American Life in the Jim Crow South*, digital collection, John Hope Franklin Research Center, Duke University Libraries, Durham, NC, https://repository.duke.edu/dc/behindtheveil/btvnc03061.

27   Ernestine Foy Clemmons and Grace Green George, interview by Karen Ferguson, July 30, 1993, *Behind the Veil: Documenting African-American Life in the Jim Crow South*, digital collection, John Hope Franklin Research Center, Duke University Libraries, Durham, NC, https://repository.duke.edu/dc/behindtheveil/btvnc05016.

28   Chafe, Gavins, and Korstad, *Remembering Jim Crow*, 16.

29   "Shot a Negro Dead," *Baltimore Sun*, July 4, 1906; "Bradley Woman Has Big Feed," *Daily Utah State Journal*, December 26, 1906.

30   William E. Garnett and Allen David Edwards, *Virginia's Marginal Population: Study in Rural Poverty* (Blacksburg: Virginia Polytechnic Institute, Virginia Agricultural Experiment Station, 1941), 65.

31   United States Bureau of the Census, *Realty Tax Delinquency*, vol. 1 (Washington, DC: Government Printing Office, 1934), 3–4, Arkansas addendum; Samuel Morris Ownbey, "'The Once Peaceful Little Town': Edmondson, Arkansas, and the Decline of African American Landownership" (MA thesis, University of Arkansas, 2020), ProQuest dissertation no. 27959673, 19; Sammy Morgan, "Elite Dominance in the Arkansas Delta, from the New Deal to the New Millennium" (PhD diss., University of Mississippi, 2005), UMI no. 3190580, 23, 24; H. W. Blalock, *Plantation Operations of Landlords and Tenants in Arkansas* (Fayetteville: University of Arkansas, May 1937), 6, 8.

32   Raper, *Preface to Peasantry*, 212.

33   On hoarding and misappropriating New Deal subsidies, see also Sarah Milov, *The Cigarette: A Political History* (Cambridge, MA: Harvard University Press, 2019).

34   On Edmonson's founding and development, see G. P. Hamilton, *Beacon Lights of the Race* (Memphis, TN: E. H. Clark and Brother, 1911), 544–56.

35   "Challenge Elections in All-Negro Town," *Atlanta Daily World*, May 9, 1943.

36   Hamilton, *Beacon Lights of the Race*, 546; Story Matkin-Rawn, "'The Great Negro State of the Country': Arkansas's Reconstruction and the Other Great Migration," *Arkansas Historical Quarterly* 72, no. 1 (2013): 39.

37   Ownbey, "'Once Peaceful Little Town,'" 17.

38   Hamilton, *Beacon Lights of the Race*, 546.

39   Workers Defense League attorney Joseph Freeland's description of the sentiments of Crittenden County's white planters, quoted in Ownbey, "'Once Peaceful Little Town,'" 27; See also "Tee Davis Got Ten Years for Defending His Home in Arkansas," *Baltimore Afro-American*, January 8, 1944.

40   Secretary (no name listed) to Hon. J. L. Bond (Superintendent of Public Instruction, Little Rock, Arkansas), April 23, 1919, in folder: NAACP Administrative File, Subject File, Discrimination (Education General, 1919–1920), part 3: Campaign for Educational Equality, series A: Legal Department and Central Office Records, 1913–1940, Papers of the NAACP, Library of Congress, Washington, DC, available in the ProQuest History Vault.

41   H. L. Mitchell, *Mean Things Happening in This Land: The Life and Times of H. L. Mitchell, Co-Founder of the Southern Tenant Farmers Union* (Montclair, NJ: Allanheld, Osmun, 1979), 201.

42   "Challenge Elections in All-Negro Town."

43   "It was not until the New Deal programs, particularly the Agricultural Adjustment Act, had revitalized the cotton industry and raised the value of the farmland around the town that whites endeavored to deprive African Americans of their property" (Ownbey, "'Once Peaceful Little Town,'" 2).

44   Edmondson Home and Improvement Company v. H. E. Weaver, complaint, Crittenden County Chancery Court, in folder "Southern Tenant Farmers' Union, Including American Farm Bureau Attacks on Union (1942)," in part 13: NAACP and Labor, series A: subject files on labor conditions and employment discrimination, 1940–1955, Papers of the NAACP, Library of Congress, Washington, DC, available in the ProQuest History Vault.

45   C. O. Brannen, *Tax Delinquent Rural Lands in Arkansas* (Fayetteville: University of Arkansas, 1934), 44; Edmondson Home and Improvement Company v. H. E. Weaver, complaint.

46   J. R. Butler, report to the Workers Defense League, October 13, 1941, in "Edmondson, Arkansas, Case, 1941–1942," box 165, folder 3, Workers' Defense League Records, Walter P. Reuther Library, Detroit, MI; "Challenge Elections in All-Negro Town."

47   Edmondson Home and Improvement Company v. H. E. Weaver, complaint.

48   Edmondson Home and Improvement Company v. H. E. Weaver, complaint.

49   H. L. Mitchell to Walter White, February 28, 1942, in "Southern Tenant Farmers' Union, Including American Farm Bureau Attacks on Union."

50   H. L. Mitchell to Walter White, February 28, 1942.

51   Mitchell, *Mean Things Happening in This Land*, 201.

52   Ownbey, "'The Once Peaceful Little Town'; for a profile of one family's journey

from Edmondson to Chicago and their experience in the northern metropolis, see William Peters, *Southern Accents—Northern Ghettos* (ABC News, released by Benchmark Films, 1969).

53 Jackson v. Day, 9 So. 2d 789 (Miss. 1942); "Duped Woman Is Granted Chance to Regain Land," *Atlanta Daily World*, October 12, 1942; "Court Grants Duped Woman Chance to Regain Land," *Norfolk Journal and Guide*, October 17, 1942.

54 *Jackson*, 9 So. 2d 789; "Duped Woman Is Granted Chance to Regain Land"; "Court Grants Duped Woman Chance to Regain Land."

55 *Jackson*, 9 So. 2d 789.

56 Marshall, "Cold, Cold Ground."

57 N. D. B. Connolly, *A World More Concrete: Real Estate and the Remaking of Jim Crow South Florida* (Chicago: University of Chicago Press, 2014), 29. See also Dylan C. Penningroth, *The Claims of Kinfolk: African American Property and Community in the Nineteenth-Century South* (Chapel Hill: University of North Carolina Press, 2003); Dylan C. Penningroth, "Everyday Use: A History of Civil Rights in Black Churches," *Journal of American History* 107, no. 4 (March 2021): 871-98.

58 *Jackson*, 9 So. 2d 789.

59 "Preacher Slain; Tongue Cut Out," *New Orleans Informer*, June 24, 1944.

60 "4 White Men Freed in Slaying of Negro Preacher," *PM*, October 8, 1944; Rose Farley, "This Land Is My Land: Murdine 'Baby Ruth' Berry Won Her Fight to Save the Family Farm Passed Down by Former Slaves, but Her Battle—Real or Imagined—Isn't Over," *Dallas Observer*, January 17, 2002; "For Justice in Mississippi," *Workers Defense Bulletin* (Fall 1944); "Mississippi Farmer Slain by Gang Who Sought His 220-Acre Farm," *Atlanta Daily World*, August 17, 1944. On the Simmons case, see also Charles M. Payne, *I've Got the Light of Freedom: The Organizing Tradition and the Mississippi Freedom Struggle* (Berkeley: University of California Press, 1995), 14-15; John Dittmer, *Local People: The Struggle for Civil Rights in Mississippi* (Urbana: University of Illinois Press, 1994), 15.

61 Dolores Barclay and Todd Lewan, "Land Taken from Blacks through Trickery, Violence and Murder: PART 1," *Los Angeles Sentinel*, December 27, 2001.

CHAPTER FOUR

1 "The Amite County Case and State Law Enforcement," *Jackson* [MS] *Advocate*, October 28, 1944.

2 J. Edwin Burton, "Tax Assessment and the Role of State Government," *State Government* 57 (1984): 23. See also Ajay K. Mehrotra, *Making the Modern American Fiscal State: Law, Politics, and the Rise of Progressive Taxation, 1877-1929* (New York: Cambridge University Press, 2013), 214-21.

3 On the localization of property taxation in the early twentieth century, see Mehrotra, *Making the Modern American Fiscal State*, 214-21. On the introduction of a state income tax in Wisconsin in 1911, see Mehrotra, 228-41.

4 By 1942, property taxes constituted less than 5 percent of all states' total revenues.

5 Frank Domurad, David Fleisher, Gene Russianoff, and Loretta Simon, *City of Unequal Neighbors: A Study of Residential Property Tax Assessments in New York City*, NYPIRG report (Albany: New York Public Interest Research Group Inc., 1981), 32.

6 Kenneth K. Baar, "Property Tax Assessment Discrimination against Low-Income Neighborhoods," *Urban Lawyer* 13 (Summer 1981): 342.

7 Richard J. Kissel, *Report on the Assessment Practices in Cook County (Illinois Department of Local Government Affairs)* (Springfield: Illinois Department of Local Government Affairs, October 1972), 780, 801, 804.

8 Martin A. Levin, "Urban Politics and Political Economy: The Politics of the Property Tax," *Policy Sciences* 9, no. April (1978): 241; Diane B. Paul, *The Politics of the Property Tax* (Washington, DC: Lexington Book, 1975), 7. For a summary of each state's statutes on property reassessments, see Justin Higginbottom, "State Provisions for Property Reassessment," Tax Foundation, Inc., April 29, 2010, https://taxfoundation.org/state-provisions-property-reassessment/.

9 George Crile, "A Tax Assessor Has Many Friends," *Harper's* (November 1972).

10 Charles Abrams, *Forbidden Neighbors* (New York: Harper, 1955).

11 On early-twentieth-century annexation of suburban areas by cities, see Jon C. Teaford, *City and Suburb: The Political Fragmentation of Metropolitan America, 1850-1970* (Baltimore, MD: Johns Hopkins University Press, 1979), 76-105; Colin Gordon, *Citizen Brown: Race, Democracy, and Inequality in the St. Louis Suburbs* (Chicago: University of Chicago Press, 2019), 23; Kenneth T. Jackson, *Crabgrass Frontier: The Suburbanization of the United States* (New York: Oxford University Press, 1985), 138-56.

12 Nancy Burns, *The Formation of American Local Governments: Private Values in Public Institutions* (New York: Oxford University Press, 1994), 5.

13 William G. Colman, *Cities, Suburbs, and States: Governing and Financing Urban America* (New York: Free Press, 1975), 23.

14 David M. P. Freund, *Colored Property: State Policy and White Racial Politics in Suburban America* (Chicago: University of Chicago Press, 2007), 217.

15 Andrew Wiese, *Places of Their Own: African American Suburbanization in the Twentieth Century* (Chicago: University of Chicago Press, 2004), 37; Andrew Wiese, "The Other Suburbanites: African American Suburbanization in the North before 1950," *Journal of American History* 85, no. 4 (1999): 1496.

16 Andrew Wiese, "Racial Cleansing in the Suburbs: Suburban Government, Urban Renewal, and Segregation on Long Island, New York, 1945-1960," in *Contested Terrain: Power, Politics, and Participation in Suburbia,* eds. Marc L. Silver and Martin Melkonian (Westport, CT: Greenwood Press, 1995), 61-70.

17 Gary J. Miller, *Cities by Contract: The Politics of Municipal Incorporation* (Cambridge, MA: MIT Press, 1981), 135. See also Gordon, *Citizen Brown*, 18; Michelle Wilde Anderson, "Mapped out of Democracy," *Stanford Law Review* 62, no. 4 (2010): 931-1003.

18 Gordon, *Citizen Brown*, 18.

19 Wiese, "Racial Cleansing in the Suburbs," 61.

20 Miller, *Cities by Contract*, 159.

21 In suburban Connecticut, more than one-half of all land zoned as residential had a minimum lot requirement of at least one acre. When existing measures were seen as insufficient to maintaining an area's "character," many suburbs increased the size and standard requirements for residential zoning. During the 1950s, the average lot size in the suburban counties surrounding New York City doubled, while in New Jersey, over 150 municipalities increased minimum lot-size requirements between 1960 and 1967 alone. By 1970, less than one percent of developable land in northeastern New Jersey permitted multifamily housing.

See Michael N. Danielson, *The Politics of Exclusion* (New York: Columbia University Press, 1976), 61; Richard Briffault, "Our Localism: Part I—The Structure of Local Government Law," *Columbia Law Review* 90, no. 1 (1990): 41.

22 Briffault, "Our Localism," 50.

23 Lily Geismer, *Don't Blame Us: Suburban Liberals and the Transformation of the Democratic Party* (Princeton, NJ: Princeton University Press, 2014), 173–97.

24 Burns, *Formation of American Local Governments*, 64, 6; Teaford, *City and Suburb*, 172; Sheryll D. Cashin, "Localism, Self-Interest, and the Tyranny of the Favored Quarter: Addressing the Barriers to New Regionalism," *Georgetown Law Journal* 88, no. 7 (1999): 1992.

25 Destin Jenkins, *The Bonds of Inequality: Debt and the Making of the American City* (Chicago: University of Chicago Press, 2021).

26 Francesca Russello Ammon, *Bulldozer: Demolition and Clearance of the Postwar Landscape* (New Haven, CT: Yale University Press, 2016); Brent Cebul, "Tearing Down Black America," *Boston Review*, July 22, 2020, http://bostonreview.net/race/brent-cebul-tearing-down-black-america.

27 Kenneth Baar, "Property Tax Assessment Discrimination against Low-Income Neighborhoods," *Clearinghouse Review* 15, no. 6 (1981): 479; George E. Peterson, *Property Taxes, Housing, and the Cities* (Lexington, MA: Lexington Books, 1973), 100–101.

28 Arthur D. Little, *A Study of Property Taxes and Urban Blight: Prepared for the U.S. Department of Housing and Urban Development* (Washington, DC: Government Printing Office, April 23, 1973), 59.

29 Peterson, *Property Taxes, Housing, and the Cities*, 92, 88.

30 Paul, *Politics of the Property Tax*, 27.

31 "How the City Assesses Real Estate: 2 Agencies Criticized," *New York Times*, February 22, 1973.

32 "NAACP Demands Lower Boston Taxes," *Boston Globe*, July 7, 1967; Oliver Oldman and Henry Aaron, "Assessment-Sales Ratios under the Boston Property Tax," *National Tax Journal* (March 1965): 36–49.

33 Emanuel Tobier, *Aspects of the New York City Property Market: A Study of Trends in Market Values, Assessments, Effective Tax Rates and Property Tax Delinquency* (New York: Citizens Housing and Planning Council of New York, Inc., December 1975); Domurad et al., "City of Unequal Neighbors," iv.

34 "Hardy Williams Says Black-Owned Real Estate Assessments Highest," *Philadelphia Tribune*, April 13, 1971.

35 Frank Butterini, Hilda Cornwell, Susan Dowd, and Robert Goch, *Anatomy of Inequity: A Study of Real Property Tax System in Buffalo, New York* (Buffalo: New York Public Interest Research Group Inc., January 1980).

36 Frank Butterini, Mary Ann Galeota, and Tom Griswold, *Assess Us as You Will: A Study of Residential Property Tax Assessments in the City of Syracuse* (New York: New York Public Interest Research Group, 1980), 9.

37 Thomas D. Pearson, "Assessment Ratios and Property Tax Burdens in Norfolk, Virginia, 1974–75," *American Real Estate and Urban Economics Association Journal* 7, no. 2 (1979): 190–230.

38 William S. Hendon, "Discrimination against Negro Homeowners in Property Tax Assessment," *American Journal of Economics and Sociology* 27, no. 2 (1968): 125–32.

39 John C. Hilke, "Determinants of Property Assessment Differentials with Emphasis on Delaware County, Pennsylvania" (Swarthmore, PA: National Science Foundation and Swarthmore College, 1973).

40 Philip Johnson Grossman, "Property Tax Assessment Bias: A Study of the Property Tax as a User Charge" (PhD diss., Charlottesville, University of Virginia, 1984), ProQuest dissertation no. 8503479, 7.

41 Val Hymes, "Ghetto Tax Used by Cities to Gouge Poor, Aid Flight," *Baltimore Afro-American*, April 28, 1973.

42 Paul, *Politics of the Property Tax*, 45.

43 Noliwe Rooks, *Cutting School: Privatization, Segregation, and the End of Public Education* (New York: New Press, 2017); Keeanga-Yamahtta Taylor, "Backstory to the Neoliberal Moment," *Souls: A Critical Journal of Black Politics, Culture, and Society* 14, no. 3-4 (2012): 185–206.

CHAPTER FIVE

1 Eugene Williams, death certificate, July 27, 1919, in "Birth and Death Records, 1916–present," Illinois Department of Public Health, Division of Vital Records, Springfield, IL.

2 Brian McCammack, *Landscapes of Hope: Nature and the Great Migration in Chicago* (Cambridge, MA: Harvard University Press, 2017).

3 St. Clair Drake and Horace R. Cayton, *Black Metropolis: A Study of Negro Life in a Northern City* (New York: Harper and Row, 1945), 65–77; William M. Tuttle, *Race Riot: Chicago in the Red Summer of 1919* (New York: Atheneum, 1970); Colin Fisher, "African Americans, Outdoor Recreation, and the 1919 Chicago Race Riot," in *"To Love the Wind and the Rain": African Americans and Environmental History*, eds. Dianne D. Glave and Mark Stoll (Pittsburgh, PA: University of Pittsburgh Press, 2006), 63–76. See also "Chicago 1919: Confronting the Race Riots," accessed March 20, 2021, https://www.chicago1919.org/.

4 Jessica Trounstine, *Segregation by Design: Local Politics and Inequality in American Cities* (New York: Cambridge University Press, 2018), 99–100.

5 Claude Brown, *Manchild in the Promised Land* (New York: Macmillan, 1965), 190.

6 Harold L. Ickes, "Address by Hon. Harold L. Ickes, Secretary of the Interior and Administrator of Public Works, before the Chicago Urban League" (speech, Chicago, IL, February 26, 1936).

7 Chicago Commission on Race Relations, *The Negro in Chicago: A Study of Race Relations and a Race Riot* (Chicago: University of Chicago Press, 1922), 194, 642.

8 Chicago Commission on Race Relations, *Negro in Chicago*, 616.

9 Daniel Wortel-London and Brent Cebul, "Cities and States Need Aid—but Also Oversight," *Washington Post*, May 4, 2020, https://www.washingtonpost.com/outlook/2020/05/04/cities-states-need-aid-also-oversight/.

10 Drake and Cayton, *Black Metropolis*, 111.

11 Sylvia Hood Washington, *Packing Them In: An Archaeology of Environmental Racism in Chicago, 1865-1954* (Lanham, MD: Lexington Books, 2005). See also Arnold R. Hirsch, *Making the Second Ghetto: Race and Housing in Chicago, 1940-1960* (Cambridge: Cambridge University Press, 1983); Beryl Satter, *Family Properties: Race, Estate, and the Exploitation of Black Urban America* (New York: Metropolitan Books, 2009).

12 Chicago Commission on Race Relations, *Negro in Chicago*, 614-15, 643.

13 "Statement by the Chicago Branch of the National Association for the Advancement of Colored People, Presented to the Members of the Board of Education at the Public Hearing on December 18, 1957 on the Tentative 1958 School Budget," p. 10, in "Chicago, Illinois Branch Operations, November-December 1957," part 27: Selected Branch Files, 1956-1965, series C: The Midwest, Papers of the NAACP, Library of Congress, Washington, DC, available in the ProQuest History Vault.

14 Drake and Cayton, *Black Metropolis*, 202.

15 "Statement by the Chicago Branch of the National Association for the Advancement of Colored People," 5.

16 Chicago Branch, National Association for the Advancement of Colored People, "De Facto Segregation in Chicago Public Schools," p. 9, in "Chicago, Illinois Branch Operations, November-December 1957."

17 Tracy L. Steffes, "Managing School Integration and White Flight: The Debate over Chicago's Future in the 1960s," *Journal of Urban History* 42, no. 4 (2016): 713; Amanda I. Seligman, *Block by Block: Neighborhoods and Public Policy on Chicago's West Side* (Chicago: University of Chicago Press, 2005), 128.

18 "Statement by the Chicago Branch of the National Association for the Advancement of Colored People," 10. See also Seligman, *Block by Block*, 125-28.

19 "Urban League Report Reveals Neglect of Schools in Atlanta," *Pittsburgh Courier*, January 27, 1945.

20 Chicago Urban League, "A Summary of An Equal Chance for Education," March 1962, in "Congress of Racial Equality Chicago Chapter and Chicago School Desegregation Plans and Documentation," CORE—Chicago Chapter: School Segregation, 1959-1966, Congress of Racial Equality papers, Chicago chapter, 1946-1966. See also Alphine Wade Jefferson, "Housing Discrimination and Community Response in North Lawndale (Chicago), Illinois, 1948-1978" (PhD diss., Duke University, 1979), ProQuest dissertation no. 8003626, 152; Beryl Satter, *Family Properties: Race, Estate, and the Exploitation of Black Urban America* (New York: Metropolitan Books, 2009), 94.

21 Chicago Commission on Race Relations, *Negro in Chicago*, 192; "Rhodes Avenue Repaired," *Chicago Defender*, August 24, 1918; "Neighborhood Pride," *Chicago Defender*, September 29, 1923; "Spring Cleaning," *Chicago Defender*, April 4, 1925.

22 Chicago Commission on Race Relations, *Negro in Chicago*, 193-94.

23 "Dayton Negroes Ask to Pay More Taxes to Secure Paved Streets," *Cleveland Call and Post*, January 27, 1945; "No Funds for Benn's Plat," *Cleveland Call and Post*, March 17, 1945; "Benn's Plat Citizens Plead for Sanitary Drinking Water," *Cleveland Call and Post*, April 14, 1945; "Benn's Plat Citizens Make 26th Appeal for Pure Drinking Water," *Cleveland Call and Post*, April 28, 1945; Leon Taylor, "Await Decision in Benn's Plat Case," *Cleveland Call and Post*, September 29, 1945.

24 "Alarms Mixed, Water Trickles as 4 Schenley Heights Homes Burn," *Pittsburgh Courier*, April 10, 1954; "Schenley Heights Citizens to Air Water Complaints," *Pittsburgh Courier*, March 24, 1962; "250 Crowd City Hall to Protest Bad Service: Schenley-Herron Residents Urge Action NOW! Water Protest Draws 250 to City Council," *Pittsburgh Courier*, April 14, 1962.

25 "Council Wages War on Unfair Shift System," *Chicago Defender*, December 30, 1939; Jefferson, "Housing Discrimination and Community Response," 154-55, 156.

26 "We Accuse!" *Chicago Defender*, August 15, 1963.

27 "16 Arrested for Sit-In in S. Side School," *Chicago Tribune*, January 17, 1962; "Halt Burnside Sit-In Arrests Temporarily," *Chicago Tribune*, January 19, 1962; "School Officials Warn 'Study-In' Parents," *Chicago Defender*, January 8, 1962; "17 Arrested at Burnside," *Chicago Defender*, January 17, 1962.

28 Webb v. Board of Education of City of Chicago, 223 F.Supp. 466 (N.D. Ill. 1963). Dionne Danns, *Desegregating Chicago's Public Schools: Policy Implementation, Politics, and Protest, 1965-1985* (New York: Palgrave Macmillan, 2014), 13-14.

29 "Pickets Protest 'Willis Wagons,'" *Chicago Defender*, May 26, 1962.

30 Steffes, "Managing School Integration," 713; Dionne Danns, *Something Better for Our Children: Black Organizing in Chicago Public Schools, 1963-1971* (New York: Routledge, 2003), 30; "Rap Cop Brutality at Protest Site," *Chicago Defender*, August 13, 1963; "Armstrong, Gregory Picket 'Willis Wagon,'" *Chicago Defender*, August 6, 1963; "Pickets Protest 'Willis Wagons.'"

31 Danns, *Something Better for Our Children*.

32 Jack Dougherty, "Shopping for Schools: How Public Education and Private Housing Shaped Suburban Connecticut," *Journal of Urban History* 38, no. 2 (2012): 205-24.

33 See Arthur E. Wise, *Rich Schools, Poor Schools: The Promise of Equal Educational Opportunity* (Chicago: University of Chicago Press, 1967), 128.

34 St. Louis Tax Reform Group and Missouri Tax Reform Group, *Understanding Missouri State Taxes* (St. Louis, MO: St. Louis Tax Reform Group, 1973), 5, box 18, folder 7, Movement for Economic Justice Records, 1972-1980, Wisconsin Historical Society, Madison, WI.

35 Richard Briffault, "Our Localism: Part I—The Structure of Local Government Law," *Columbia Law Review* 90, no. 1 (1990): 21n66.

36 Virginia Fleming, *The Cost of Neglect, the Value of Equity: A Guidebook for School Finance Reform in the South* (Atlanta, GA: Southern Regional Council, 1974), 18.

37 Nancy Folbre, "Remembering the Alamo Heights," *Texas Observer*, November 13, 1992.

38 Richard C. Schragger, "*San Antonio v. Rodriguez* and the Legal Geography of School Finance Reform," in *Civil Rights Stories*, eds. Myriam E. Gilles and Risa Goluboff (New York: Foundation Press, 2008), 85-110; San Antonio Independent School District et al. v. Rodriguez et al., 411 U.S. 1 (1973); Folbre, "Remembering the Alamo Heights"; Charles J. Ogletree, "The Legacy and Implications of San Antonio Independent School District v. Rodriguez," *Richmond Journal of the Law and the Public Interest* 17, no. 2 (January 2014): 515-48.

39 Dick Netzer and Paul H. Douglas, *Impact of the Property Tax: Its Economic Implications for Urban Problems; Research Report Supplied by the National Commission on Urban Problems to the Joint Economic Committee, Congress of the United States* (Washington, DC: Government Printing Office, 1968), 26.

40 Tracy L. Steffes, "Assessment Matters: The Rise and Fall of the Illinois Resource Equalizer Formula," *History of Education Quarterly* 60, no. 1 (2020): 29.

41 Sheryll D. Cashin, "Localism, Self-Interest, and the Tyranny of the Favored Quarter: Addressing the Barriers to New Regionalism," *Georgetown Law Journal* 88, no. 7 (1999): 1985-2048. On the "the cumulative advantages and disadvantages . . . that flow from economic segregation" and metropolitan fragmentation, see also Colin Gordon, *Citizen Brown: Race, Democracy, and Inequality in the St. Louis Suburbs* (Chicago: University of Chicago Press, 2019), 21-22.

42 Emily E. Straus, *Death of a Suburban Dream: Race and Schools in Compton, California* (Philadelphia: University of Pennsylvania Press, 2014), 5.

43 Charles Tiebout, "A Pure Theory of Local Expenditures," *Journal of Political Economy* 64, no. 5 (October 1956): 416–24. On the influence of Tiebout's model, see William A. Fischel, ed., *The Tiebout Model at Fifty: Essays in Public Economics in Honor of Wallace Oates* (Cambridge, MA: Lincoln Institute of Land Policy, 2006).

44 Gary J. Miller, *Cities by Contract: The Politics of Municipal Incorporation* (Cambridge, MA: MIT Press, 1981), 63.

45 Leon H. Washington Jr., "Eastside—Los Angeles' Stepchild: Sanitation, Noise, Zoning Evils Described by Sentinel Publisher," *Los Angeles Sentinel*, October 2, 1947; Leon H. Washington Jr., "Eastside, Watts Communities Cite Safety, Traffic Needs," *Los Angeles Sentinel*, November 6, 1947; Edith Smith, "Some Sober Reflections," *Cleveland Call and Post*, September 25, 1965.

46 Ron Seigel, "Says City Departments Don't Help Self-Help," *Michigan Chronicle*, March 2, 1968.

47 "Clogged Sewers Bring Vermin, Rats into West Phila. Section: Charges Jim Crow," *Philadelphia Tribune*, July 20, 1968.

48 United States Commission on Civil Rights, *A Time to Listen . . . A Time to Act* (Washington, DC: Government Printing Office, 1967), 18–19.

49 United States Commission on Civil Rights, *Time to Listen*, 19.

50 "Ike Told Corona Biased to Negroes," *New York Amsterdam News*, October 17, 1953.

51 The National Advisory Commission on Civil Disorders, *The Kerner Report* (Princeton, NJ: Princeton University Press, 2016 [1968]), 3.

52 Dayton Committee on Civil Rights, *Dayton's Call to Action: Recommendations for the Solution to Human Problems in the Community* (Dayton: Ohio State Advisory Committee to the United States Commission on Civil Rights, April 1967).

53 National Advisory Commission on Civil Disorders, *The Kerner Report*, 1.

54 Andrew W. Kahrl, *Free the Beaches: The Story of Ned Coll and the Battle for America's Most Exclusive Shoreline* (New Haven, CT: Yale University Press, 2018), 73–74.

55 Jefferson, "Housing Discrimination and Community Response," 181–82.

56 National Advisory Commission on Civil Disorders, *Kerner Report*, 149.

57 George Todd, "After the Violence, City Sweeps Clean: Brownsville Blasts Off on Garbage Bit," *New York Amsterdam News*, June 20, 1970. See also Johanna Fernández, *The Young Lords: A Radical History* (Chapel Hill: University of North Carolina Press, 2020); Robert R. Gioielli, *Environmental Activism and the Urban Crisis: Baltimore, St. Louis, Chicago* (Philadelphia, PA: Temple University Press, 2014).

CHAPTER SIX

1 Louis Balthazar, deposition, May 19, 1969, box 44, folder 12, Business and Professional People for the Public Interest, University of Illinois at Chicago Special Collections; "Chicago West Side Families Celebrate 70 Years of Peace and Unity," *AP News*, August 5, 2021.

2 Balthazar, deposition; on contract sales, see Beryl Satter, *Family Properties: Race,*

Estate, and the Exploitation of Black Urban America (New York: Metropolitan Books, 2009); and Samuel DuBois Cook Center on Social Equity, *The Plunder of Black Wealth in Chicago: New Findings on the Lasting Toll of Predatory Housing Contracts* (Durham, NC: Duke University, May 2019).

3   Balthazar, deposition.

4   Hugh Hough, "Tax-Delinquent Law Evils Face a Grim Accuser," *Chicago Sun-Times*, April 23, 1969.

5   Balthazar, deposition.

6   Hough, "Tax-Delinquent Law Evils Face a Grim Accuser."

7   Robert P. Swierenga, "Acres for Cents: Delinquent Tax Auctions in Frontier Iowa," *Agricultural History* 48, no. 2 (April 1974): 247–66, at 250.

8   On Glos, see "Tax Shark Operates," *Chicago Tribune*, March 1, 1912; "Jacob Glos, Tax Shark, Gets Jolt," *Chicago Tribune*, June 3, 1916; "Jacob Glos, Tax Speculator, Is Dead, Aged 72," *Chicago Tribune*, October 7, 1928.

9   "Tax Shark Operates," *Chicago Tribune*, March 1, 1912; "Jacob Glos, Tax Shark, Gets Jolt," *Chicago Tribune*, June 3, 1916.

10   W. H. Speck, *Tax Sales and Tax Titles in Illinois* (Chicago: University of Chicago Law School, 1948), 25.

11   Speck, *Tax Sales and Tax Titles in Illinois*, 25–26.

12   "Refuses Big Dividend," *New York Times*, November 18, 1911.

13   Cook County, Illinois, assistant state's attorney Marshall Kearney, quoted in Robert Cushman, "Panel: Receivership versus Sales as a Collection Device," in *Illinois Tax Problems*, ed. Illinois Tax Commission, 221.

14   "We Need Mr. Wiltsie," *Detroit Free Press*, June 6, 1905.

15   "Tax Sale 'King' Loses," *Washington Post*, August 15, 1913.

16   Louis F. Alyea, *Enforcement of Real Estate Tax Liens* (Chicago: Municipal Finance Officers Association, 1939); Frederick L. Bird, "Extent and Distribution of Urban Tax Delinquency," *Law and Contemporary Problems* 3 (1936): 337–46; Speck, *Tax Sales and Tax Titles in Illinois*, 5; "Find North Side Farthest Behind in Paying Taxes," *Chicago Tribune*, July 26, 1931.

17   David T. Beito, *Taxpayers in Revolt: Tax Resistance during the Great Depression* (Chapel Hill: University of North Carolina Press, 1989).

18   Cushman, "Panel," 220.

19   Beito, *Taxpayers in Revolt*, 9–10.

20   For a full list of all state legislation, see Alyea, *Enforcement of Real Estate Tax Liens*.

21   Willard Christopher Weckmueller, "Property Tax Delinquency in Wisconsin" (PhD diss., University of Wisconsin–Madison, 1938), ProQuest dissertation no. 0135981, 283.

22   "Tax Buyers Quit," *Milwaukee Journal*, August 2, 1933.

23   "Tax Buyers Quit."

24   A. U. Rodney, "The Tax Lien Investor's Relation to the Collection of Delinquent Taxes," *Law and Contemporary Problems* 3 (1936): 429–35; Paul Studenski, "A New Plan for the Private Financing of Delinquent Tax Payments," *Law and Contemporary Problems* 3 (1936): 364; Bird, "Extent and Distribution of Urban Tax Delinquency," 338; Donald Jackson, "Tax Delinquency of Rural Real Estate," *Law and Contemporary Problems* 3 (1936): 348; "Boston Credit Up as Dealers Show More Confidence," *Wall Street Journal*, March 1, 1938.

25   "Ending Tax Delinquency," *Chicago Bar Record* 29 (September 1948): 333–34.

26   Charles L. Savage, "How to Perfect Tax Titles," *St. John's Law Review* 18 (November 1943): 18.

27   "Tax Buyers Are Active," *Chicago Daily Herald*, April 19, 1940.

28   "Bond Company Makes Specialty of Taxes," *Atlanta Constitution*, May 11, 1931.

29   "Interstate Company Aids Land Owners," *Atlanta Constitution*, September 14, 1931.

30   William Clements and Terry Shaffer, "Tax-Sale Evictee Gets Reprieve," *Chicago Daily News*, April 25, 1969; "U.S. Nabs Fox as Income Levy Dodger," *Chicago Tribune*, September 25, 1915.

31   Speck, *Tax Sales and Tax Titles in Illinois*, 26.

32   "County Holds Tax Writ Sale," *Milwaukee Journal*, October 3, 1939.

33   "Tax Arrearage in Cook County Poses Problem," *Chicago Tribune*, November 24, 1946; "Seek Changes to Speed Tax Sales of Land," *Chicago Tribune*, April 7, 1947; "Sterile Land," *Chicago Tribune*, April 8, 1947; "Action Urged on Delinquent Realty Taxes," *Chicago Tribune*, June 13, 1948; "Taxpayers Who Don't Pay," *Chicago Tribune*, August 12, 1948; "How Tax Payments Are Discouraged," *Chicago Tribune*, December 1, 1949; "How to Collect Taxes," *Chicago Tribune*, January 16, 1950; Kermit Holt, "Why the Annual Tax Sale Fails to Get Buyers," *Chicago Tribune*, January 19, 1950; "To Improve Tax Collections," *Chicago Tribune*, May 26, 1951.

34   "Chicago Drives for Collection of $435,000,000 Unpaid Taxes," *Christian Science Monitor*, June 17, 1939.

35   Paul O'Connor, "A Plague on All Your Houses," *Chicagoan* (September 1974); Guerino J. Turano, "Equitable Relief, Collateral Attack and the Illinois Tax Deed," *Chicago-Kent Law Review* 51, no. 3 (January 1975): 726.

36   On Black housing as an extractive asset in mid-twentieth-century US cities, see Keeanga-Yamahtta Taylor, *Race for Profit: How Banks and the Real Estate Industry Undermined Black Homeownership* (Chapel Hill: University of North Carolina Press, 2019); N. D. B. Connolly, *A World More Concrete: Real Estate and the Remaking of Jim Crow South Florida* (Chicago: University of Chicago Press, 2014); and Leif Michael Fredrickson, "The Age of Lead: Metropolitan Change, Environmental Health and Inner City Underdevelopment in Baltimore" (PhD diss., University of Virginia, 2017), ProQuest dissertation no. 10668400.

37   "Slum Apartments Bring Widow $50,000 Year," *Baltimore Afro-American*, February 12, 1949; *The Slums: The Road Back* (Chicago: Metropolitan Housing and Planning Council of Chicago, 1954), box 153, folder 4, Hyde Park-Kenwood Community Conference Records, University of Chicago Special Collections.

38   Andrew Wiese, "Black Housing, White Finance: African American Housing and Home Ownership in Evanston, Illinois, before 1940," *Journal of Social History* 33, no. 2 (1999): 430-31.

39   Taylor, *Race for Profit*, 31.

40   See Satter, *Family Properties*; Connolly, *World More Concrete*.

41   Sharon Bobbitt, "How Harsh Tax Deed Law Smoothes Way for Buyers," *Suburbanite Economist*, December 16, 1970.

42   Guerino Turano, "Redemption from Tax Sales in Illinois—Confusion Galore," *John Marshall Law Review* 23, n. 1 (Fall 1989): 118-19.

43   "Applications for Membership," *Chicago Bar Record* 38 (October 1956), 12; Paul O'Connor, "First and Second Drafts of Article on Allan Blair," unpublished

notes, 1974, box 4, Paul O'Connor Papers, Chicago Historical Society Research Center.

44   Southmoor Bank and Trust Co. v. Willis, 155 N.E.2d 308; 15 Ill.2d 388 (1958).

45   Clements and Shaffer, "Tax-Sale Evictee Gets Reprieve"; see also Marshall Patner, "Blair Complaint v. MP," memo, 1973, Marshall Patner Collection, University of Illinois at Chicago Special Collections.

46   These figures are based on records from the 1970 Cook County Tax Sale, found in the Cook County Tax Sale Judgment Books housed in the Cook County Clerk's Office, Hawthorne Warehouse, Cicero, IL.

47   Hugh Hough, "How Law Cost Him His Home," *Chicago Sun-Times*, April 27, 1969; *Hawthorn Lane & Co. v. William and Nancy Parks*, Report of Proceedings, February 21, 1968, box 44, folder 6, Business and Professional People for the Public Interest, University of Illinois at Chicago Special Collections.

48   Allan Blair, "Deposition, *In the Matter of the Application of the County Collector, Etc.*," December 1, 1967, box 44, folder 5, Business and Professional People for the Public Interest, University of Illinois at Chicago Special Collections; *Hawthorn Lane & Co. v. William and Nancy Parks*, Report of Proceedings; Patner, "Blair Complaint v. MP."

49   On the concept of "dignity taking," see Bernadette Atuahene, *We Want What's Ours: Learning from South Africa's Land Restitution Program* (New York: Oxford University Press, 2014).

50   Hugh Hough, "At Christmastime—Tax Slip Costs Family Its Home," *Chicago Sun-Times*, May 1, 1969.

51   William Clements, "Blair Deals Downstate Also," *Chicago Daily News*, May 1, 1969. As Keeanga-Yamahtta Taylor notes, "The financial exploitation of Black communities, particularly in the housing market, contributed to resentments that ultimately boiled over into the rebellions that shook the United States through the second half of the 1960s." See Keeanga-Yamahtta Taylor, "Backstory to the Neoliberal Moment," *Souls: A Critical Journal of Black Politics, Culture, and Society* 14, nos. 3–4 (2012): 198.

52   John Simon, "Deposition, *Rufus Thomas v. Lois, Inc., Allan Blair, and Bruce Buyer*," September 24, 1969, box 44, folder 19, Business and Professional People for the Public Interest, University of Illinois at Chicago Special Collections.

53   "Wreck King Flats, Receiver Declares," *Washington Afro-American*, April 19, 1966.

54   Blair v. Commissioner of Internal Revenue, 63 T.C. 214 (1974); "Women's Boards Opt for Pirates, Gangsters," *Chicago Tribune*, March 8, 1968; Mike Royko, "Chicago: City With 'I Will,'" *Chicago Daily News*, March 4, 1969; Paul O'Connor, "Draft of Story on Catherine Catoor" (unpublished manuscript, 1973), box 4, Paul O'Connor Papers, Chicago Historical Society Research Center.

CHAPTER SEVEN

1   Lois Flagg, interview by Andrew Kahrl, Edwards, MS, July 10, 2013.

2   Jean White, interview by Andrew Kahrl, Edwards, MS, July 10, 2013; Lois Flagg, interview by Andrew Kahrl, July 10, 2013.

3   Charles M. Payne, *I've Got the Light of Freedom: The Organizing Tradition and the Mississippi Freedom Struggle* (Berkeley: University of California Press, 1995), 392.

4 Jefferson Cowie, *Freedom's Dominion: A Saga of White Resistance to Federal Power* (New York: Basic Books, 2022).

5 N. D. B. Connolly, *A World More Concrete: Real Estate and the Remaking of Jim Crow South Florida* (Chicago: University of Chicago Press, 2014), 121.

6 "Segregation Balks School Bond Issue," *Chicago Defender*, October 8, 1938.

7 "Suit to Halt Election on School Bonds Fails," *Muskogee* [OK] *Daily Phoenix and Times-Democrat*, September 16, 1938.

8 Simmons v. Board of Education of City of Muskogee of State of Oklahoma, 306 U.S. 617 (1939); Thurgood Marshall, "Memorandum to Secretary, Mr. White from Mr. Marshall, Re: Muskogee Oklahoma School Bond Case," January 19, 1939, in part 3: The Campaign for Educational Equality, series A: Legal Department and Central Office Records, 1913–1940, Papers of the NAACP, Library of Congress, Washington, DC, available in the ProQuest History Vault.

9 "$100,000 for Schools," *Atlanta Daily World*, July 7, 1940; "Atlanta NAACP Goes on Record as Opposing School Bond Issue: Calls Attention to Immediate Needs of Negroes," *Atlanta Daily World*, August 8, 1940; "Atlantans Defeat $6,000,000 Bond Issue," *Chicago Defender*, September 14, 1940.

10 "State-Wide Mass Meeting Petitions Legislature for Better Negro Education," *Atlanta Daily World*, February 23, 1946; "Mississippi Negroes Gird for War with Jim Crow," *Chicago Defender*, March 9, 1946. Black Mississippians who came of age in the postwar era, historian Charles Payne notes, "exhibited a great deal more resentment at their station in life. They considered themselves entitled to equal treatment and were much less comfortable than their parents had been with the elaborate codes of ritual deference . . . [and] tended to be more visibly angry about the injustices and indignities of the system" (Charles M. Payne, *I've Got the Light of Freedom: The Organizing Tradition and the Mississippi Freedom Struggle* [Berkeley: University of California Press, 1995], 23).

11 Federal Bureau of Investigation, "Protest March, Thomasville, Alabama, April 13, 1966, Protesting Discrimination in Public Facilities and Employment," memorandum, April 22, 1966, Centers of the Southern Struggle: FBI Files on Montgomery, Albany, St. Augustine, Selma, and Memphis, Federal Bureau of Investigation, Washington, DC, available in ProQuest History Vault.

12 "Race 'Rioting' and Threat of Death Penalty," *Atlanta Journal and Constitution*, November 3, 1963.

13 James Farmer, *Louisiana Story 1963* (New York: CORE, November 1964).

14 Judi Burken, "Clinton Girl Works With CORE," *Clinton* [IA] *Herald*, August 20, 1964, in folder 132, Congress of Racial Equality Papers, 1941–1967, Wisconsin Historical Society, Library-Archives Division, available in ProQuest History Vault.

15 Farmer, *Louisiana Story 1963*.

16 Farmer, *Louisiana Story 1963*.

17 "College Students and Others Needed for CORE Summer Program," CORE summer program brochure, n.d., in the Congress of Racial Equality Papers, Martin Luther King, Jr. Center for Nonviolent Social Change, Inc., Atlanta, GA.

18 "Voter Rolls Reopen," *Voice of Americus*, July 1, 1964.

19 Student Nonviolent Coordinating Committee, *The City Must Provide: South Atlanta: The Forgotten Community* (Atlanta, GA: SNCC, 1963), Student Nonviolent Coordinating Committee Papers, 1959–1972, Martin Luther King, Jr.

Center for Nonviolent Social Change, Inc., Atlanta, GA, in ProQuest History Vault.

20 "Proposed Statement to Be Issued by Mayor and Board of Aldermen of Edwards, Mississippi," 1966, Mississippi State Sovereignty Commission, Mississippi Department of Archives and History, Jackson.

21 Erle Johnston Jr., "Edwards, Mississippi, Investigation," declassified agency file, August 25, 1966, Mississippi State Sovereignty Commission, Mississippi Department of Archives and History, Jackson.

22 "Town of Edwards, Minute Book 12," 1964–1968, City Hall, Town of Edwards, Mississippi, March 12, 1964; December 7, 1965.

23 "Town of Edwards, Minute Book 12," April 28, 1964; May 20, 1964; June 2, 1964; July 7, 1964; April 6, 1965; May 4, 1965.

24 White, interview, July 10, 2013. On the racial politics of swimming pools in the civil rights South, see also Timothy B. Tyson, *Radio Free Dixie: Robert F. Williams and the Roots of Black Power* (Chapel Hill: University of North Carolina Press, 1999); Jeff Wiltse, *Contested Waters: A Social History of Swimming Pools in America* (Chapel Hill: University of North Carolina Press, 2007); Rebecca Retzlaff, "Desegregation of City Parks and the Civil Rights Movement: The Case of Oak Park in Montgomery, Alabama," *Journal of Urban History* 47, no. 4 (2021); P. Caleb Smith, "Reflections in the Water: Society and Recreational Facilities, a Case Study of Public Swimming Pools in Mississippi," *Southeastern Geographer* 52, no. 1 (2012).

25 Mark Newman, *Divine Agitators: The Delta Ministry and Civil Rights in Mississippi* (Athens: University of Georgia Press, 2004).

26 Chester Higgins, "Negro Buying Shuts Down a Mississippi Town," *Jet*, September 29, 1966.

27 K. C. Morrison, interview by Andrew Kahrl, Starkville, MS, July 8, 2013.

28 White, interview, July 10, 2013.

29 "Mary White v. City of Edwards, Civil Action No. 3973," assorted case documents, 1966, TO 35, box 19, folder 1, Lawyers' Committee for Civil Rights under Law, Tougaloo College Civil Rights Collection, housed at the Mississippi Department of Archives and History, Jackson; Johnston, "Edwards, Mississippi, Investigation."

30 "Town of Edwards, Minute Book 12," July 5, 1966.

31 Tom Scarbrough, "Edwards, Mississippi," declassified agency file, July 12, 1966, Mississippi State Sovereignty Commission, Mississippi Department of Archives and History, Jackson.

32 White, interview, July 10, 2013.

33 Jean Phillips, affidavit, September 30, 1969, TO 35, box 19, folder 18, Lawyers' Committee for Civil Rights under Law, Tougaloo College Civil Rights Collection.

34 Higgins, "Negro Buying Shuts Down a Mississippi Town."

35 Johnston, "Edwards, Mississippi, Investigation."

36 "Affidavits," 1970, TO 35, box 19, series: Unlawful Taxation, folder: Bland v. Angelo Opposition to Defendant's Motion, Dates: 1970, Lawyers' Committee for Civil Rights under Law, Tougaloo College Civil Rights Collection.

37 Town of Edwards, "Curfew Ordinance" (August 10, 1966), TO 35, box 19, folder 2, Lawyers' Committee for Civil Rights under Law, Tougaloo College Civil Rights Collection.

38 Delta Ministry, "Some Facts about Mt. Beulah" (1970), box 2, folder 39, Charles Horwitz Papers, Tougaloo College Civil Rights Collection.

39 Higgins, "Negro Buying Shuts Down a Mississippi Town."

40 James Saggus, "Negro Boycott Stalls Trade in Miss. Town," *Washington Post*, August 23, 1966.

41 White, interview, July 10, 2013.

42 Charles Horwitz, "A New Approach to Community Development," position paper, 1967, box 1, folder 7, Charles Horwitz Papers, Tougaloo College Civil Rights Collection.

43 "A Small Town Is Dying," *Amarillo* [TX] *Globe-Times*, August 19, 1966.

44 "Negro Girl Leading Successful Boycott," *Providence* [RI] *Journal*, August 31, 1966, TO 35, box 19, series: Unlawful Taxation, folder 2, Lawyers' Committee for Civil Rights under Law, Tougaloo College Civil Rights Collection.

45 "We, the Negro Citizens and Tax Payers of Edwards, Mississippi, Demand," organizers' list of reform demands, 1966, Mississippi State Sovereignty Commission, Mississippi Department of Archives and History, Jackson.

46 White, interview, July 10, 2013.

47 Connie Thompson, interview by Andrew Kahrl, Edwards, MS, July 10, 2013.

48 A. L. Hopkins, "Investigation in Edwards, Mississippi, to Determine Whether or Not Known Subversives Are Participating in the Boycott of the White Business Establishments," declassified agency file, October 6, 1966, Mississippi State Sovereignty Commission, Mississippi Department of Archives and History, Jackson.

49 "Town of Edwards, Minute Book 12," February 7, 1967.

50 A. L. Hopkins, "Investigator A. L. Hopkins's Report," declassified agency file, November 4, 1966, Mississippi State Sovereignty Commission, Mississippi Department of Archives and History, Jackson.

51 "March Incident Summary," Student Nonviolent Coordinating Committee Wide Area Telephone Service report, 1967, folder WATS Reports March 1965, Student Nonviolent Coordinating Committee Papers, 1959–1972, Martin Luther King, Jr. Center for Nonviolent Social Change, Inc., Atlanta, GA, available in ProQuest History Vault.

52 Erle Johnston Jr., "Edwards Boycott," declassified agency file, September 19, 1966, Mississippi State Sovereignty Commission, Mississippi Department of Archives and History, Jackson.

53 Clark E. Robbins, "Statement of the Mayor and Board of Aldermen to the Citizens of Edwards, Mississippi," 1966, Mississippi State Sovereignty Commission, Mississippi Department of Archives and History.

54 Testimony of W. H. Montgomery, in "Appendix, in the United States Court of Appeals for the Fifth Circuit no. 30429 Percy Bland, et al, v. Robert McHann, et al Appeal from the United States District Court for the Southern District of Mississippi" (November 26, 1969). See Bland v. McHann, 63 F.2d 21 (1972).

55 David Magee, affidavit, in "Affidavits."

56 "List of Property Owners' Assessed Values," compiled by Lawyers' Committee and Mt. Beulah residents, 1967, TO 35, box 19, folder 8, Lawyers' Committee for Civil Rights under Law, Tougaloo College Civil Rights Collection. See also "Appendix, in the United States Court of Appeals for the Fifth Circuit no. 30429 Percy Bland, et al."

57 "Town of Edwards, Minute Book 12," November 14, 1966 and November 29, 1966.

58 Miss. Code (1942) § 1858, 3742, 3742–17. See also "Why Didn't Negroes in Edwards Know About This?" *Edwards* [MS] *MFDP Black and White Hummer*, January 25, 1967, folder 69, box 2, Charles Horwitz Papers, Tougaloo College Civil Rights Collection.

59 David McGee, deposition, in "Appendix, in the United States Court of Appeals for the Fifth Circuit no. 30429 Percy Bland, et al."

60 Charles Horwitz, affidavit, in "Affidavits."

61 "Review Form, Proposed Affirmative Action," November 17, 1967, TO 35, box 19, folder 20, Lawyers' Committee for Civil Rights under Law, Tougaloo College Civil Rights Collection.

62 Horwitz, affidavit.

63 Langston Hughes, *Victory Poses Problems* (Columbia: University of Missouri Press, 1959), 155.

64 Samantha Barbas, *Actual Malice: Civil Rights and Freedom of the Press in New York Times v. Sullivan* (Oakland: University of California Press, 2023).

65 "Segregation Up in 5 States," *Baltimore Sun*, January 22, 1956; "Mixed Churches Must Pay Mississippi Tax," *Baltimore Afro-American*, April 7, 1956; Stan Opotowsky, "Inside the White Citizens Councils: The Big Pocketbook Squeeze," *Baltimore Afro-American*, March 16, 1957.

66 Congress of Racial Equality, "Chronology of Violence and Intimidation in Mississippi since 1961," June 6, 1962, Mississippi local chapter, Community Relations Department, folder: 252251-021-0788, June 2, 1962–December 7, 1965, Congress of Racial Equality Papers, 1941–1967, Wisconsin Historical Society, Library-Archives Division, available in ProQuest History Vault; "News Release, Ruleville, Mississippi," SNCC, September 17, 1962, Student Nonviolent Coordinating Committee Papers, 1959–1972, Martin Luther King, Jr. Center for Nonviolent Social Change, Inc., Atlanta, GA, available in ProQuest History Vault.

67 "Candidate Criticizes Rights Enforcement," *Student Voice*, May 19, 1964.

68 Evan Doss, interview by Andrew Kahrl, Port Gibson, MS, July 15, 2013.

69 Lawyers' Committee for Civil Rights under Law, *Report on Edwards Tax Assessments* (Washington, DC: Lawyers' Committee, February 2, 1967), TO 35, box 19, folder 22, Lawyers' Committee for Civil Rights under Law, Tougaloo College Civil Rights Collection.

70 Delta Ministry, "News in Hinds County," internal report, 1967, box 1, folder 41, Charles Horwitz Papers, Tougaloo College Civil Rights Collection.

71 "Town of Edwards, Minute Book 12," January 3, 1967.

72 Bland v. McHann, 463 F.2d 21 (1972), at 28.

73 Lawyers' Committee for Civil Rights under Law, "Complaint on Discriminatory Tax Assessment of Property in Edwards," July 31, 1968, TO 35, box 19, folder 21, Lawyers' Committee for Civil Rights under Law, Tougaloo College Civil Rights Collection; Lawyers' Committee for Civil Rights under Law, "Bland v. Angelo, Complaint," January 13, 1969, TO 35, box 19, series: Unlawful Taxation, folder: Bland v. Angelo Complaint and Verification, 1968–1969, Lawyers' Committee for Civil Rights under Law, Tougaloo College Civil Rights Collection.

74 Lawyers' Committee for Civil Rights under Law, "Notes on Testimony, James W. Loewen," 1967, TO 35, box 19, series: Unlawful Taxation, folder: Bland v. Angelo Evidence: Land Assessment and Questionnaires, 1966 and ?, Lawyers' Committee for Civil Rights under Law, Tougaloo College Civil Rights Collection; Lawyers' Committee for Civil Rights under Law, "Procedures for Appraisals (in Loewen's Study)," 1969, TO 35, box 19, series: Unlawful Taxation, folder 10, Lawyers' Committee for Civil Rights under Law, Tougaloo College Civil Rights

Collection; Lawyers' Committee for Civil Rights under Law, "Notes on Testimony, James W. Loewen," 1970, TO 35, box 19, folder 14, Lawyers' Committee for Civil Rights under Law, Tougaloo College Civil Rights Collection; Lawyers' Committee for Civil Rights under Law, "Findings of Facts," July 22, 1970, TO 35, box 19, folder 20, Lawyers' Committee for Civil Rights under Law, Tougaloo College Civil Rights Collection; and James Loewen, interview by Andrew Kahrl, Washington, DC, June 5, 2013. See also James W. Loewen, *Social Science in the Courtroom: Statistical Techniques and Research Methods for Winning Class-Action Suits* (Lexington, MA: Lexington Books, 1982).

75 "Minutes of Meeting of Mayor and Board of Aldermen," Edwards, MS, February 7, 1967, TO 35, box 19, series: Unlawful Taxation, folder: Bland v. Angelo Evidence: Land Assessment and Questionnaires, 1966 and ?, Lawyers' Committee for Civil Rights under Law, Tougaloo College Civil Rights Collection; "Bland v. Angelo Answer to Plaintiffs' Second and Third Interrogatories," 1969, TO 35, box 19, series: Unlawful Taxation, folder ½, Lawyers' Committee for Civil Rights under Law, Tougaloo College Civil Rights Collection.

76 Lawyers' Committee for Civil Rights under Law, *Report on Edwards Tax Assessments*; and Mary Blue, affidavit, in "Affidavits."

77 See Michael J. Bednarz, "Comity Bars Federal Damages for Section 1984 Discriminatory State Tax Assessments," *Boston University Journal of Tax Law* 1 (1983): 147–65.

78 Frank Parker to James Loewen, re: Bland v. McHann, August 11, 1970, TO 35, box 19, series: Unlawful Taxation, folder 31, Lawyers' Committee for Civil Rights under Law, Tougaloo College Civil Rights Collection. On Cox, see Jere Nash and Andy Taggart, *Mississippi Politics: The Struggle for Power, 1976–2008* (Jackson: University Press of Mississippi, 2009), 112.

79 *Bland v. McHann*, 463 F.2d, at 29, 24.

80 Bland v. McHann, 410 U.S. 966 (1973); Lynch v. Household Financial Corp. et al., 405 U.S. 538 (1972), at 542n6.

81 "Mississippi—Agriculture," January 1, 1965, folder in record group 453, records of the US Commission on Civil Rights, National Archives, College Park, MD, available in ProQuest History Vault; "Related Organizations and Activities: Law Students Civil Rights Research Council," January 1, 1965, folder in Congress of Racial Equality Papers, Wisconsin Historical Society, Library-Archives Division, available in ProQuest History Vault.

82 Roy Reed, "Equal Service Edict Irks Town," *New York Times*, March 2, 1971.

83 "Showdown Comes to Shaw, Miss.," *Cleveland Call and Post*, January 16, 1971.

84 "Suits Asks Equal Service by Cities," *Baltimore Afro-American*, December 2, 1967.

85 "Where a Minority Drags Its White Feet," *Boston Globe*, July 30, 1972.

86 "LDF Sues to End Dual City Services, Police Duties," *Baltimore Afro-American*, April 5, 1969.

87 Hawkins v. Town of Shaw, Mississippi, 303 F. Supp. 1162 (N.D. Miss. 1969); "Showdown Comes to Shaw, Miss."

88 Hawkins v. Town of Shaw, 303 F. Supp. 1162; Jack Rosenthal, "Appeals Court Bids Town Give Races Equal Services," *New York Times*, February 2, 1971; John P. MacKenzie, "Ruling on Equalizing Town Services Is Major Rights Victory," *Washington Post*, February 16, 1971. See also Charles M. Haar and Daniel W. Fessler, *The Wrong Side of the Tracks: A Revolutionary Rediscovery of the Common*

Law Tradition of Fairness in the Struggle against Inequality (New York: Simon and Schuster, 1986).

89 Rosenthal, "Appeals Court Bids Town Give Races Equal Services"; Whitney M. Young, "Ruling Against Miss. Town Applies to Others," *Chicago Defender*, February 27, 1971; William O. Walker, "It's All a Matter of Law," *Cleveland Call and Post*, March 20, 1971; "Revolution by Court Order," *New York Times*, February 7, 1971; "Meaning of the Shaw Case," *Baltimore Afro-American*, April 10, 1971.

90 "Equal City Services Upheld," *Washington Post*, March 28, 1972.

91 "Where a Minority Drags Its White Feet"; "For Immediate Release, to All Media, from the Concerned Citizens of Shaw, MS," press release, June 1, 1972, box 1, folder 38, Charles Horwitz Papers, Tougaloo College Civil Rights Collection; James M. Mohead, "Weekly Report," declassified agency file, May 1, 1972, Mississippi State Sovereignty Commission, Mississippi Department of Archives and History, Jackson; "Shaw Marshal Acquitted," *Greenville* [MS] *Delta Democrat-Times*, May 5, 1972.

92 "Where a Minority Drags Its White Feet"; "For Immediate Release, to All Media, from the Concerned Citizens of Shaw, MS."

93 R. Dennis Anderson, "Toward an Equalization of Municipal Services: Variations on a Theme by Hawkins," *Journal of Urban Law* 50 (November 1972): 177–97; Lawrence P. Simon, "Equal Protection in the Urban Environment: The Right to Equal Municipal Services," *Tulane Law Review* 46 (1972): 496–525; "Equality for the Other Side of the Tracks," *Focus* (November 1975); Ammons v. Dade City, Fla., 594 F. Supp. 1274 (M.D. Fla. 1984).

94 San Antonio Independent School District et al. v. Rodriguez et al., 411 U.S. 1 (1973); Daniel L. Rubinfeld and Robert P. Inman, "The Judicial Pursuit of Local Fiscal Equity," *Harvard Law Review* 92 (1979): 1662–750; Robert L. Lineberry, "Mandating Urban Equality: The Distribution of Municipal Public Services," *Texas Law Review* 53 (1974): 34.

CHAPTER EIGHT

1 Evan Doss, interview by Andrew Kahrl, Port Gibson, MS, July 15, 2013.

2 Jonathan Rowe, "Black Assessor Rallies Reform," *People and Taxes*, 1974.

3 "Fairness by Blacks Promised," *Austin* [TX] *Statesman*, January 2, 1972.

4 Freedom Information Service, "County Government in Mississippi," pamphlet, October 1966, box 5, series 3, folder 8, Rims Barber Collection, Mississippi Department of Archives and History, Jackson; Freedom Information Service, "Municipal Government in Mississippi," pamphlet, 1969, box 5, series 3, folder 9, Rims Barber Collection, Mississippi Department of Archives and History, Jackson.

5 Stokely Carmichael, quoted in Benjamin Muse, *The American Negro Revolution: From Nonviolence to Black Power, 1963–1967* (Bloomington: Indiana University Press, 1968), 244.

6 "Plan to Tax Whites into Losing Property Bared by Carmichael," *Philadelphia Tribune*, January 21, 1967.

7 Hugh Stephen Whitaker, "A New Day: The Effects of Negro Enfranchisement in Selected Mississippi Counties" (PhD diss., Florida State University, 1965), ProQuest dissertation no. 6602102, 150.

8 In Lowndes County, Alabama, the first African American elected tax assessor in 1978 found, upon entering office, "egregious errors that universally advantaged

whites and disadvantaged African Americans." See Hasan Kwame Jeffries, *Bloody Lowndes: Civil Rights and Black Power in Alabama's Black Belt* (New York: New York University Press, 2009), 235–36.

9 The 1970 US census listed the number of majority-Black counties (in relation to all counties) in the following states as: Mississippi (25 of 82), South Carolina (12 of 46), Alabama (10 of 67), Louisiana (9 of 64), Georgia (22 of 159). See Social Explorer and US Census Bureau, "Census 1970," Social Explorer tables (SE), https://www.socialexplorer.com/tables/C1970/R11343312.

10 Allen v. State Board of Elections, 393 U.S. 544 (1969); Ari Berman, *Give Us the Ballot: The Modern Struggle for Voting Rights in America* (New York: Farrar Straus Giroux, 2015), 55–64.

11 Charles S. Aiken, "Race as a Factor in Municipal Underbounding," *Annals of the Association of American Geographers* 77, no. 4 (1987): 566.

12 "Equality for the Other Side of the Tracks," *Focus* (November 1975); Donald G. Hagman, "The Use of Boundary Lines to Discriminate in the Provision of Services by Race," *University of Detroit Journal of Urban Law* 54 (1977): 849–97; Aiken, "Race as a Factor in Municipal Underbounding"; Daniel T. Lichter, Domenico Parisi, Steven Michael Grice, and Michael Taquino, "Municipal Underbounding: Annexation and Racial Exclusion in Small Southern Towns," *Rural Sociology* 72, no. 1 (2007): 47–68; Michelle Wilde Anderson, "Mapped Out of Democracy," *Stanford Law Review* 62, no. 4 (2010): 931–1003.

13 "Why Don't Negroes in Edwards Go to the Board of Aldermen Meetings Every First Tuesday in the Month?" *Edwards* [MS] *MFDP Black and White Hummer*, January 25, 1967, box 2, folder 69, Charles Horwitz Papers, Tougaloo College Civil Rights Collection.

14 Perkins v. Matthews, 400 U.S. 379 (1971).

15 J. Todd Moye, *Let the People Decide: Black Freedom and White Resistance Movements in Sunflower County, Mississippi, 1945-1986* (Chapel Hill: University of North Carolina Press, 2004), 166.

16 "Carver Randle in Mayor Race," *Indianola* [MS] *Enterprise-Tocsin*, December 28, 1967; "Vote Carver Randle for Mayor," *Greenville* [MS] *Delta Democrat-Times*, January 3, 1968.

17 Chris Danielson, *After Freedom Summer: How Race Realigned Mississippi Politics, 1965-1986* (Gainesville: University Press of Florida, 2011), 55.

18 "Bolton Mayor Finally Takes Office," *Focus* 1, no, 11 (September 1973); John Kincaid, "Beyond the Voting Rights Act: White Responses to Black Political Power in Tchula, Mississippi," *Publius: The Journal of Federalism* 16, no. 4 (Fall 1986): 155–72; Minion K. C. Morrison, "Preconditions for Afro-American Leadership: Three Mississippi Towns," *Polity* 17, no. 3 (1985): 504–29.

19 Rims Barber, interview by Andrew Kahrl, Jackson, MS, July 7, 2013; Bennie Thompson, telephone interview by Andrew Kahrl, May 12, 2022.

20 Owen Brooks, interview by Andrew Kahrl, Jackson, MS, July 14, 2013.

21 Thompson, interview, May 12, 2022.

22 Thompson, interview, May 12, 2022; Brooks, interview, July 14, 2013. See also Danielson, *After Freedom Summer*, 68–69.

23 Danielson, *After Freedom Summer*, 70.

24 Minion K. C. Morrison, "Federal Aid and Afro-American Political Power in Three Mississippi Towns," *Publius: The Journal of Federalism* 17, no. 4 (1987): 97–111.

25 Doss, interview, July 15, 2013.

26 Barbara Phillips and Joseph Huttie Jr., *Mississippi Property Tax: Special Burden for the Poor* (Jackson, MS: Black Economic Research Center, 1973), 49.

27 Doss, interview, July 15, 2013; Jesse Morris to Harry Bowie and Rims Barber, "Re: Meeting on April 21st Concerning Tax Assessor of Claiborne County," April 1972, box 34, folder 11, Black Economic Research Center Records, Schomburg Center for Research in Black Culture, New York.

28 "Fairness by Blacks Promised."

29 Barbara Phillips, interview by Andrew Kahrl, Chicago, IL, November 16, 2013; James Miller, telephone interview by Andrew Kahrl, August 7, 2013.

30 Jesse Morris to Robert Browne, "Re: Claiborne County, Mississippi," January 27, 1972, box 34, folder 9, Black Economic Research Center Records, Schomburg Center.

31 Morris to Browne.

32 Morris to Browne.

33 Phillips, interview, November 16, 2013.

34 Doss, quoted in Thomas F. Gustafson Jr. to Michael McIntosh, "Subject: Ad Valorem Taxation Practices in Jefferson County, Mississippi," November 1, 1973, box E18, folder misc. corresp. 11/73, Emergency Land Fund Records, Amistad Research Center, New Orleans, LA.

35 Phillips and Huttie, *Mississippi Property Tax*, 51.

36 Rowe, "Black Assessor Rallies Reform."

37 Evan Doss to State Tax Commission, March 10, 1972, box 34, folder 11, Black Economic Research Center Records, Schomburg Center.

38 W. Hamp King to Evan Doss, "Re: His Letter to Gov. Waller," March 16, 1972, box 34, folder 11, Black Economic Research Center Records, Schomburg Center.

39 "Editorial: Vote 'No' on Reappraisal," *Port Gibson Reveille*, November 14, 1972.

40 Morris to Bowie and Barber; Phillips and Huttie, *Mississippi Property Tax*, 50.

41 "Writ of Mandamus Sought: Hearing Set for 9:00 A.M. Monday before Judge Guider," *Port Gibson Reveille*, October 12, 1972.

42 Barbara Phillips to Robert Browne, "Re: Claiborne County Report," May 14, 1973, box 34, folder 10, Black Economic Research Center Records, Schomburg Center.

43 Barbara Phillips, *Report on Claiborne County Situation*, internal report, May 15, 1972, box 34, folder 12, Black Economic Research Center Records, Schomburg Center.

44 "Black Assessor Shakes Up County," *Focus* 3 (December 1974).

45 "Black Assessor Shakes Up County"; "Tax Collector Jailed; Out on $10,000 Bond," *Port Gibson Reveille*, November 7, 1974; Doss, interview, July 15, 2013; "Jailed Miss. Assessor Charges Harassment," *Baltimore Afro-American*, November 30, 1974.

46 *People's Action Council Team* [Jackson, MS], newsletter, January 29, 1975, box 7, folder 49, Rims Barber Collection, Mississippi Department of Archives and History, Jackson; Mary R. Warner, *The Dilemma of Black Politics: A Report of Harassment of Black Elected Officials* (Sacramento, CA: National Association of Human Rights Workers, 1977). In 1980, the Mississippi Supreme Court upheld a lower court ruling finding that the lack of uniformity in assessment formulas among counties violated the state's constitution and ordered that all counties reassess properties at a uniform percentage. See State Tax Commission v. Fondren, 387

So.2d 712 (Mississippi Supreme Court 1980). See also "Supreme Court Upholds Reappraisal Ruling," *Clarksdale* [MS] *Press Register*, August 20, 1980.

47 Morrison, "Preconditions for Afro-American Leadership"; Kincaid, "Beyond the Voting Rights Act"; Morrison, "Federal Aid and Afro-American Political Power"; Clyde Woods, *Development Arrested: The Blues and Plantation Power in the Mississippi Delta* (London: Verso, 1998), 221.

48 Manning Marable, "The Tchula Seven: Harvest of Hate in the Mississippi Delta" (Boulder, CO: Westview Press, 1982); Sheila D. Collins, "Revenge of the Good Ole Boys," *In These Times*, January 20, 1982.

49 Morrison, "Federal Aid and Afro-American Political Power"; Collins, "Revenge of the Good Ole Boys."

50 Frank Chapman, "The Ordeal of Eddie James Carthan and the Fight for Democratic Rights," *Freedomways* 23, no. 1 (1983): 10-13.

51 Chapman, "Ordeal of Eddie James Carthan."

52 Regina Devoual, "The People of Claiborne County," *Southern Exposure* 10 (April/May 1982): 35-38.

53 David Moberg, "Nuclear Plant in Mississippi Draws Black Opposition," *In These Times*, September 19, 1979.

54 Devoual, "People of Claiborne County"; Regina Devoual, "After the Port Gibson, Miss., Boycott Victory . . . New Strength for NAACP and the Black Economy," *Crisis* (October 1982), 372-73; "Court Upholds Ruling against Mostly Black Miss. County," *Baltimore Afro-American*, June 20, 1987.

55 Barber, interview, July 7, 2013.

56 "Court Upholds Ruling against Mostly Black Miss. County."

57 "Court Upholds Ruling against Mostly Black Miss. County"; Doug McAdam and Hilary Boudet, *Putting Social Movements in Their Place: Explaining Opposition to Energy Projects in the United States, 2000-2005* (New York: Cambridge University Press, 2012), 82.

58 "Court Upholds Ruling against Mostly Black Miss. County."

59 Barber, interview, July 7, 2013.

60 Doss, interview, July 15, 2013.

61 Deborah H. Bell, "The Law Clinic as a Regional Center: Looking for Solutions to Rural Southern Housing Problems," *Journal of Urban and Contemporary Law* 42 (1992): 118-19.

62 "Miss. Town Has Millions in Federal Funds, but Won't Spend a Dime in Worst Area," *Atlanta Daily World*, November 25, 1984.

63 Alfreda L. Madison, "The President's 'New Federalism' Does Not Work," *Washington Informer* 21, no. 11 (January 2, 1985): 15.

64 "Sugarditch - 'Showcase of the Delta'?" *Memphis Tri-State Defender*, May 22, 1985; "Life in Shantytown, USA," *New York Newsday*, July 15, 1985.

65 Joseph Delaney Jr., "Says Law Abused in Mississippi," *Chicago Defender*, April 18, 1985.

66 "The Shacks Disappear, but the Poverty Lives On," *New York Times*, March 10, 1991.

67 Woods, *Development Arrested*, 225-26; "Miss. Town Has Millions in Federal Funds."

68 Joseph Delaney Jr., "Says Law Abused in Mississippi," *Chicago Defender*, April 18, 1985.

69 "Tunica, MS; 'Forgotten World,'" *Memphis Tri-State Defender*, July 31, 1985;

"Residents Deplore Sugar Ditch," *Memphis Tri-State Defender*, September 4, 1985.

70 *60 Minutes*, "There for All to See," produced by Marti Galovic Palmer, aired December 8, 1985, on CBS, https://www.youtube.com/watch?v=O3VR7gcwE2Q.

71 "Alvin Chambliss Charges; Sugar Ditch Grants Aimed at Weakening Black Voting Rights," *Memphis Tri-State Defender*, October 9, 1985.

72 "Sugarditch—'Showcase of the Delta'?" *Memphis Tri-State Defender*, May 22, 1985.

73 Bell, "Law Clinic as a Regional Center," 118.

CHAPTER NINE

1 Margaret Newkirk, "How Generations of Black Americans Lost Their Land to Tax Liens," *Bloomberg.com*, June 29, 2022; Leo McGee and Robert Boone, "A Study of Rural Land Ownership, Control Problems and Attitudes of Blacks toward Rural Land," in *The Black Rural Landowner—Endangered Species: Social, Political, and Economic Implications*, eds. Leo McGee and Robert Boone (Westport, CT: Greenwood Press, 1979), 99; Roy Reed, "Blacks in South Struggle to Keep the Little Land They Have Left," *New York Times*, December 7, 1972; "Lost: Precious Land," *Norfolk Journal and Guide*, January 6, 1973.

2 Pete Daniel, *Dispossession: Discrimination against African American Farmers in the Age of Civil Rights* (Chapel Hill: University of North Carolina Press, 2013); Valerie Grim, "Between Forty Acres and a Class Action Lawsuit," in *Beyond Forty Acres and a Mule: African American Landowning Families since Reconstruction*, eds. Debra A. Reid and Evan P. Bennett (Gainesville: University Press of Florida, 2012), 271–96; Adrienne M. Petty, *Standing Their Ground: Small Farmers in North Carolina since the Civil War* (New York: Oxford University Press, 2013).

3 Robert G. Healy, *Competition for Land in the American South: Agriculture, Human Settlement, and the Environment* (Washington, DC: Conservation Foundation, 1985).

4 Black Economic Research Center, *Only Six Million Acres: The Decline of Black-Owned Land in the Rural South* (New York: Black Economic Research Center, 1973), 3.

5 Lester M. Salamon, *Land and Minority Enterprise: The Crisis and the Opportunity* (Washington, DC: Office of Minority Business Enterprise, US Department of Commerce, 1976), 7.

6 Emergency Land Fund, Mississippi state branch, "Explanation of 'Results Sheet,'" 1974, box E45, folder Tax Sale Data 1973–74, Emergency Land Fund Records, Amistad Research Center, New Orleans, LA; Jesse Morris to Burt Neuborne, December 27, 1973, box E18, folder Misc. Corresp. 12/73, Emergency Land Fund Records, Amistad Research Center.

7 Michael A. Figures, *Final Report: Southern Land Project/Alabama Region* (New York: Black Economic Research Center, April 1973), 2, box 46, folder 3, Black Economic Research Center Records, Schomburg Center for Research in Black Culture, New York.

8 Black Economic Research Center, *Three Associated Black Institutions: A Comprehensive Effort in Black Economic Development; Report of Activities, 1972–73* (New York: Black Economic Research Center, 1973), 15, box 5, folder 6, Movement for Economic Justice Records, 1972–1980, Wisconsin Historical Society, Madison.

9   "Works Progress Administration Federal Writers' Project Correspondence Regarding the Publication of Beaufort, South Carolina State Guide," September 1, 1935, 4–6, Works Progress Administration record group 69, WPA, Federal Writers Project, Negro Studies, 1936–1941, New Deal Agencies and Black America, available at ProQuest History Vault.

10 Joe McDomick, interview by Andrew Kahrl, St. Helena Island, SC, April 17, 2014.

11 Vann R. Newkirk II, "The Great Land Robbery: The Shameful Story of How 1 Million Black Families Have Been Ripped from Their Farms," *Atlantic*, September 2019.

12 Elizabeth Leland, *The Vanishing Coast* (Winston-Salem, NC: John F. Blair, 1996), 13.

13 Analysis of South Carolina tax code by Agricultural Extension Service of Clemson University, as quoted in June Manning Thomas, "Effects of Land Development on Black Land Ownership in the Sea Islands of South Carolina," *Review of Black Political Economy* 8, no. 3 (Spring 1978): 266–76, at 275.

14 Faith R. Rivers, "Public Trust: Where Has It Been and Where Is It Going?" (panel presentation, University of South Carolina School of Law Southeastern Environmental Law Journal Symposium, *Bridging the Divide: Public and Private Interest in Coastal Marshes and Marsh Islands*, Columbia, September 7, 2006).

15 Michael N. Danielson, *Profits and Politics in Paradise: The Development of Hilton Head Island* (Columbia: University of South Carolina Press, 1995); Margaret A. Shannon and Stephen W. Taylor, "Astride the Plantation Gates: Tourism, Racial Politics, and the Development of Hilton Head Island," in *Southern Journeys: Tourism, History, and Culture in the Modern South* (Tuscaloosa: University of Alabama Press, 2003), 177–95.

16 Wine, quoted in Michael C. Wolfe, *The Abundant Life Prevails: Religious Traditions of Saint Helena Island* (Waco, TX: Baylor University Press, 2000), 123.

17 William E. Schmidt, "The Rise of the Low Country," *New York Times*, June 1, 1986.

18 Emory Campbell, interview by Andrew Kahrl, Hilton Head Island, SC, April 17, 2014.

19 In 1960, Beaufort County auctioned tax liens on forty-six properties, with twenty-nine of those properties redeemed by the owner. In 1968, the county auctioned tax liens on 138 properties, with only forty-five of those properties redeemed. See Beaufort County Tax Sales Book 4 (December 1959–October 1984), Beaufort County Office of Register of Deeds, Beaufort, SC.

20 Charles S. Johnson, *Negro Housing: Report of the Committee on Negro Housing, Nannie H. Burroughs, Chairman*, eds. John M. Gries and James Ford (New York: Negro Universities Press, 1969), 253.

21 McDomick, interview, April 17, 2014.

22 Barbara Phillips to Robert Browne, *Report: The Mound Bayou Development Corporation Land Fund, 1971–1973* (New York: Emergency Land Fund, April 15, 1973), box E18, folder Misc. Corresp. 4/73, Emergency Land Fund Records, Amistad Research Center.

23 "Many states . . . have statutory or common law rulings stating that the failure of a taxpayer to receive notice of the sale will not invalidate the sale." Emergency Land Fund, *The Impact of Heir Property on Black Rural Land Tenure in the Southeastern Region of the United States* (New York: Black Economic Research Center, 1980), 258.

24 "Case: Mrs. Gladys Williams," ELF intake notes, 1973, box E18, folder Misc. Corresp. 6/73, Emergency Land Fund Records, Amistad Research Center.

25 "Case: Mr. Cecil Taylor," ELF intake notes, 1973, box E18, folder Misc. Corresp. 6/73, Emergency Land Fund Records, Amistad Research Center.

26 Faith R. Rivers, "Restoring the Bundle of Rights: Preserving Heirs' Property in Coastal South Carolina," paper presented at the Property Preservation Task Force Program: Preservation and Development of Tenancy in Common Property—Societal, Real Estate and Tax Considerations, San Diego, CA, 2006, p. 25. Copy in author's possession.

27 Emergency Land Fund, *Impact of Heir Property on Black Rural Land Tenure*, 256.

28 Harold R. Washington and Paris Favors Jr., "Forty Acres, No Mule," *North Carolina Central Law Journal* 5 (1973–1974): 62; Rivers, "Restoring the Bundle of Rights," 14; Black Economic Research Center, *Only Six Million Acres*, 11–12.

29 Thomas W. Mitchell, Stephen Malpezzi, and Richard K. Green, "Forced Sale Risk: Class, Race, and the 'Double Discount,'" *Florida State Law Review* 37 (Spring 2010): 589–658.

30 Thomas W. Mitchell, "From Reconstruction to Deconstruction: Undermining Black Landownership, Political Independence, and Community through Partition Sales of Tenancies in Common," *Northwestern University Law Review* 95 (Winter 2001): 505–80.

31 Joe McDomick, interview by Andrew Kahrl, St. Helena Island, SC, June 24, 2019.

32 McDomick, interview, April 17, 2014.

33 McDomick, interview, April 17, 2014. On African Americans' engagement with the legal system and local courts during the Jim Crow era, cf. Dylan C. Penningroth, "Everyday Use: A History of Civil Rights in Black Churches," *Journal of American History* 107, no. 4 (March 2021): 871–98.

34 Harold R. Washington, *Black Land Manual: 'Got Land Problems?'* (Frogmore, SC: Penn Community Services, 1973); McDomick, interview, June 24, 2019.

35 *1974 Annual Report, Penn Community Services, Inc.* (Frogmore, SC: Penn Community Services, 1974), box 9, folder 2, Septima Poinsette Clark Papers, Avery Research Center for African American History and Culture, Charleston, SC.

36 McDomick, interview, April 17, 2014; McDomick, interview, June 24, 2019.

37 Reed, "Blacks in South Struggle to Keep the Little Land They Have Left."

38 McDomick, interview, April 17, 2014; Washington, *Black Land Manual*, 17–19; Brian Grabbatin, "'The Land Is Our Family and the Water Is Our Bloodline': The Dispossession and Preservation of Heirs' Property in the Gullah-Geechee Communities of Lowcountry South Carolina" (PhD diss., University of Kentucky, 2016), ProQuest dissertation no. 10103960, 93.

39 Russell Rickford, "'We Can't Grow Food on All This Concrete': The Land Question, Agrarianism, and Black Nationalist Thought in the Late 1960s and 1970s," *Journal of American History* 103 (March 2017): 956, 957.

40 Greta de Jong, *You Can't Eat Freedom: Southerners and Social Justice after the Civil Rights Movement* (Chapel Hill: University of North Carolina Press, 2016), 141–42.

41 McGee and Boone, "Study of Rural Land Ownership," 89. See also Edward Onaci, *Free the Land: The Republic of New Afrika and the Pursuit of a Black Nation-State* (Chapel Hill: University of North Carolina Press, 2020).

42 Monica M. White, *Freedom Farmers: Agricultural Resistance and the Black Freedom Movement* (Chapel Hill: University of North Carolina Press, 2018), 19.

43 Black Economic Research Center, *Only Six Million Acres*, 5; Alec Fazackerley

Hickmott, "Black Land, Black Capital: Rural Development in the Shadows of the Sunbelt South, 1969-1976," *Journal of African American History* 101 (Fall 2016): 505.

44 Hickmott, "Black Land, Black Capital: Rural Development in the Shadows of the Sunbelt South, 1969-1976," 505. On Forman's influence on Browne and the founding of the Black Economic Research Center, see Martha Biondi, "Preliminary Comments on Black Intellectuals and Reparation in the Black Power Era" (presentation at the *Seventh Annual Gilder Lehrman Center International Conference* [*Repairing the Past: Confronting the Legacies of Slavery, Genocide, & Caste*], Yale University, New Haven, CT, October 27-29, 2005). See also John W. Handy, "The Emergence of the Black Economic Research Center and the Review of Black Political Economy," *Review of Black Political Economy* 35, no. 2/3 (2008): 75-89.

45 Hickmott, "Black Land, Black Capital," 516.

46 "Must All Blacks Flee the South?" *New York Times*, April 26, 1970.

47 Black Economic Research Center, *Three Associated Black Institutions*.

48 Black Economic Research Center, *Only Six Million Acres*, 7-13.

49 Black Economic Research Center, *Only Six Million Acres*, 22.

50 Joe Brooks, telephone interview by Andrew Kahrl, November 21, 2013.

51 Joe Brooks, "The Emergency Land Fund: Robert S. Browne, the Idea and the Man," *Review of Black Political Economy* 35, no. 2/3 (2008): 68-69.

52 Hickmott, "Black Land, Black Capital," 507.

53 Yvonne Shinhoster, "Growing Loss of Land Plagues Southern Rural Blacks," *Atlanta Daily World*, August 28, 1975.

54 Eleanor Clift, "Black Land Loss: 6,000,000 Acres and Fading Fast," *Southern Exposure* 2 (Fall 1974): 109.

55 Brooks, "Emergency Land Fund," 69.

56 Emergency Land Fund, Mississippi state branch, "Explanation of 'Results Sheet.'"

57 Black Economic Research Center, *Three Associated Black Institutions*, 22.

58 Phillips to Browne, *Report: The Mound Bayou Development Corporation Land Fund*.

59 Jesse Morris, interview by Andrew Kahrl, Jackson, MS, July 14, 2013.

60 Black Economic Research Center, *Only Six Million Acres*, J-8.

61 Morris, interview, July 14, 2013.

62 Black Economic Research Center, *Three Associated Black Institutions*, 23.

63 Brooks, "Emergency Land Fund," 122.

64 William H. McGee to Jesse Morris, *Report on Leflore County Tax Sale* (New York: Emergency Land Fund, April 2, 1973), box E18, folder Misc. Corresp. 3/73, Emergency Land Fund Records, Amistad Research Center.

65 Black Economic Research Center, *Three Associated Black Institutions*, 23.

66 Jesse Morris, "Memorandum Re: April 2nd Tax Sale," April 9, 1973, box E18, folder Misc. Corresp. 4/73, Emergency Land Fund Records, Amistad Research Center.

67 Velma Payne, "The History of the ELF," *Forty Acres and a Mule* (November 1980).

68 Joe Brooks, interview, November 21, 2013.

69 Joseph Brooks, "The Emergency Land Fund: A Rural Land Retention and Development Model," in *The Black Rural Landowner*, eds. McGee and Boone, 117-34.

70 Morris, interview, July 14, 2013.

71 Joseph Adams to county contacts of the Emergency Land Fund, "Tax Sale on September 16, 1974," August 28, 1974, box E45, folder Tax Sale 9–16–74 Pike, Emergency Land Fund Records, Amistad Research Center.

72 Randolph Walker to Joseph Adams, "Memorandum," October 1, 1974, box E45, folder Tax Sale 9–16–74 Pike, Emergency Land Fund Records, Amistad Research Center.

73 Emergency Land Fund, "Brief Summary, Client: Ullysses Smith," n.d., box 42, folder Problem Cases Summary, Emergency Land Fund Records, Amistad Research Center.

74 James Miller to Jesse Morris, "Tax Sale in Claiborne County," September 16, 1974, box E45, folder Tax Sale 9–16–74 Chickasaw, Emergency Land Fund Records, Amistad Research Center.

75 Emergency Land Fund, "Other Activities and Information: May 1–May 31, 1978," May 31, 1978, box 51, folder ELF-Land Problems, Emergency Land Fund Records, Amistad Research Center.

76 Emergency Land Fund, quoted in Hickmott, "Black Land, Black Capital," 521.

77 Black Economic Research Center, *Only Six Million Acres*, I–2.

78 Emory S. Campbell to Board of Trustees, Penn Community Services, Inc., quarterly report (July–September 1980), October 17, 1980, box 11, folder 98, William ("Bill") Saunders Papers, circa 1950–2004, Avery Research Center for African American History and Culture.

79 Penn Community Services, *South Carolina Report for November, December and January to the National Association of Landowners* (Frogmore, SC: Penn Community Services, Inc., January 1978), box 77, folder South Carolina NAL Reports, Emergency Land Fund Records, Amistad Research Center; Penn Community Services, *South Carolina Association of Landowners, Report for November, 1977* (Frogmore, SC: Penn Community Services, Inc., November 1977), box 77, folder ELF/Reports, Emergency Land Fund Records, South Carolina Association of Landowners, 1977, Amistad Research Center.

80 Penn Community Services, *South Carolina Association of Landowners, Quarterly Report* (Frogmore, SC: Penn Community Services, Inc., December 5, 1979), box E80, folder ELF Reports, Emergency Land Fund Records, Amistad Research Center.

81 Joe Brooks, interview, November 21, 2013.

82 Emergency Land Fund, *The Emergency Land Fund: A Five Year Report, 1972–1977* (New York: Emergency Land Fund, 1978), box 81, folder South Carolina State Reports, Emergency Land Fund Records, Amistad Research Center.

83 Joe Brooks, interview, November 21, 2013.

84 Clift, "Black Land Loss," 109.

85 Salamon, *Land and Minority Enterprise*, 3.

86 Salamon, *Land and Minority Enterprise*, 55, 15, 25.

87 On the Washington family estate saga, see generally Emergency Land Fund Records, box 18, Amistad Research Center.

88 Hickmott, "Black Land, Black Capital," 528.

89 Richard Porter, "The Emergency Land Fund: The Struggle to Preserve Black Ownership of Land," *Forty Acres and a Mule* (December 1979).

90 Emergency Land Fund, *Five Year Report*; Emory Campbell, "Penn Center—Proposed Activities for the '80s," internal report, April 15, 1980, box 11, folder 98,

William ("Bill") Saunders Papers, circa 1950-2004, Avery Research Center for African American History and Culture.

91 Campbell, interview, April 17, 2014.

92 Grabbatin, "'Land Is Our Family,'" 94.

93 Beaufort County Tax Sales Book 4 (December 1959-October 1984), Beaufort County Office of Register of Deeds, Beaufort, SC.

94 "Hilton Head Islanders Split Racially over Incorporation Vote," *New York Times*, May 10, 1983. See also Vernie Singleton, "We Are an Endangered Species: An Interview with Emory Campbell," *Southern Exposure* 10 (May-June 1982): 37-39.

95 "NAACP Housing Corp. Drafts Black Agenda," *Pittsburgh Courier*, March 28, 1981.

96 Gunnar Hansen, *Islands at the Edge of Time: A Journey to America's Barrier Islands* (Washington, DC: Island Press, 1993), 142.

97 "Hilton Head Islanders Split Racially over Incorporation Vote."

98 "Development, Taxes Threaten a Black Bastion in S.C.," *Philadelphia Tribune*, July 21, 1989.

99 Patricia Jones-Jackson, *When Roots Die: Endangered Traditions on the Sea Islands* (Athens: University of Georgia Press, 1987), xiii.

CHAPTER TEN

1 Edward Greer, *Big Steel: Black Politics and Corporate Power in Gary, Indiana* (New York: Monthly Review Press, 1979), 161.

2 Raymond A. Mohl and Neil Betten, *Steel City: Urban and Ethnic Patterns in Gary, Indiana, 1906-1950* (New York: Holmes and Meier, 1986).

3 Thomas J. Sugrue, *Sweet Land of Liberty: The Forgotten Struggle for Civil Rights in the North* (New York: Random House, 2008), 461.

4 Bell v. School City of Gary, Indiana, 324 F.2d 209 (N.D. Ind. 1963). See also Sugrue, *Sweet Land of Liberty*, 461-62.

5 Richard A. Cloward and Frances Fox Piven, *The Politics of Turmoil: Essays on Poverty, Race, and the Urban Crisis* (New York: Pantheon, 1974), 325-28.

6 Josh Mound, "Stirrings of Revolt: Regressive Levies, the Pocketbook Squeeze, and the 1960s Roots of the 1970s Tax Revolt," *Journal of Policy History* 32 (2020): 105-50.

7 Cloward and Piven, *Politics of Turmoil*, 329-54. See also Sugrue, *Sweet Land of Liberty*, 400-448.

8 James Boggs and Grace Lee Boggs, "The City Is the Black Man's Land," *Monthly Review* 17 (April 1966): 42.

9 James Turner, "Black in the Cities: Land and Self-Determination," *Black Scholar* 1, no. 6 (1970): 9-13.

10 Cloward and Piven, *Politics of Turmoil*, 254.

11 Kevin M. Kruse, *White Flight: Atlanta and the Making of Modern Conservatism* (Princeton, NJ: Princeton University Press, 2005), 37-38.

12 Robert L. Lineberry, "Reforming Metropolitan Governance: Requiem or Reality," *Georgetown Law Journal* 58 (1970): 693-95. In regionally governed cities like Nashville, Tennessee, Black neighborhoods were less subject to overassessments and the tax revenues from regional growth remained within a single jurisdiction. But, as the historian Ansley T. Erickson notes, "when faced with questions of how to allocate resources—in the form of schools, fire stations, or sanitary sewers—the metropolitan political structure often tilted to the white suburban majority" (*Making the Unequal Metropolis: School Desegregation and Its Limits* [Chicago: University of Chicago Press, 2016], 5).

13 Francesca Russello Ammon, *Bulldozer: Demolition and Clearance of the Postwar Landscape* (New Haven, CT: Yale University Press, 2016); Brent Cebul, "Tearing Down Black America," *Boston Review*, July 22, 2020, http://bostonreview.net/race/brent-cebul-tearing-down-black-america.

14 Charles L. Schultze, "Fiscal Problems of Cities," in *The Fiscal Crisis of American Cities: Essays on the Political Economy of Urban America with Special Reference to New York*, eds. Roger E. Alcaly and David Mermelstein (New York: Vintage, 1977), 192; Cloward and Piven, *Politics of Turmoil*, 325–27; John Oliver, "Behind the Urban School Squeeze," *American Teacher* (March 1973).

15 Greer, *Big Steel*, 164. This trend held true nationwide. By 1971, the year when it elected its first Black mayor, Newark, New Jersey, boasted a property tax rate the second highest of any city in the nation, an incredible $8.44 per $100 of assessed value. See Cloward and Piven, *Politics of Turmoil*, 328; "Outmoded Levy: Rising Property Taxes Burden Many but Fail to Raise Enough Money," *Wall Street Journal*, January 15, 1971.

16 "Games Companies Play: A Taxing Look at U.S. Steel," *Chicago Free Press*, October 19, 1970.

17 Greer, *Big Steel*, 161.

18 Edward Rohrbach, "Gary, U.S. Steel Clash," *Chicago Tribune*, June 27, 1972.

19 "Race Is Cited as the Biggest Gary Problem: Gary's No. 1 Problem Is Racial," *Chicago Tribune*, July 16, 1973.

20 Joseph McLaughlin, "Gary's Mayor Hatcher: New Breed of Politician," *Chicago Tribune*, December 20, 1970.

21 McLaughlin, "Gary's Mayor Hatcher."

22 "Gary in Black and White," *Newsweek*, April 21, 1969.

23 "Secession Campaign Threatens Gary, Ind.," *Christian Science Monitor*, April 10, 1969; "Gary Mayor Battles to Block Secession of Tax-Irked Suburb," *Christian Science Monitor*, March 21, 1969.

24 "Secession In Gary? Mayor Hatcher Faces New Fight," *Chicago Defender*, May 31, 1969; "Gary's Black Mayor Gives Lesson on Suburban Secessionists' Folly," *Daily World*, June 10, 1969.

25 H. Paul Friesema, "Black Control of Central Cities: The Hollow Prize," *Journal of the American Institute of Planners* (March 1969): 75–79.

26 Richard Hatcher, "The Black City Crisis," *Black Scholar* 1 (April 1970): 54–62.

27 Charles Howard Levine, "Community Conflict and Mayoral Leadership: A Theoretical Examination with Applications to Black Mayoral Leadership in Gary, Indiana, and Cleveland, Ohio" (PhD diss., Indiana University, 1971), 201; Edward Greer, "Citizens Taxpayer Association," internal memo, October 1, 1968, box 87, folder 18, Business and Professional People for the Public Interest, University of Illinois at Chicago Special Collections.

28 Greer, *Big Steel*, 166–67.

29 "Gary, Indiana Property Assessments," unpublished anonymous manuscript, 1971, box 87, folder 11, Business and Professional People for the Public Interest, University of Illinois at Chicago Special Collections; Greer, *Big Steel*, 170.

30 Greer, *Big Steel*, 169–80.

31 "Gary, Indiana Property Assessments."

32   Peter Braestrup, "Nader Urges Local Tax Probe," *Washington Post*, August 10, 1970; "Impact and Administration of the Property Tax," in "Property Taxes: Hearings before the Subcommittee on Intergovernmental Relations of the Committee on Government Operations, United States Senate, Ninety-Second Congress, Second Session," US Senate transcript, June 26, 1972. On tax assessor scandals and the 1967 tax assessment reforms enacted in California, see Robert O. Self, *American Babylon: Race and the Struggle for Postwar Oakland* (Princeton, NJ: Princeton University Press, 2003), 286–87; Isaac William Martin, *The Permanent Tax Revolt: How the Property Tax Transformed American Politics* (Stanford, CA: Stanford University Press, 2008). On Ralph Nader and public-interest group formation and activism in the 1970s, see Paul Sabin, *Public Citizens: The Attack on Big Government and the Remaking of American Liberalism* (New York: Norton, 2021).

33   Jesse Jackson, "What the Assessor's Office Scandal Really Means," *Chicago Defender*, October 10, 1970.

34   Robert McClory, "Blacks Hang Cullerton in Effigy," *Chicago Defender*, May 9, 1972.

35   "Impact and Administration of the Property Tax."

36   Sugrue, *Sweet Land of Liberty*, 470.

37   Arthur E. Wise, *Rich Schools, Poor Schools: The Promise of Equal Educational Opportunity* (Chicago: University of Chicago Press, 1967), 7, 164.

38   Quoted in Virginia Fleming, *The Cost of Neglect, the Value of Equity: A Guidebook for School Finance Reform in the South* (Atlanta, GA: Southern Regional Council, 1974), 28.

39   Vernon Jordan, "Inequality in Educational Opportunity," *Los Angeles Sentinel*, November 11, 1971.

40   Fleming, *Cost of Neglect*, 17.

41   "Tax 'Revolution': School Ruling Is Seen Changing the Nature of U.S. Cities, Suburbs," *Wall Street Journal*, March 13, 1972.

42   San Antonio Independent School District et al. v. Rodriguez et al., 411 U.S. 1 (1973).

43   *San Antonio Independent School District*, 411 U.S.

44   Milliken v. Bradley, 48 U.S. 717 (1974).

45   See Tracy L. Steffes, "Assessment Matters: The Rise and Fall of the Illinois Resource Equalizer Formula," *History of Education Quarterly* 60, no. 1 (2020): 24–57; James E. Ryan, *Five Miles Away, A World Apart: One City, Two Schools, and the Story of Educational Opportunity in Modern America* (New York: Oxford University Press, 2010), 145–80.

46   Martin A. Schwartz, "Municipal Services Litigation after Rodriguez," *Brooklyn Law Review* 40 (1973): 93–114.

47   Mary Bowen Little, "Potholes, Lampposts and Policemen: Equal Protection and the Financing of Basic Municipal Services in the Wake of Hawkins and Serrano," *Villanova Law Review* 17, no. 4 (1972): 680.

48   Little, "Potholes, Lampposts and Policemen," 656.

49   Palmer v. Thompson, 403 U.S. 217 (1971); Washington v. Davis, 426 U.S. 229 (1976); Charles M. Haar and Daniel W. Fessler, *The Wrong Side of the Tracks: A Revolutionary Rediscovery of the Common Law Tradition of Fairness in the Struggle against Inequality* (New York: Simon and Schuster, 1986), 48–49.

50   Greer, *Big Steel*, 176.

51 Carroll Harvey, "Watching Cities Go Broke," *Focus* (October 1975).

52 John H. Mollenkopf, "The Crisis of the Public Sector in America's Cities," in *Fiscal Crisis of American Cities*, eds. Alcaly and Mermelstein, 1977), 113-31; Cloward and Piven, *Politics of Turmoil*, 332-37.

53 Godfrey Hodgson and George Crile, "Gary: Epitaph for a Model City," *Washington Post*, March 4, 1973.

CHAPTER ELEVEN

1 Josh Levin, *The Queen: The Forgotten Life behind an American Myth* (New York: Little, Brown and Company, 2019), 90-91; Ian Haney Lopez, *Dog Whistle Politics: How Coded Racial Appeals Have Reinvented Racism and Wrecked the Middle Class* (New York: Oxford University Press, 2015).

2 Movement for Economic Justice, *Organizing Community Tax Clinics: A Manual Prepared for the Tax Justice Project* (Washington, DC: Movement for Economic Justice, 1973), box 42, folder 8, George Wiley Papers, Movement for Economic Justice Records, Wisconsin Historical Society, Madison.

3 Nick Kotz and Mary Lynn Kotz, *A Passion for Equality: George A. Wiley and the Movement* (New York: Norton, 1977), 295-96; Simon Hall, *American Patriotism, American Protest: Social Movements since the Sixties* (Philadelphia: University of Pennsylvania Press, 2011), 104-5.

4 George A. Wiley, *Progress Report on the Planning Phase for the Movement for Economic Justice* (Washington, DC: Movement for Economic Justice, June 20, 1973), box 41, folder 4, George Wiley Papers, Movement for Economic Justice Records, Wisconsin Historical Society; Kotz and Kotz, *Passion for Equality*, 295-96.

5 George Wiley, "Speech March 5, Statler Hilton," March 5, 1973, box 40, folder 3, George Wiley Papers, Movement for Economic Justice Records, Wisconsin Historical Society, Madison.

6 Wiley, "Speech March 5, Statler Hilton."

7 Wiley, "Speech March 5, Statler Hilton."

8 Annelise Orleck, *Storming Caesars Palace: How Black Mothers Fought Their Own War on Poverty* (Boston, MA: Beacon Press, 2005).

9 Movement for Economic Justice, *Organizing Community Tax Clinics*.

10 John Shannon, *Property Taxation: Reform and Relief; Comments on S. 1255* (Washington, DC: Government Printing Office, May 7, 1973), 14498; "Financial Crisis Now Confronting Schools Explained," *Louisville Defender*, August 17, 1972; Josh Mound, "Stirrings of Revolt: Regressive Levies, the Pocketbook Squeeze, and the 1960s Roots of the 1970s Tax Revolt," *Journal of Policy History* 32 (2020): 105-50, at 108.

11 Isaac William Martin, *The Permanent Tax Revolt: How the Property Tax Transformed American Politics* (Stanford, CA: Stanford University Press, 2008).

12 "Negroes Hit Hardest by Planned Tax Hike," *Michigan Chronicle*, March 18, 1967.

13 United States Advisory Commission on Intergovernmental Relations, *The Property Tax in a Changing Environment: Selected State Studies; an Information Report* (Washington, DC: Government Printing Office, 1974), 2-3.

14 Elizabeth Tandy Shermer, *Sunbelt Capitalism: Phoenix and the Transformation of American Politics* (Philadelphia: University of Pennsylvania Press, 2013), 179.

15 Eva Galambos, *The Tax Structure of the Southern States: An Analysis* (Atlanta, GA: Southern Regional Council, November 1969), 13.

16 Mound, "Stirrings of Revolt."

17 Howard H. Carwile, "They Soak the Poor," *Baltimore Afro-American*, February 14, 1970.

18 Mound, "Stirrings of Revolt," 124. Mound's findings challenge prevailing assumptions about Black voter preferences for tax increases, rooted in racist renderings of Blacks as "benefit recipients rather than 'taxpayers,'" and complicate claims that voter rejection of school levies were rooted in racial animus. Cf. Camille Walsh, *Racial Taxation: Schools, Segregation, and Taxpayer Citizenship, 1869-1973* (Chapel Hill: University of North Carolina Press, 2018), 141.

19 "Unfair Tax Bite No News in South Shore, Beverly," *Chicago Sun-Times*, October 16, 1972.

20 Citizens Action Program (CAP), *CAP Yearly Report—Second Half of 1972*, newsletter, 1972, box 1, folder 2, Citizens Action Program Records, University of Illinois at Chicago Special Collections.

21 "Unfair Tax Bite No News in South Shore, Beverly"; "Beverly Area Residents Form Tax Protest Unit," *Chicago Tribune*, November 20, 1972; "Beverly Citizens Hit Assessing," *Chicago Tribune*, November 28, 1972; Constance Lauerman, "Beverly Hills Strives for Stability," *Chicago Tribune*, November 30, 1972; "CAP to 'Visit' Cullerton Today," *Chicago Defender*, December 5, 1972; "CAP Again," *People and Taxes* (1973); W. F. (Skip) Bossette, "Stage Tax Revolt in Packed Hall," *Chicago Defender*, June 26, 1972.

22 Arthur Lyons, "The Urban Property Tax and Minorities," in *Housing: Chicago Style—A Consultation Sponsored by the Illinois Advisory Committee to the United States Commission on Civil Rights*, ed. United States Commission on Civil Rights, Illinois Advisory Commission (Washington, DC: US Commission on Civil Rights, 1982), 73-78; Dona P. Gerson, "Tax Revolt in Cook County: Inflation of Property Values Combined with Increased Tax Levies," *Illinois Issues* (1978).

23 Robert McClory, "Blacks Hang Cullerton in Effigy," *Chicago Defender*, May 9, 1972; "Residents Form Tax Protest Unit," *Chicago Tribune*, November 20, 1972; "Carey Vows Homeowner Tax Probe," *Chicago Daily News*, December 5, 1972; David Emmons, "Community Organizing and Urban Policy: Saul Alinsky and Chicago's Citizens Action Program" (PhD diss., University of Chicago, 1986), ProQuest dissertation no. T-30105, 202.

24 National Black Political Convention, *The National Black Political Agenda* (Gary, IN: National Black Political Convention, 1972); "We Must Pave the Way so That Others May Follow," *Chicago Defender*, March 18, 1972.

25 "A 'New' Bobby Seale Running in Oakland," *Philadelphia Inquirer,* April 2, 1973; "Panther Runs for Mayor in Oakland," *Norfolk Journal and Guide*, April 21, 1973.

26 Arthur D. Little, Inc., *A Study of Property Taxes and Urban Blight: Report to the U.S. Department of Housing & Urban Development* (Washington, DC: Government Printing Office, January 1973).

27 Orleck, *Storming Caesars Palace*, 110-11.

28 Wiley, "Speech March 5, Statler Hilton."

29 Movement for Economic Justice, "Why You Should Organize a Tax Clinic," flyer, February 16, 1973, box 11, folder 2, Movement for Economic Justice Records, 1972-1980, Wisconsin Historical Society.

30 "Black Leaders Boost TEA Party Convention," *Philadelphia Tribune*, December 15, 1973. On low-income taxpayer clinics, see also Keith Fogg, "Taxation with Representation: The Creation and Development of Low-Income Taxpayer Clinics," *Tax Lawyer* 67 (Fall 2013): 3-64.

31   Kotz and Kotz, *Passion for Equality*, 304.

32   Research Atlanta, *Assessment-Sales Ratios in Fulton County and the City of Atlanta* (Atlanta. GA: Research Atlanta, 1975); "Mayor Raps Tax Assessing Methods," *Atlanta Constitution*, February 8, 1975; "NAACP Suit Attacks Inequity in County's Tax Assessments," *Atlanta Daily World*, February 9, 1975.

33   Charles Hayslett, "Reappraisals Reaping Resentment," *Atlanta Constitution*, March 23, 1975; "Assessment Rollbacks Held Illegal," *Atlanta Constitution*, May 20, 1975; Jim Gray, "NAACP Suit Blasts 'Outlaw' Reappraisal," *Atlanta Constitution*, May 13, 1975; Jim Gray, "Suit Hits Northside Assessing," *Atlanta Constitution*, May 30, 1975; Yvonne Shinhoster, "NAACP Hits Rollback in Northside Property Taxes," *Atlanta Daily World*, June 6, 1976.

34   Mound, "Stirrings of Revolt."

35   See Robert Kuttner, *Revolt of the Haves: Tax Rebellions and Hard Times* (New York: Simon and Schuster, 1980); Robert O. Self, *American Babylon: Race and the Struggle for Postwar Oakland* (Princeton, NJ: Princeton University Press, 2003); Bruce J. Schulman, *The Seventies: The Great Shift in American Culture, Society, and Politics* (Cambridge, MA: De Capo, 2001).

36   Bay Area Urban League, *Proposition 13: Impact on Minorities* (Davis: Institute of Governmental Affairs and the UCD Kellogg Program, University of California, 1979), 5, 88, 96.

37   Emmons, "Community Organizing and Urban Policy," 204, 335-48.

38   Arthur Lyons, *Assessment Ratios for Townships and Selected Neighborhoods in Cook County, Illinois: A Study in Nonuniformity* (Chicago: School of Urban Sciences, University of Illinois at Chicago Circle, August 1978).

39   Arthur Lyons, interview by Andrew Kahrl, Chicago, IL, January 8, 2015.

40   Ed McManus, "Discrimination in Property Assessment: Human or Computer Bias?" *Illinois Issues* (August 1979); Lyons, interview, January 8, 2015.

41   Fred Bremer, Ed Dolan, Thelma Karson, Toni Mahan, and Larry Wenderski, *Relative Tax Burdens in Black and White Neighborhoods of Cook County* (Chicago: School of Urban Sciences, University of Illinois at Chicago Circle, April 24, 1979); McManus, "Discrimination in Property Assessment."

42   Lyons, interview, January 8, 2015.

43   Ed McManus, "Property Tax Rate Higher in Black Areas, Study Says," *Chicago Tribune*, April 14, 1979.

44   "Schedule Public Hearings: Plan to Investigate Overassessment of Black-Owned Homes," *Chicago Defender*, April 17, 1979; Roy Harvey, "Residents of Evanston, Englewood Unite in Drive," *Chicago Defender*, May 5, 1979; "Black Leaders Seek Probe of Cook Assessor," *Chicago Sun-Times*, April 17, 1979.

45   Arvis Averette, interview by Andrew Kahrl, Chicago, IL, May 12, 2015. On rising property taxes as a percentage of household income in South Shore, see Norman A. Katz, *Urban Neighborhoods: An Action Report on the Impact of Tax Assessment and Tax Delinquency Policies; Recommendations for Changes in the Property Tax System to Encourage Housing Conservation and Neighborhood Revitalization* (Chicago: Trust, Inc., April 1978).

46   Averette, interview, May 12, 2015.

47   Faith Christmas, "Metcalfe: Unity Victory Key," *Chicago Defender*, May 8, 1972. Vernon Jarret quoted in Simon Balto, *Occupied Territory: Policing Black Chicago from Red Summer to Black Power* (Chapel Hill: University of North Carolina Press, 2020), 250.

48 Roger Biles, *Mayor Harold Washington: Champion of Race and Reform in Chicago* (Urbana: University of Illinois Press, 2018), 29.

49 Averette, interview, May 12, 2015; Lori Granger, "Chicago, Evanston Groups Join in 'Black Tax' Rally," *Chicago Defender*, May 19, 1979.

50 Averette, interview, May 12, 2015.

51 Lyons, interview, January 8, 2015.

52 Lyons, interview, January 8, 2015; Averette, interview, May 12, 2015.

53 "Black Property Owners Unite to Fight Tax 'Bias,'" *Chicago Tribune*, June 18, 1979; "'Black Tax' Is Target of Lawsuit," *Chicago Defender*, June 18, 1979; "Sen. Washington Forms Black Taxpayers Coalition," *Chicago Weekend*, June 22, 1979, box 13, folder 8, Harold Washington Archives and Collections, Pre-Mayoral Records, Illinois State Senate Records, 1976-1980, Chicago Public Library Special Collections and Preservation Division; James Yuenger, "Assessor Is Facing Black Protest Blitz," *Chicago Tribune*, August 5, 1979; "Black Tax Issue Builds Steam: Citizens in Mass Protest," *Chicago Defender*, August 25, 1979; Sylvia Mills, "Homeowners Hold Meet," *Chicago Defender*, August 27, 1979; "Black Taxpayers Revolt: Charge Assessor Discriminates," *Keep Strong* (September 1979); "Averette to Head Taxpayers Group," *Chicago Defender*, September 10, 1979; Lyons, interview, January 8, 2015; Averette, interview, May 12, 2015.

54 Harold Washington, transcripts of debates, June 1979, box 4, folder 12, Harold Washington Archives and Collections, Pre-Mayoral Records, Illinois State Senate Records, 1976-1980, Chicago Public Library Special Collections and Preservation Division; Averette, interview, May 12, 2015.

55 "New Tax Group Getting Wide Participation in Black Areas," *Chicago Defender*, August 25, 1979.

56 "New Tax Group Getting Wide Participation in Black Areas."

57 Lyons, interview, January 8, 2015; Arthur Lyons, "Some Questions Raised by 'A Report to the Assessor on Assessment Practices & Procedures for Residential Properties in Cook County,'" press release, January 17, 1980, box 9, folder 6, Harold Washington Archives and Collections, Pre-Mayoral Records, Illinois State Senate Records, 1976-1980, Chicago Public Library Special Collections and Preservation Division.

58 Lyons, "Some Questions Raised"; Tom Granatir, "Taxing Questions," *Chicago Journal*, May 14, 1980; Harold Washington, "Some More Taxes," *Chicago Journal*, May 21, 1980, box 37, folder 3, Harold Washington Archives and Collections, Mayoral Campaign Records, Chicago Public Library Special Collections and Preservation Division.

59 Gary Adkins, "Taxes and Tirades: Thompson v. Bakalis," *Illinois Issues* (1978), 4-6; Gerson, "Tax Revolt in Cook County"; Charles Minert, "Illinois Tax Revolt—the 8% Solution: Totten Calls for Limits on State Revenues and Property Tax Rates," *Illinois Issues* (1978), 10-12. See also Tracy L. Steffes, "Assessment Matters: The Rise and Fall of the Illinois Resource Equalizer Formula," *History of Education Quarterly* 60, no. 1 (2020): 24-57.

60 Lyons, interview, January 8, 2015.

CHAPTER TWELVE

1 David Balin, telephone interview by Andrew Kahrl, June 16, 2021.

2 See Keeanga-Yamahtta Taylor, *Race for Profit: How Banks and the Real Estate*

Industry Undermined Black Homeownership (Chapel Hill: University of North Carolina Press, 2019).

3 Louis Balthazar, deposition, May 19, 1969, box 44, folder 12, Business and Professional People for the Public Interest, University of Illinois at Chicago Special Collections.

4 The group was later renamed Business and Professional People for the Public Interest.

5 William Clements and Terry Shaffer, "Tax-Sale Evictee Gets Reprieve," *Chicago Daily News*, April 25, 1969.

6 *Hawthorn Lane & Co. v. William and Nancy Parks*, Report of Proceedings, February 21, 1968, box 44, folder 6, Business and Professional People for the Public Interest, University of Illinois at Chicago Special Collections; Hugh Hough, "How Law Cost Him His Home," *Chicago Sun-Times*, April 27, 1969; Marshall Patner, "Blair Complaint v. MP," 1973, Marshall Patner Collection, University of Illinois at Chicago Special Collections.

7 F. Raymond Marks, Kirk Leswing, and Barbara A. Fortinsky, *The Lawyer, the Public, and Professional Responsibility* (Chicago: American Bar Foundation, 1972), 161–63; "Public-Interest Lawyer Marshall Patner, 69," *Chicago Tribune*, December 28, 2000; Patner, "Blair Complaint v. MP"; see also Paul Sabin, *Public Citizens: The Attack on Big Government and the Remaking of American Liberalism* (New York: W. W. Norton and Company, 2021).

8 Balthazar, deposition.

9 Marshall Patner and Joseph Karaganis, complaint, *Balthazar v. Mari Ltd.*, box 44, folder 27, Scholarship, Education and Defense Fund for Racial Equality Records, 1944–1983, Wisconsin Historical Society, Madison.

10 "U.S. Courts to Review Tax-Sale Law," *Chicago Daily News*, May 5, 1969.

11 Mike Royko, "Chicago: City with 'I Will,'" *Chicago Daily News*, March 4, 1969.

12 Mike Royko, "Compassion: A Lost Virtue," *Chicago Daily News*, July 1, 1969; Mike Royko, "Meet a Ghost: Henry Riedl," *Chicago Daily News*, April 30, 1969.

13 Royko, "Compassion."

14 Hugh Hough, "How an Aged Widow Was Evicted for Back Taxes," *Chicago Sun-Times*, April 24, 1969.

15 Clements and Shaffer, "Tax-Sale Evictee Gets Reprieve."

16 Royko, "Compassion"; Hugh Hough, "Blair Lawyer Pledges Eviction Moratorium," *Chicago Sun-Times*, April 26, 1969.

17 Hough, "How an Aged Widow Was Evicted for Back Taxes"; Royko, "Chicago"; Mike Royko, "Arrest Bares a Sad Story," *Chicago Daily News*, March 12, 1969; Jack Schnedler and Terry Shaffer, "Housing 'Tax Buys' by Blair Hit," *Chicago Daily News*, April 24, 1969.

18 Clements and Shaffer, "Tax-Sale Evictee Gets Reprieve."

19 Robert Cushman, *Amicus Curiae, Balthazar v. Mari Ltd.* (brief, 1969), box 44, folder 14, Business and Professional People for the Public Interest, University of Illinois at Chicago Special Collections.

20 Marshall Patner, "Motion to Extend Time for Filing Petition, *Balthazar v. Mari Ltd.*," 1969, box 44, folder 15, Business and Professional People for the Public Interest, University of Illinois at Chicago Special Collections; Marshall Patner, "Reply in Support of Jurisdictional Statement, *Balthazar v. Mari Ltd.*," 1969, box 44, folder 14, Business and Professional People for the Public Interest, University of Illinois at Chicago Special Collections.

21   Howard C. Emmerman, "Revenue and Taxation—Collection of Delinquent
      Real Estate Taxes—Legislating Protection of the Delinquent Property Owner in
      an Era of Super- Marketable Tax Titles," *DePaul Law Review* 19, (Winter 1969):
      348–76.

22   Hugh Hough, "Tax-Delinquent Law Evils Face a Grim Accuser," *Chicago
      Sun-Times*, April 23, 1969; Hough, "How an Aged Widow Was Evicted for Back
      Taxes"; Schnedler and Shaffer, "Housing 'Tax Buys' by Blair Hit"; Clements and
      Shaffer, "Tax-Sale Evictee Gets Reprieve"; "Injustice Can Be Legal (Editorial),"
      Chicago Daily News, April 25, 1969; Frank Maier, "Revival of Bill to Curb Tax-Sale
      Abuses Sought," *Chicago Daily News*, June 20, 1969.

23   Hough, "Tax-Delinquent Law Evils Face a Grim Accuser."

24   "Bill to End Tax-Delinquency Abuses Okd by House Unit," *Chicago Sun-Times*,
      May 8, 1969; Patner, "Blair Complaint v. MP"; Taxpayers' Federation of Illinois,
      "Guest Editorial: Tax Delinquencies," *Chicago Tribune*, May 17, 1969; "New Law
      to Protect Home Owners," *Chicago Defender*, June 29, 1970; Joseph Karaganis to
      Geraldine Hoffman, January 26, 1970, box 44, folder 16, Business and Profes-
      sional People for the Public Interest, University of Illinois at Chicago Special
      Collections.

25   Sheldon Karon, "Claim of Allan Blair," June 28, 1973, box 43, folder 20, Business
      and Professional People for the Public Interest, University of Illinois at Chicago
      Special Collections.

26   Robert McClory, "Land Grabbers 'Rook' Ghetto," *Chicago Defender*, Sep-
      tember 22, 1973; Paul O'Connor, "First and Second Drafts of Article on Allan
      Blair," 1974, box 4, Paul O'Connor Papers, Chicago Historical Society Research
      Center.

27   Timothy E. Gray, *No Redemption: Tax Lien Auctions, Evictions, and Lessons from
      the Foreclosure Crisis* (Chicago: Windy City Publishers, 2016), 3, 17, 53.

28   Balin, interview, June 16, 2021; Gray, *No Redemption*, 16–17.

29   Peter Benjaminson, "How to Lose Your Home for $18: The Law and the Tax
      Buyers," *Detroit Free Press*, May 16, 1971.

30   Balin, interview, June 16, 2021; Peter Benjaminson, "Tax Sale System
      Denounced," *Detroit Free Press*, November 4, 1971.

31   Taylor, *Race for Profit*.

32   Satter, *Family Properties*, 343.

33   Satter, *Family Properties*, 335–36.

34   Pamela Zekman and Jerry Thornton, "Winning Con Game in Slums," *Chicago
      Tribune*, May 11, 1973; David Young, "City Tax Buyer Sues Firm for Slum Fire
      Loss," *Chicago Tribune*, June 25, 1974.

35   "5 Slumlord Empires Linked by Legal Maze," *Chicago Tribune*, May 7, 1973;
      "Slumlord Guide—8 Steps to Profit: A Manual for Slumlords," *Chicago Tribune*,
      May 9, 1973; Balin, interview, June 16, 2021.

36   Commission to Study the Property Tax, *Final Report Submitted to the Assessor of
      Cook County* (Chicago: Cook County Assessors Office, January 18, 1978).

37   John J. Lawlor, "Real Property Tax Delinquency and the Rehabilitation of Multi-
      Family Housing Stock in Chicago, Illinois: The Role of the Collection Provisions
      of the Illinois Revenue Act," *DePaul Law Review* 26, no. 1 (1976–1977), 3; Com-
      mission to Study the Property Tax, *Final Report Submitted to the Assessor of Cook
      County*, 7.

38   McClory, "Land Grabbers 'Rook' Ghetto."

39 "Delinquent Tax Loser Sues to Regain Home," *Freeport* [IL] *Journal-Standard*, April 21, 1973; Mike Royko, "Allan Blair Strikes Again!" *Chicago Daily News*, February 27, 1973, p. 36, box 43, folder 19, Business and Professional People for the Public Interest, University of Illinois at Chicago Special Collections.

40 Illinois-Legislative Investigating Commission, *Delinquent Tax Sales: A Report to the Illinois General Assembly* (Chicago: Illinois-Legislative Investigating Commission, September 1976), 11; Ronald Yates, "Woman's $25,000 Home Sold for $59," *Chicago Tribune*, September 5, 1973; O'Connor, "First and Second Drafts of Article on Allan Blair"; "Mrs. Ware Will Never Surrender," *Chicago Defender*, July 1, 1974.

41 O'Connor, "First and Second Drafts of Article on Allan Blair"; Illinois-Legislative Investigating Commission, *Delinquent Tax Sales*, 11, 51; BPI, "*Lilian K. Ware v. DRG, Inc.*, Memorandum in Support of Preliminary Injunction and Temporary Restraining Order," 1973, box 44, folder 1, Business and Professional People for the Public Interest, University of Illinois at Chicago Special Collections.

42 Illinois-Legislative Investigating Commission, *Delinquent Tax Sales*, 13.

43 Dolores McCahill, "Blair Brandished a Gun, Hearing Is Told," *Chicago Sun-Times*, October 18, 1974; "*Lilian K. Ware v. DRG, Inc.*, Memorandum."

44 "Funds Pouring In to Save Her Home," *Chicago Daily News*, September 8, 1973; "*Lilian K. Ware v. DRG, Inc.*, Transcript of Hearing," August 15, 1972, box 44, folder 1, Business and Professional People for the Public Interest, University of Illinois at Chicago Special Collections.

45 "Funds Pouring In to Save Her Home"; "The Lillian Ware Case," *Chicago Defender*, September 15, 1973.

46 "Mrs. Ware Will Never Surrender." Estimate of the number of newspapers that reported on Ware's case based on search in https://www.newspapers.com.

47 William Juneau, "2 in Ware Case Sue Walker for Slander, Libel," *Chicago Tribune*, June 18, 1974. In response to Walker's press conference, Blair and Gray filed a $6 million lawsuit against the governor over his "false, defamatory and libelous" public comments, one that was ultimately tossed when the state supreme court ruled that the public statements of a sitting governor were protected under free speech.

48 "Taxpayers Face License Loss," *Chicago Defender*, October 23, 1974; "Complaint Filed against Tax Buyer and His Lawyer," *Chicago Tribune*, June 13, 1974.

49 "Mrs. Ware Will Never Surrender"; "Mrs. Ware Buys Back Home," *Chicago Tribune*, July 12, 1974.

50 Robert McClory, "Lose $30,000 Home: $30,000 Home Lost in Tax Trap," *Chicago Defender*, April 27, 1976; Illinois-Legislative Investigating Commission, *Delinquent Tax Sales*, 20–21; "People of the State of Illinois Ex Rel Warren Hardie and Mattie Hardie, His Wife, Petitioners, vs. Stanley T. Kusper, Jr., County Clerk, Cook County, Illinois, Respondent. Suggestions in Support of Motion for Leave to File Petition for Writ of Mandamus," December 8, 1976, box 1, folder 2, Marshall Patner Collection, University of Illinois at Chicago Special Collections.

51 McClory, "Lose $30,000 Home: $30,000 Home Lost in Tax Trap"; Illinois-Legislative Investigating Commission, *Delinquent Tax Sales*, 22.

52 Robert McClory, "Defy Tax Trap Eviction: Defy Eviction in Tax Trap 'Steal,'" *Chicago Defender*, April 29, 1976; Basil Talbott Jr., "Tax Dispute May Cost Man His Home," *Chicago Sun-Times*, May 1, 1976, box 1, folder 2, Marshall Patner Collection, University of Illinois at Chicago Special Collections.

53 Talbott, "Tax Dispute May Cost Man His Home"; Robert McClory, "Move to

Outlaw Tax Grabs: Ask Daley, Dunne Fight Tax Grabs," *Chicago Defender*, May 5, 1976; Jan Faller, "Seek Fair Deal for Evicted Westsider, 72," *Chicago Defender*, June 26, 1976; "Evict Man, 72, in Tax Case: Evict Man, 72, in New Tax Seizure," *Chicago Defender*, June 23, 1976.

54 David Young, "Tax Buyer Wants New Image," *Chicago Tribune*, June 10, 1974.

55 Illinois-Legislative Investigating Commission, *Delinquent Tax Sales*, 44.

56 Robert W. Lake, *Real Estate Tax Delinquency: Private Disinvestment and Public Response* (New Brunswick, NJ: Center for Urban Policy Research, 1979); Susan Olson and M. Leanne Lachman, *Tax Delinquency in the Inner City: The Problem and Its Possible Solutions* (Lexington, MA: Lexington Books, 1976); Lawlor, "Real Property Tax Delinquency"; George Sternlieb and Robert W. Lake, "The Dynamics of Real Estate Tax Delinquency," *National Tax Journal* 29, (September 1976): 261–71.

57 "Arson Report Links Tax Debtors to Fires, Raps Hub Title Office," *Boston Globe*, July 27, 1985; Jeff Lyon, "Notorious Landlord," *Chicago Tribune*, November 10, 1996, http://articles.chicagotribune.com. On arson as an instrument of profit in urban housing markets in the 1970s, see Bench Ansfield, "The Crisis of Insurance and the Insuring of the Crisis: Riot Reinsurance and Redlining in the Aftermath of the 1960s Uprising," *Journal of American History* 107 (March 2021): 899–921; Bench Ansfield, "Born in Flames: Arson, Racial Capitalism, and the Reinsuring of the Bronx in the Late Twentieth Century" (PhD diss., Yale University, 2021), ProQuest dissertation no. 28322008; Daniel Kerr, "Who Burned Cleveland, Ohio? The Forgotten Fires of the 1970s," in *Flammable Cities: Urban Conflagrations and the Making of the Modern World*, ed. Greg Bankoff, Uwe Lübken, and Jordan Sand (Madison: University of Wisconsin Press, 2012), 332–52.

58 Lake, *Real Estate Tax Delinquency*, 13. See also Destin Jenkins, *The Bonds of Inequality: Debt and the Making of the American City* (Chicago: University of Chicago Press, 2021).

59 Illinois-Legislative Investigating Commission, *Delinquent Tax Sales*, 51.

60 Illinois-Legislative Investigating Commission, *Delinquent Tax Sales*, vi, 51.

61 Illinois-Legislative Investigating Commission, *Delinquent Tax Sales*, 54–58.

62 Andrew Patner, interview by Andrew Kahrl, Chicago, IL, February 21, 2014; "Chicago Lawyer Killed in Wisconsin Plane Crash," *Chicago Tribune*, January 28, 1979.

63 David R. Gray, "Remembering Mr. Blair," *Chicago Tribune*, February 7, 1979.

64 "Court Urged to Apply Reform Law," *Daytona Beach News-Journal*, November 26, 1980; "Speculator Fights for Old Couple's Home," *Norwalk Hour*, November 26, 1980.

65 "A House Lost for $92.07," *New York Newsday*, June 29, 1986; "The Young Champions of Annie Kennedy," *New York Newsday*, November 30, 1986; "The Plate Is Passed: Congregants at 108 Black Churches Contribute so Annie Kennedy Can Get Her House Back," *New York Newsday*, December 22, 1986; "End the Tax Speculators' Feast in Nassau," *New York Newsday*, September 30, 1986.

66 "No More: County Changes System That Victimized Homeowners Who Owed Property Taxes," *New York Newsday*, November 18, 1986; "Nassau County Ends Home Tax-Lien System," *New York Times*, November 24, 1986.

67 "Scavenger Sale Might Be Sure Bet," *Chicago Tribune*, August 30, 1987; Maria Pappas, *How Wealthy Investors Are Making Millions Exploiting Illinois' Property Tax Law: Their Profits Come at the Expense of Black and Latino Communities* (Chicago: Cook County Treasurer's Office, October 2022), 7.

68   Chinta Strausberg, "Steele Seeks Fed Probe of Tax 'Scam' on Black Churches," *Chicago Defender*, July 14, 1997; "State Cuts Red Tape to Assist Churches," *Chicago Tribune*, October 28, 2001; Chinta Strausberg, "Tax Attack on Area Churches? Clergyman Says African Americans Are Victims of Back-Tax Buy-outs," *Chicago Defender*, June 26, 1997; Chinta Strausberg, "Shaw Asks Devine to Probe Black Church Tax Sale Scam," *Chicago Defender*, May 3, 1999; Chinta Strausberg, "Alderman to Help Churches in Income Tax Bind: Smith Seeks to Aid Ministers Fighting Scavenger Sales," *Chicago Defender*, July 19, 1997; Sarah Karp, "Some Landlords Called into the Court-Again and Again," *Chicago Reporter*, September 17, 2007, http://www.chicagoreporter.com/some-landlords-called-court-again-and-again/.

CHAPTER THIRTEEN

1   "'Fresh Air' Remembers 'Boyz N The Hood' Director John Singleton," *Fresh Air*, May 3, 2019, https://www.npr.org/2019/05/03/719986809/fresh-air-remembers-boyz-n-the-hood-director-john-singleton.

2   "Parks Panel Studies Ways to Raise Money," *Los Angeles Times*, October 26, 1981; "City Department Heads Plead Cases," *Los Angeles Times*, June 10, 1978.

3   "'Fresh Air' Remembers 'Boyz N The Hood' Director John Singleton." See also Robin D. G. Kelley, *Race Rebels: Culture, Politics, and the Black Working Class* (New York: Free Press, 1994), 183–228.

4   David Johnston, "The Dead Parks: Insufficient Funding, Drugs and Violence Drive Many Away from City Recreation Areas," *Los Angeles Times*, September 3, 1987.

5   Josh Mound, "Stirrings of Revolt: Regressive Levies, the Pocketbook Squeeze, and the 1960s Roots of the 1970s Tax Revolt," *Journal of Policy History* 32 (2020): 105–50; David O. Sears and Jack Citrin, *Tax Revolt: Something for Nothing in California* (Cambridge, MA: Harvard University Press, 1982).

6   Isaac William Martin and Kevin Beck, "Property Tax Limitation and Racial Inequality in Effective Tax Rates," *Critical Sociology* 43, no. 2 (2017): 221–36; Shayak Sarkar and Josh Rosenthal, "Exclusionary Taxation," *Harvard Civil Rights and Civil Liberties Law Review* 53 (2018): 619–80.

7   Hellerstein v. Assessor of Islip, 37 N.Y. 2d 1 (N.Y. 1975).

8   Sarkar and Rosenthal, "Exclusionary Taxation." 663.

9   "Property Taxes: The Unbalanced Burden," *New York Newsday*, May 12, 1985.

10   "Fear of Reassessment Disaster Prompts Tolerance of Inequity," *New York Newsday*, May 17, 1985.

11   "Critics Say Little-Known State Cap, over Time, Will Aid Wealthy," *New York Newsday*, December 6, 2002.

12   Bethany P. Paquin, *Chronicle of the 161-Year History of State-Imposed Property Tax Limitations* (Cambridge, MA: Lincoln Institute of Land Policy, April 2015), 21–22.

13   Center for Urban Policy and the Environment, Indiana University, *Tax and Expenditure Limits on Local Governments* (Washington, DC: Advisory Commission on Intergovernmental Relations, March 1995), iii.

14   Bernadette Atuahene, "Predatory Cities," *California Law Review* 108, no. 1 (2020): 136–37.

15   US Commission on Civil Rights, *Targeted Fines and Fees Against Low-Income*

Communities of Color: Civil Rights and Constitutional Implications (Washington, DC: US Commission on Civil Rights, 2017), 9.

16 TEL-induced funding reductions have been linked to increases in student-teacher ratios, decreases in teacher salaries, and reductions in average teacher tenures. See Bing Yuan, Joseph Cordes, David Brunori, and Michael E. Bell, "Tax and Expenditure Limitations and Local Public Finances," in *Erosion of the Property Tax Base*, eds. Nancy Y. Augustine, Michael E. Bell, David Brunori, and Joan M. Youngman (Cambridge, MA: Lincoln Institute of Land Policy, 2009), 162–67. See, in general, Mark Haveman and Terri A. Sexton, *Property Tax Assessment Limits: Lessons from Thirty Years of Experience* (Cambridge, MA: Lincoln Institute of Land Policy, 2008), https://www.lincolninst.edu/publications/policy-focus-reports/property-tax-assessment-limits.

17 Destin Jenkins, *The Bonds of Inequality: Debt and the Making of the American City* (Chicago: University of Chicago Press, 2021), 200–16.

18 Josiah Rector, *Toxic Debt: An Environmental Justice History of Detroit* (Chapel Hill: University of North Carolina Press, 2022), 142; Ester R. Fuchs, *Mayors and Money: Fiscal Policy in New York and Chicago* (Chicago: University of Chicago Press, 1992), 211; G. Ross Stephens, "New Federalism by Default, Little OPEC States, and Fiscal Darwinism," in *Public Policy Across States and Communities*, ed. Dennis R. Judd (Greenwich, CT: Jai Press, 1985), 49; Timothy Conlan, *From New Federalism to Devolution: Twenty-Five Years of Intergovernmental Reform* (Washington, DC: Brookings Institution Press, 1998), 147.

19 Robin D. G. Kelley, "Neo-Cons of the Black Nation," *Black Renaissance*, October 31, 1997; R. C. Longworth, "City's Needs Grow while Tax Sources Dwindle," *Chicago Tribune*, May 12, 1981; Thomas J. Sugrue, *Sweet Land of Liberty: The Forgotten Struggle for Civil Rights in the North* (New York: Random House, 2008), 523–24.

20 Harold Washington, "Position Paper: Taxes and Budget," January 3, 1983, box 43, folder 13, Harold Washington Archives and Collections, Mayoral Campaign Records, Chicago Public Library Special Collections and Preservation Division.

21 George E. Peterson and Carol W. Lewis, *Reagan and the Cities* (Washington, DC: Urban Institute Press, 1986), 231.

22 See Gary Rivlin, *Fire on the Prairie: Chicago's Harold Washington and the Politics of Race* (New York: Henry Holt, 1992); Roger Biles, *Mayor Harold Washington: Champion of Race and Reform in Chicago* (Urbana: University of Illinois Press, 2018).

23 Pierre Clavel and Wim Wiewel, eds., *Harold Washington and the Neighborhoods: Progressive City Government in Chicago, 1983–1987* (New Brunswick, NJ: Rutgers University Press, 1991), 19; Longworth, "City's Needs Grow while Tax Sources Dwindle." On the changing political and economic landscape that urban Black regimes navigated in the 1980s, and their contested embrace of neoliberal approaches to addressing urban inequality, see Danielle Wiggins, "'Save Auburn Avenue for Our Black Heritage': Debating Development in Post–Civil Rights Atlanta," *Journal of African American History* 107, no. 1 (2022): 79–104; Adolph L. Reed Jr., "The Black Urban Regime: Structural Origins and Constraints," in Reed, *Stirrings in the Jug: Black Politics in the Post-Segregation Era* (Minneapolis: University of Minnesota Press, 1999), 79–116. See also Lester K. Spence, *Knocking the Hustle: Against the Neoliberal Turn in Black Politics* (Brooklyn, NY: Punctum

Books, 2015); Michael C. Dawson and Megan Ming Francis, "Black Politics and the Neoliberal Racial Order," *Public Culture* 28, no. 1 (2016): 23–62.

24   Dennis R. Judd, "Electoral Coalitions, Minority Mayors, and the Contradictions in the Municipal Policy Arena," in *Cities in Stress: A New Look at the Urban Crisis*, ed. Mark Gottdiener (Beverly Hills, CA: Sage, 1986), 147.

25   Larry Bennett, "Harold Washington and the Black Urban Regime," *Urban Affairs Quarterly* 28 (March 1993): 423–40.

26   Andrew J. Diamond, *Chicago on the Make: Power and Inequality in a Modern City* (Oakland: University of California Press, 2017), 147–48.

27   Arthur Lyons, "The Urban Property Tax and Minorities," in *Housing: Chicago Style—A Consultation Sponsored by the Illinois Advisory Committee to the United States Commission on Civil Rights*, ed. United States Commission on Civil Rights, Illinois Advisory Commission (Washington, DC: US Commission on Civil Rights, 1982), 76; Arthur Lyons and Charles J. Orlebeke, *Chicago Area Public Finances, 1970–1990: Trends and Prospects* (Chicago: Metropolitan Housing and Planning Council of Chicago, October 1981), 22.

28   "Walker Enacts Tax, Wage Bills as Term Ends," *Chicago Tribune*, January 11, 1977.

29   Reed Jr., "Black Urban Regime," 102. A 1981 study by the Council of State Planning Agencies found that only 3.3 percent of the companies it surveyed said that taxes affected location decisions. See John Curley, "Tax Breaks Aims at Luring Firms Increasingly Attacked as a Giveaway," *Wall Street Journal*, November 2, 1981; Michael Peter Smith, Randy L. Ready, and Dennis R. Judd, "Capital Flight, Tax Incentives and the Marginalization of American States and Localities," in *Public Policy across States and Communities*, ed. Judd, 190–91.

30   Smith, Ready, and Judd, "Capital Flight," 185–86.

31   Smith, Ready, and Judd, "Capital Flight," 194.

32   "Reagan Cuts Blasted at Chicago Meet," *Daily World*, February 14, 1986; Bill Barnhart, "Chicago's Stock Rises on Wall St.," *Chicago Tribune*, August 25, 1985.

33   Bennett, "Harold Washington and the Black Urban Regime."

34   Reed Jr., "Black Urban Regime."

35   Judd, "Electoral Coalitions," 146.

36   Donal Malone, "Neoliberal Governance and Uneven Development in Jersey City," *Theory in Action* 10 (January 2017): 36.

37   Malone, "Neoliberal Governance," 36–37.

38   State laws governing how often—and how thoroughly—local governments were required to conduct reassessments varied considerably, from annual reassessments (eight states) to six-to-ten-year cycles (four states) to no requirements for updating assessment rolls at all (seven states).

39   "Three N.J. Localities Face Property Tax Revaluation," *Dow Jones Institutional News*, April 4, 2016; Terrence T. McDonald, "Fulop, Jersey City Pastor Spar over Revaluation," *Jersey Journal*, April 12, 2016.

40   Bruce Bartlett, *Reagan's Tax Revolution: Ending the Free Ride for State and Local Taxes* (Washington, DC: Heritage Foundation, June 14, 1985), https://www.heritage.org/taxes/report/reagans-tax-revolution-ending-the-free-ride-state-and-local-taxes.

41 Peter J. Ferrara, *Tax Reform's Next Step: End State and Local Tax Deductions and Boost the Personal Exemption* (Washington, DC: Heritage Foundation, February 5, 1988), https://www.heritage.org/taxes/report/tax-reforms-next-step-end-state-and-local-tax-deductions-andboost-the-personal.

42 Jacob Javits, "The Treasury's Trojan Horse," *New York Times*, May 14, 1985.

43 William W. Ellis and Darlene Colbert, *Blacks and Tax Reform, 1985-1986: An Assessment of Possible Impacts on Blacks of Selected Proposals by the President and Provisions of the Tax Reform Act of 1985 (H.R. 3838)* (Washington, DC: Congressional Research Service, May 3, 1986), 24, 26.

44 Alicia Parlapiano and K. K. Rebecca Lai, "Among the Tax Bill's Biggest Losers: High-Income, Blue State Taxpayers," *New York Times*, December 5, 2017.

45 Esther Cyna, "Shortchanged: Racism, School Finance and Educational Inequality in North Carolina, 1964-1997" (PhD diss., Columbia University, 2021), ProQuest dissertation no. 28414738, 4.

46 Bruce D. Baker and Sean P. Corcoran, *The Stealth Inequities of School Funding: How State and Local School Finance Systems Perpetuate Inequitable Student Spending* (Washington, DC: Center for American Progress, September 2012); Sheryll Cashin, *White Space, Black Hood: Opportunity Hoarding and Segregation in the Age of Inequality* (Boston, MA: Beacon Press, 2021), 127-44; James E. Ryan, *Five Miles Away, A World Apart: One City, Two Schools, and the Story of Educational Opportunity in Modern America* (New York: Oxford University Press, 2010).

CHAPTER FOURTEEN

1 *60 Minutes*, "The New Plantations," aired March 31, 1991, on CBS, https://www.imdb.com/title/tt12885860/.

2 Gayle Krotkin to Tia [no last name], 1989, folder Daufuskie: Property Taxes, box 31, Southern Justice Institute Records, Southern Historical Collection, University of North Carolina, Chapel Hill.

3 Samuel Stein, *Capital City: Gentrification and the Real Estate State* (New York: Verso, 2019).

4 Isaac William Martin and Kevin Beck show that the relationship between property taxes and gentrification defies easy explanations. Their research—which finds no clear evidence that property taxes lead to displacement in gentrifying housing markets—has offered an important corrective to prevailing assumptions that property taxes fuel gentrification by taxing longtime residents out of their homes. See Isaac William Martin and Kevin Beck, "Property Tax Limitation and Racial Inequality in Effective Tax Rates," *Critical Sociology* 43, no. 2 (2017): 221-36; Isaac William Martin and Kevin Beck, "Gentrification, Property Tax Limitation, and Displacement," *Urban Affairs Review* 54, no. 1 (2018): 33-73. Focusing on gentrifying markets in states with assessment caps and phase-ins, Andrew Hayashi argues that property tax systems can act as subsidies to owners of property in areas undergoing gentrification. See Andrew Hayashi, "Dynamic Property Taxes and Racial Gentrification," *Notre Dame Law Review* 96, no. 4 (2021): 1517-38. By treating gentrification as strictly a market dynamic and not also as a set of governing rationales and priorities, these studies tend to overlook the other features of local tax systems under neoliberalism that fuel gentrification and its upward redistributional effects, and they do not account for the discretionary powers that local tax administrators enjoy or the political economy they operate within. In contrast, see Dan Immergluck, *Red Hot City: Housing, Race, and Exclusion in the Twenty-First Century* (Oakland: University of California Press, 2022); Cameron Hightower and James C. Fraser, "The Raced-Space of Gentrification: 'Reverse Blockbusting,' Home Selling, and Neighborhood Remake in North Nashville," *City and Community* 19, no. 1 (2020): 223-44.

5 On the political economy of rural and urban real property ownership and the need for more comparative analysis that bridges the artificial divide between rural land and urban housing in the literature, see Levi Van Sant, Taylor Shelton, and Kelly Kay, "Connecting Country and City: The Multiple Geographies of Real Property Ownership in the US," *Geography Compass* 17, no. 2 (February 2023) 1-15, https://doi.org/10.1111/gec3.12677.

6 On the use of direct taxes as a mechanism for imposing market-based relations on indigenous populations and putting new commodities (such as land) into circulation, see Mathew Forstater, "Taxation and Primitive Accumulation: The Case of Colonial Africa," *Research in Political Economy*, 22 (2005), 51-65; Leigh Gardner, *Taxing Colonial Africa: The Political Economy of British Imperialism* (New York: Oxford University Press, 2012); and Steven Stoll, *Ramp Hollow: The Ordeal of Appalachia* (New York: Hill and Wang, 2017), 90-126.

7 "Daufuskie Island: Barrier Islanders Fear They Cannot Block Progress," *Atlanta Constitution*, August 1, 1982.

8 James Ceruti, "Sea Islands: Adventuring along the South's Surprising Coast," *National Geographic* (March 1971), 366-93; "An Island Time Has Forgotten," *Washington Post*, December 25, 1978; Jeanne Moutoussamy-Ashe, *Daufuskie Island: A Photographic Essay* (Columbia: University of South Carolina Press, 1982); Sabra Conway Slaughter, "'The Old Ones Die and the Young Ones Leaving': The Effects of Modernization on the Community of Daufuskie Island, South Carolina" (PhD diss., University of Michigan, 1985), ProQuest dissertation no. 8600554; Joyce Hollyday, "A Plague in Paradise: Development Endangers a Way of Life on South Carolina's Daufuskie," *Sojourners* 21 (August 1992): 12-18.

9 Skip Rozin, "Daufuskie Island: The Next Hilton Head?" *Historic Preservation* (March-April 1983): 20-25; "Daufuskie Island: Barrier Islanders Fear They Cannot Block Progress," *Atlanta Constitution*, August 1, 1982; "The Rise of the Low Country," *New York Times*, June 1, 1986; "An Unspoiled Oasis Braces for Resort," *Philadelphia Inquirer*, April 9, 1985.

10 Hollyday, "A Plague in Paradise," 12-18.

11 Henrietta Canty to unnamed filmmaker, "The Real Daufuskie Island," unpublished letter draft, 1989, box 31, folder Daufuskie: History and General Articles, Southern Justice Institute Records, Southern Historical Collection, University of North Carolina, Chapel Hill.

12 "South Carolina African-American Community Threatened by Developers," *Pittsburgh Courier*, December 5, 1992; Holly Morris, "An Island's Double Standard: Black Landowners of Daufuskie, S.C., Fight to Hold On against Inequitable Taxes," *Atlanta Journal and Constitution*, June 3, 1990; "Opinion Spilt on '60 Minutes' Story about S.C.," *Philadelphia Tribune*, April 12, 1991.

13 Canty, "Real Daufuskie Island"; Henrietta Canty, "History of Daufuskie Island in the Area of Human Relations," 1989, box 31, folder Daufuskie: History and General Articles, Southern Justice Institute Records, Southern Historical Collection; Henrietta Canty, "Property Assessments Exorbitant, Absurd," *Island Packet*, November 25, 1988.

14   Morris, "Island's Double Standard."

15   "Developers Sued for Desecrating Black Cemetery," *Christic Institute South: The People's Advocate* (September–October 1990); Morris, "Island's Double Standard"; Gayle Korotkin to Kathy C. Fisher, February 28, 1990, box 31, folder Correspondence, Southern Justice Institute Records; John P. Smith, "Cultural Preservation of the Sea Island Gullahs: A Black Social Movement in the Post-Civil Rights Era," *Rural Sociology* 56 (Summer 1991): 284–98.

16   "Rising Property Tax Taking Toll on S.C. Island Slave Descendants," *Wilmington Star-News*, August 14, 1990; Morris, "Island's Double Standard."

17   W. A. Caton Jr., "A Fight between Old and New, Rich and Poor," *Savannah Morning News*, October 28, 1990, box 28, folder [unnamed], Southern Justice Institute Records, Southern Historical Collection; Nelson B. Rivers III, *Monthly Report, Charleston Branch of the NAACP* (Charleston, SC: NAACP, December 8, 1990), box 2, folder 14, Charleston Branch of the NAACP, Avery Research Center for African American History and Culture; Joyce Hollyday, "A Plague in Paradise: Development Endangers a Way of Life on South Carolina's Daufuskie," *Sojourners* 21 (August 1992): 12–18; Jeffrey Gettleman, "Fighting against the Tide," *St. Louis Post-Dispatch*, January 10, 2002; Roger Pinckney, "Burying Miss Louise: Transcendence and Regeneration in the Rural South," *Orion*, 2004; Yvonne Wilson, interview by Andrew Kahrl, Daufuskie Island, SC, April 1, 2019.

18   Lewis Pitts to "Dear friends," November 13, 1990, box 28, folder [unnamed], Southern Justice Institute Records.

19   "Developers Sued for Desecrating Black Cemetery," *People's Advocate*, October 1990; "Daufuskie Wins Allies," *People's Advocate*, June 1990, box 28, folder Correspondence, Southern Justice Institute Records.

20   Alan Jenkins, telephone interview by Andrew Kahrl, September 8, 2014.

21   Sonya Ross, "South Carolina African-American Community Threatened by Developers," *Pittsburgh Courier*, December 5, 1992; John C. Williams, "NAACP, Beaufort Officials to Debate Daufuskie Charges," *Savannah Morning News*, December 1, 1992; Nelson B. Rivers III, *Annual Report of Nelson B. Rivers, III, Executive Director of the South Carolina Conference of Branches of the NAACP* (Charleston, SC: NAACP, October 9, 1993), box 2, folder 15, Charleston Branch of the NAACP, Avery Research Center for African American History and Culture.

22   See also Russ Bynum, "Slave Descendants on Sapelo Island Stunned by Property Tax Increase," *Augusta Chronicle*, January 29, 2013, https://www.augustachronicle.com/story/news/2013/01/30/slave-descendants-sapelo-island-stunned-property-tax-increase/14466710007/; R. Robin McDonald, "Sapelo's Historic Former Slave Community Sues State, Claiming Discrimination," *Daily Report*, December 9, 2015, http://www.dailyreportonline.com/id=1202744428733/Sapelos-Historic-Former-Slave-Community-Sues-State-Claiming-Discrimination?slreturn=20151110192013.

23   Trace Gibson, "Poor Tenants Are the Real Losers," *Philadelphia Tribune*, January 15, 1980. See also Trace Gibson, "Land Developers Find the Elderly Easy Prey," *Philadelphia Tribune*, January 18, 1980.

24   Gerald Horne, "Whither Black Political Power," *Pittsburgh Courier*, March 21, 1981.

25   Arthur Lyons and Jason Hardy, Center for Economic Policy Analysis, and Chicago Rehab Network, "Solving the Right Problems: Making the Property Tax Fair for Everyone" (Chicago: Chicago Rehab Network, August 1999), 27.

26 By 1974, all states had adopted measures offering some form of property tax relief for elderly homeowners. United States Advisory Commission on Intergovernmental Relations, "The Property Tax in a Changing Environment," Selected State Studies: An Information Report (Washington: US Government Printing Office, 1974), 2–3.

27 Mark Haveman and Terri A. Sexton, *Property Tax Assessment Limits: Lessons from Thirty Years of Experience* (Cambridge, MA: Lincoln Institute of Land Policy, 2008), 11, https://www.lincolninst.edu/publications/policy-focus-reports/property-tax-assessment-limits.

28 For an overview of state homestead exemption and circuit breaker programs, see David Baer, *State Programs and Practices for Reducing Residential Property Taxes* (Washington, DC: AARP Public Policy Institute, 2003); John H. Bowman, Daphne A. Kenyon, Adam Langley, and Bethany P. Paquin, *Property Tax Circuit Breakers: Fair and Cost-Effective Relief for Taxpayers* (New York: Columbia University Press, 2009).

29 "Grassroots Group Sets Property Tax Revolt," *Chicago Defender*, January 13, 2004; Haveman and Sexton, *Property Tax Assessment Limits*, 15.

30 Karen Lyons, Sarah Farkas, and Nicholas Johnson, *The Property Tax Circuit Breaker: An Introduction and Survey of Current Programs* (Washington, DC: Center on Budget and Policy Priorities, March 21, 2007), https://www.cbpp.org/sites/default/files/archive/3-21-07sfp.pdf; Haveman and Sexton, *Property Tax Assessment Limits*, 33–34.

31 Andrew Hayashi, "Property Taxes and Their Limits: Evidence from New York City," *Stanford Law and Policy Review* 25 (2014): 33–52.

32 David Baer, "Awareness and Popularity of Property Tax Relief Programs," *Assessment Journal* 5 (July–August 1998): 47.

33 Haveman and Sexton, *Property Tax Assessment Limits*, 35.

34 Alexa Eisenberg, Roshanak Mehdipanah, and Margaret Dewar, "'It's Like They Make It Difficult for You on Purpose': Barriers to Property Tax Relief and Foreclosure Prevention in Detroit, Michigan," *Housing Studies* 35, no. 8 (2020): 1415–41.

35 Eisenberg, Mehdipanah, and Dewar, "'It's Like They Make It Difficult,'" 1420.

36 Eisenberg, Mehdipanah, and Dewar, "'It's Like They Make It Difficult,'" 1427.

37 Bernadette Atuahene, "Predatory Cities," *California Law Review* 108, no. 1 (2020): 125–26, 136–37, 150, 149, 138–39.

38 Timothy R. Hodge, Mark Skidmore, Gary Sands, and Daniel McMillen, "Assessment Inequity in a Declining Housing Market: The Case of Detroit," *Real Estate Economics* 45, no. 2 (June 2017): 237, 254.

39 "Detroit Homeowners Overtaxed $600 Million," *Detroit News*, January 9, 2020; Nancy Kaffer, "Wayne County Tax Auction: Why the Treasurer Should Stop Holding It," *Detroit Free Press*, August 26, 2018, https://www.freep.com/story/opinion/columnists/nancy-kaffer/2018/08/26/wayne-county-tax-foreclosure-auction-detroit/1066345002/; Bernadette Atuahene, "Compensate Detroiters Who Illegally Lost Their Homes," *Detroit News*, June 13, 2018.

40 Between 2014 and 2017, Jersey City's poorest wards paid $143 million more in property taxes than they should have had the update been completed (with the average homeowner in the city's poorest neighborhoods paying $9,176 in excess taxes over this time period), while commercial property owners and downtown homeowners saved another $143 million. Aaron Morrill, "How the Mayor Stuck

Wards A, B, C and D With $143 Million In Taxes," *Jersey City Times*, October 19, 2021.

41 Center for Economic Policy Analysis, *Property Tax Assessments in Jersey City: An Analysis of Impact* (Chicago: Center for Economic Policy Analysis, 2016).

42 Tom Moran, "In Jersey City, Poor Blacks Subsidize Rich Whites," *Jersey Journal*, April 17, 2016.

43 Real Garden State, "Rev. Alonzo Perry Sr. and Mayor Steven Fulop Debate Reval at Jersey City Together," April 11, 2016, YouTube video, 13:51, https://www .youtube.com/watch?v=XR1f2qS6zvA; Terrence T. McDonald, "Fulop, Jersey City Pastor Spar over Revaluation," *Jersey Journal*, April 12, 2016.

44 McDonald, "Fulop, Jersey City Pastor Spar over Revaluation."

45 "Jersey City Divided as New Tax Assessments Finally Roll Out," *NJ.Com*, February 13, 2018.

46 Robert P. Strauss, "Restoring the Public Trust in Allegheny County's Real Estate Assessments" (speech, annual dinner of the League of Women Voters of Greater Pittsburgh, Pittsburgh, PA, May 15, 2002), 12.

47 Lee Harris, "'Assessing' Discrimination: The Influence of Race in Residential Property Tax Assessments," *Journal of Land Use and Environmental Law* 20, no. 1 (2004): 15–16.

48 Robert P. Strauss and David A. Strauss, "Residential Real Estate Assessment Fairness in Four Urban Areas," *National Tax Association Proceedings* 96 (2003): 303.

49 Jason Grotto, "An Unfair Burden: Cook County Failed to Value Homes Accurately for Years. The Result: A Property Tax System That Harmed the Poor and Helped the Rich," *Chicago Tribune*, June 7, 2017.

50 Jason Grotto, "The Problem with Appeals: Assessor Joseph Berrios Encourages Homeowners to File Appeals. But the Process Makes the Property Tax System Even Less Fair," *Chicago Tribune*, June 8, 2017.

51 "Investigation: Madigan Firm the Biggest Player in Commercial Property Tax Appeals," *Illinois Policy*, December 8, 2017.

52 Grotto, "Problem with Appeals."

53 Bernadette Atuahene and Christopher Berry, "Taxed Out: Illegal Property Tax Assessments and the Epidemic of Tax Foreclosures in Detroit," *UC Irvine Law Review* 9, no. 4 (May 2019), https://scholarship.law.uci.edu/ucilr/vol9/iss4/3/.

54 Grotto, "Problem with Appeals."

55 "Cook County Assessor Berrios Implements New State of the Art Residential Assessment Models," *News Release*, July 9, 2015.

56 Curtis Black, "What It'll Take to Root Out Discriminatory Property Taxes in Cook County," *Chicago Reporter*, August 3, 2017.

57 David Roeder, "Reform-Minded Assessor Tackles Chicago Valuations and Clout," *Chicago Sun-Times*, July 12, 2021.

58 Christine MacDonald, "ACLU, NAACP Sue to Stop Wayne County Tax Auction," *Detroit News*, July 13, 2016, http://www.detroitnews.com/story/news/ local/wayne-county/2016/07/13/aclu-naacp-sue-wayne-county-tax-auction/ 87027282/; "ACLU, NAACP Ask State High Court to Look at Tax Auction," *Detroit Informer*, November 1, 2017.

59 Bernadette Atuahene, "Detroit's Tax Foreclosures Indefensible," *Detroit Free Press*, September 1, 2016, http://www.freep.com/story/opinion/contributors/ 2016/09/01/detroits-tax-foreclosures-indefensible/89717644/; Violet Ikonomova, "Study Finds Detroit's Foreclosure Crisis Fueled by Illegal Tax Assessments," *Detroit Metro Times*, July 12, 2017, https://www.metrotimes.com/detroit/could-detroits-tax-foreclosures-be-unconstitutional/Content?oid=4522278; Bernadette Atuahene, "Don't Let Detroit's Revival Rest on an Injustice," *New York Times*, July 22, 2017, https://www.nytimes.com/2017/07/22/opinion/sunday/dont-let-detroits-revival-rest-on-an-injustice.html?_r=0; Bernadette Atuahene, "Compensate Detroiters Who Illegally Lost Their Homes," *Detroit News*, June 13, 2018, https://www.detroitnews.com/story/opinion/2018/06/13/compensate-detroiters-who-illegally-lost-their-homes/695810002/; Ken Coleman, "Anti-Foreclosure Activists Demand More Help in Detroit," *Michigan Advance*, January 16, 2021, https://michiganadvance.com/2021/01/16/anti-foreclosure-activists-demand-more-help-in-detroit/.

60 For the legal argument that racially inequitable property assessments violate the Fair Housing Act's disparate impact liability, see Shayak Sarkar and Josh Rosenthal, "Exclusionary Taxation," *Harvard Civil Rights and Civil Liberties Law Review* 53 (2018): 619–80.

61 Robert F. Williams, "The Tax Injunction Act and Judicial Restraint: Property Tax Litigation in Federal Courts," *Rutgers Law Journal* 12 (Summer 1981): 653–95.

62 Sarkar and Rosenthal, "Exclusionary Taxation," 641.

63 Michael McCabe, "'Little Woman' Wins in Property Tax Case," *Chicago Tribune*, October 11, 1979; "'Little Person' Is Winner in Big Property Tax Case," *Chicago Tribune*, October 11, 1979; "Federal Injunctive Relief in State Tax Cases: LaSalle v. Rosewell," *Harvard Law Review* 93 (1980): 1016–27.

64 "Assessment System Penalizes Minorities, Feds Charge," *New York Newsday*, March 8, 1999; "Judge: State Case on Assessment Bias Takes Precedence," *New York Newsday*, January 12, 2000; "Nassau Tax Base: The People Were Heard," *New York Times*, April 2, 2000.

65 Atuahene, "Predatory Cities."

66 United States Department of Justice, Civil Rights Division, *Investigation of the Ferguson Police Department* (Washington, DC: Department of Justice, March 4, 2015), 11.

67 Colin Gordon, "Ferguson Revisited," *Dissent*, August 9, 2015.

68 A 2019 study on Governing.com found that in nearly six hundred jurisdictions in the US, fines account for over 10 percent of general revenues; they account for over 20 percent in 284 jurisdictions. Mike Maciag, "Addicted to Fines," *Governing.com*, August 19, 2019.

69 The authors of this study defined "Black suburbs" as those with at least a 15 percent Black population. Mark Schneider and John R. Logan, "Suburban Racial Segregation and Black Access to Local Public Resources," *Social Science Quarterly* 63, no. 4 (1982): 762, 766.

70 Diana Jean Schemo, "Suburban Taxes Are Higher for Blacks, Analysis Shows," *New York Times*, August 17, 1994.

71 C. S. Ponder, "Spatializing the Municipal Bond Market: Urban Resilience under Racial Capitalism," *Annals of the American Association of Geographers*, March 31, 2021, 1–18.

72 Nora E. Taplin-Kaguru, *Grasping for the American Dream: Racial Segregation, Social Mobility, and Homeownership* (New York: Routledge, 2021), 114.

73 Josh Pacewicz and John N. Robinson, "Pocketbook Policing: How Race Shapes

Municipal Reliance on Punitive Fines and Fees in the Chicago Suburbs," *Socio-Economic Review* 19, no. 3 (2021): 995.

74   Andre M. Perry, *Know Your Price: Valuing Black Lives and Property in America's Black Cities* (Washington, DC: Brookings Institution, 2020), 116.

75   Benedict S. Jimenez, "Separate, Unequal, and Ignored? Interjurisdictional Competition and the Budgetary Choices of Poor and Affluent Municipalities," *Public Administration Review* 74, no. 2 (2014): 251.

76   Sheryll Cashin, *The Failures of Integration: How Race and Class Are Undermining the American Dream* (New York: Public Affairs Press, 2004), 135.

77   Pacewicz and Robinson, "Pocketbook Policing," 977-80, 993.

78   Walter Johnson, "Ferguson's Fortune 500 Company," *Atlantic*, April 26, 2015.

79   Joe Soss and Joshua Page, "The Predator State: Race, Class and the New Era of Indentured Citizenship" (unpublished paper presented at the 2015-16 Neoliberalism Seminar at CUNY—Hunter College, New York, 2016), 9.

80   Mike Maciag, "Skyrocketing Court Fines Are Major Revenue Generator for Ferguson," *Governing*, August 22, 2014, http://www.governing.com/topics/public-justice-safety/gov-ferguson-missouri-court-fines-budget.html.

81   Pacewicz and Robinson, "Pocketbook Policing," 986.

82   "Skyrocketing Court Fines Are Major Revenue Generator for Ferguson."

83   Jodi Rios, *Black Lives and Spatial Matters: Policing Blackness and Practicing Freedom in Suburban St. Louis* (Ithaca, NY: Cornell University Press, 2020), 100.

84   "Skyrocketing Court Fines Are Major Revenue Generator for Ferguson."

85   Radley Balko, "How Municipalities in St. Louis County, Mo., Profit from Poverty," *Washington Post*, September 3, 2014, http://www.washingtonpost.com/news/the-watch/wp/2014/09/03/how-st-louis-county-missouri-profits-from-poverty/.

86   Keeanga-Yamahtta Taylor, *From #BlackLivesMatter to Black Liberation* (Chicago: Haymarket Books, 2016), 105; Pacewicz and Robinson, "Pocketbook Policing," 986.

87   Dan Kopf, "The Fining of Black America," *Priceonomics*, June 24, 2016; Rios, *Black Lives and Spatial Matters*, 82-110.

CHAPTER FIFTEEN

1   Brad Westover, "NTLA in Action" (presented at the annual meeting of the National Tax Lien Association, Fort Lauderdale, FL, February 25, 2016).

2   Works that tie tax-lien sales and privatization of tax enforcement to broader patterns and practices characteristic of neoliberal urbanism include Hilary Botein and C. Patrick Heidkamp, "Tax Lien Sales as Local Neoliberal Governance Strategy: The Case of Waterbury, Connecticut," *Local Economy* 28, no. 5 (2013): 488-98; and Irene Tung, "Financializing Urban Governance: Cities, Capital Markets and Property Tax Liens" (New Brunswick, NJ: Rutgers University, 2014). On histories of urban neoliberalism in the US, see Andrew J. Diamond, *Chicago on the Make: Power and Inequality in a Modern City* (Berkeley: University of California Press, 2017); Andrew J. Diamond and Thomas J. Sugrue, eds., *Neoliberal Cities: The Remaking of Postwar Urban America* (New York: New York University Press, 2019); and Benjamin Holtzman, *The Long Crisis: New York City and the Path to Neoliberalism* (New York: Oxford University Press, 2021).

3 "Tax Sale Auction Higher Than Last Year," *Chicago Metro News*, May 22, 1982; Jane Bryant Quinn, "Road to Tax-Lien Sales Paved with Risks as Well as Gold," *Washington Post*, March 17, 1986.

4 "How Firm Came to Rule Tax-Buying Kingdom with a Secret Strategy and Deep Pockets," *Chicago Tribune*, October 29, 1995; "Gentle Giant or Ruthless Investor?" *Business Florida*, May 1, 1996.

5 "How Firm Came to Rule Tax-Buying Kingdom"; "Gentle Giant or Ruthless Investor?"

6 "Skandalakis, Campbell and Watson Endorse Bulk Sale," *Atlanta Daily World*, June 26, 1994.

7 "Tax Lien Sale Plan Vote Delayed by Fulton County," *Atlanta Daily World*, August 21, 1994.

8 Frank S. Alexander, *Project Status Report* (Atlanta, GA: Land Bank Authority, July 25, 1994).

9 Alan S. Oser, "The New Approach on Tax-Delinquent Property," *New York Times*, March 3, 1996; Georgette C. Poindexter, LizabethAnn Rogovoy, and Susan Wachter, "Selling Municipal Property Tax Receivables: Economics, Privatization, and Public Policy in the Era of Urban Distress," *Connecticut Law Review* 30 (Fall 1997): 191–93; Amy B. Resnick, "Municipal Securitization: Governments' Desperation May Determine Future Use of Lien Securitizations," *Bond Buyer*, October 27, 1998. On Schundler, see Ruth Shalit, "Schundler's Lust," *New Republic*, May 9, 1994.

10 "Capital Asset Seeking to Continue Success with Lien Purchasing, Service," *Bond Buyer*, January 20, 1998.

11 Amy B. Resnick, "Selling Liens Gives Municipalities Alternatives to Tax Hikes," *Bond Buyer*, October 9, 1996.

12 "Service Considered to Collect Delinquent Tax," *Pittsburgh Post-Gazette*, January 21, 1998.

13 Poindexter, Rogovoy, and Wachter, "Selling Municipal Property Tax Receivables," 161.

14 Resnick, "Selling Liens Gives Municipalities Alternatives to Tax Hikes"; "How Firm Came to Rule Tax-Buying Kingdom"; Oser, "New Approach on Tax-Delinquent Property"; Steven Lee Myers, "Giuliani's Spending Plan Is Approved Nearly Intact," *New York Times*, March 7, 1996; Matt Pacenza, "The Lien Machine: The City's Private Tax Collectors Turn Landlords' Debts into Dollars—But Tenants Pay the Price," *City Limits: New York's Urban Affairs News Magazine*, November 30, 2001; Frank S. Alexander, "Tax Liens, Tax Sales, and Due Process," *Indiana Law Journal* 75 (2000): 762; Amy B. Resnick, "Governments Avoid Securitizations, Despite Projected Growth Potential," *Bond Buyer*, July 28, 1998.

15 Paul Hughes, "Florida Firm Buys Property Tax Liens," *Meriden* [CT] *Record-Journal*, July 1, 1995; "Politics, Race Hamper Fulton's Efforts High Stakes," *Atlanta Journal and Constitution*, June 15, 1997; Botein and Heidkamp, "Tax Lien Sales as Local Neoliberal Governance Strategy: The Case of Waterbury, Connecticut."

16 Resnick, "Governments Avoid Securitizations."

17 Deepak Karamcheti, "NAACP: Company Unfairly Targets Poor," *Pittsburgh Courier*, April 25, 1998; Christine Richard, "MBIA Debt Backed by Crack Houses Perpetuates Blight," *Bloomberg*, November 29, 2006.

18 John Kromer, *Vacant-Property Policy and Practice: Baltimore and Philadelphia*

(Washington, DC: Brookings Institution, Center on Urban and Metropolitan Policy, October 2002), 39.

19 "Tax Liens Put 100 Properties on Auction Block," *Greensburg* [PA] *Tribune-Review*, July 27, 1997, 100; Christine S. Richard, *Confidence Game: How a Hedge Fund Manager Called Wall Street's Bluff* (New York: John Wiley and Sons, Inc., 2010), 119.

20 Amy B. Resnick, "National Tax Lien Association Elects Officers," *Bond Buyer*, April 9, 1997.

21 In 1995, Georgia lawmakers increased interest penalties to 60 percent after thirteen months. In 1998, Ohio permitted counties with populations of over two hundred thousand to conduct bulk sales of tax liens. See Richard Whitt, "Investors Can Reap 60 Percent Profit on Tax Liens: Predatory 'a Very Kind Word' for State Law," *Atlanta Journal and Constitution*, April 1, 2002; Joshua J. Miller, "The Cost of Delinquent Property Tax Collection: Three Essays in Local Public Finance" (PhD diss., University of Illinois at Chicago, 2012), ProQuest dissertation no. 3552481, 72–76.

22 "E. Ky. Cheating Rest of State's Children: Lax Tax Collection Stiffs Citizens Who Pay Up, School Funding Deal," *McClatchy-Tribune Business News*, August 6, 2006.

23 "Companies Buy Late Tax Bills," *Louisville Courier-Journal*, May 11, 2005; "Tax Lien Sales Cloud City Control over Houses," *Louisville Courier-Journal*, June 19, 2011.

24 Fred Schulte and June Arney, "Probe Targets Tax-Lien Sales," *Baltimore Sun*, September 7, 2007, http://www.baltimoresun.com/business/real-estate/bal -taxsale-probe-090707-story.html.

25 Mark Belko, "Tax Liens Buyer Sued: Costs Called Improper," *Pittsburgh Post-Gazette*, April 4, 1998.

26 Jack Healy, "Tax Collectors Put Squeeze on Homeowners: Buying Up City Debts, Private Firms Are Quick to Foreclose to Make a Profit," *International Herald Tribune*, August 19, 2009; Charles D. Rittenhouse, "The True Costs of Not Paying Your Property Taxes in Ohio," *University of Dayton Law Review* 36, no. 2 (January 2011): 221–47.

27 "Tax Collection Cleanup: No-Nonsense Commissioner Brings Aggressive Tactics," *Atlanta Journal and Constitution*, April 3, 1997; "Pay Delinquent Property Taxes, Owners Warned," *Atlanta Daily World*, April 20, 1997.

28 Johnny Edwards, "Sale of Small Debts Stokes Criticism," *Atlanta Journal and Constitution*, March 6, 2013.

29 "Sale of Fulton Tax Liens Surprises Property Owners," *Atlanta Journal and Constitution*, October 24, 1996; "Tax-Sale Tales Pour in Mail: Fulton County Threatened to Sell or Placed Liens on Homes of More than a Dozen Who Had Paid Up," *Atlanta Journal and Constitution*, November 27, 2000.

30 "A Play on Tax Liens by Wall Street Types Blows Up in Their Face," *Wall Street Journal*, November 30, 2000.

31 Varsolona v. Breen Capital Services Corp., 180 N.J. 605 (N.J. 2004); "Play on Tax Liens by Wall Street Types Blows Up in Their Face."

32 *Varsolona*, 180 N.J.; Tito Pollice v. National Tax Funding, 225 F.3d 379 (3rd Cir. 2000).

33 "N.Y. Firm's Liens Are City's Blight," *Pittsburgh Tribune*, December 1, 2006.

34 "N.Y. Firm's Liens Are City's Blight."

35   Rev. Charles R. Davis Sr., "The Tax Lien Line," *Pittsburgh Post-Gazette*, August 29, 2006; Richard, "MBIA Debt Backed by Crack Houses Perpetuates Blight."

36   "Lien Sale Looked Good Then," *McClatchy-Tribune Business News*, December 1, 2006.

37   "Finder's Fee Used in Privatizing Tax Collections in Waterbury," *Meriden* [CT] *Record-Journal*, August 20, 2001; State of Connecticut Task Force to Study Municipal Tax Collection, *Final Report* (Connecticut General Assembly, January 1, 2001), https://doksi.net/hu/get.php?lid=32514; Botein and Heidkamp, "Tax Lien Sales as Local Neoliberal Governance Strategy," 496.

38   "City Council Gets Serious about Delinquent Taxpayers," *Philadelphia Tribune*, May 2, 1997; Dianna Marder, "Council to Rethink Its Proposal to Sell Real Estate Tax Liens," *Philadelphia Inquirer*, June 5, 1997.

39   Cynthia Burton, "City Aims Selectively at Its Tax Delinquents: Proponents Say Exemptions Stabilize Neighborhoods, Critics Say They Breed Cynicism," *Philadelphia Inquirer*, September 21, 1998.

40   Marder, "Council to Rethink Its Proposal to Sell Real Estate Tax Liens."

41   Burton, "City Aims Selectively at Its Tax Delinquents."

42   "As Predicted, Philadelphia Agency Defaults on $46M of Insured Tax- Lien Debt," *Bond Buyer*, July 27, 2004.

43   Fred Schulte and June Arney, "Small Unpaid Bills Put Residents at Risk," *Baltimore Sun*, March 25, 2007.

44   Schulte and Arney, "Probe Targets Tax-Lien Sales"; Fred Schulte and June Arney, "Guilty Plea in Tax Sale Rigging," *Baltimore Sun*, June 4, 2008; Fred Schulte, "Baltimore Lawyer Admits to Rigging Tax Sales," *Baltimore Sun*, March 4, 2011.

45   Schulte and Arney, "Small Unpaid Bills Put Residents at Risk"; "Tax-Lien Bid-Rigging Paid Off," *Baltimore Sun*, May 18, 2010.

46   "City Profits on Tax Lien Misery," *Baltimore Sun*, May 18, 2010.

47   Fred Schulte, Ben Protess, and Lagan Sebert, "The Other Foreclosure Menace: Mortgage Paid Off, Woman Loses Home—Over a Small Water Bill," *Center for Public Integrity*, May 18, 2010, http://www.publicintegrity.org/2010/05/18/7082/other-foreclosure-menace; Fred Schulte, Lagan Sebert, and Ben Protess, "Follow-Up: Baltimore Lawmakers Seek Overhaul of Tax Lien Sale," *Center for Public Integrity*, July 7, 2010, http://www.publicintegrity.org/2010/07/07/7092/follow-baltimore-lawmakers-seek-overhaul-tax-lien-sale; Fred Schulte and Ben Protess, "The New Tax Man: Big Banks and Hedge Funds," *Huffington Post*, October 18, 2010, http://www.huffingtonpost.com/2010/10/18/the-new-tax-man-big-banks_n_766169.html; Fred Schulte, "Wall Street Quietly Creates a New Way to Profit from Homeowner Distress," *Center for Public Integrity*, December 9, 2010, http://www.publicintegrity.org/2010/12/09/2263/wall-street-quietly-creates-new-way-profit-homeowner-distress.

48   Fern Shen, "In Baltimore, Water Rates Rose but Relief Measures Lagged, Study Finds," *BaltimoreBrew*, November 16, 2016, https://www.baltimorebrew.com/2016/11/16/in-baltimore-water-rates-rose-but-relief-measures-lagged-study-finds/; Joan Jacobson, *The Steep Price of Paying to Stay: Baltimore City's Tax Sale, the Risks to Vulnerable Homeowners, and Strategies to Improve the Process* (Baltimore, MD: Abell Foundation, October 2014), http://www.abell.org/sites/default/files/publications/ec-taxsale1014.pdf; Schulte, Protess, and Sebert, "Other Foreclosure Menace."

49 Schulte, Sebert, and Protess, "Follow-Up."

50 "City Profits on Tax Lien Misery."

51 Kathleen C. Engel and Patricia A. McCoy, "From Credit Denial to Predatory Lending: The Challenge of Sustaining Minority Homeownership," in *Segregation: The Rising Costs for America*, eds. James H. Carr and Nandinee K. Kutty (New York: Routledge, 2008), 81–123; Devin Fergus, "Financial Fracking in the Land of the Fee, 1980–2008," in *The Assets Perspective: The Rise of Asset Building and Its Impact on Social Policy*, eds. Reid Cramer and Trina R. Williams Shanks (New York: Palgrave Macmillan, 2014), 67–95; Kendra Strauss, "Accumulation and Dispossession: Lifting the Veil on the Subprime Mortgage Crisis," *Antipode* 41, no. 1 (2009): 10–14; Ruby Mendenhall, "The Political Economy of Black Housing: From the Housing Crisis of the Great Migrations to the Subprime Mortgage Crisis," *Black Scholar* 40, no. 1 (2010): 20–37.

52 Audrey G. McFarlane, "The Properties of Instability: Markets, Predation, Racialized Geography, and Property Law," *Wisconsin Law Review*, no. 5 (2011): 855–928; Gary A. Dymski, "Racial Exclusion and the Political Economy of the Subprime Crisis," *Historical Materialism* 17 (2009): 149–79; Benjamin Howell, "Exploiting Race and Space: Concentrated Subprime Lending as Housing Discrimination," *California Law Review* 94 (2006): 101–48. See also Louise Seamster, "Black Debt, White Debt," *Contexts* 18, no. 1 (2019): 30–35.

53 Kai Wright, "The Subprime Swindle," *Nation*, July 14, 2008; Rick Brooks and Ruth Simon, "Subprime Debacle Traps Even Very Credit-Worthy: As Housing Boomed, Industry Pushed Loans to a Broader Market," *Wall Street Journal*, December 3, 2007.

54 John Rao, *The Other Foreclosure Crisis: Property Tax Liens* (Boston, MA: National Consumer Law Center, July 2012).

55 Nathan B. Anderson and Jane K. Dokko, *Liquidity Problems and Early Payment Default among Subprime Mortgages* (Washington, DC: Federal Reserve Board, November 22, 2010), https://www.federalreserve.gov/pubs/feds/2011/201109/index.html.

56 Center for Responsible Lending, *Losing Ground: Foreclosures in the Subprime Market and Their Cost to Homeowners* (Durham, NC: Center for Responsible Lending, December 2006), https://www.responsiblelending.org/sites/default/files/nodes/files/research-publication/foreclosure-paper-report-2-17.pdf.

57 *American Casino*, directed by Leslie Cockburn (2009; Austin, TX: Table Rock Films).

58 Thriving Communities Institute, *Property Tax Delinquency and Tax Lien Sales in Cuyahoga County, Ohio* (Cleveland, OH: Thriving Communities Institute, March≈1, 2015).

59 "Delinquent Tax Bills on Rise: Unpaid Debts, Higher Values Can Mean Big Business for Investors," *Daytona Beach News-Journal*, May 16, 2007.

60 Marc Hochstein, Kate Berry, and Harry Terris, "Taxing Times," *American Banker*, August 6, 2009.

61 Schulte, "Wall Street Quietly Creates a New Way to Profit from Homeowner Distress."

62 Jacobson, *Steep Price of Paying to Stay*.

63 "Wall Street Finds Lucrative Market in Tax Liens," *Fresh Air*, December 14, 2010; Lynnley Browning, "The Lucrative Investment Trend Hedge Funds Don't Want

You to Know About," *Fortune*, May 2, 2013, http://fortune.com/2013/05/01/the
-lucrative-investment-trend-hedge-funds-dont-want-you-to-know-about/.

64 Scott Suttell, "Cleveland Suffers from an 'Extra-Vicious' Aeon Financial," *Crain's
Cleveland Business*, December 9, 2013, http://www.crainscleveland.com/article/
20131209/BLOGS03/131209828; NAACP Legal Defense Fund, "LDF Urges
Changes to Cuyahoga County's Property Tax Lien Sales System," press release,
March 3, 2014, https://www.naacpldf.org/press-release/ldf-urges-changes-to
-cuyahoga-countys-property-tax-lien-sales-system/.

65 Michael Sallah and Debbie Cenziper, "Debt Collecting Machine," *Washington
Post*, December 8, 2013, http://www.washingtonpost.com/sf/investigative/2013/
12/08/debt-collecting-machine/.

66 Suttell, "Cleveland Suffers from an 'Extra-Vicious' Aeon Financial."

67 Thriving Communities Institute, *Property Tax Delinquency and Tax Lien Sales*, 28.

68 NAACP Legal Defense Fund, "LDF Urges Changes to Cuyahoga County's Property Tax Lien Sales System."

69 Rea Zaimi, "Rethinking 'Disinvestment': Historical Geographies of Predatory
Property Relations on Chicago's South Side," *EPD: Society and Space* 40, no. 2
(2022): 245–57.

70 Michael Sallah, Debbie Cenziper, and Steven Rich, "Left with Nothing," *Washington Post*, September 8, 2013.

71 Sallah, Cenziper, and Rich, "Left with Nothing."

72 "D.C. Officials Express Anger over Lost Homes; Group Sounded Alarm in 2012,"
Washington Post, September 10, 2013.

73 Cameron LaPoint, "Property Tax Sales, Private Capital, and Gentrification in the
U.S." (working paper, Yale School of Management, revised March 20, 2023), 6,
https://papers.ssrn.com/sol3/papers.cfm?abstract_id=.

74 LaPoint, "Property Tax Sales," 38.

75 Michael Sallah, Debbie Cenziper, and Mike DeBonis, "D.C. Council Orders
Review of Cases Where People Lost Homes over Small Tax Debts," *Washington
Post*, September 17, 2013; Debbie Cenziper and Michael Sallah, "Citing Abuses,
Federal Lawmakers Call for Examination of Tax-Lien Programs Nationwide,"
Washington Post, September 19, 2013; Jonetta Rose Barras, "What Lies beneath
D.C.'s Tax-Lien Abuses," *Washington Post*, September 20, 2013; NAACP Legal
Defense Fund, "LDF Urges D.C. Mayor and Council to Change D.C.'s Property
Tax Lien Sales System"; Michael Sallah, Debbie Cenziper, and Steven Rich,
"Lawsuit Challenges the District's Tax-Lien Program, Seeks Compensation for
Families," *Washington Post*, September 24, 2013.

76 Coleman v. District of Columbia, 70 F.Supp. 3d 58 (D.D.C. 2014).

77 LaPoint, "Property Tax Sales."

78 See, for example, Brad Westover, "Tax Lien Sales Are Efficient, Fair and Rebuild
Communities: Column," *Poughkeepsie* [NY] *Journal*, October 2, 2018.

79 "Response to National Consumer Law Center," NTLA press release, July 20,
2012, https://www.ntla.org/news/news.asp?id=170067&hhSearchTerms=%22
%22national+consumer+law+center%22%22. See also "The Uneventful Foreclosure Crisis," NTLA press release, October 27, 2015, https://www.ntla.org/
news/news.asp?id=257428&hhSearchTerms=%22%22national+consumer+law
+center%22%22.

80 Westover, "NTLA in Action."

81 Elected officials and representatives from the following cities and counties attended and/or spoke on panels at the 2016 NTLA Annual Conference and Meeting: Summit County, Ohio; Clay County, Florida; Franklin County, Ohio; Philadelphia, Pennsylvania; West Haven, Connecticut; Highlands County, Florida. Copy of conference program in author's possession.

CONCLUSION

1 Rick Rojas, "Mississippi's Capital Loses Water as a Troubled System Faces a Fresh Crisis," *New York Times*, August 30, 2022, https://www.nytimes.com/2022/08/30/us/mississippi-jackson-water.html; Aubri Juhasz, "Philadelphia Schools Close Due to High Temperatures and No Air Conditioning," *NPR*, August 31, 2022, https://www.npr.org/2022/08/31/1120355494/philadelphia-schools -close-due-to-high-temperatures-and-no-air-conditioning.

2 Emmanuel Felton and Bryan Pietsch, "Jackson's Water Crisis Comes after Years of Neglect: 'We've Been Going It Alone,'" *Washington Post*, August 30, 2022, https://www.washingtonpost.com/nation/2022/08/30/jackson-mississippi -water-crisis-update/; Jason Breslow, "The Water Crisis in Jackson Follows Years of Failure to Fix an Aging System," *NPR*, August 31, 2022, https://www.npr.org/2022/08/31/1120166328/jackson-mississippi-water-crisis.

3 Maia Bloomfield Cucchiara, "Cities Are Trying to Fix Their Schools by Luring the Middle Class: It Won't Work," *Atlantic*, October 15, 2013, https://www .theatlantic.com/education/archive/2013/10/cities-are-trying-to-fix-their -schools-by-luring-the-middle-class-it-wont-work/280390/; Queen Muse, "Budget Cuts Set to Silence the Music at Philly Schools," *NBC10 Philadelphia*, updated June 21, 2013, https://www.nbcphiladelphia.com/news/local/philly -students-face-uncertainties-school-cutbacks-music/1984816/.

4 Sophie Kasakove and Nick Thieme, "How a Small Group of Investors Turned Distressed Baltimore Neighborhoods into Profit Centers," *Baltimore Banner*, March 29, 2023, https://www.thebaltimorebanner.com/community/housing/tax -investors-distressed-neighborhoods-D47ZGPFQBZEBHKLG7IKMTFSLJA/; Nick Thieme and Sophie Kasakove, "Tax Sale Nightmare: How an Unpaid Bill Can Cost Baltimore Homeowners Thousands, or Even Their Homes," *Baltimore Banner*, January 26, 2023, https://www.thebaltimorebanner.com/community/ housing/baltimore-tax-sale-lien-auction-64APUHOPUFB6VJ4Z6IX6WC7NMU/; Lorraine Mirabella, "Advocates Rally to Remove Homeowners from City Tax Sale," *Baltimore Sun*, March 22, 2021, https://www.baltimoresun .com/coronavirus/bs-md-homeowners-tax-sale-rally-20210322 -n2rzanddqzbodbm35s7hqy32nq-story.html.

5 Emily Sullivan, "Activists Plead Scott to Follow Promise to Remove Some Homeowners from Tax Sale," *WYPR*, April 30, 2021, https://www.wypr.org/wypr -news/2021-04-30/activists-plead-scott-to-follow-promise-to-remove-some -homeowners-from-tax-sale; Allison Harris, "How We Can Fix Maryland's Terrible Tax Sale System," *Baltimore Brew*, May 7, 2021, https://baltimorebrew.com/ 2021/05/07/how-we-can-fix-marylands-terrible-tax-sale-system/; Kasakove and Thieme, "How a Small Group of Investors."

6 Yvonne Wenger and Hallie Miller, "Advocates Make Last-Minute Push to Delay Baltimore's Tax Sale That Could Cost Vulnerable Residents Their Homes,"

Baltimore Sun, July 16, 2020, \https://www.baltimoresun.com/maryland/
baltimore-city/bs-md-ci-tax-sale-delay-20200716-b272iunly5dtjovspvof25khwi
-story.html; Mirabella, "Advocates Rally to Remove Homeowners"; Margaret
Henn, "Baltimore's Black Homeowners Deserve an Equitable Property Tax
System," *Baltimore Afro-American*, May 2, 2023, http://afro.com/baltimores
-black-homeowners-deserve-an-equitable-property-tax-system/; Hieu Truong
and Allison Harris, "Give Housing Assistance Programs a Chance to Work:
Cancel Baltimore's May Tax Sale," *Baltimore Sun*, March 21, 2022, https://
www.baltimoresun.com/opinion/op-ed/bs-ed-op-0322-baltimore-tax-sale
-20220321-rle573cxivghvnv5qxzhvpru3i-story.html.

7   Lillian Reed, "Baltimore's Tax Sale Proceeds despite Pressure from Hous-
ing Advocates, Brings in $18.8M," *Baltimore Sun*, May 19, 2021, https://www
.baltimoresun.com/maryland/baltimore-city/bs-md-ci-baltimore-tax-sale
-20210518-20210519-d4w6wgpfq5fzpapzfpto5ytwka-story.html; Henn,
"Baltimore's Black Homeowners Deserve"; Thieme and Kasakove, "Tax
Sale Nightmare"; Sophie Kasakove, Emily Sullivan, Nick Thieme, and Adam
Willis, "Proposal to Overhaul Tax Sale Fails to Pass after Baltimore City
Pumps Breaks on Own Legislation," *Baltimore Banner*, updated April 11, 2023,
https://www.thebaltimorebanner.com/community/housing/baltimore-tax
-sale-reform-legislation-stalled-7Y3HYTVTCFHM7GSBUGRIKRQ7AM/;
Sophie Kasakove and Nick Thieme, "Board OKs Plan to Exclude Most Balti-
more Homeowners from Controversial Tax Sale," *Baltimore Banner*, May 10,
2023, https://www.thebaltimorebanner.com/community/housing/board-oks
-plan-to-exclude-most-baltimore-homeowners-from-controversial-tax-sale
-PFZATFA62VHO7GTR3N7IDIDMFE/.

8   See also Brian Highsmith, "The Implications of Inequality for Fiscal Federalism
(or Why the Federal Government Should Pay for Local Public Schools)," *Buffalo
Law Review* 67 (April 2019): 101–45; Brian Highsmith, "The Structural Violence of
Municipal Hoarding," *American Prospect*, July 6, 2020, https://prospect.org/api/
content/111183a6-bca6-11ea-9cf6-1244d5f7c7c6/.

9   Colin Gordon, *Citizen Brown: Race, Democracy, and Inequality in the St. Louis
Suburbs* (Chicago: University of Chicago Press, 2019), 10.

10 See William A. Fischel, *The Homevoter Hypothesis: How Home Values Influence
Local Government Taxation, School Finance, and Land-Use Policies* (Cambridge,
MA: Harvard University Press, 2001); William A. Fischel, ed., *The Tiebout Model
at Fifty: Essays in Public Economics in Honor of Wallace Oates* (Cambridge, MA:
Lincoln Institute of Land Policy, 2006); Judge Glock, "A Benefit, Not a Burden,"
City Journal, October 7, 2021, https://www.city-journal.org/property-taxes
-should-be-benefit-not-burden.

11 Daniel Béland and André Lecours, "Fiscal Federalism and American Excep-
tionalism: Why Is There No Federal Equalisation System in the United States?"
Journal of Public Policy 34, no. 2 (2014): 303–29.

12 Kirk J. Stark, "Rich States, Poor States: Assessing the Design and Effect of a U.S.
Fiscal Equalization Regime," *Tax Law Review* 63 (2010): 957.

13 Jacob M. Grumbach, *Laboratories against Democracy: How National Parties
Transformed State Politics* (Princeton, NJ: Princeton University Press, 2022);
David Pepper, *Laboratories of Autocracy: A Wake-Up Call from behind the Lines*
(Cincinnati, OH: St. Helena Press, 2021); Richard C. Schragger, "Federalism,
Metropolitanism, and the Problem of States," *Virginia Law Review* 105, no. 8

(2019): 1537–1604; Richard C. Schragger, "Localism All the Way Up: Federalism, State-City Conflict, and the Urban-Rural Divide," *Wisconsin Law Review* 2021, no. 5 (2021): 1283–1313.

14 Emmanuel Saez and Gabriel Zucman, *The Triumph of Injustice: How the Rich Dodge Taxes and How to Make Them Pay* (New York: Norton, 2019), xii.

ILLUSTRATION CREDITS

Figure 1.1   Sarin Images/GRANGER

Figure 2.1   Library of Virginia, Richmond

Figure 2.2   African Americans segregated school, 1939, Charles Johnson Faulk Collection, Manuscripts Division, Archives and Special Collections, Mississippi State University

Figure 3.1   Louis Round Wilson Special Collections Library, University of North Carolina at Chapel Hill

Figure 3.4   Southern Tenant Farmers' Union records, Southern Historical Collection, Louis Round Wilson Special Collections Library, University of North Carolina at Chapel Hill

Figure 5.1   Central Press/Stringer

Figure 5.2   ST-15002998-0003, *Chicago Sun-Times* collection, Chicago History Museum

Figure 5.3   Associated Press

Figure 5.4   Photograph by Afro American Newspapers/Gado/Getty Images

Figure 6.1   University of Illinois at Chicago Special Collections

Figure 7.3   Folder 28, box 19, Lawyers' Committee for Civil Rights Under Law Records (T/035), Tougaloo College Civil Rights Collection, Mississippi Department of Archives and History

Figure 7.4   Folder 28, box 19, Lawyers' Committee for Civil Rights Under Law Records (T/035), Tougaloo College Civil Rights Collection, Mississippi Department of Archives and History

Figure 8.1   Associated Press

Figure 9.3   Amistad Research Center, New Orleans, LA

Figure 9.4   Amistad Research Center, New Orleans, LA

Figure 10.1   ST-19031773-0031, *Chicago Sun-Times* collection, Chicago History Museum

Figure 11.1   Photograph by Leslie Leon, Keystone Press Agency, Inc.

Figure 11.2   ST-12006200-0019, *Chicago Sun-Times* collection, Chicago History Museum

Figure 12.2   University of Illinois at Chicago Special Collections

Figure 13.1   Bettmann/Contributor

Figure 13.2   Photograph by Peter J. Schulz, Harold Washington Archives and Collections, Mayoral Records, Press Office Photographs, box 52, folder 8, Special Collections, Chicago Public Library

Figure 14.1   From *The Atlanta Journal-Constitution.* © 1990 *The Atlanta Journal-Constitution.* All rights reserved. Used under license.

Figure 15.2   Marilyn F. Hartley, July 9, 2012, courtesy John Young, Esq., Legal Aid Society, Louisville, Kentucky

Figure 15.4   Photograph by Michael Williamson

INDEX

Page numbers in italics refer to figures.